100 CHALLENGES TO FIND YOUR ARTISTIC STYLE

3dtotalPublishing

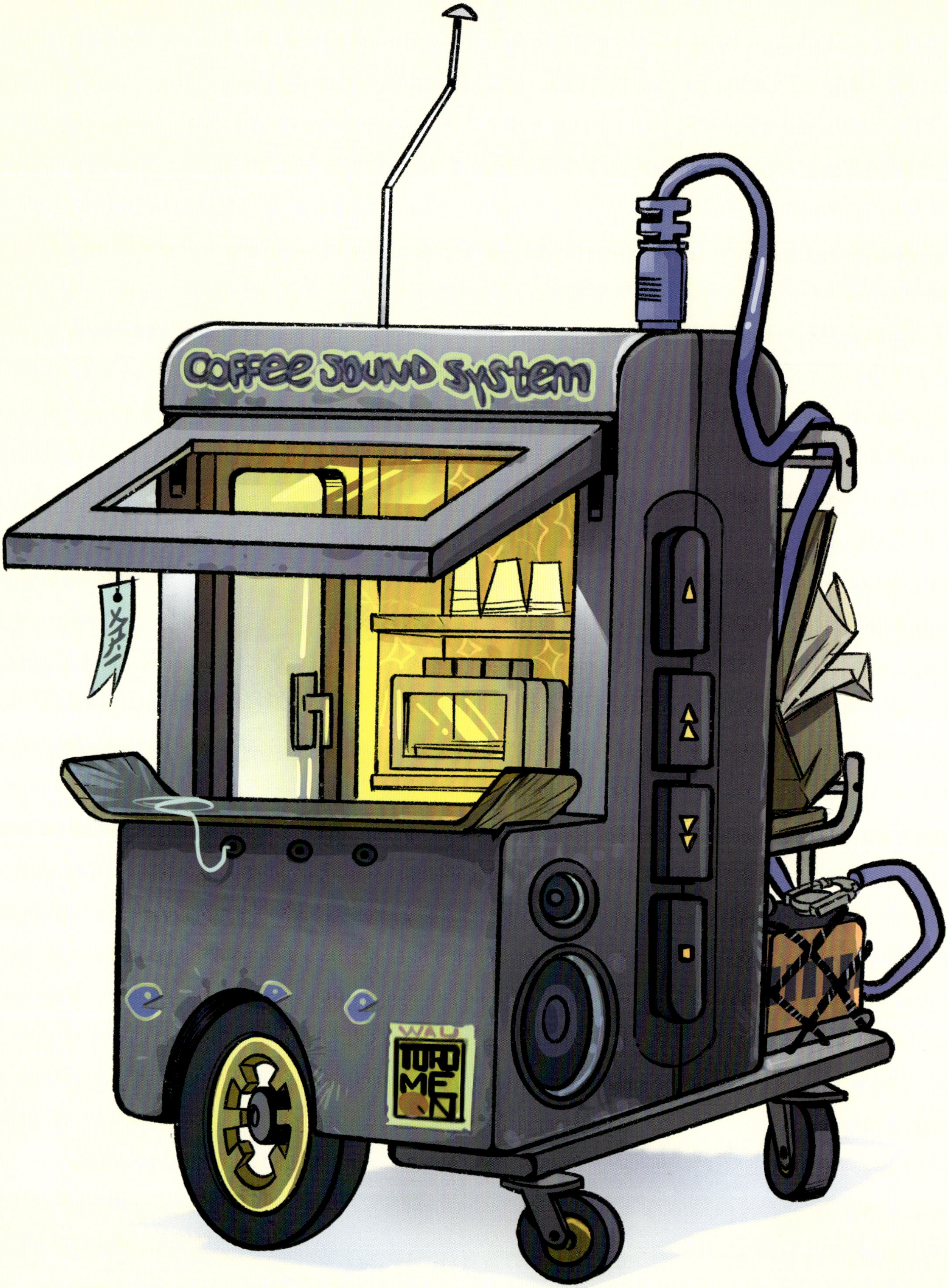
Coffee Sound System
WAU
TURN ME ON

100 CHALLENGES TO FIND YOUR ARTISTIC STYLE

3dtotalPublishing

3dtotal Publishing

Correspondence: **publishing@3dtotal.com**
Website: **store.3dtotal.com**

First published in the United Kingdom, 2026, by 3dtotal Publishing.

Address: 3dtotal.com Ltd,
6 Sansome Street, Worcester,
WR1 1UH, United Kingdom.

Hard cover ISBN: 978-1-915992-26-0

Printed and bound in Shanghai, China, by KS Printing.

Visit **store.3dtotal.com** for a complete list of available book titles.

Editor: Philippa Barker
Designer: Fiona Tarbet
Lead Editor: Rhiannon Joseph
Lead Designer: Joseph Cartwright
Studio Manager: Simon Morse
Managing Director: Tom Greenway

Front and back cover artwork by individual artists as credited throughout the book.

MIX
Paper from responsible sources
FSC® C151298

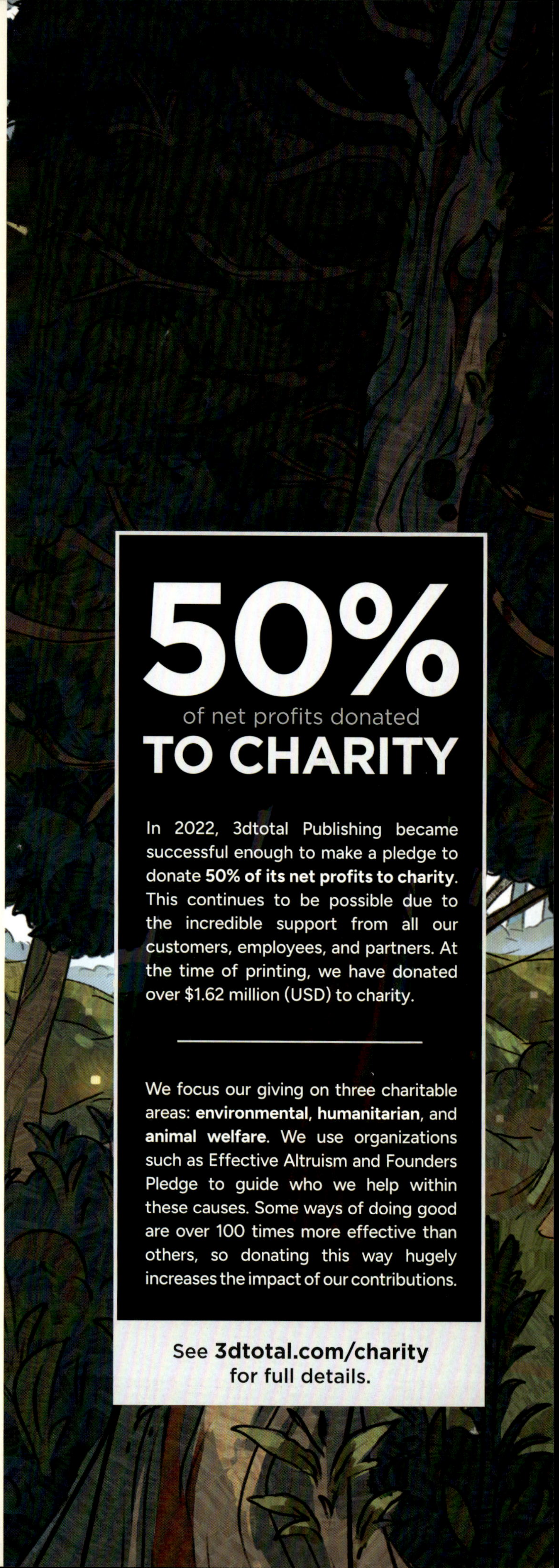

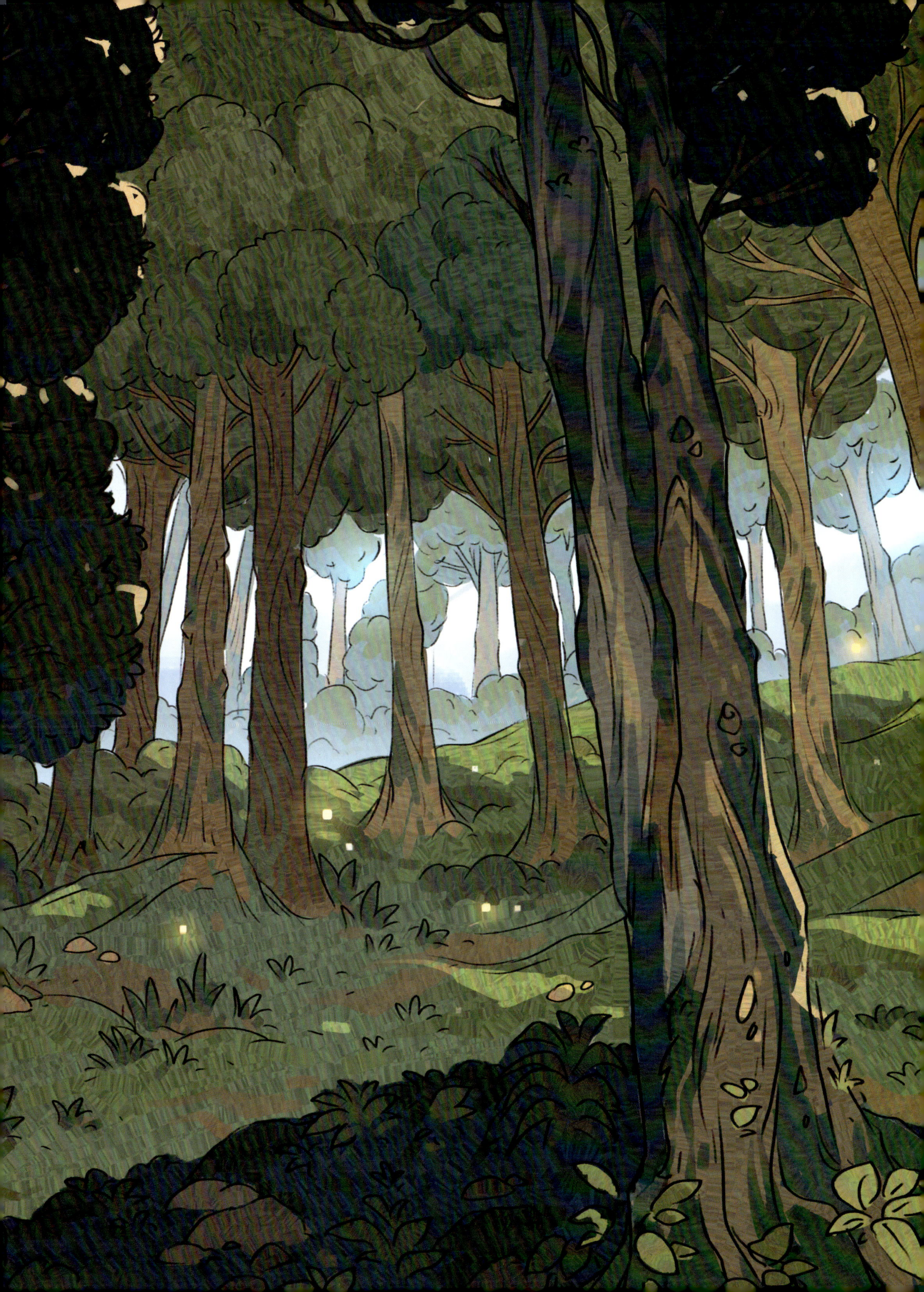

CONTE

NTS

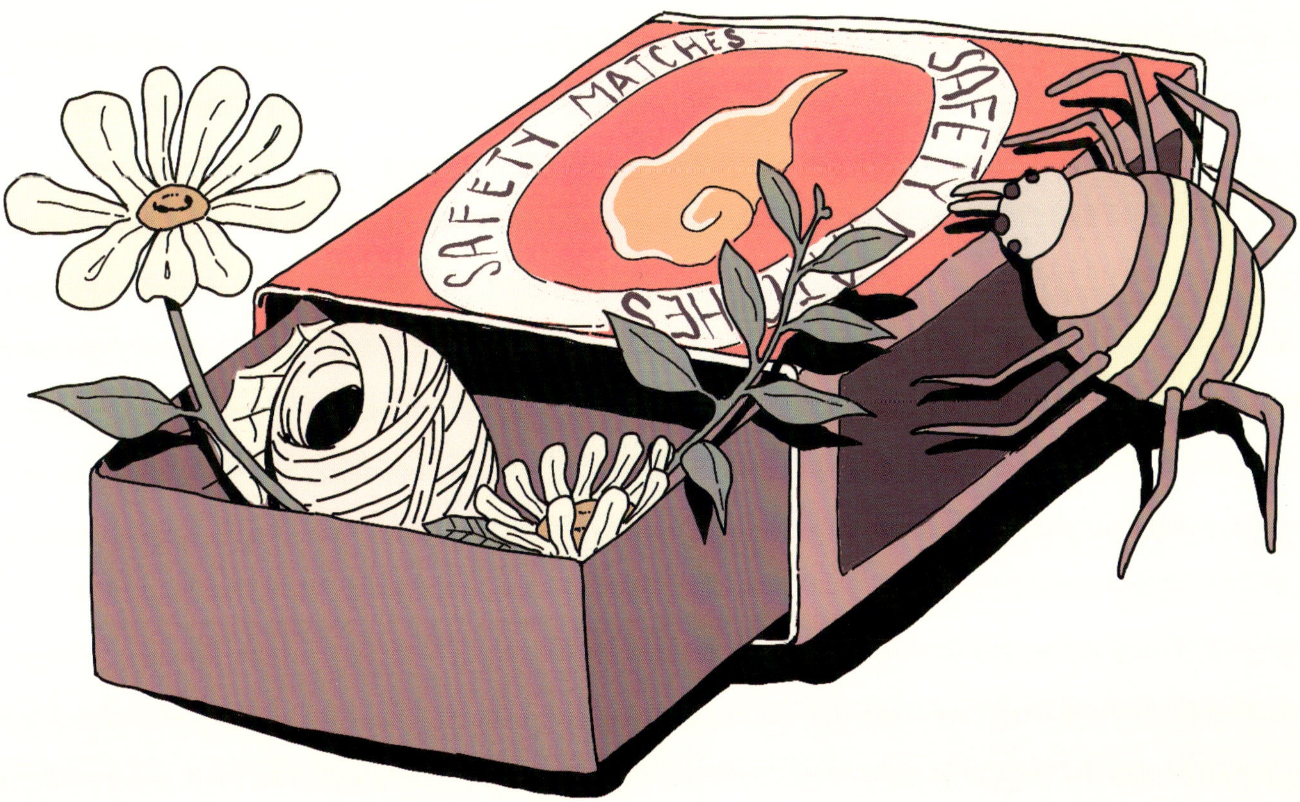

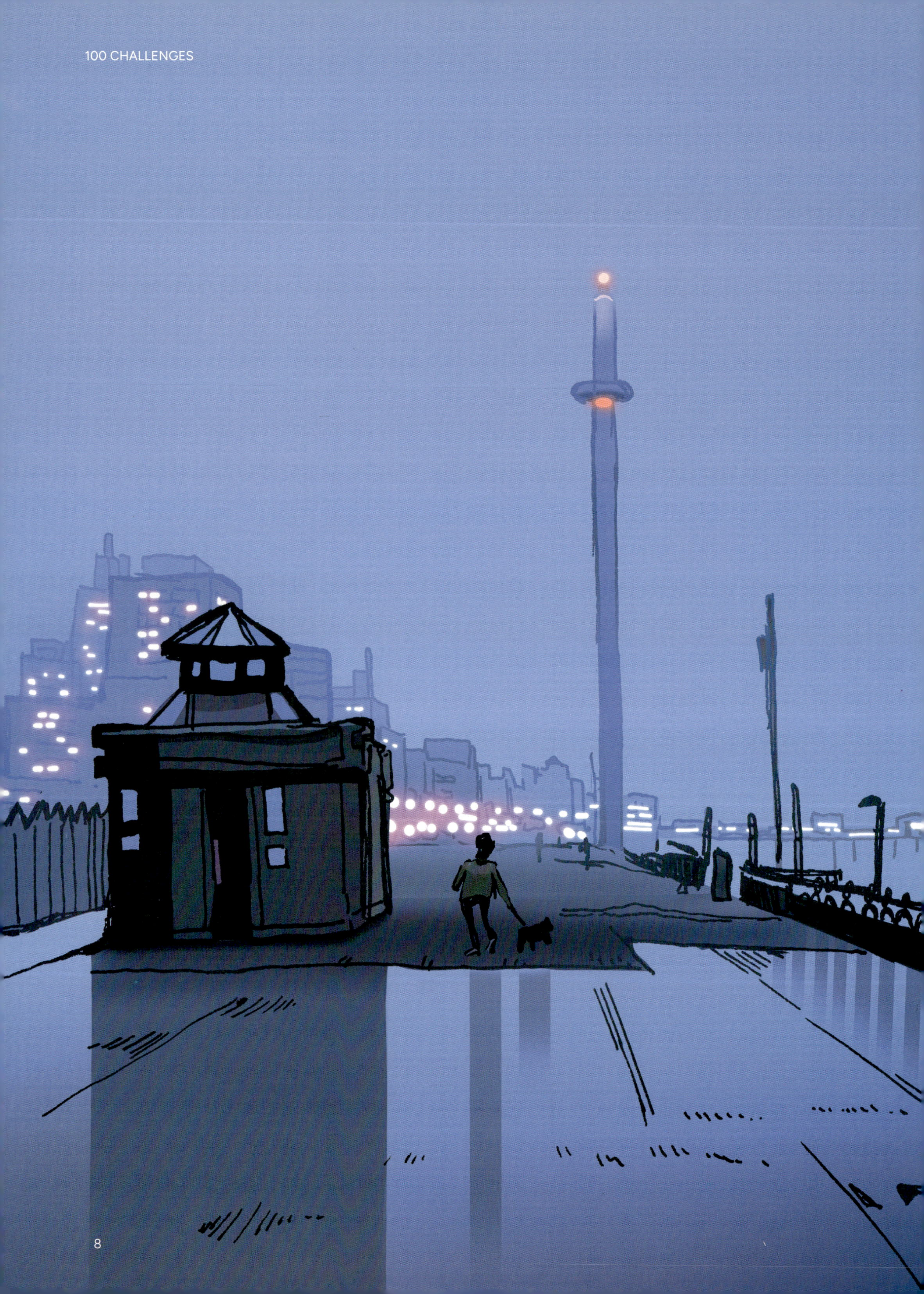

HOW TO USE THIS BOOK

While there's no one right pathway or fixed end point to discovering your own artistic style, the following pages contain 100 challenges that will encourage you to try out different techniques, tackle new subjects, and push yourself out of your creative comfort zone.

Every artist has a personal style that evolves over many years of working on their craft – whether it's due to the continued use of exaggerated shapes, simplified anatomy, reoccurring subject matter, dramatic lighting, or countless other artistic elements. While it may look effortless, and like they've never made art any other way, the qualities and quirks of what gives their artwork its characteristic look is no doubt the result of experimentation, inspiration, and a great deal of practice.

The challenges in this book are split between five themes:

- Shape & form
- Colour, value & light
- Composition, framing & perspective
- Characters & creatures
- Storytelling

The challenges in each chapter are graded as being at either a **beginner**, **intermediate**, or **advanced** level. You may decide to complete the beginner challenges in each of the five chapters before progressing to intermediate and advanced. Another route is to focus on one chapter at a time, completing all of its themed challenges before moving on to the next. As long as you take the time to explore, experiment, and, most importantly, have fun, there's no right or wrong way to learn.

Open yourself up to fresh approaches and ideas, and don't be afraid to make 'mistakes'. Follow your interests and pay attention to what you enjoy. By the end of this book, we hope you'll find yourself a few steps further along in the journey towards your artistic style.

PHILIPPA BARKER, EDITOR

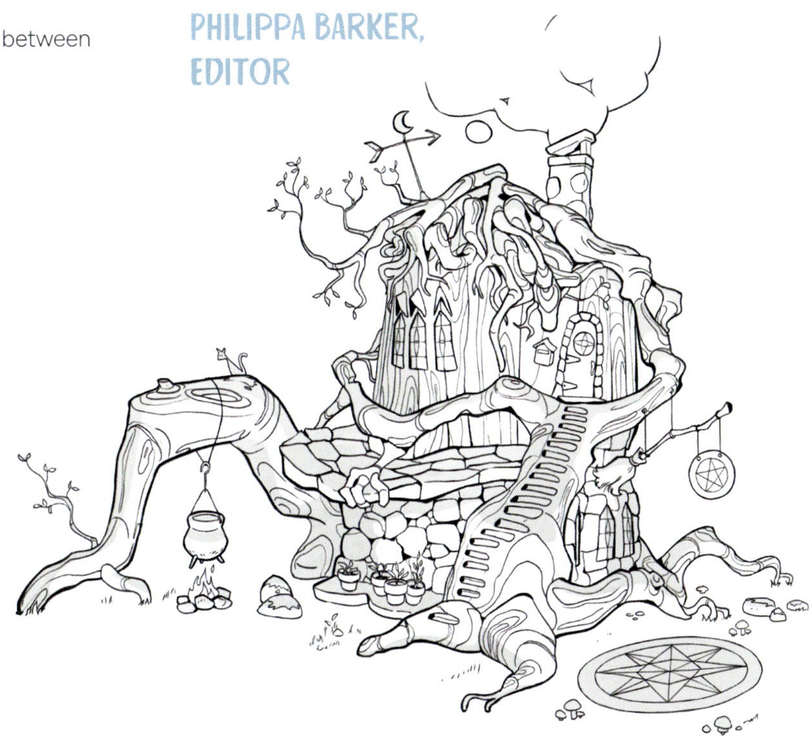

SHAPE &

Step-by-step challenges:

FORM

One-page challenges:

USING RANDOM SHAPES

BEGINNER ●

Fill a page with random, abstract shapes, then select three to turn into characters or creatures.

This task encourages you to explore shapes in your art that you may not usually use. It also helps you to examine shapes more closely, seeing the potential for a unique design in each one.

01 Start by drawing a page of random, organic shapes without a specific goal in mind. Let your hand move freely to create a variety of forms, focusing on lines, curves, and angles.

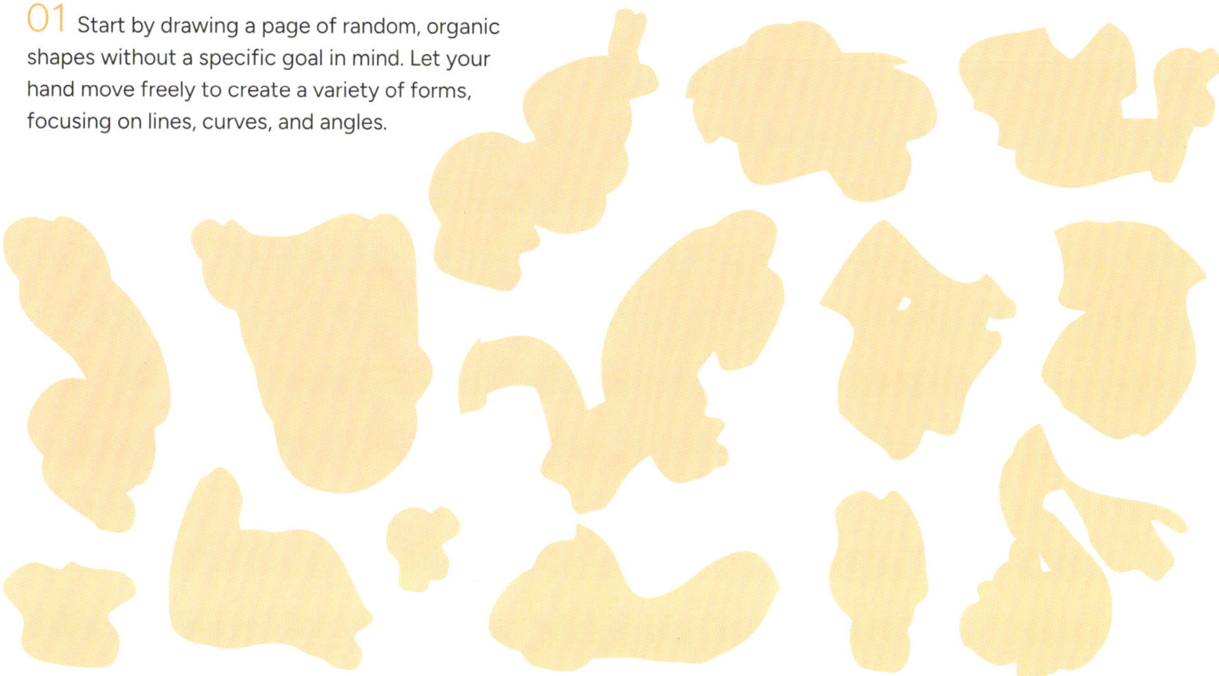

02 Review your shapes, looking for interesting forms that could be developed into a character or creature. Choose three and start to roughly sketch in some features.

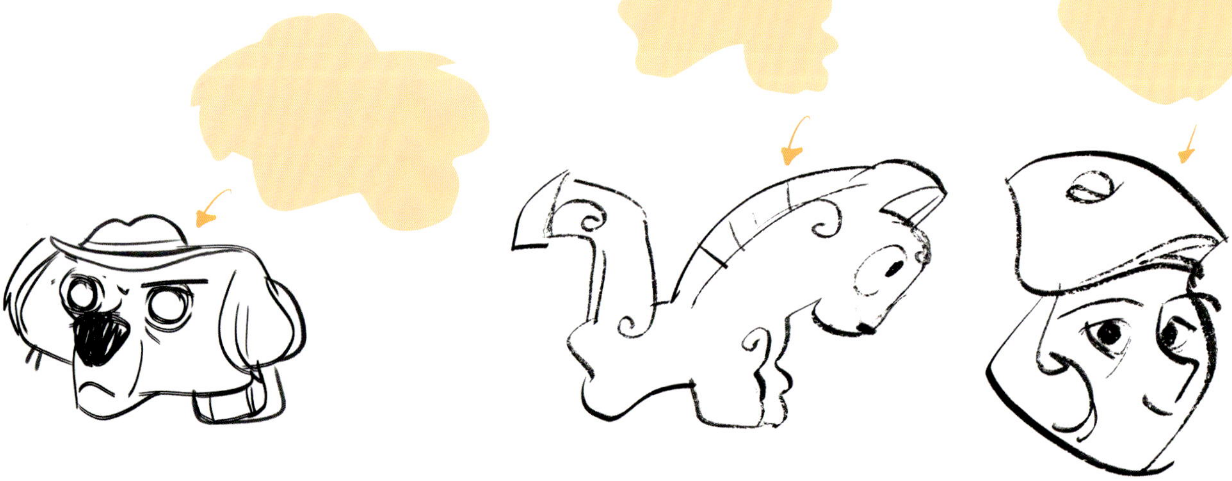

03 Think about how each shape could evolve into a design, adjusting proportions, adding limbs, or drawing in more defined facial features to add personality. Assign a colour to each design.

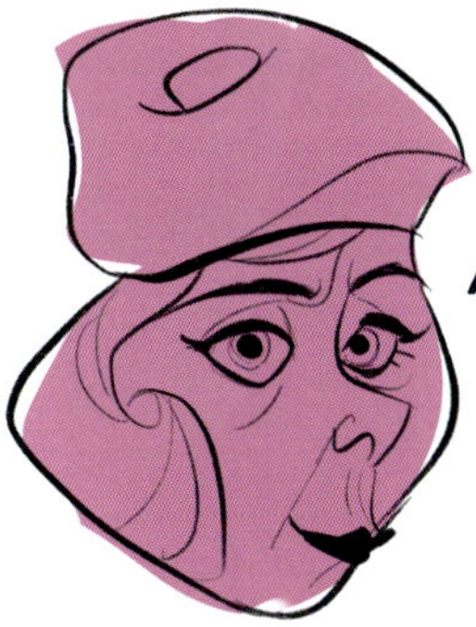
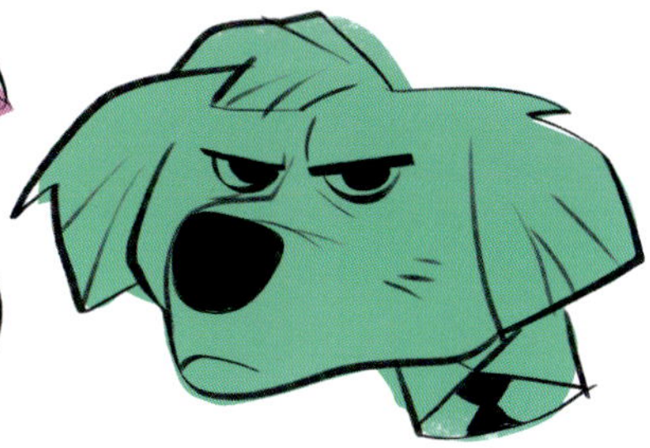
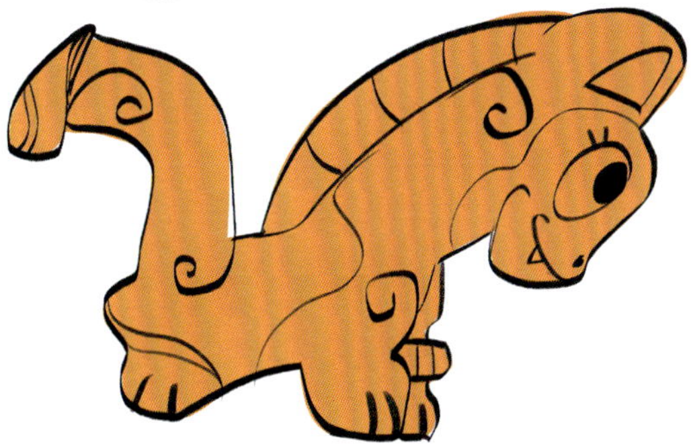

04 Refine the overall shapes as well as the details within.

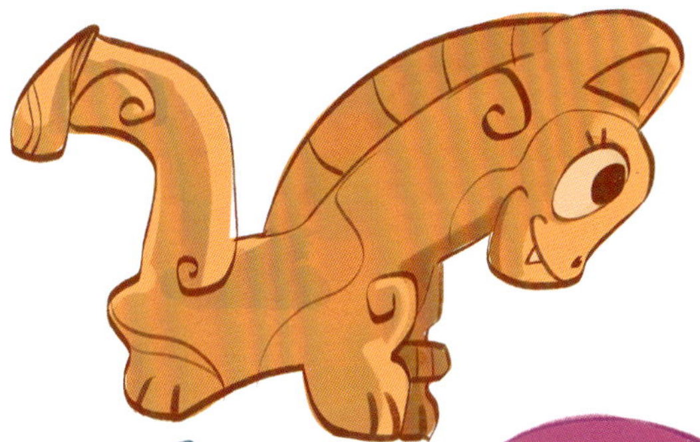
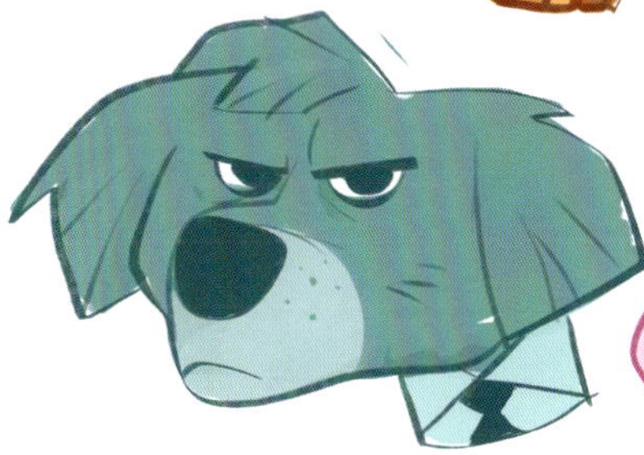
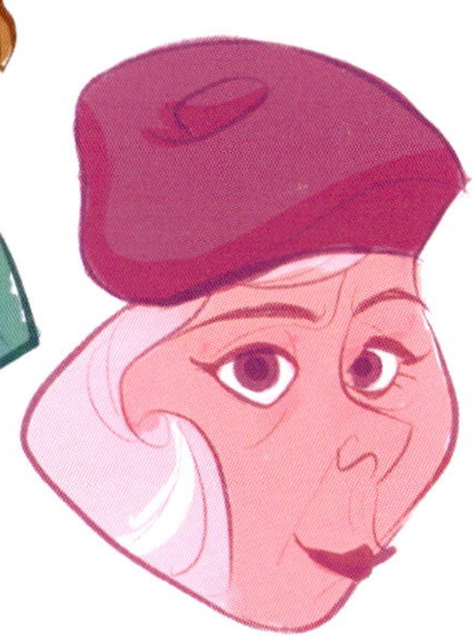

05 Define textures, lines, colour, and shading to create depth. Do the resulting images tell you anything new about your shape style?

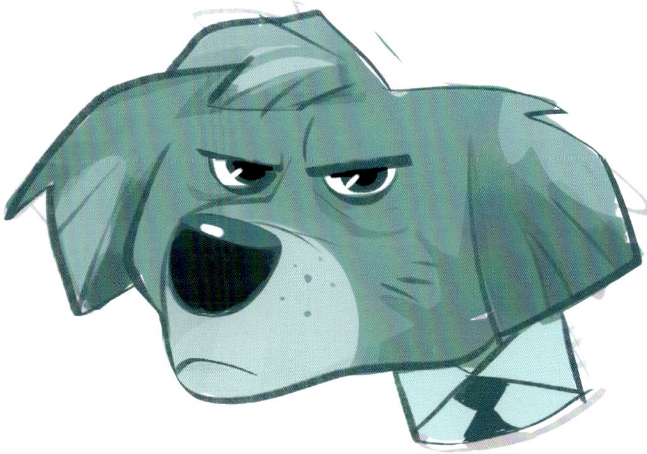
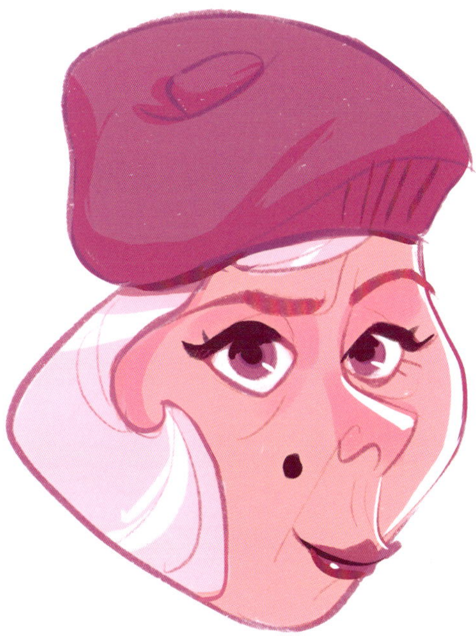
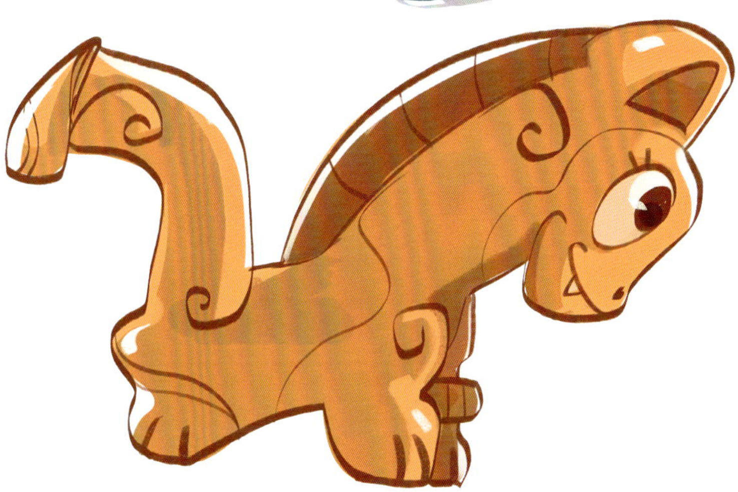

ART: TARANEH KARIMI

A TREE FROM THREE LINES

BEGINNER ●

Draw three harmonious, flowing lines, then use them to construct a tree.

The lines can form part of the tree, or simply be used as abstract silhouette outlines. The goal is to design a tree that has a visually pleasing flow and rhythm of shapes. Consider the general movement and line of action, as well as balance and composition. Think about shape language – will your tree be sharp and angular, or soft and rounded?

01 Sketch three flowing lines, arranging them in a way that sparks an idea for an interesting silhouette.

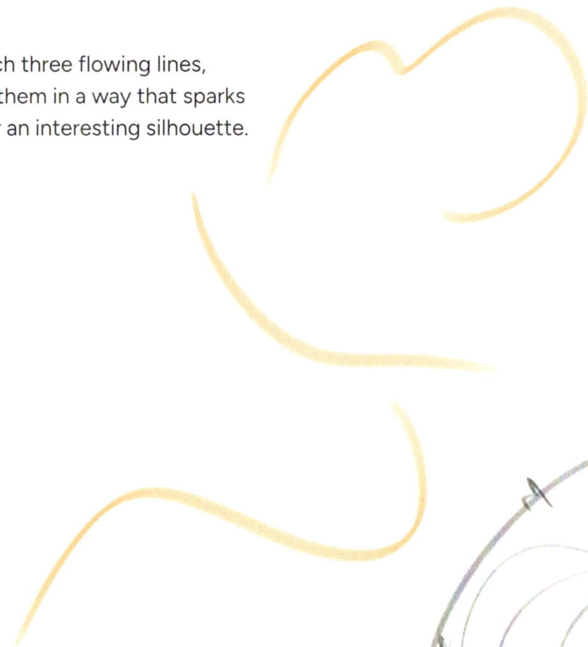

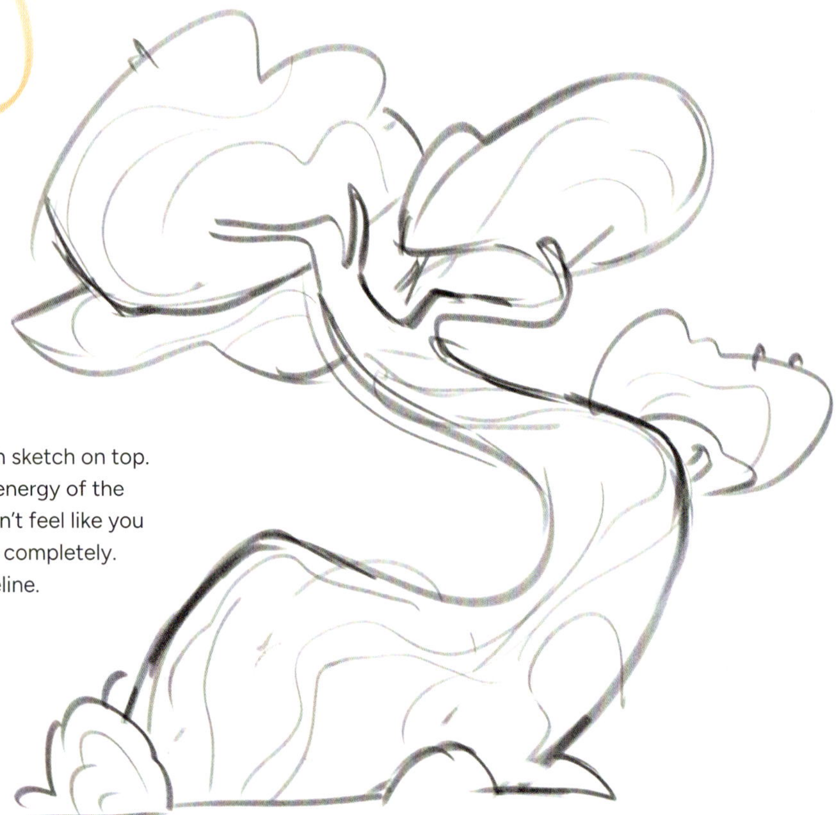

02 Create a rough sketch on top. Try to preserve the energy of the original lines, but don't feel like you have to follow them completely. Use them as a guideline.

03 Draw lots of dynamic overlaps to prevent the drawing from looking flat and two-dimensional.

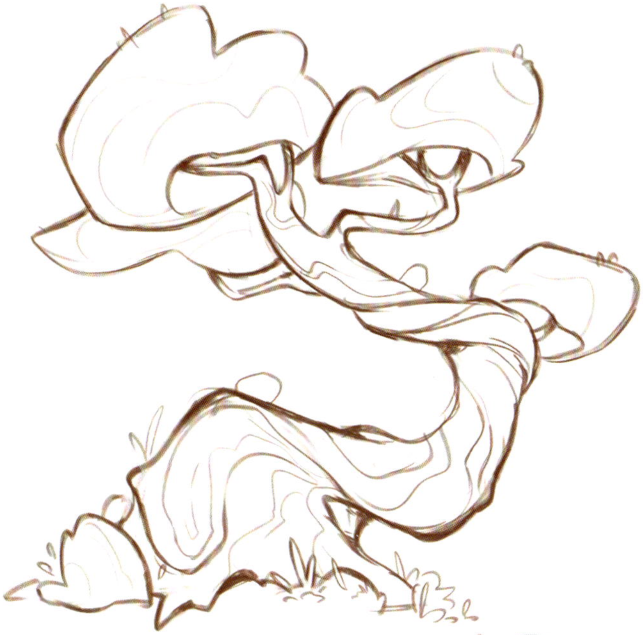

04 Add flat colours. You can use realistic greens and browns, or a more stylized colour palette.

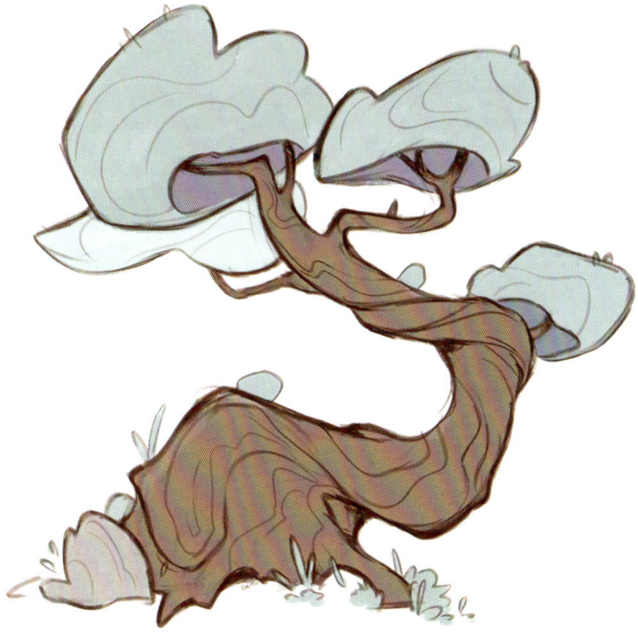

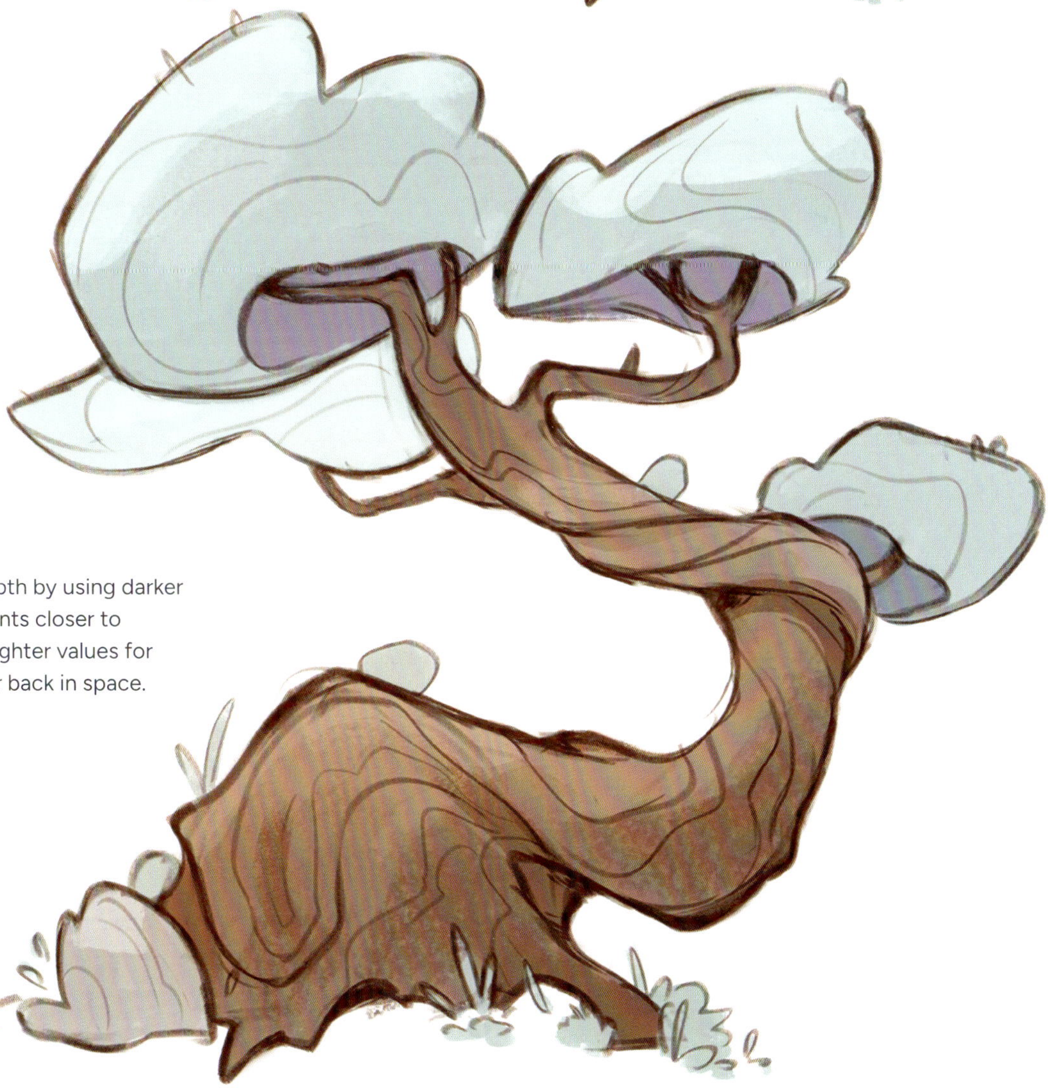

05 Create depth by using darker values for elements closer to the viewer and lighter values for elements further back in space.

ART: MAGDALINA DIANOVA

TURN IT INTO A TOY

BEGINNER ●

Choose an object and draw it as simply as possible – like a children's toy.

With no tiny details or intricate parts, toys typically have clean, simple designs with exaggerated proportions. This task will force you to simplify your chosen object into an unfussy prop design. Being able to draw simplified shapes and express yourself in a minimal style is an important part of stylization.

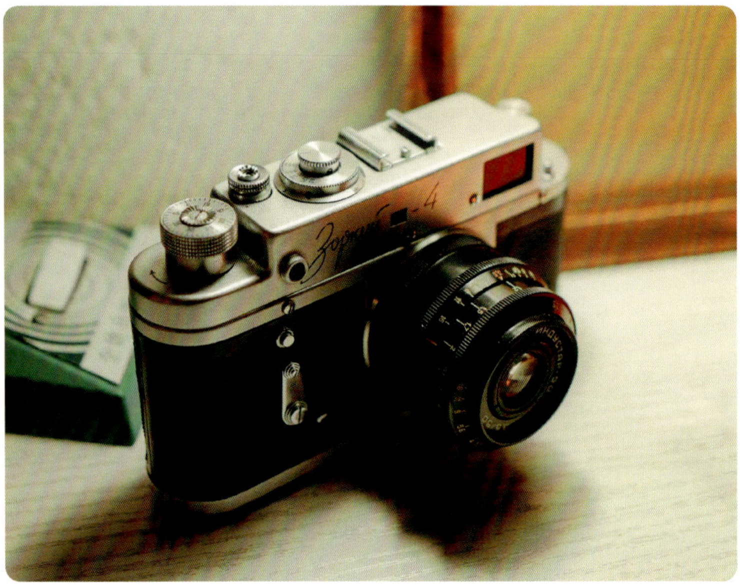

PHOTO BY DONGSH ON UNSPLASH

01 First sketch a reasonably detailed version of the object. The purpose of this is to review what lines you could remove without altering the silhouette. Feel free to add elements to make it your own!

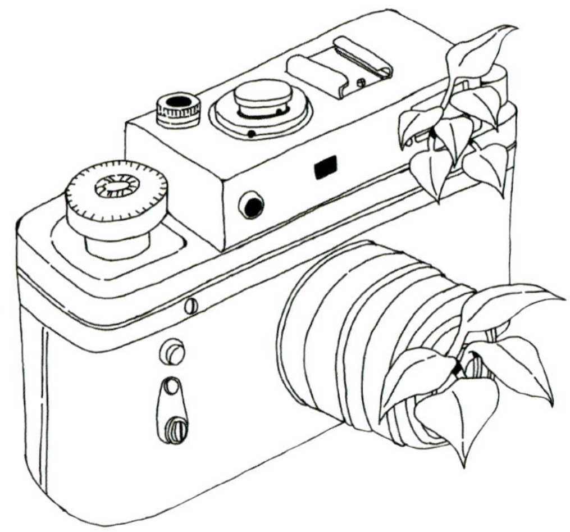

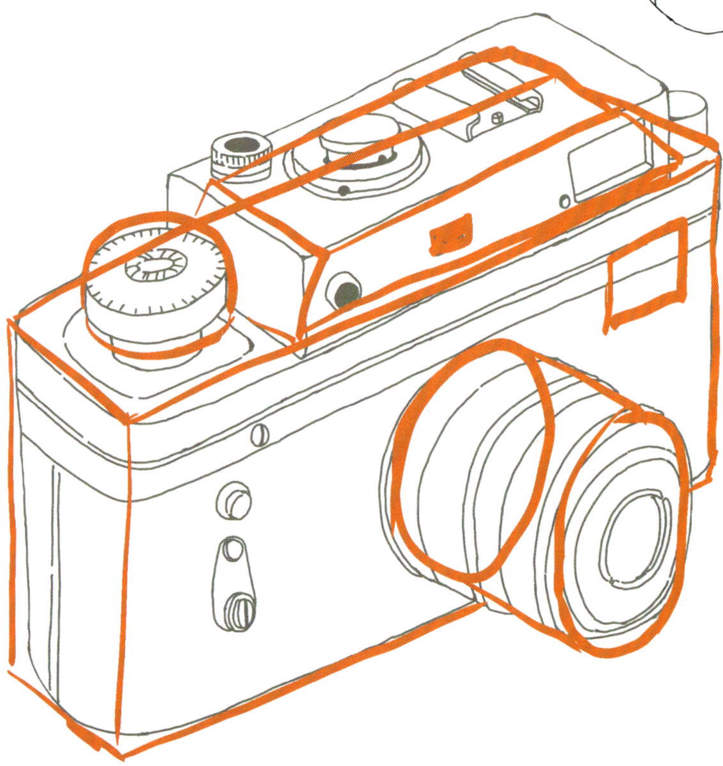

02 Now use a coloured pen and draw over your initial sketch to outline the object's basic shapes, highlighting its building blocks.

03 Use the basic shapes identified in the previous step to draw a simplified line-art version.

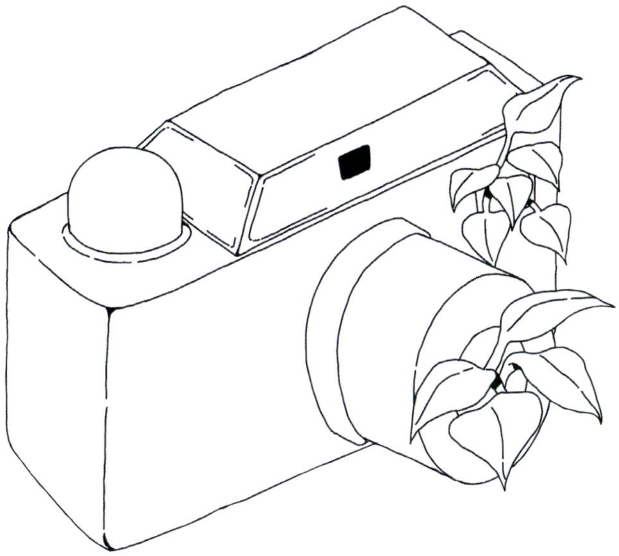

04 Add in flat base colours. Introducing pops of colour will compensate for the lack of detail and make it look more like a toy.

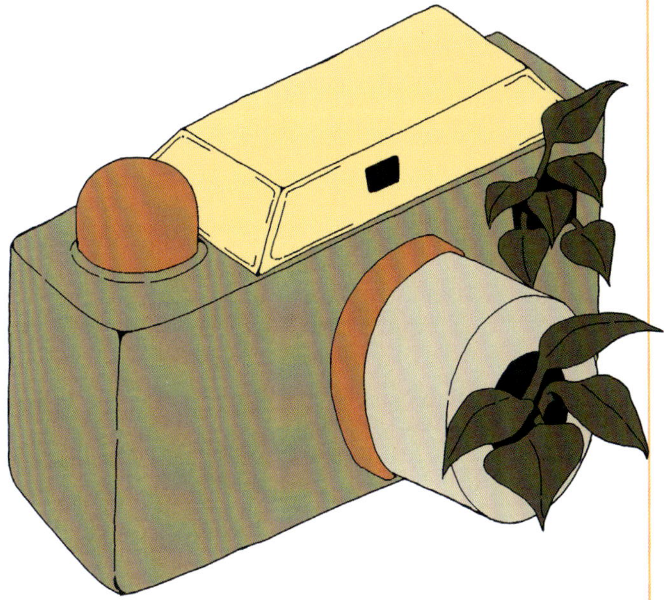

05 Finally, add highlights and shadows to give the object some depth and three-dimensionality.

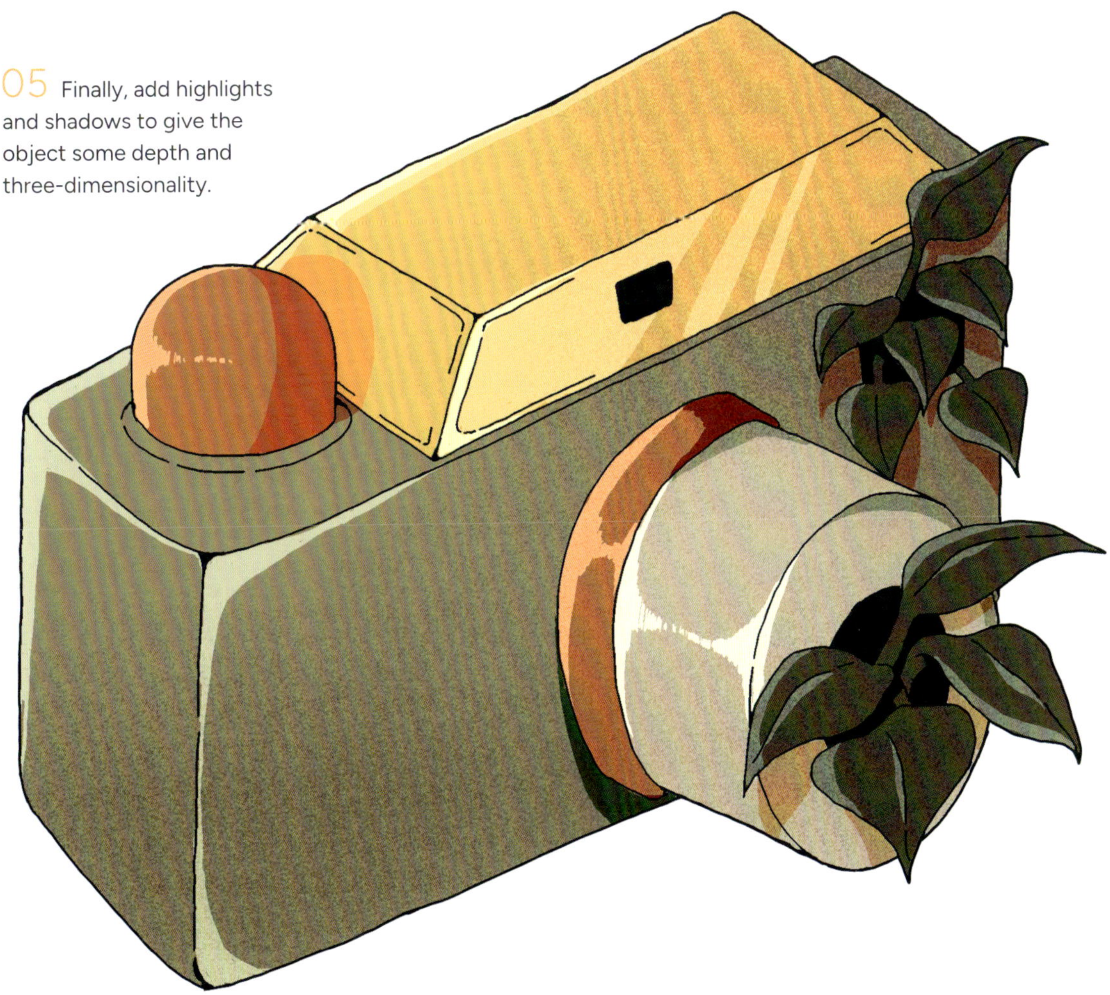

ART: ELLA OHWELLADAYS

WILD SHAPES

BEGINNER ●

With wildlife photography for reference, create a series of rough shape studies using digital brushes.

Use a variety of brushes, such as textured watercolours or pastels set to a large, painterly size. Don't erase any strokes or hit Undo – allow the shapes to emerge randomly. Then use a more controlled brush to turn those rough shapes into new creatures or characters.

01 Choose a photo of a wild animal, then use a digital brush that you can't quite control to paint rough shape studies. There are three examples shown here.

PHOTO BY FRIDA LANNERSTROM ON UNSPLASH

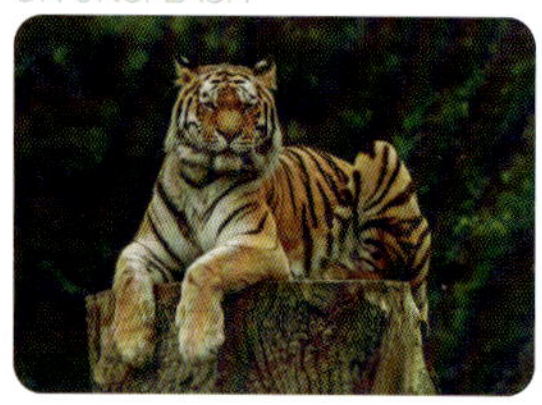

PHOTO BY JEAN WIMMERLIN ON UNSPLASH

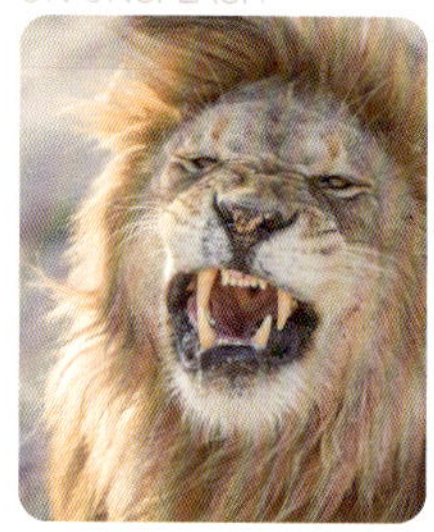

PHOTO BY NICOLE WREYFORD ON UNSPLASH

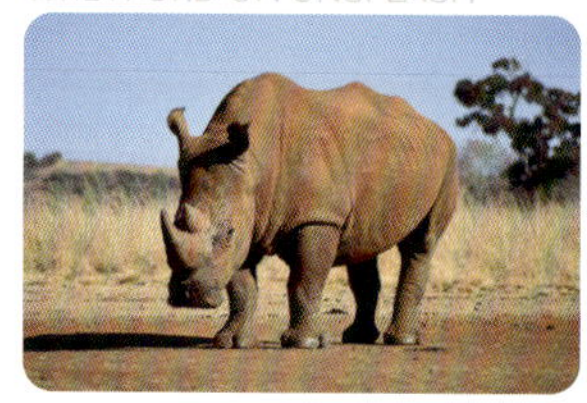

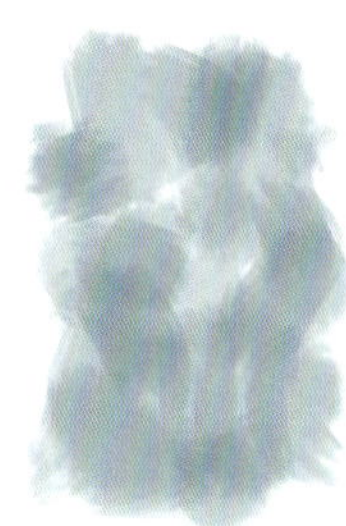

02 Rotate the canvas and observe the shapes in different orientations, exploring possible interpretations. Once you spot elements that could be made recognizable, divide up the organic shapes to create faces, bodies, and items of clothing.

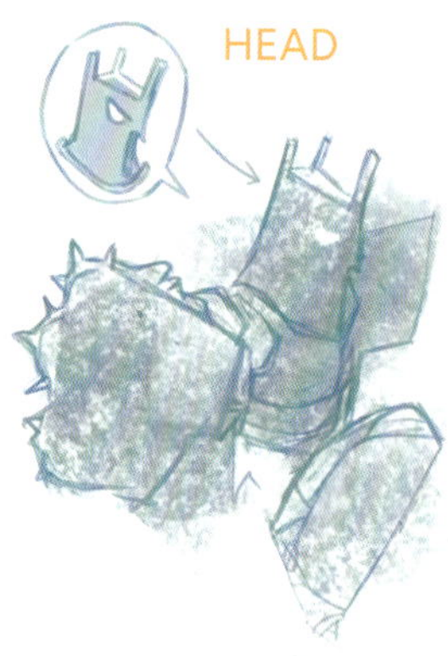

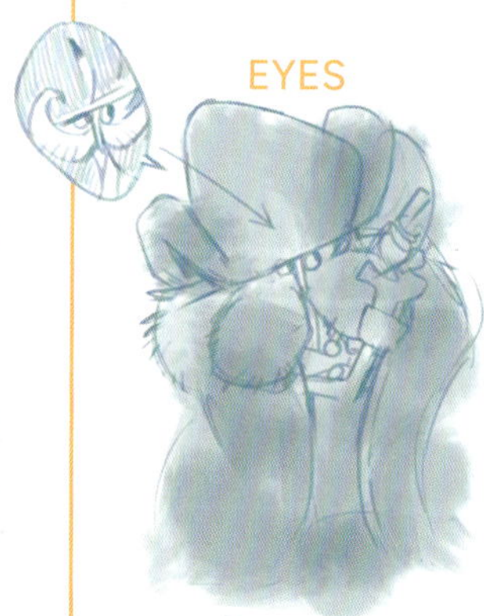

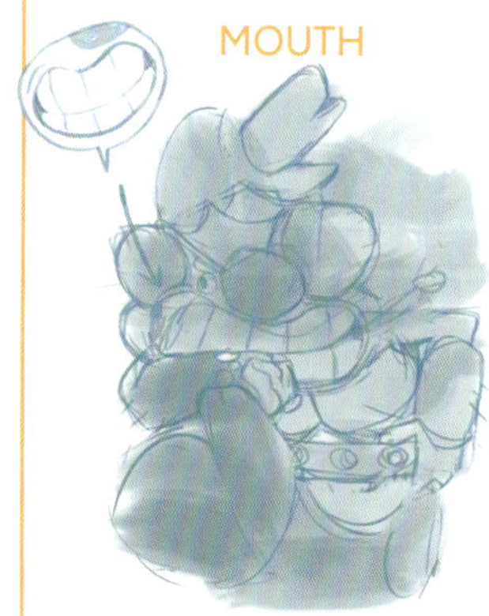

03 Continue to define your new creation, making sure it has a strong silhouette.

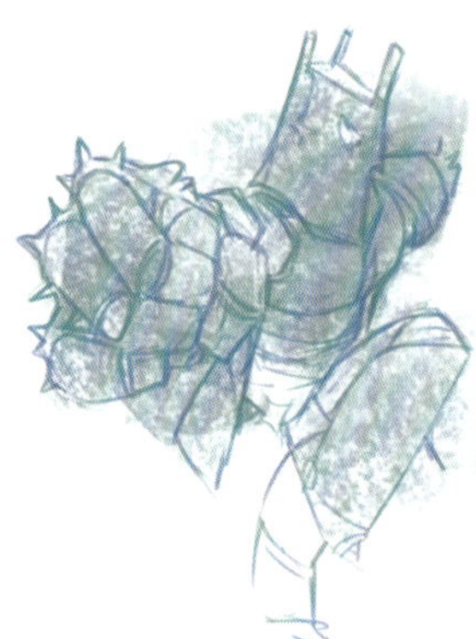

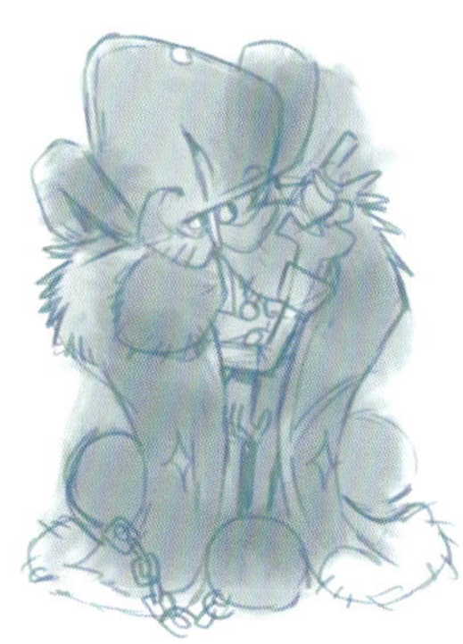

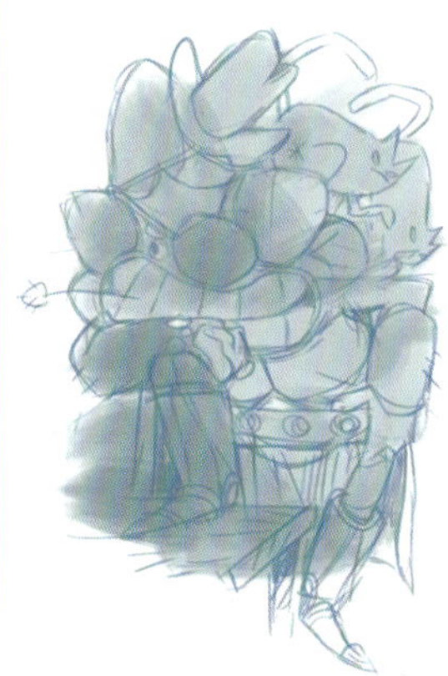

04 Working from the outside inwards, refine the outer contour then the inner details of your new creature or character.

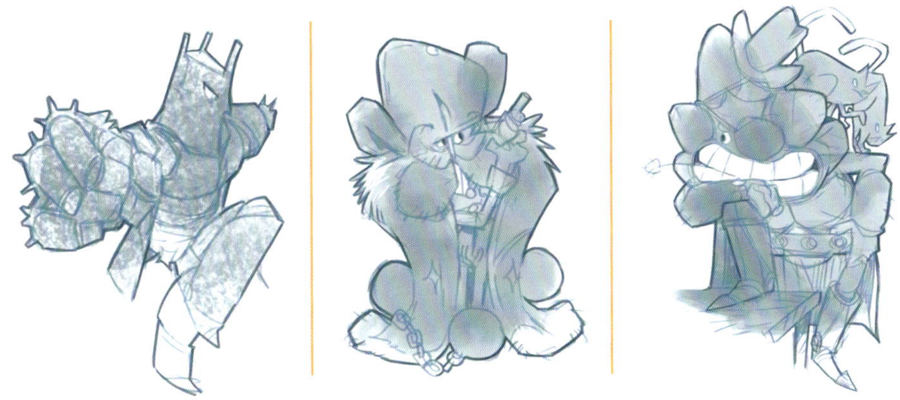

05 Add detail and shading to finish. Have you created something you wouldn't have normally considered?

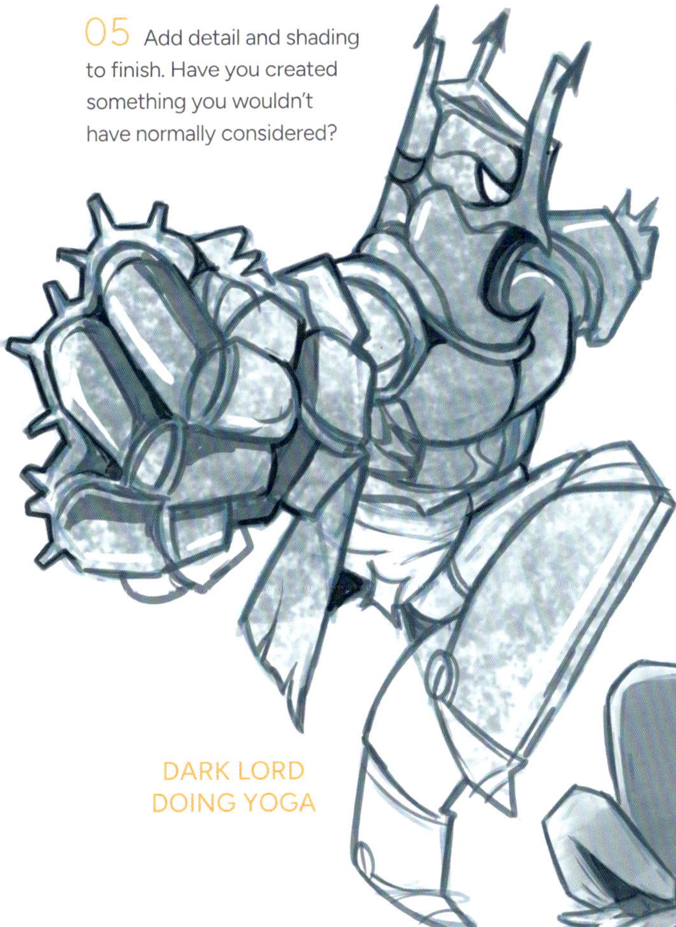

DARK LORD DOING YOGA

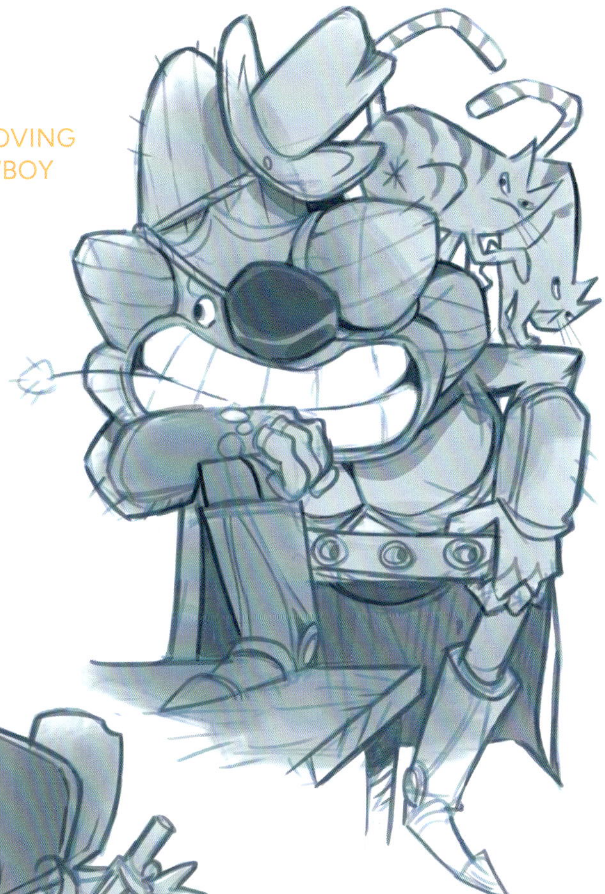

CAT-LOVING COWBOY

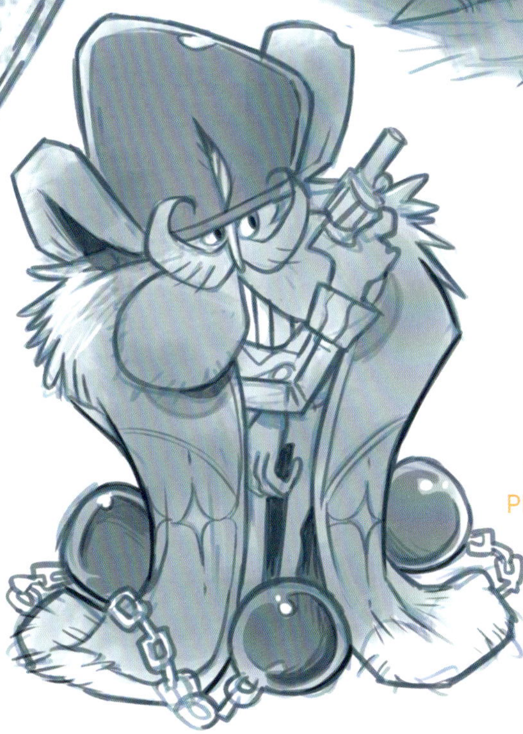

PIRATE PRISONER

SHAPING A LANDSCAPE

INTERMEDIATE ●●

Using a reference photo of a landscape, create three versions of an image: one using triangular and circular shapes, the second using rectangular and circular, and the third using rectangular and triangular.

This is a great exercise for discovering which shape language you like to use, as well as for visualizing depth within a space. It forces you to turn elements of a scene into clearly defined planes, helping you work out where the light will hit.

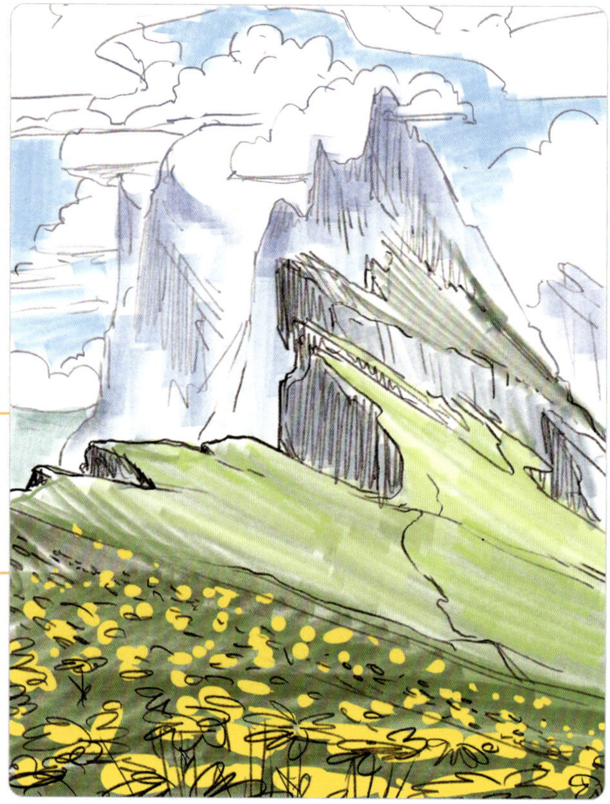

01 Start by creating a loose sketch of your reference photo to form a rough idea of the composition. This will give you something to build on.

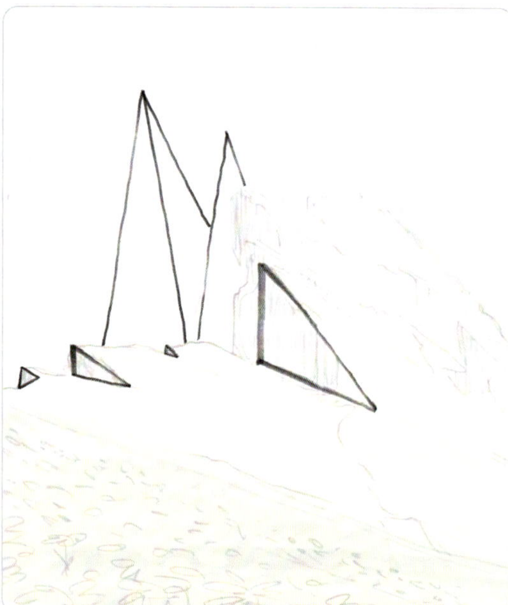

02 Create a white layer at 15% opacity over your loose sketch, then draw simple triangular shapes over the top. Follow the existing shapes of your sketch but simplify them greatly.

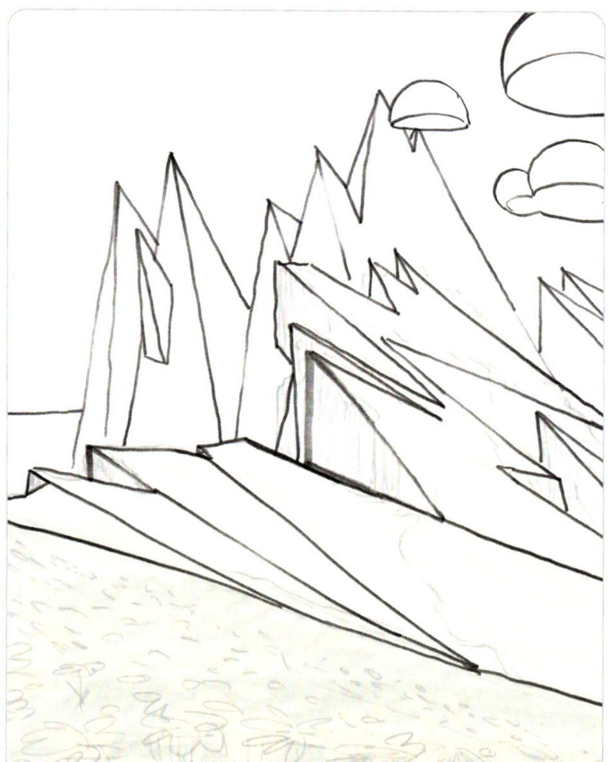

03 You could draw clouds as circular shapes, like spheres with the lower half chopped off. Making the shapes solid will help when it comes to lighting.

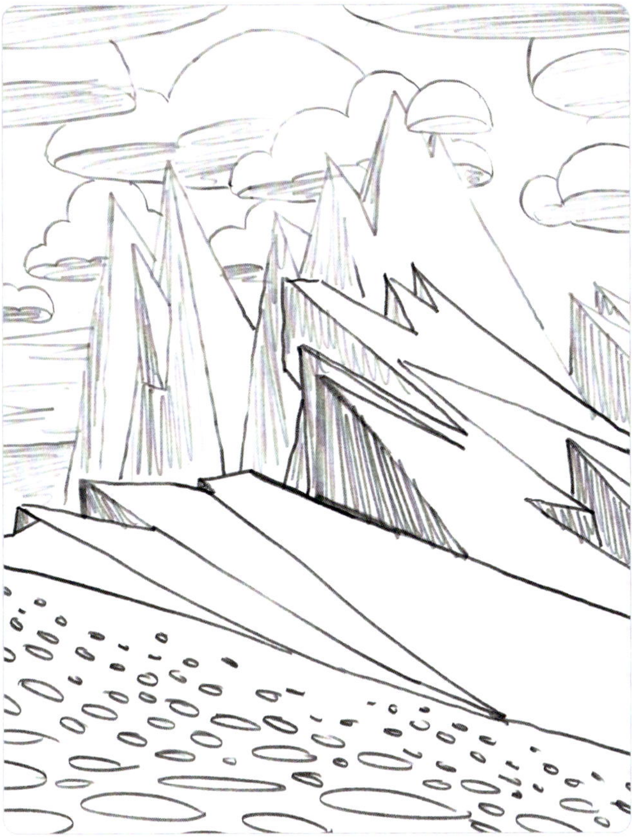

TRIANGULAR & CIRCULAR

04 Fill every part of your image with triangular and circular shapes, then add some simple shading to finish. Repeat this process using the other shape combinations – rectangular/circular and rectangular/triangular. How does the different shape language change the feel or mood of the same landscape?

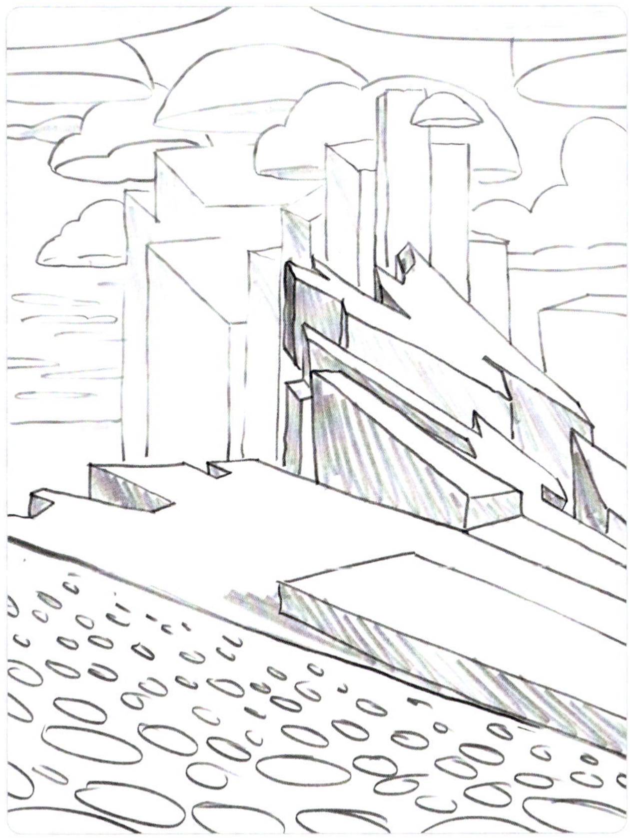

RECTANGULAR & CIRCULAR

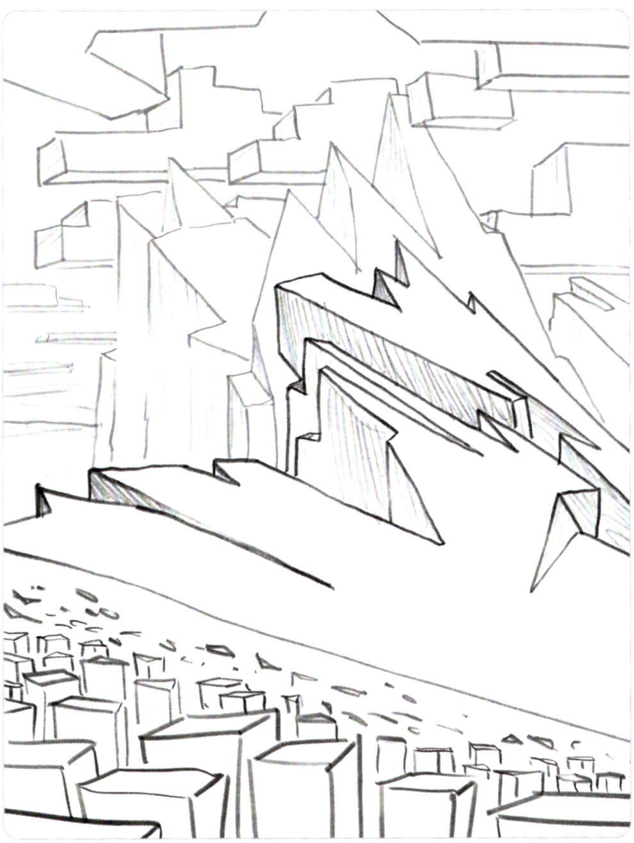

RECTANGULAR & TRIANGULAR

MAKE IT WONKY

INTERMEDIATE ●●

Pick an object and draw it. Then draw it again, but make it wonkier. Draw it a third time, exaggerating the form to make it even wonkier still.

See how far you can push the design without losing the essence of the original object. There are limits – push too far and the design will fail. This task is about distorting the shapes and overall silhouette, while ensuring the object is still recognizable.

01 Draw your chosen object. Use line work, shadow, and light to define its various shapes.

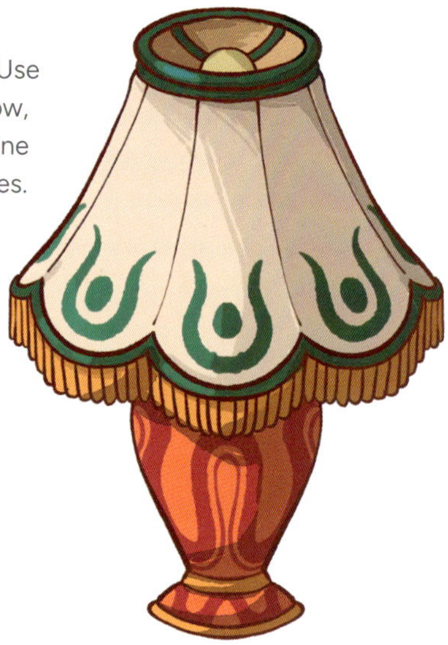

02 Push the silhouette, narrowing certain areas and widening others. The aim is to alter the design while preserving its essence.

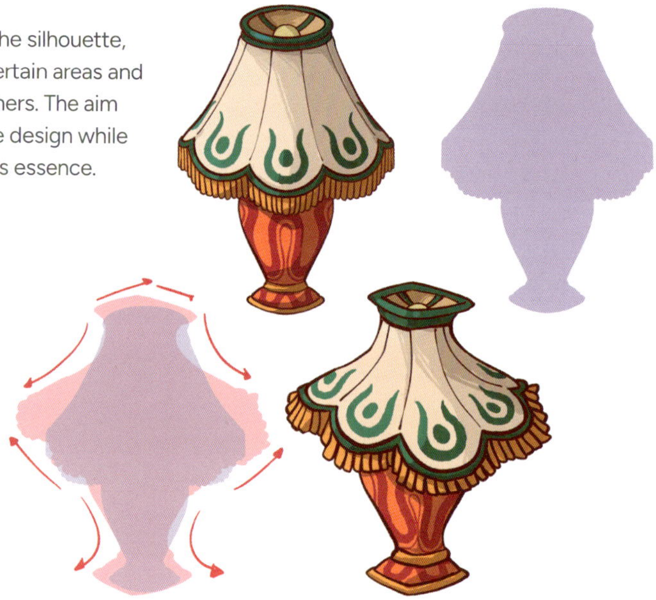

03 Exaggerate the shapes further to make it even wonkier and more stylized.

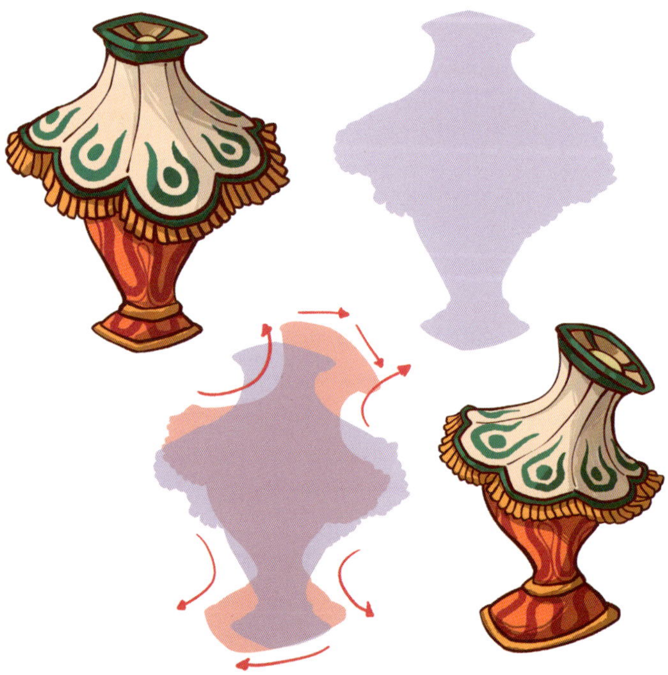

04 Check the silhouette of each design side by side. Is it still recognizable?

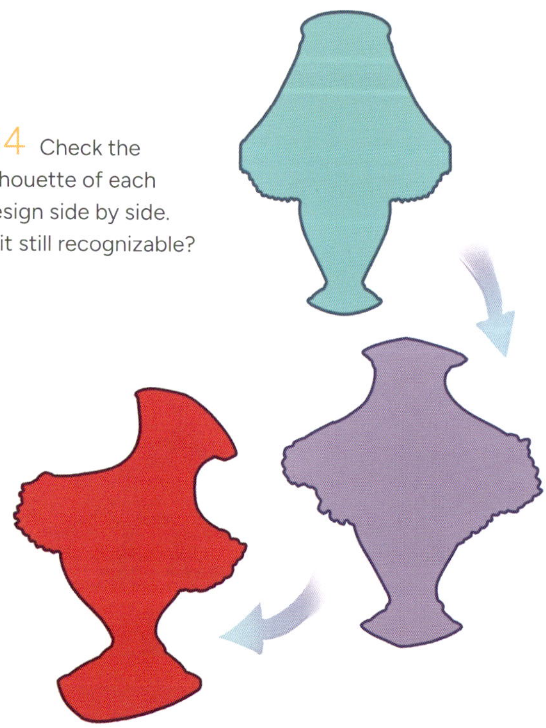

05 Compare the three final coloured designs, observing how the increased distortion and exaggeration makes the lamp appear more stylized.

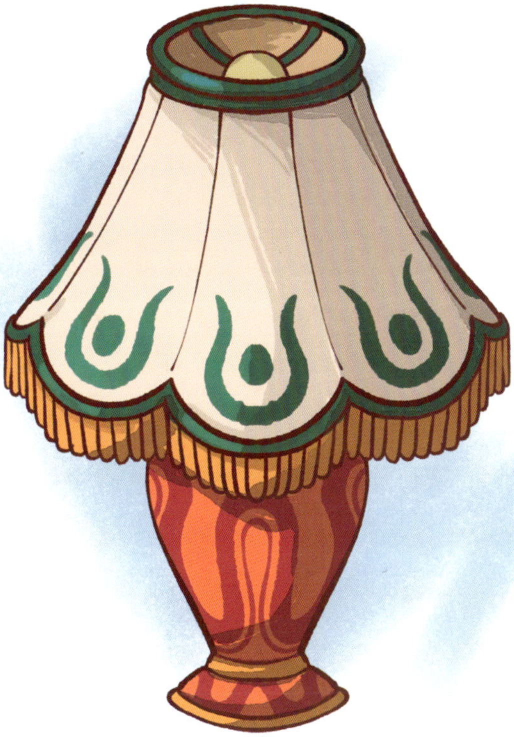

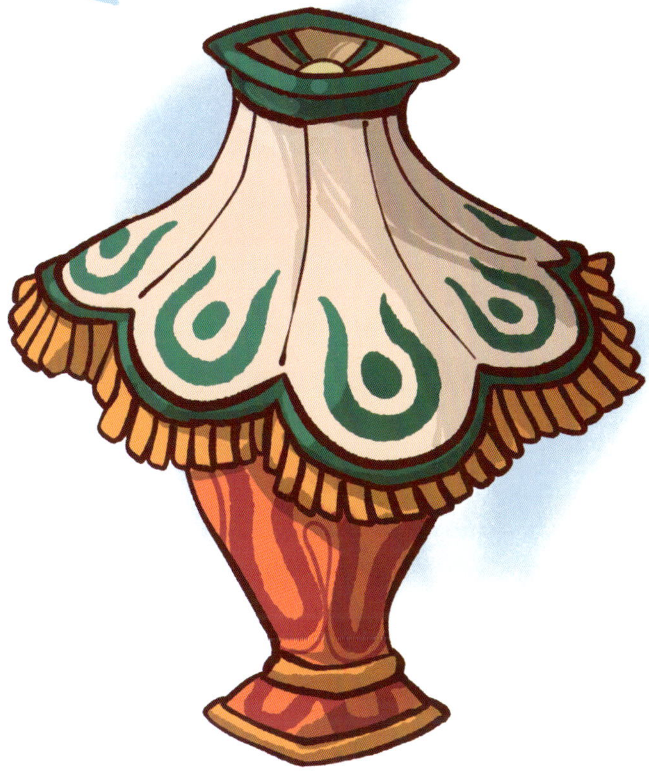

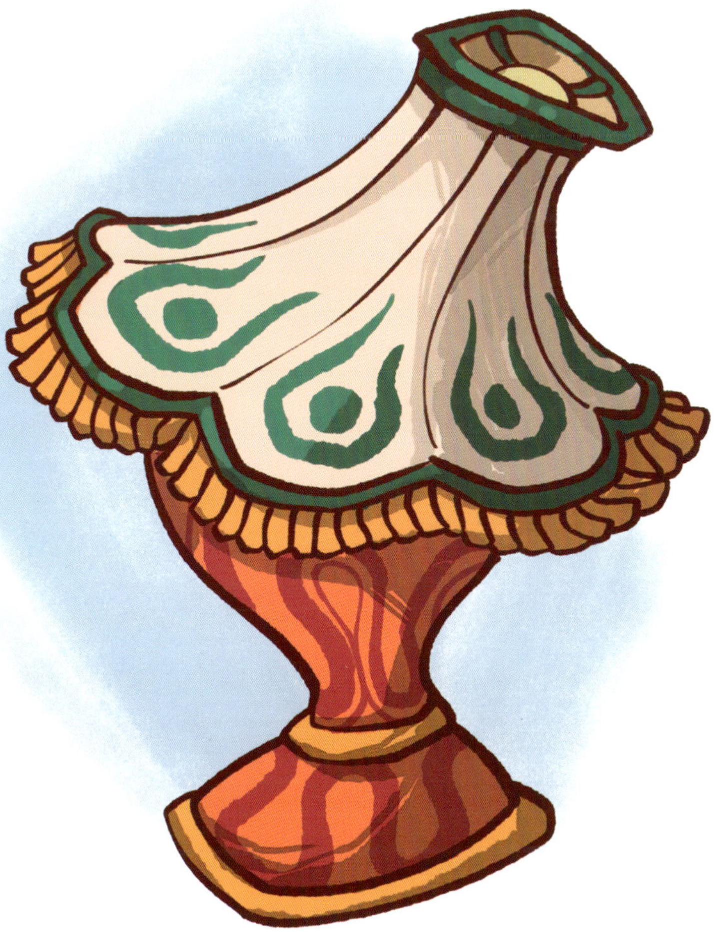

ART: JULIAN DEL REY

A SIMPLER CHARACTER

INTERMEDIATE ●●

Create a new, highly simplified version of an existing character (one of your own or borrowed from another artist).

Reduce the character to big, simple volumes, clear concrete shapes, and only a few small details. Aim to preserve the likeness and most defining features of the character. This challenge will help you define your character-design style, encouraging you to try a new approach.

01 Examine the original character design and identify the features that stand out.

02 If overwhelmed by the amount of detail, break the design down into simple volumes.

03 Push the shapes to their simplest possible forms, then bring back some of the detail where needed to add more interest.

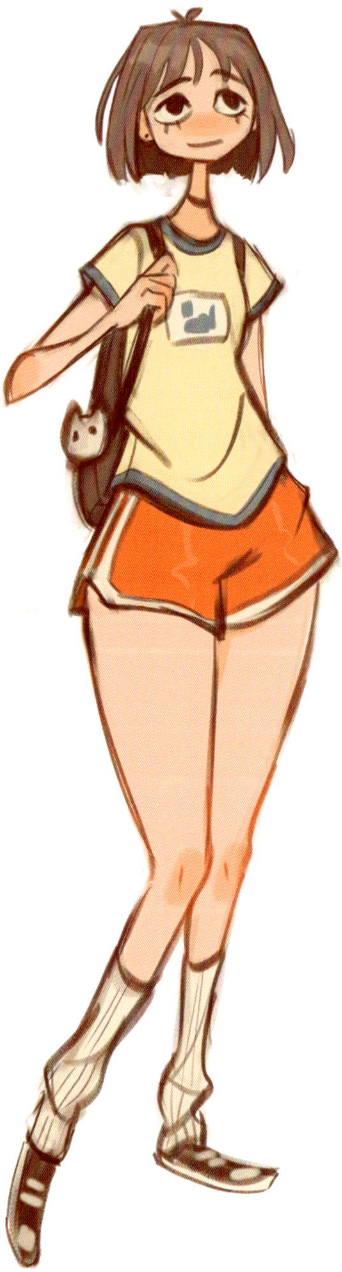

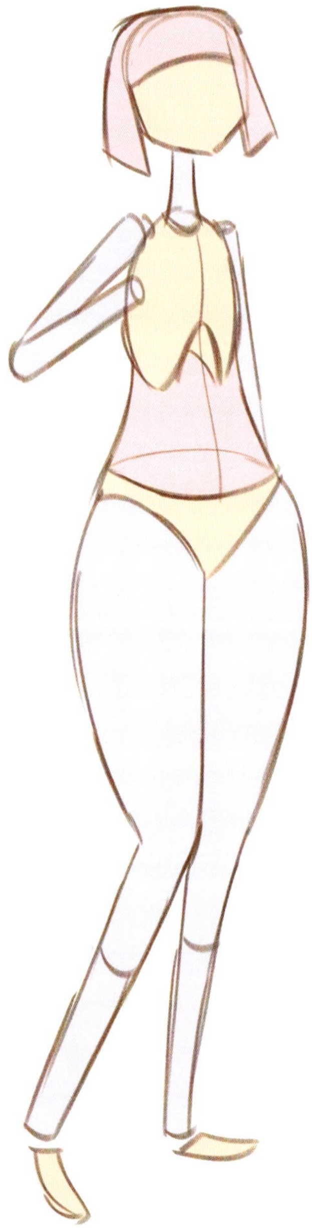

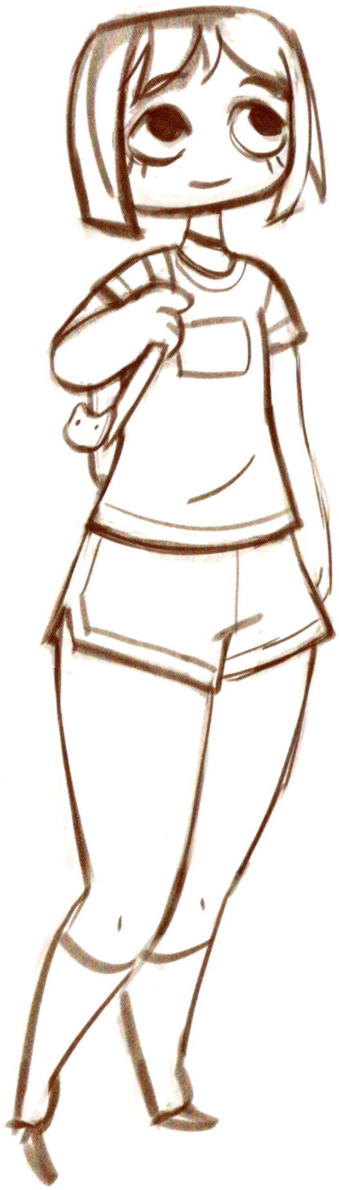

04 Avoid drawing overly complicated clothing folds and creases or too many strands of hair. Keep it simple.

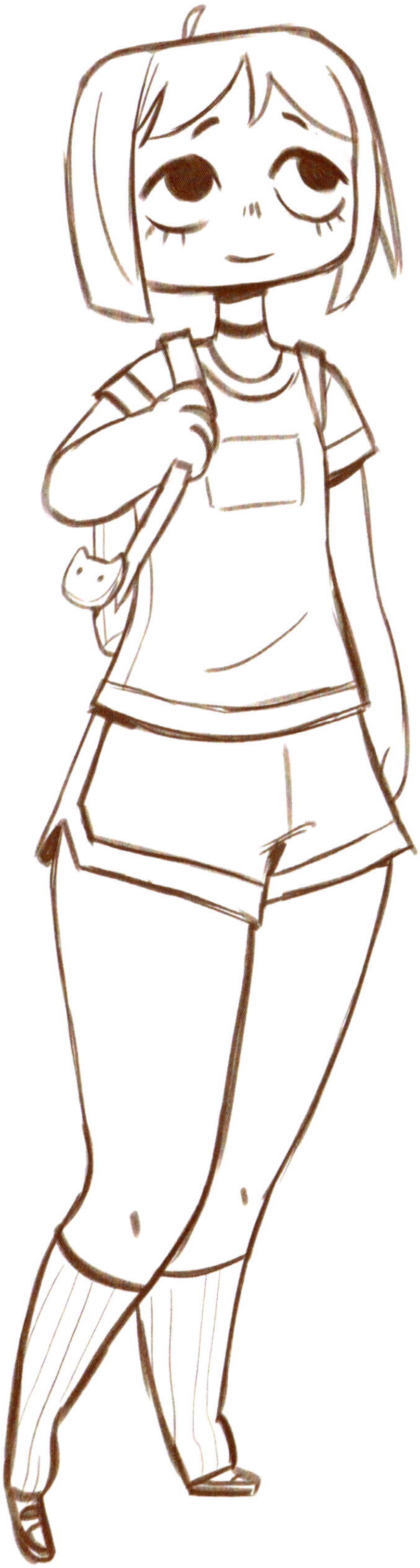

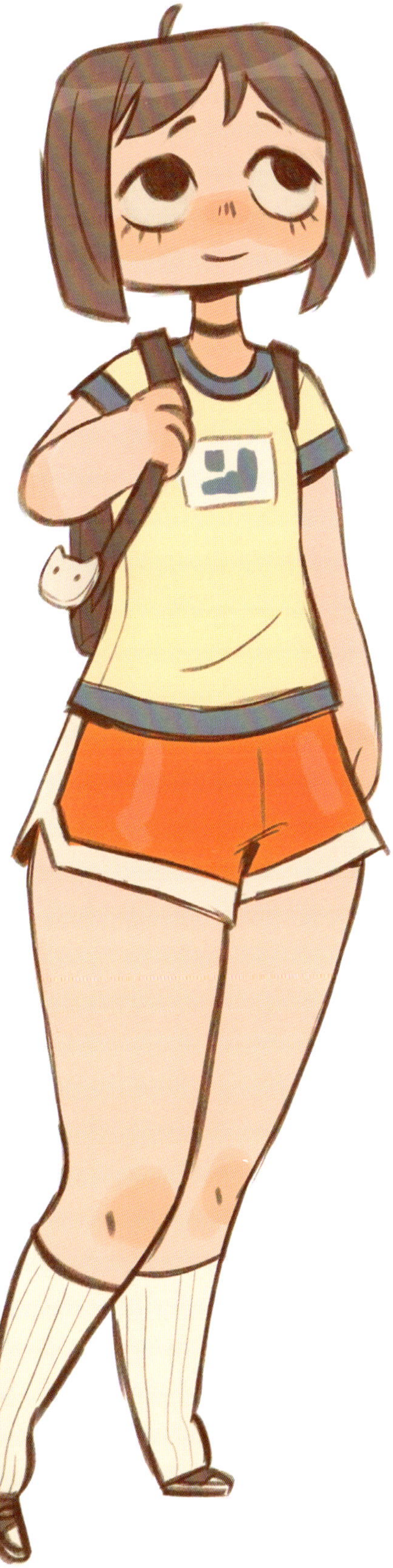

05 Finish by reintroducing colour, then compare your final version to the original design. Could this level of simplicity be a new approach for you?

ART: MAGDALINA DIANOVA

THE SHAPES OF A FACE

INTERMEDIATE ●●

Draw the simple shapes of a face over a photo reference, then convert the shapes into a stylized portrait.

The goal is to stylize through the use of simple shapes, rather than being guided by real-life anatomy. Simplify what you see into big abstract forms, describing each feature with a single shape. For example, the nose could be a triangle, rather than a combination of shapes. Save details and nuances for the final step.

01 Sketch loosely over your reference photo, simplifying what you see into big geometric shapes instead of using the standard methods for drawing a face.

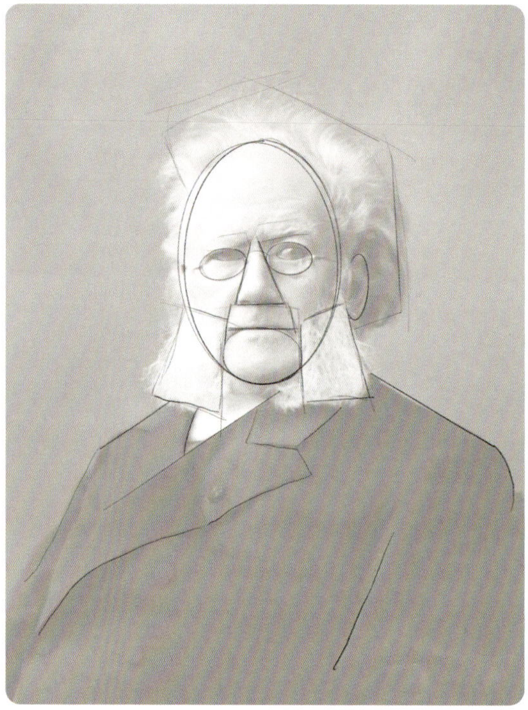

PHOTO BY GUSTAV BORGEN, 1901, ON UNSPLASH

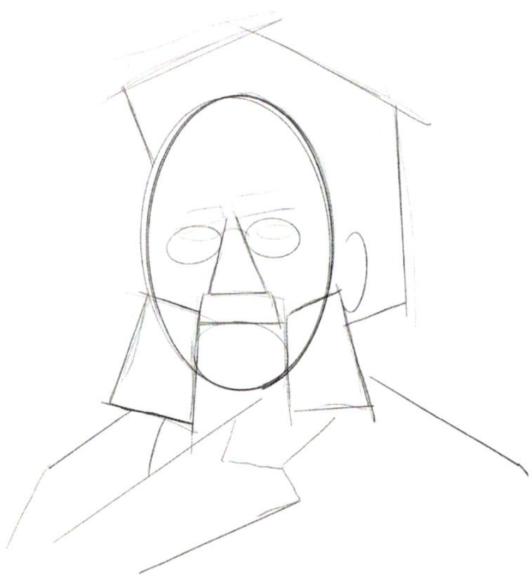

02 Remove the reference and draw back over the shapes, exaggerating the forms and proportions.

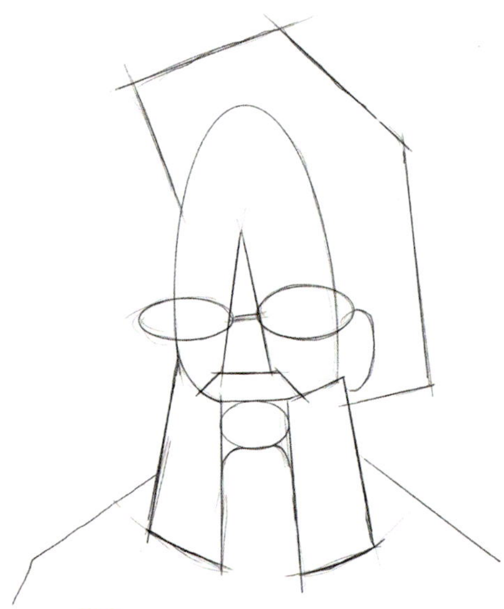

03 Push and stylize each shape again, developing the sketch into a unique character.

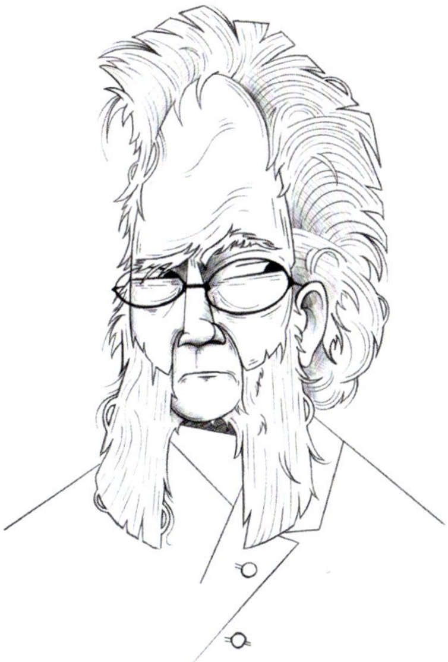

04 Add details to bring your new character to life, using your shapes as a guide.

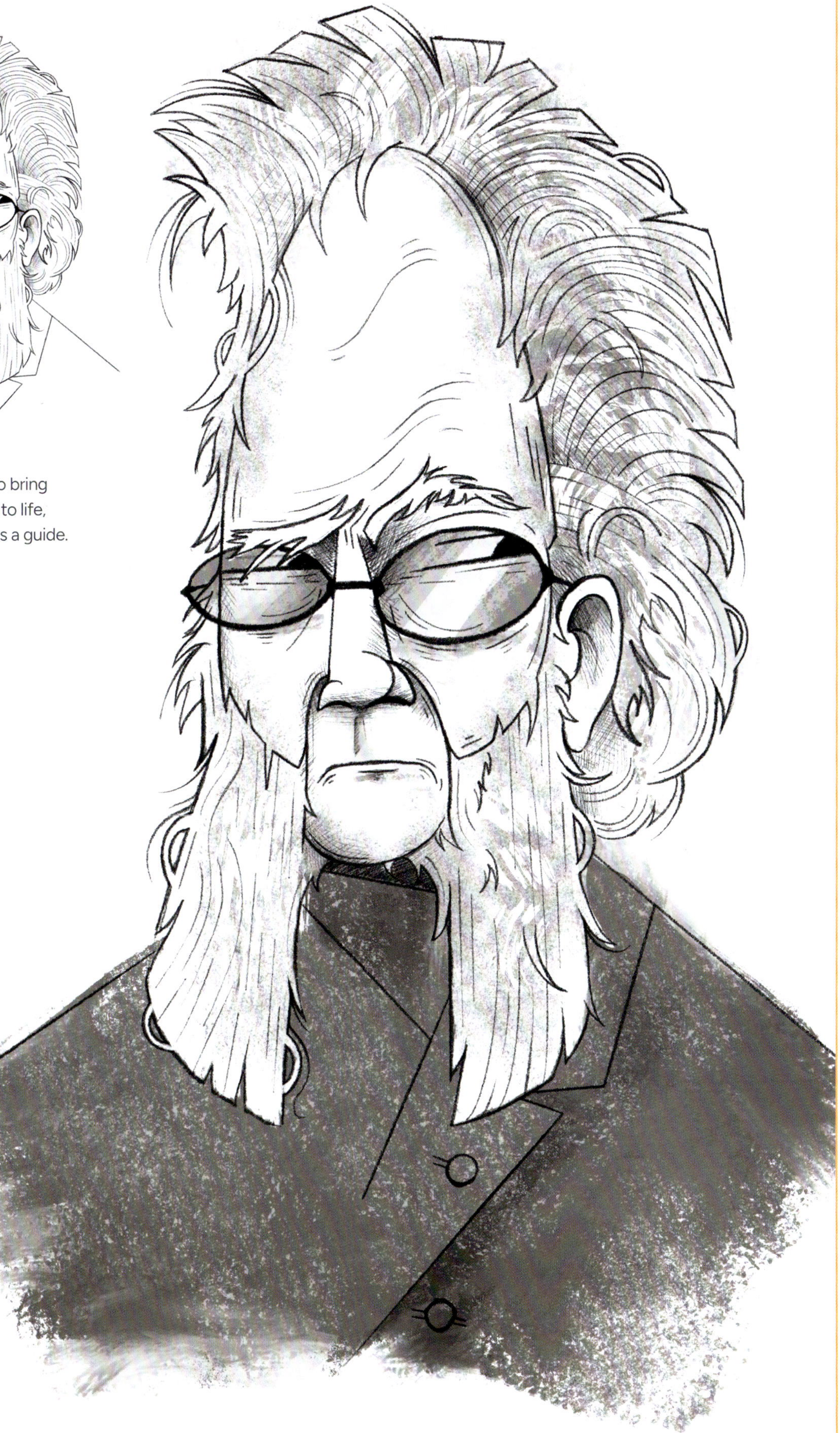

05 Increase the level of detail and shading to finish your stylized portrait.

ART: LANDER STRIJBOL

VEHICLE MIX-UP

ADVANCED ●●●

Choose two very different vehicles and merge them into one new one.

In this example, a modern-day food stand is mixed with a vintage car. Using the shapes and forms of two very different vehicles will help you develop your own style in bringing them together. This is also good practice for ensuring a vehicle stays functional and recognizable while being stylized.

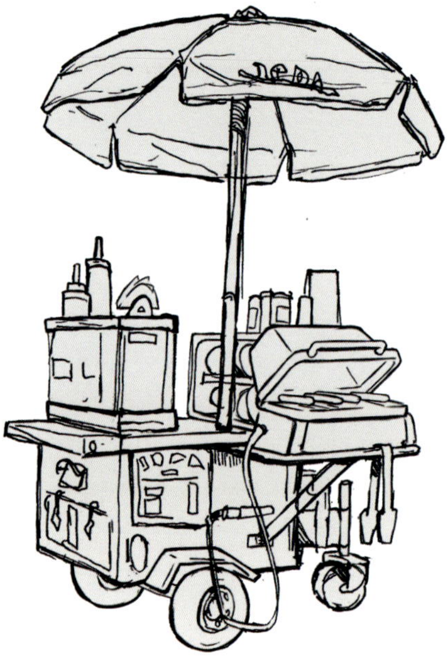

01 Sketch your chosen subjects. In this case, a modern-day hot-dog stand and a vintage car. Study the elements that make each object unique.

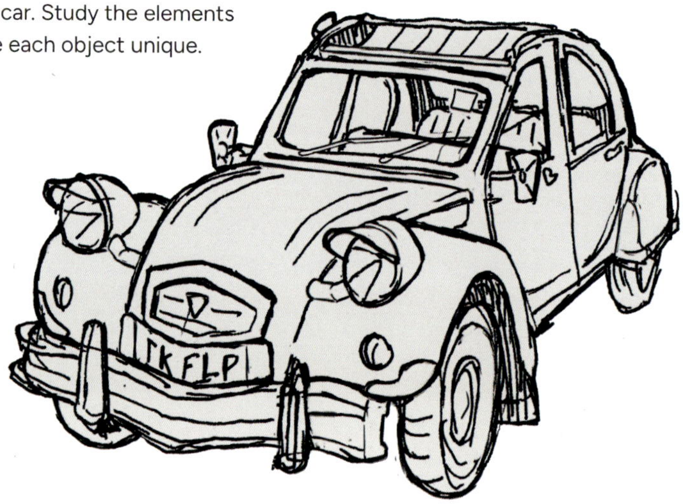

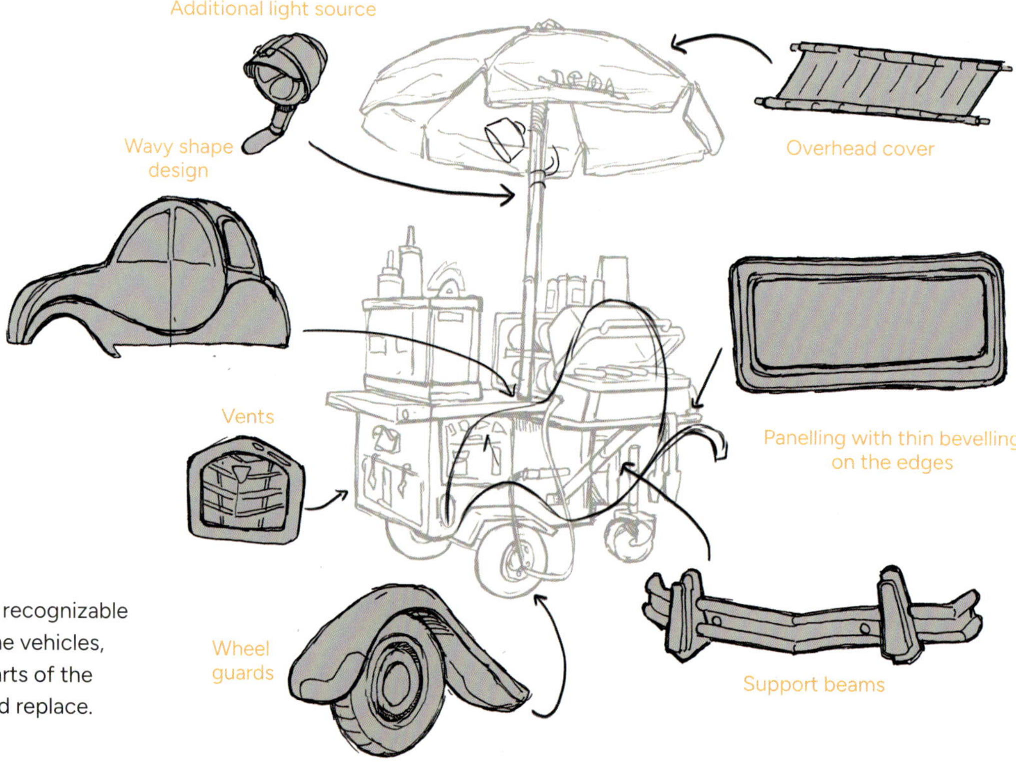

02 Extract the most recognizable features from one of the vehicles, then consider which parts of the other vehicle they could replace.

03 Create a rough sketch combining features from both vehicles without worrying about technical accuracy. Is the hot-dog stand still recognizable? Are the vintage-car elements obvious?

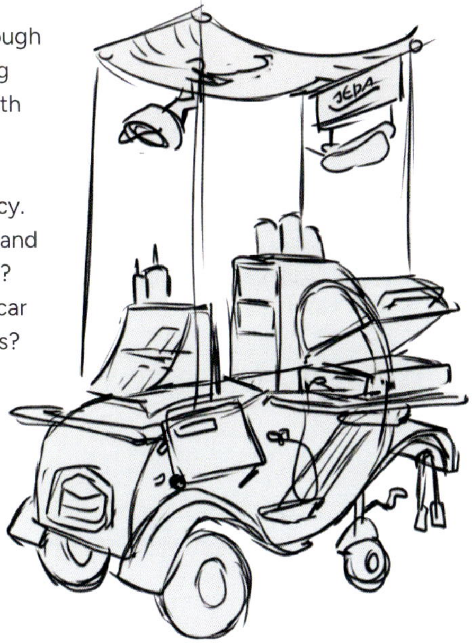

04 To help you visualize the design in three-dimensional space, group the features into simple, coloured solids.

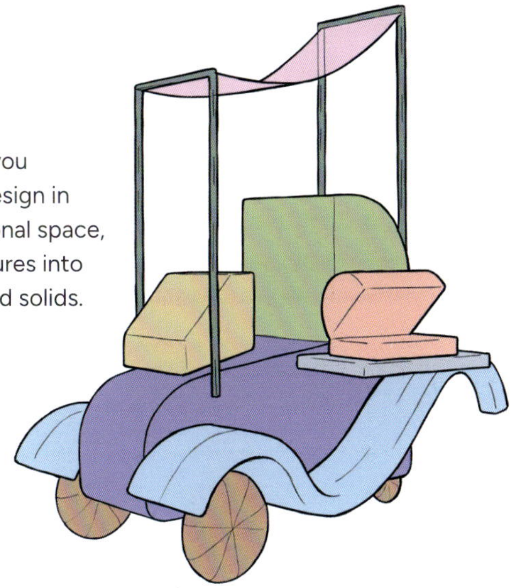

05 Add functional details to ensure the new vehicle still serves its purpose, and add simple shading to finish.

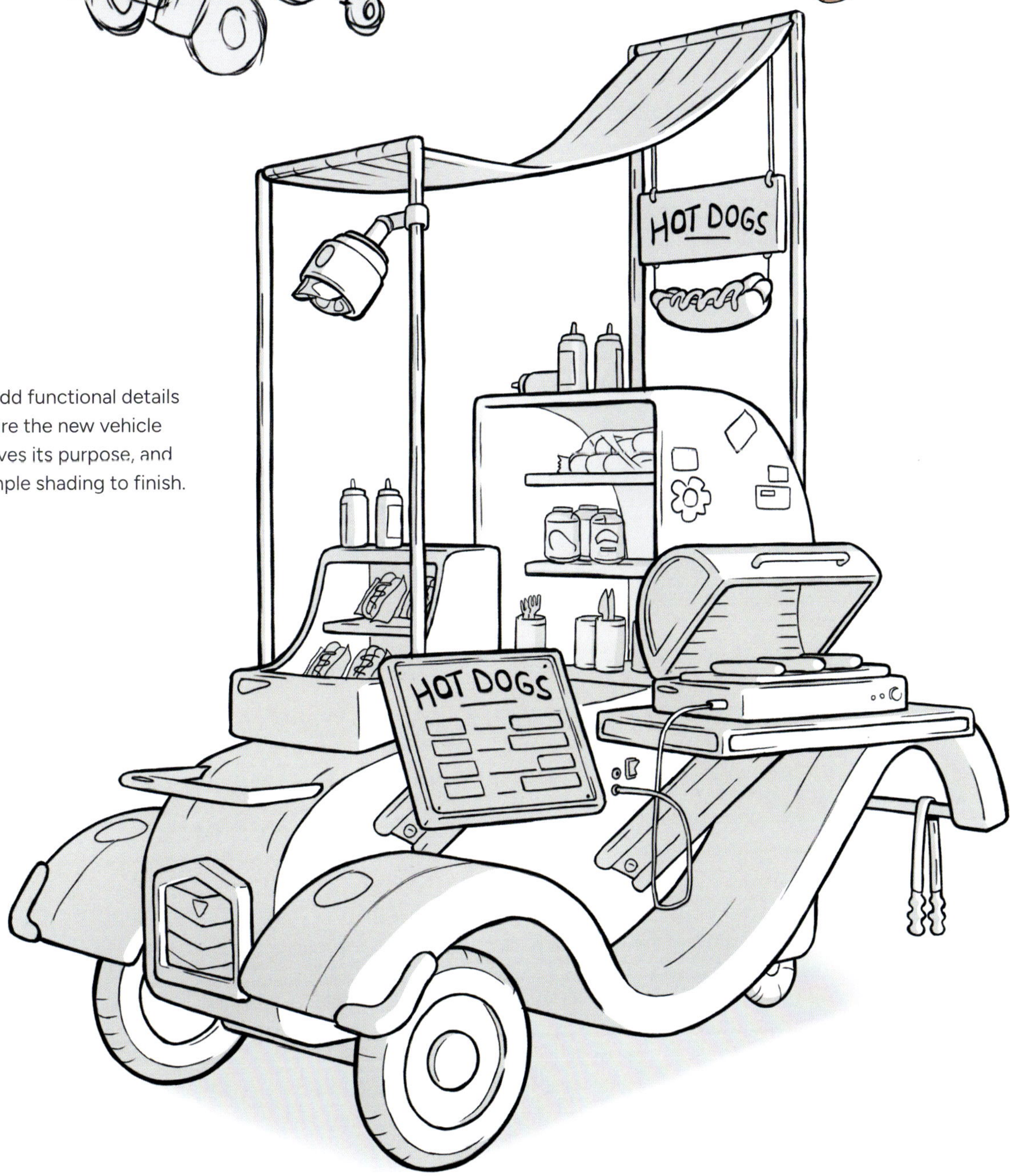

ART: MARIANA NORONHA

DELETE THE DETAIL

ADVANCED ●●●

Create a detailed sketch of a building, then gradually remove the detail until you're left with a very simplified version.

This challenge will help you to draw in the simplest way possible, minimizing the components of a subject while maintaining the recognizability. Notice how this simplification changes the style of the building and perhaps helps you discover a new element of your style.

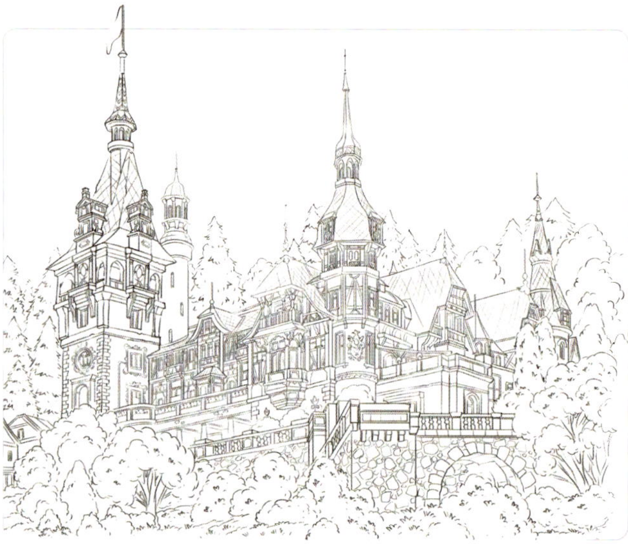

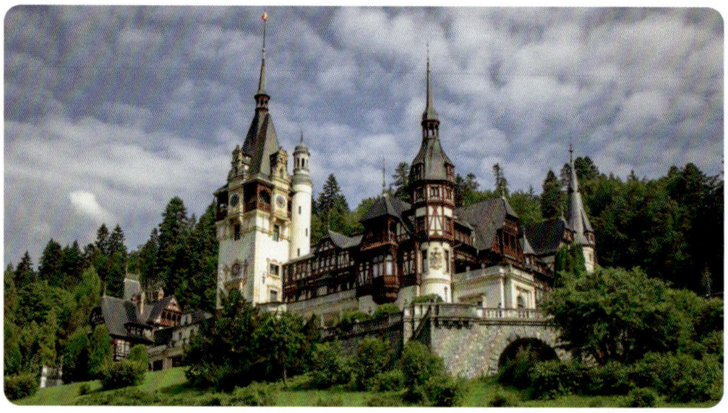

PHOTO OF PELES CASTLE BY REANIMATED MAN X ON UNSPLASH

01 Choose a reference photo and sketch your building, including as much detail as possible. Pay attention to the intricacies as you try to capture the identity of the building.

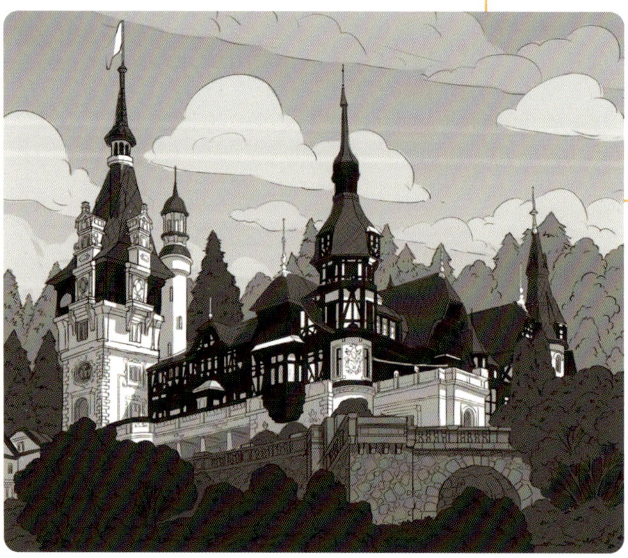

02 Using digital-painting software, add simple tones for each element, including windows, roofs, walls, trees, clouds, and the sky. Introducing these tones will make it easier to understand the structure of the image as you begin to think about how to simplify it.

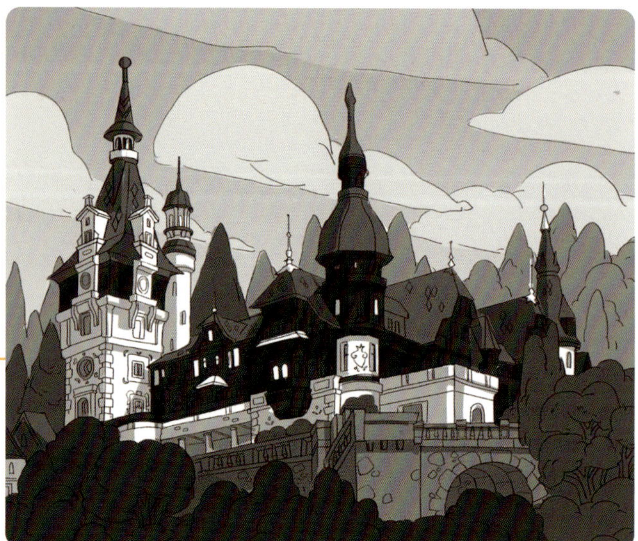

03 Start to decrease the level of detail in the image. Reduce the amount of windows and decor. Simplify any detailed brickwork, tiling, or panelling. Make tweaks to the main shapes, being careful not to lose the character of the building.

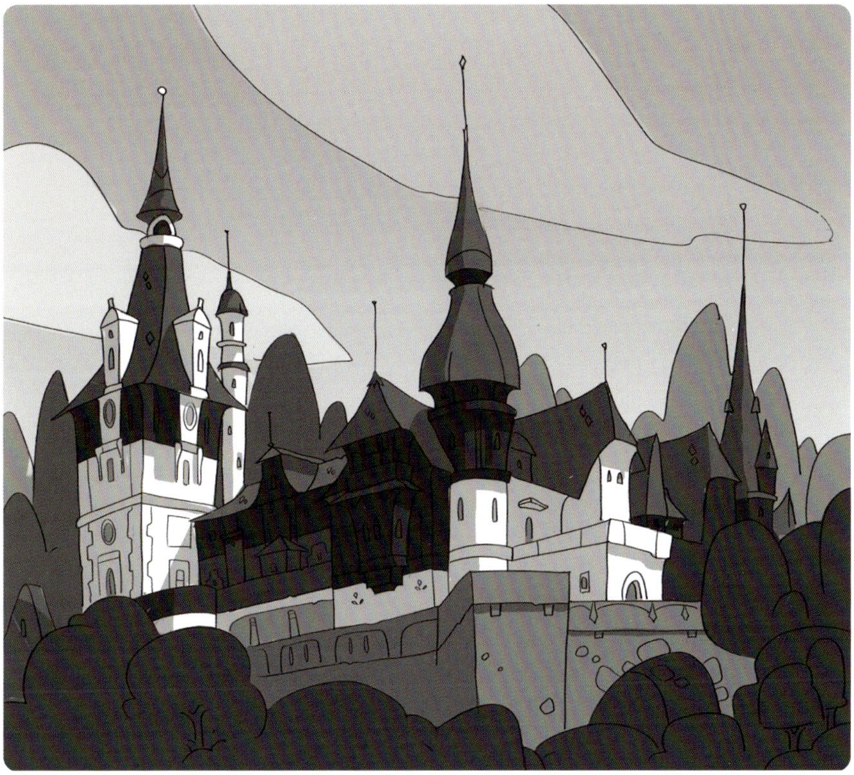

04 Further reduce the amount of detail, simplifying each element into even more basic forms. Replace ornate and complex details with more straightforward shapes, but avoid changing the forms to the extent that the building is no longer recognizable.

05 Add simple colours and basic shading to finish. Do you prefer your detailed or simplified version of the building? Which better suits your style?

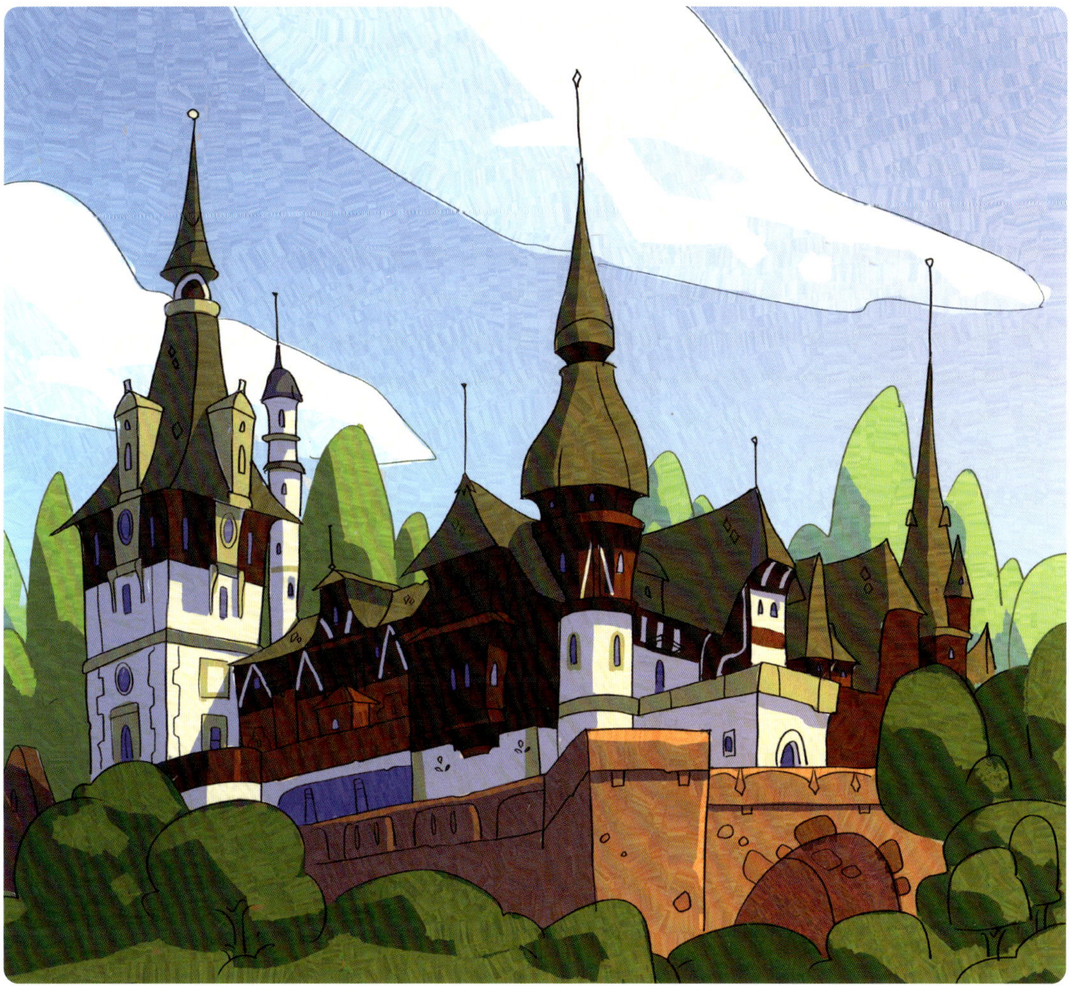

ART: ALFRED FERNANDES

FROM BUG TO BIKE

ADVANCED ●●●

Select a reference photo of an insect, then turn the bug into a bike – or any other vehicle design!

Experiment with how you can blend the function of the vehicle with the shape and flow of the insect. The example shown begins as a praying mantis – its unique form makes a great starting point. Using nature as inspiration can be a great tool in testing your art style and making new creative discoveries.

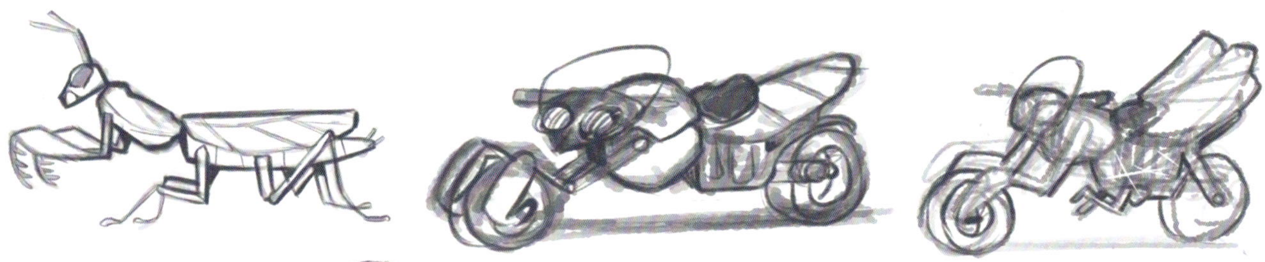

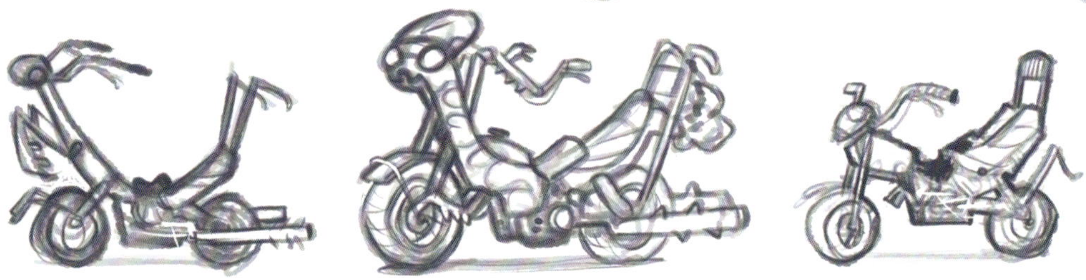

01 Start by making a profile sketch of the insect's body, then draw several vehicle designs that incorporate elements of its shape.

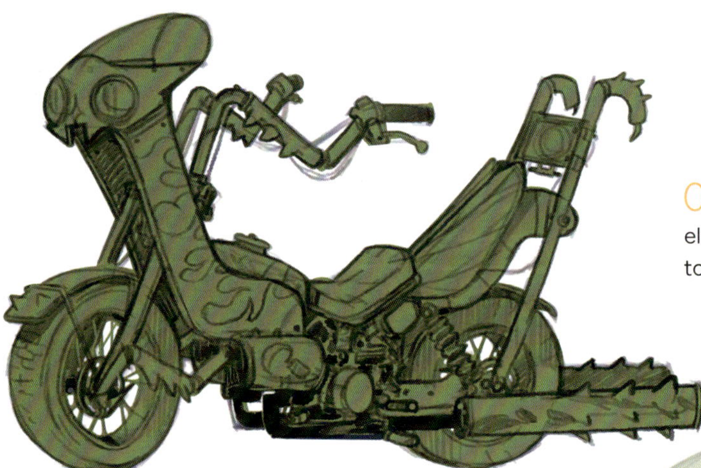

02 Combine your favourite elements from each sketch to create a final drawing.

03 Introduce colour to further suggest the look and feel of the chosen insect.

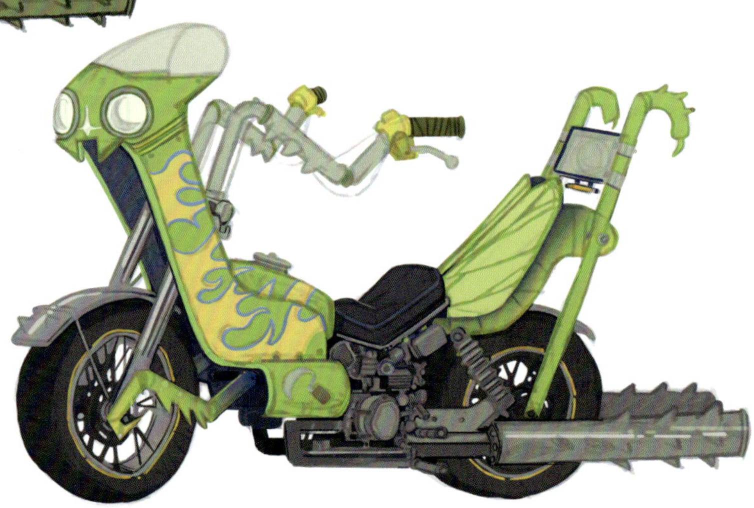

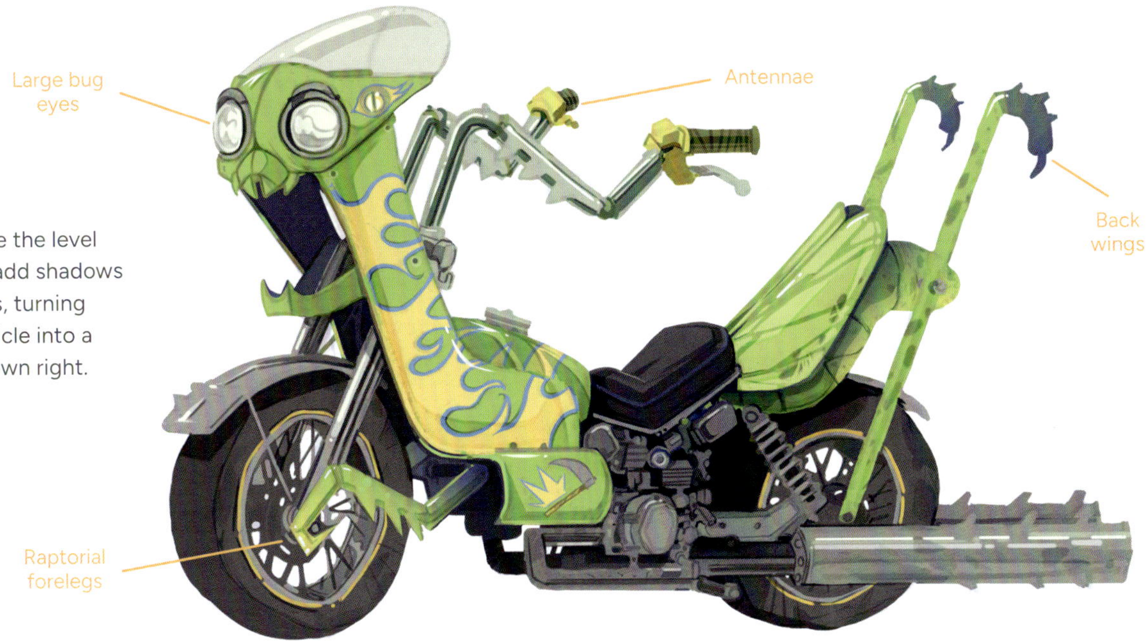

04 Increase the level of detail and add shadows and highlights, turning your new vehicle into a design in its own right.

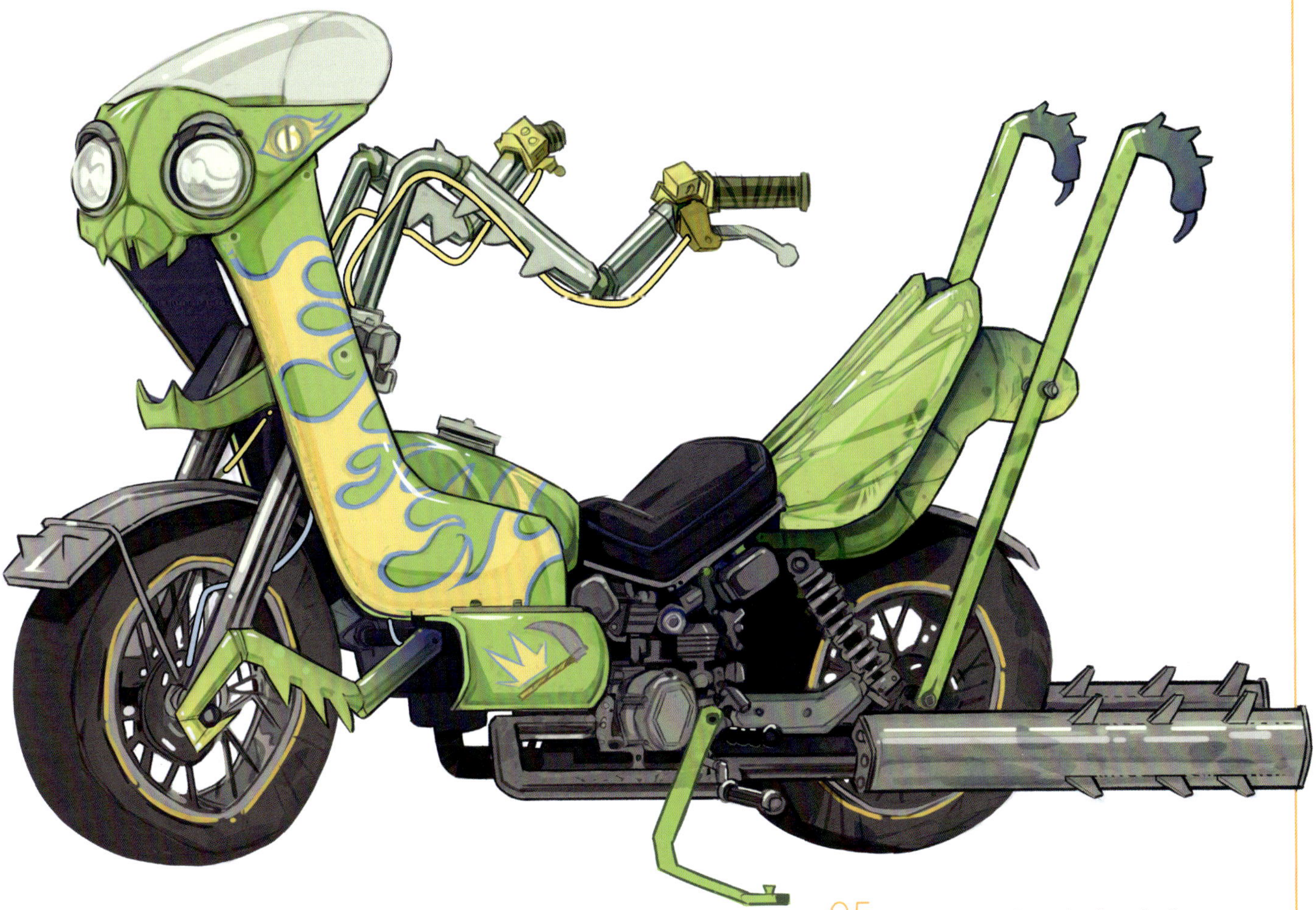

05 Add final details and refine the line work to finish. Does your new design feature shapes and forms you wouldn't usually have included in your art?

ART: LOEON LEAL

STYLE SWITCH-UP

ADVANCED ●●●

Find a historical painting you admire, then recreate it in a different, more modern style.

For example, try redrawing a Renaissance painting in the style of an anime movie, or a Pre-Raphaelite painting in a dynamic comic-book style. What elements can you carry over, and what must change? Adapting art styles in this way will help you practise different shape language, colour palettes, and compositions to develop your own favourite approach.

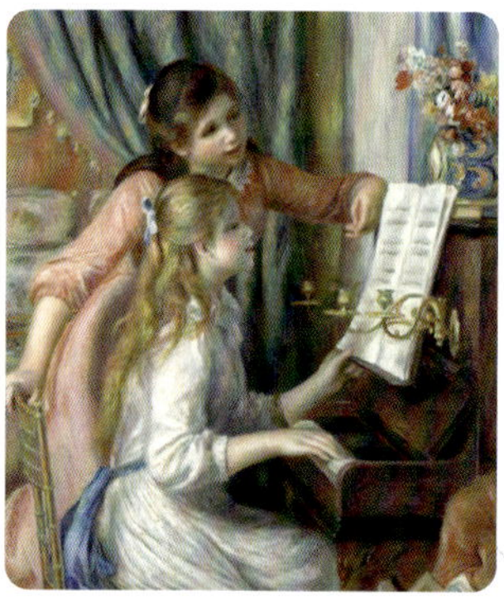

TWO YOUNG GIRLS AT THE PIANO BY PIERRE-AUGUSTE RENOIR, 1892

01 Start by sketching out the rough composition of your chosen image. This example will look at how to recreate *Two Young Girls at the Piano* by Renoir in the style of a 2D Disney movie.

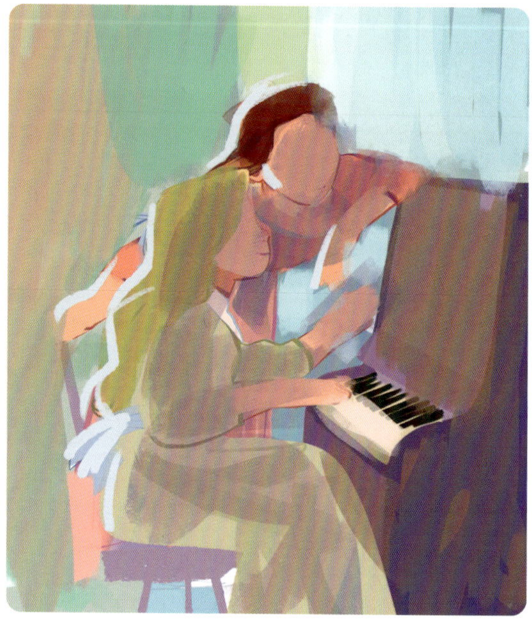

02 Next, roughly paint the basic colours of your new painting, identifying elements of the original you can use in the new style. In this example, the gentle shapes and soft, colourful tones can be carried over to maintain the calm, tenderness of the scene.

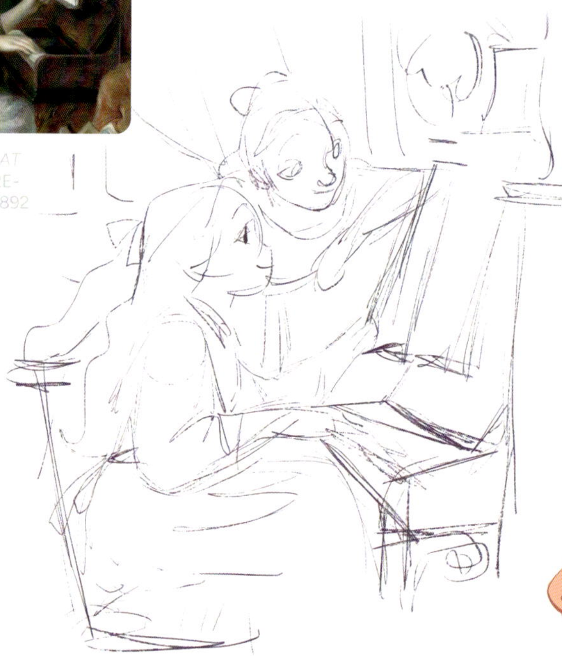

03 If there are people in your chosen painting, they are likely to remain as the main focus. Study their forms, posture, and gesture, then redraw them using shapes and features characteristic of the chosen style.

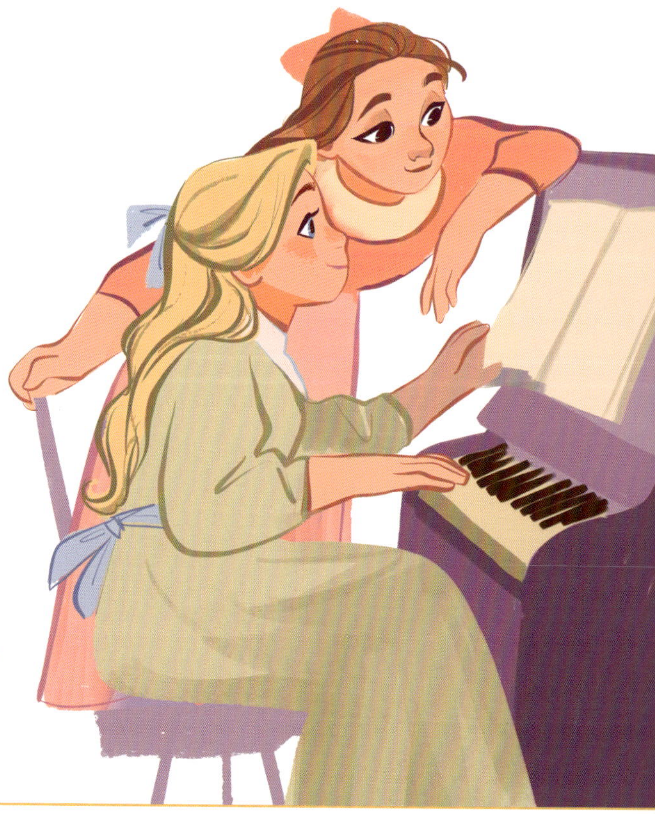

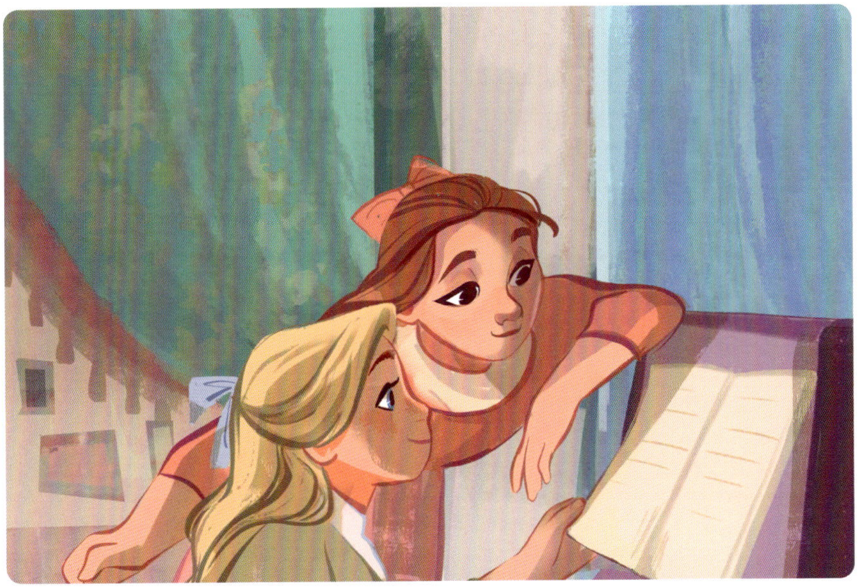

04 As you add a background and more detail to your new version, pay close attention to how the shapes and forms differ in the new style – for example, what is it that makes these shapes more 'Disney'?

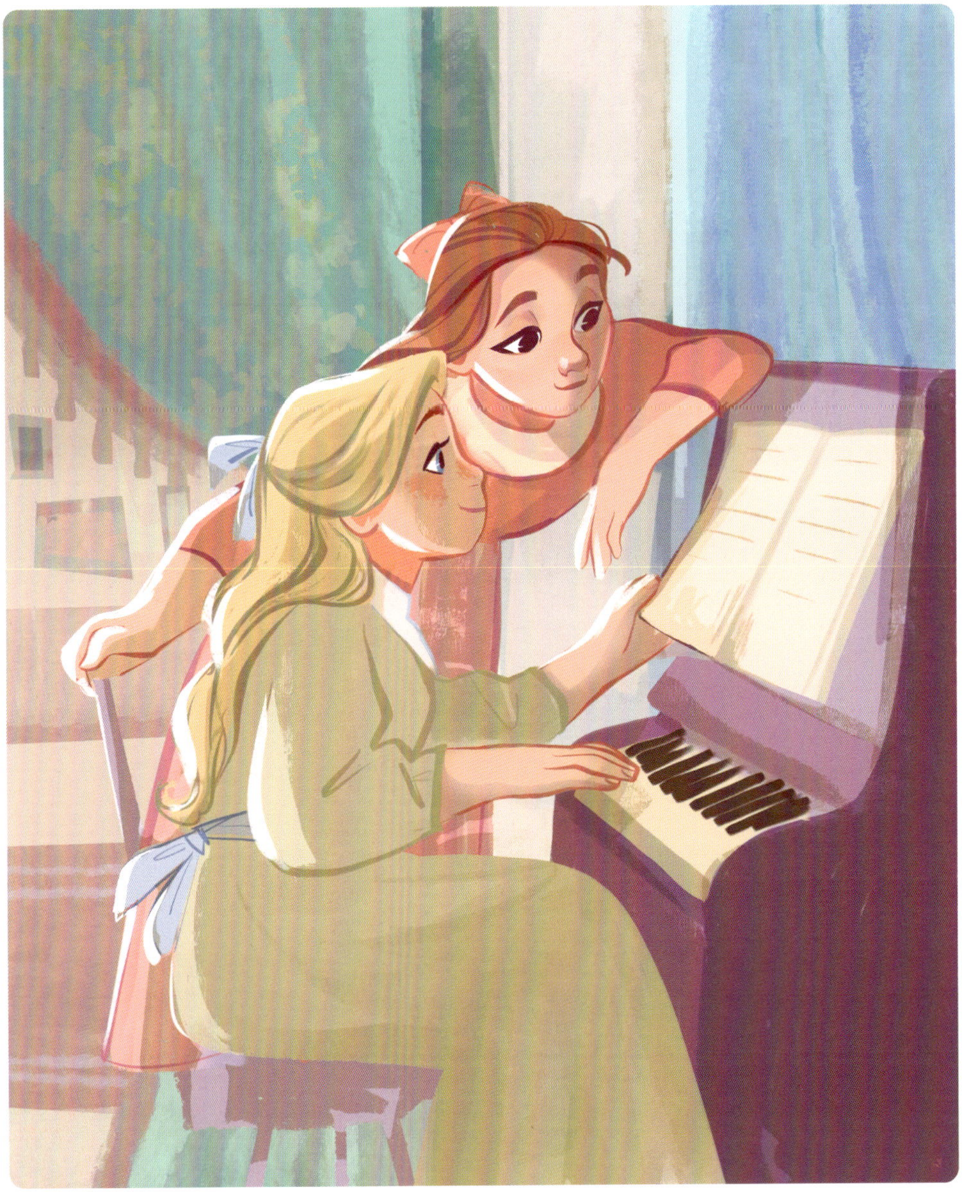

05 To finish, try to add highlights and shading that reflect the original painting but suit the new style.

SPARE PARTS

ADVANCED ●●●

Choose an interesting object, break it down into parts, and then use the parts to create a completely different item.

De-constructing an object in this way is a great method for coming up with a new design inspired by an everyday item. It's as simple as observing its qualities or functions from another angle, and exploring your personal art style as you create something entirely new from its parts.

01 Start by sketching the chosen object – in this case, a portable cassette player. Study the shapes that make up its design, looking for inspiration. The oven-like tape-deck door sparks an idea ... a musical mobile coffee cart!

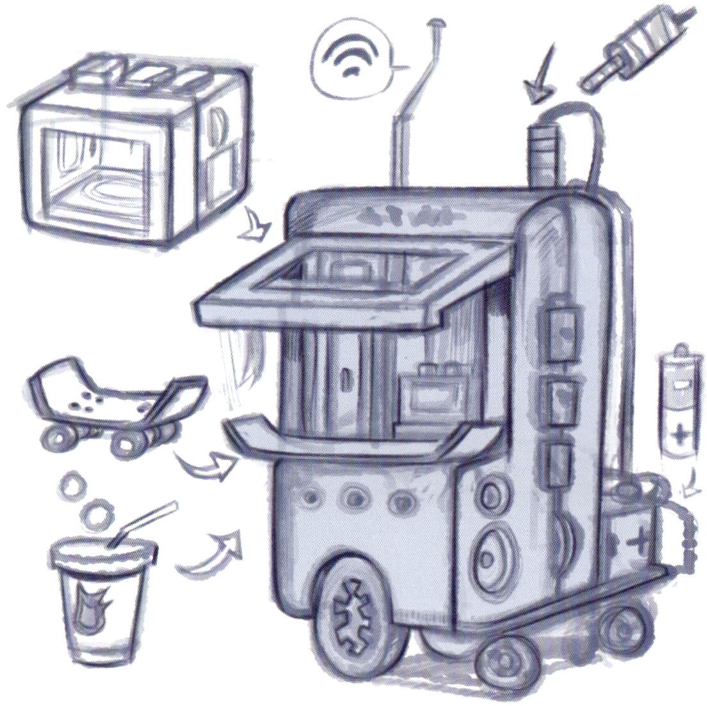

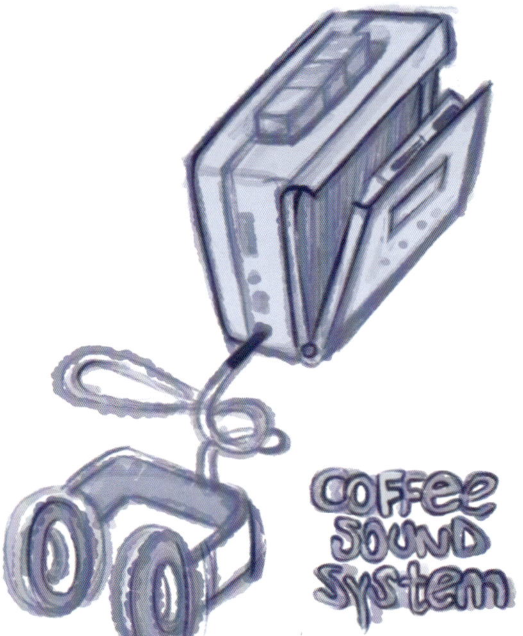

02 Refine the sketch of your new design to define the elements, incorporating shapes and details from the original object into its design.

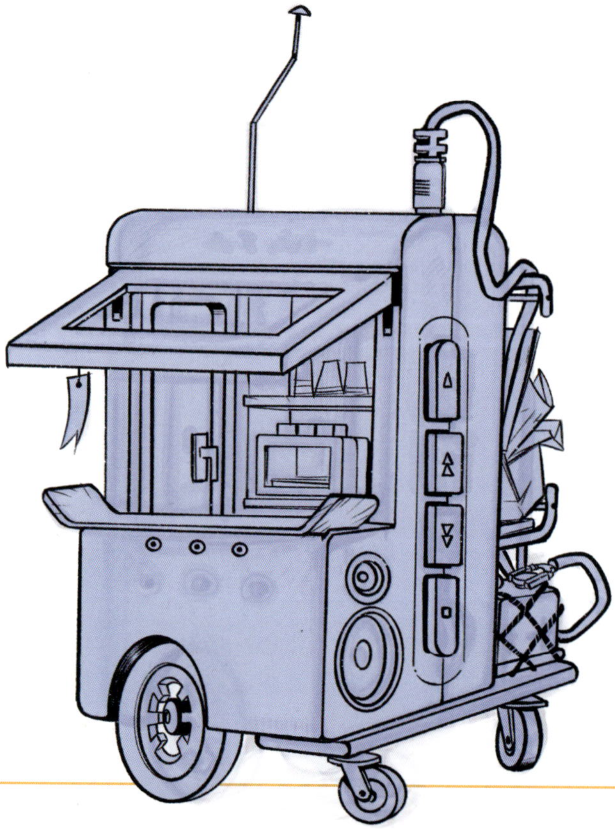

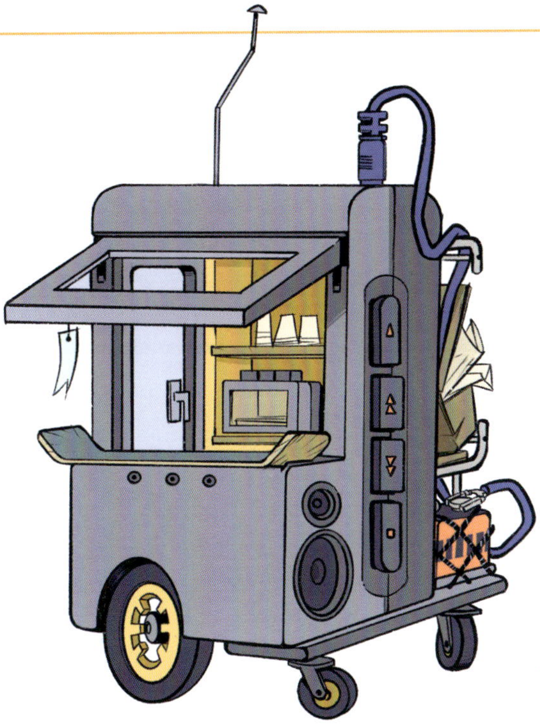

03 Go over the line work, then introduce flat base colours. Refer back to the original object when choosing a colour palette.

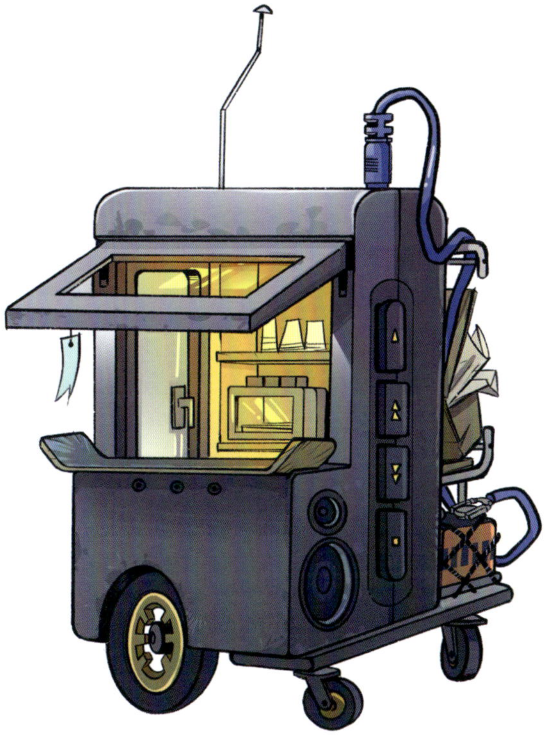

04 Introduce simple highlights and shadows to give your new design some three-dimensionality. Add textures to make it feel more 'real'.

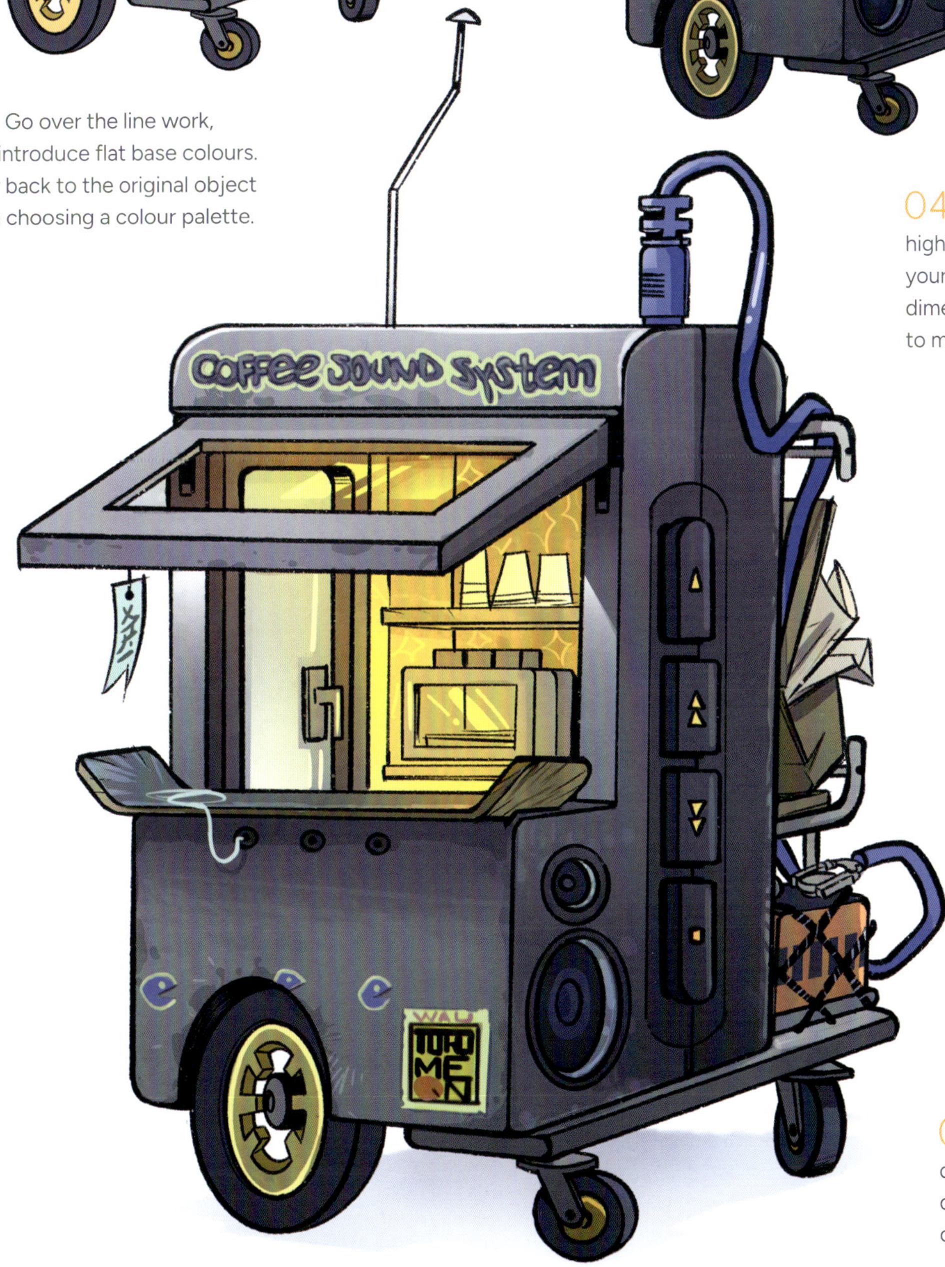

05 Add final details that demonstrate the functionality of the new design, such as cables, decor, and paintwork.

One-page challenges:

HATCHING THE FORM

BEGINNER ●

Choose an object and draw it using only hatching, following the contours of the object like a wire frame.

If drawing an apple, for example, hatch curved lines that hug the round shape of the fruit. Also try adding hatched shadows under the objects, providing information about lighting, shape, and volume with only these simple lines.

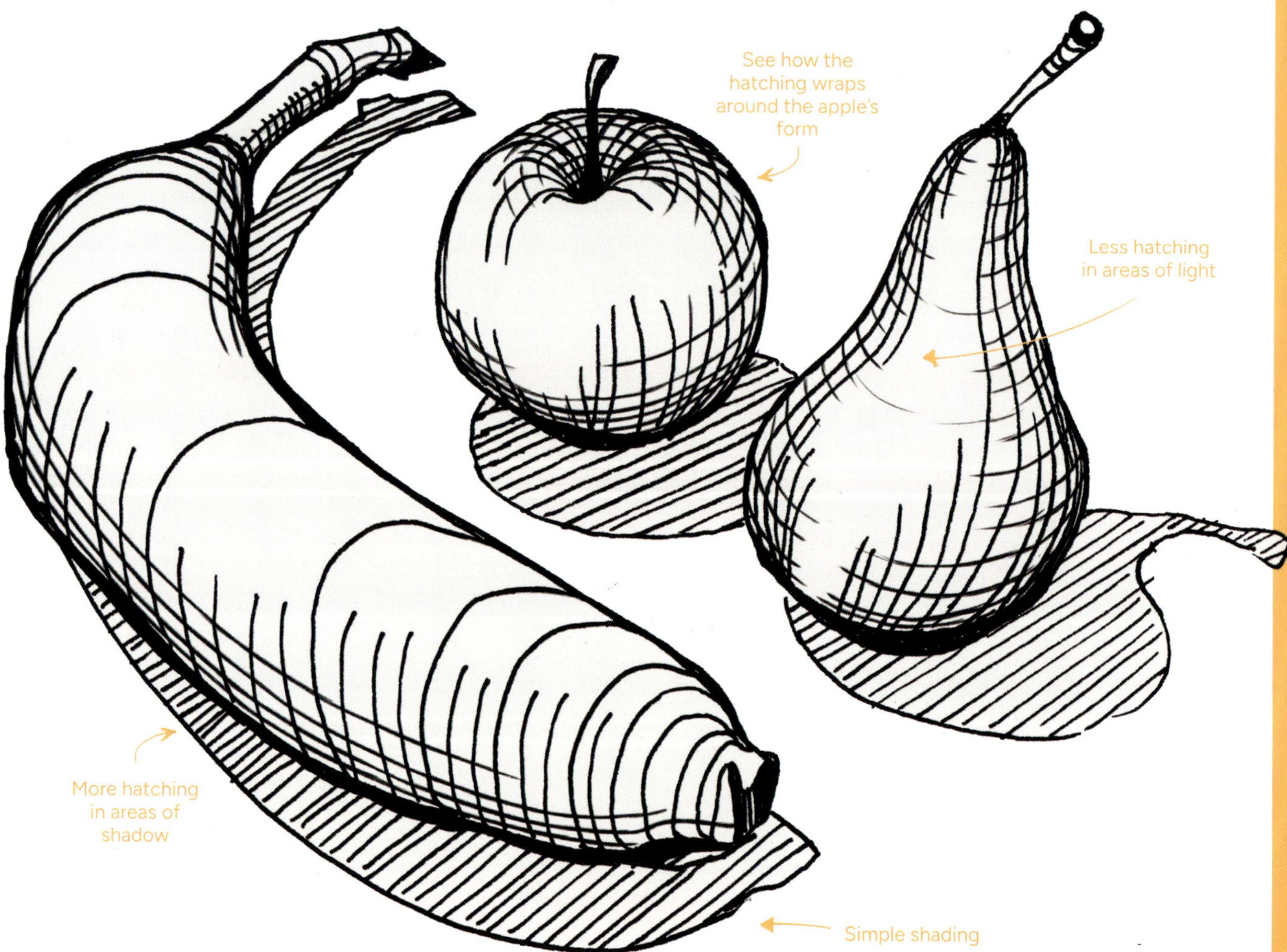

ART: MARIANA NORONHA

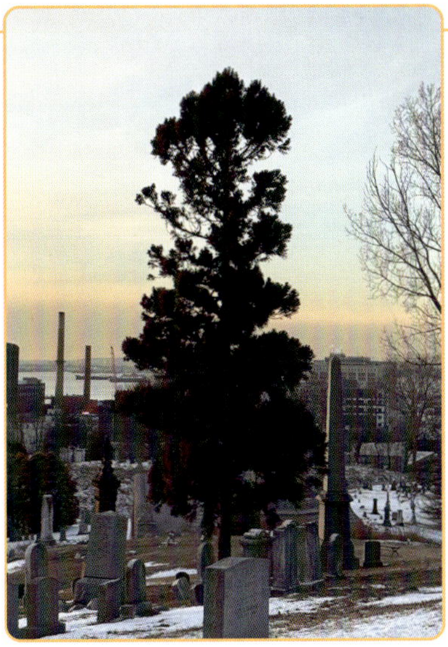

THREE TREES

BEGINNER ●

Draw three versions of the same tree: one using only straight lines, one using only curved lines, and one using both straight and curved lines.

You can use a photo reference or find a tree to draw from life. Notice how the shape language changes the mood in each version – which style did you enjoy drawing the most?

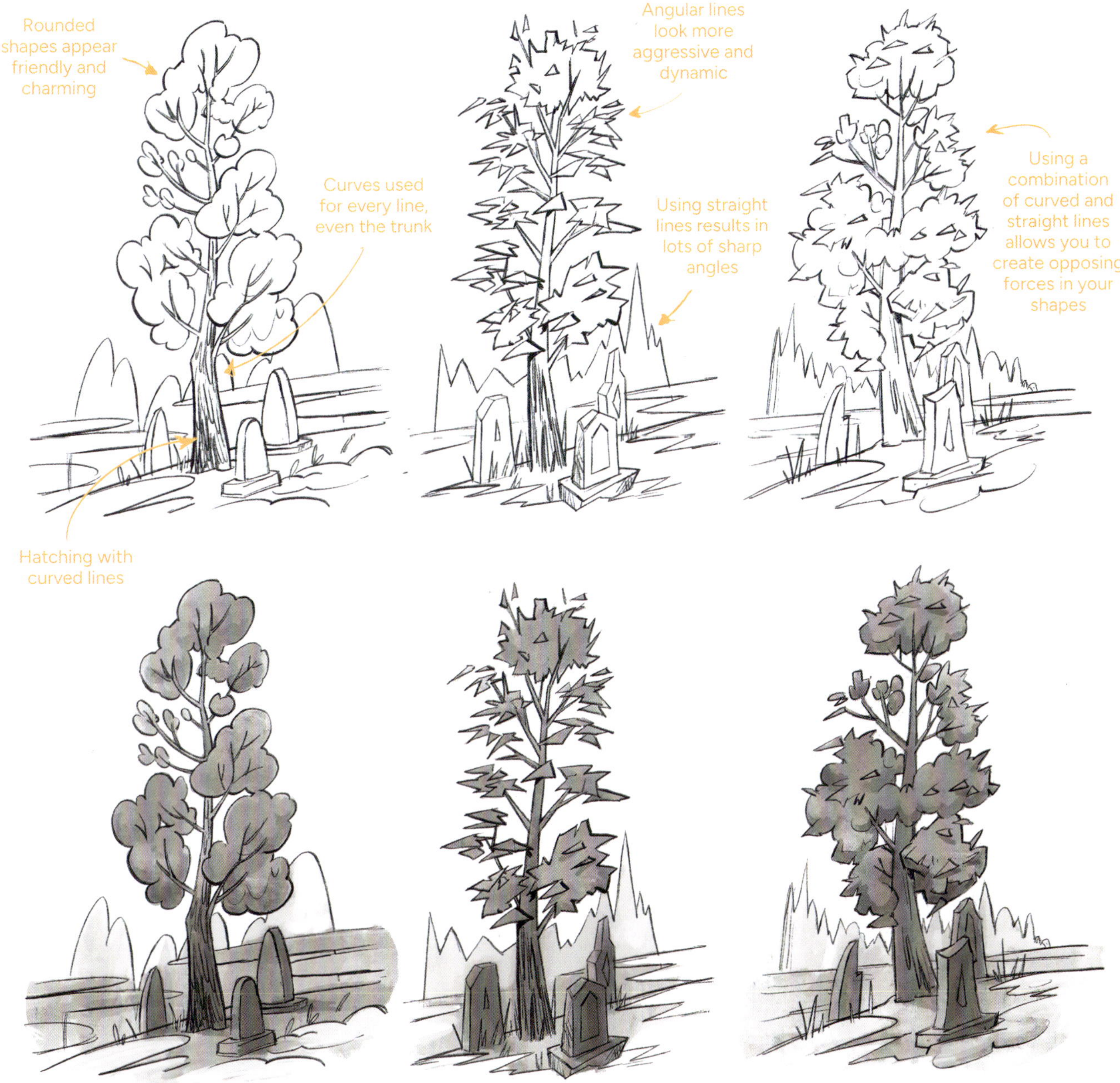

SILHOUETTES

BEGINNER ●

Fill a page with various silhouettes of the same creature, character, or object.

Try to create shapes and forms that are recognizable and easy to understand, as this is crucial for a strong design. This challenge should make you think differently about the shapes you create in your art.

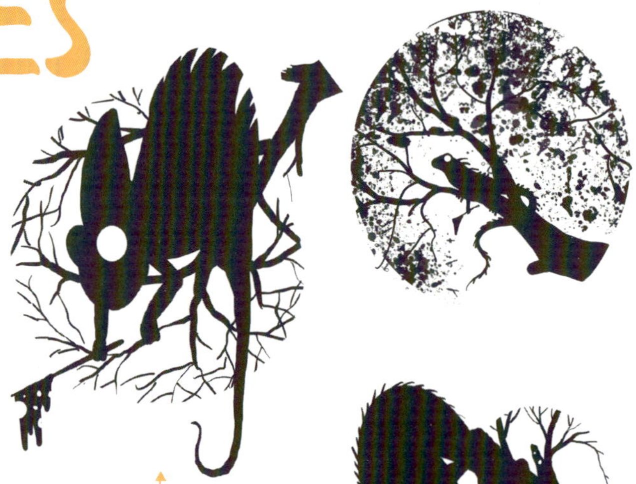

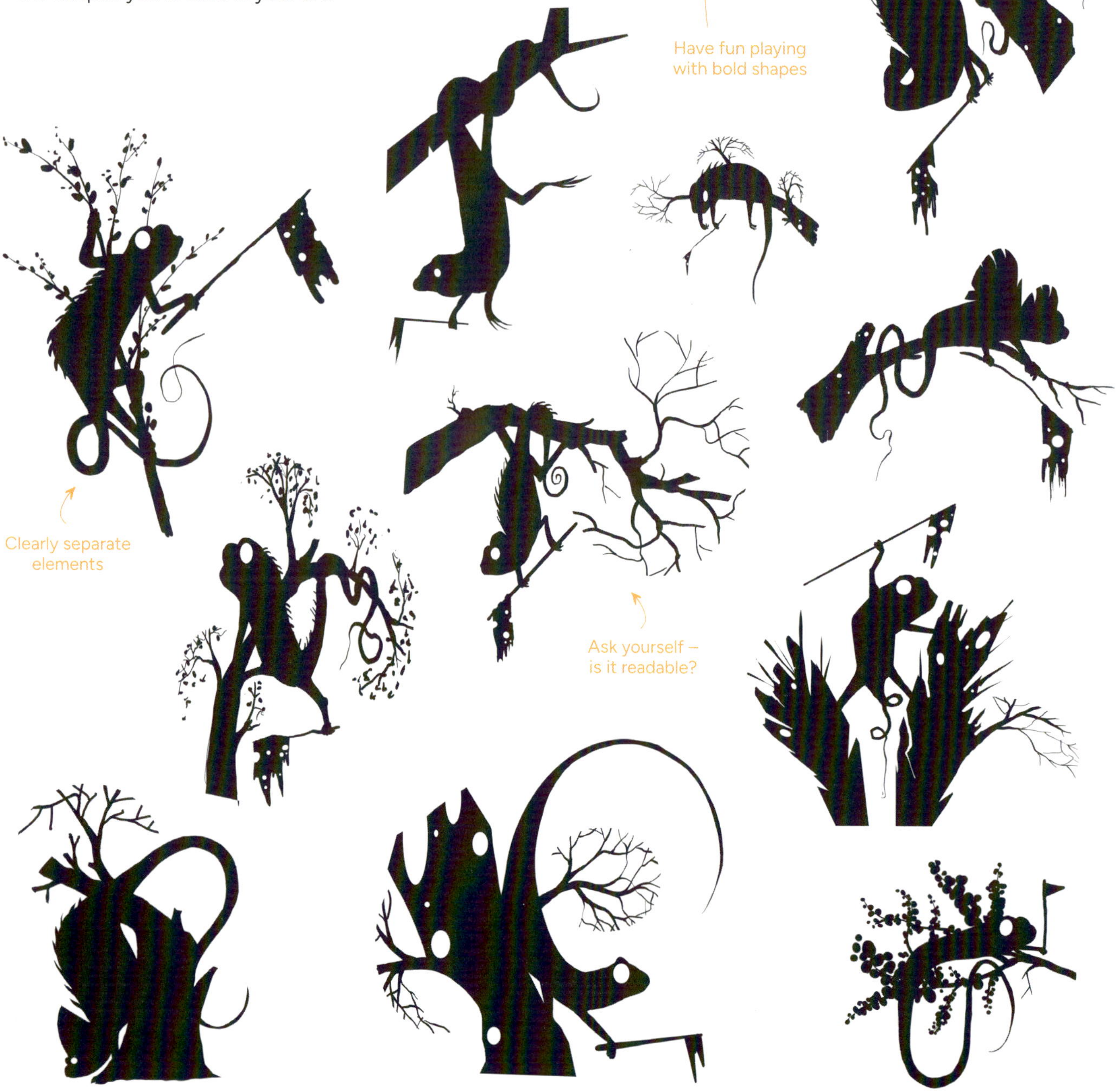

ART: LANDER STRIJBOL

TURNING A NEW LEAF

BEGINNER ●

Find an interestingly shaped leaf and use it to create a new drawing.

Draw a loose outline sketch of the leaf's shape, then design a creature or character that fits inside the shape. This challenge will encourage you to use unusual shapes in your art – experimenting with shape is an important part of developing your own style.

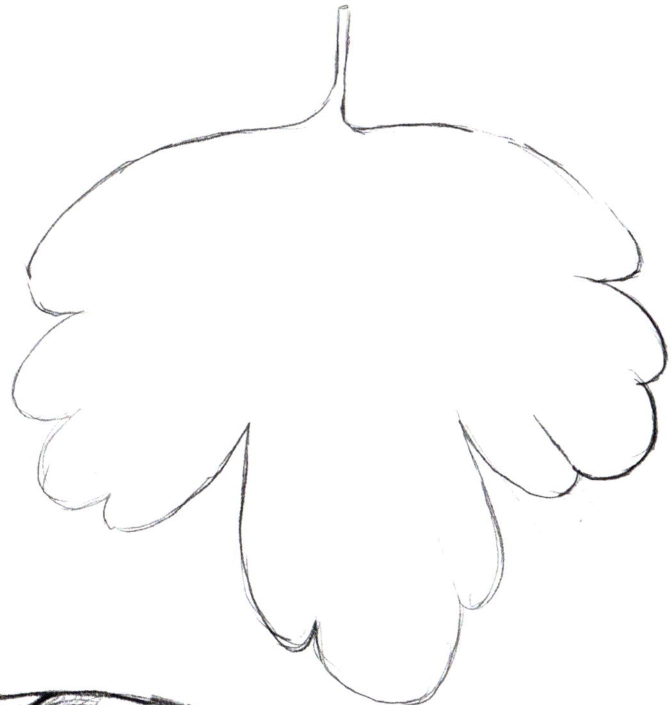

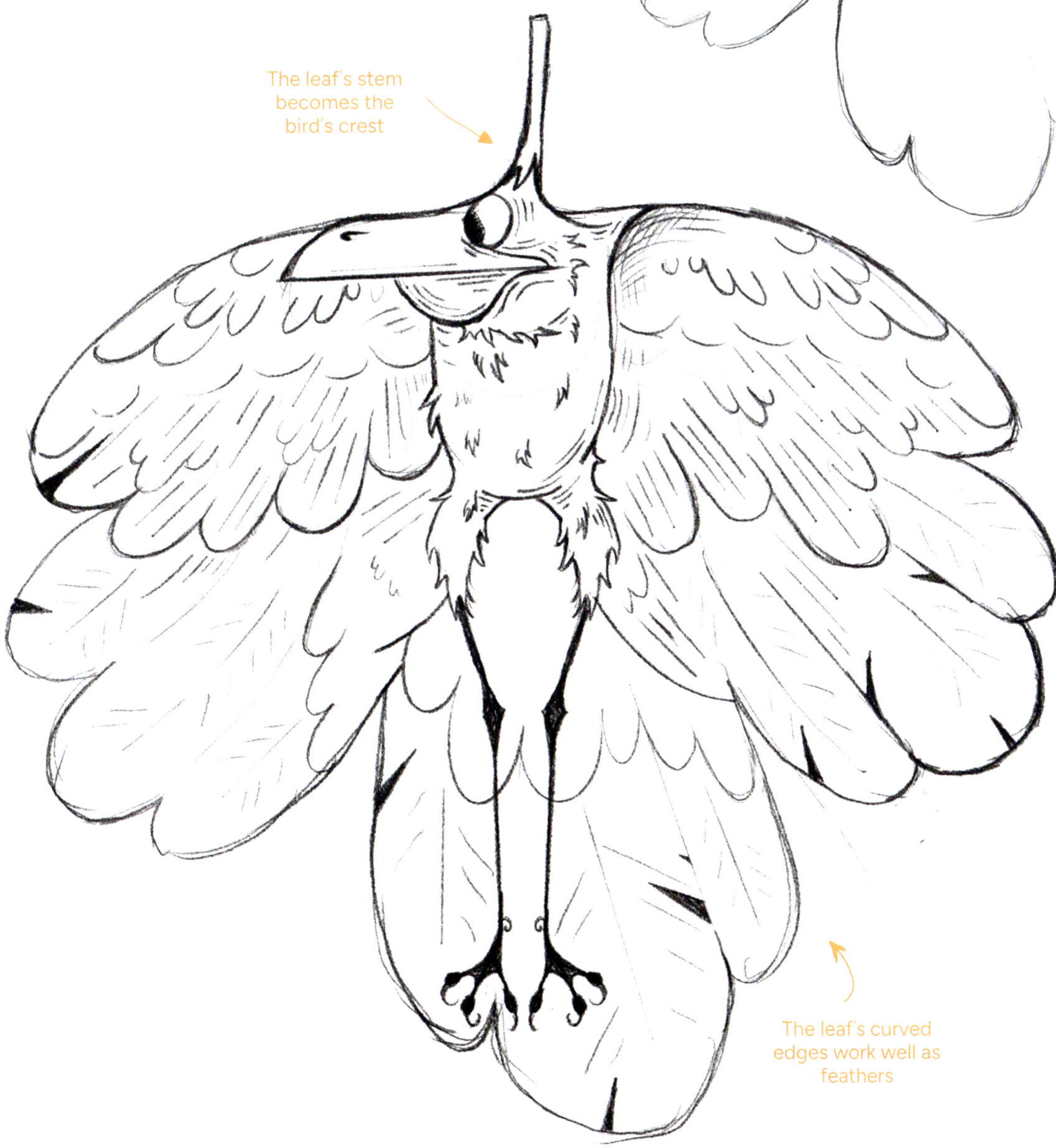

ART: LANDER STRIJBOL

AGAINST THE CLOCK

BEGINNER ●

Draw the same figure pose three times – first in one minute, then in five minutes, then in ten minutes.

This is a useful way to loosen up and learn to be okay with making mistakes. When you only have a set amount of time, you're forced to draw fast and make quick choices, meaning 'mistakes' are bound to happen. When you repeat this challenge, you will naturally start to fix things you didn't get right on the first go, making different choices. This repetitive practice will gradually reveal elements of your personal form-drawing style.

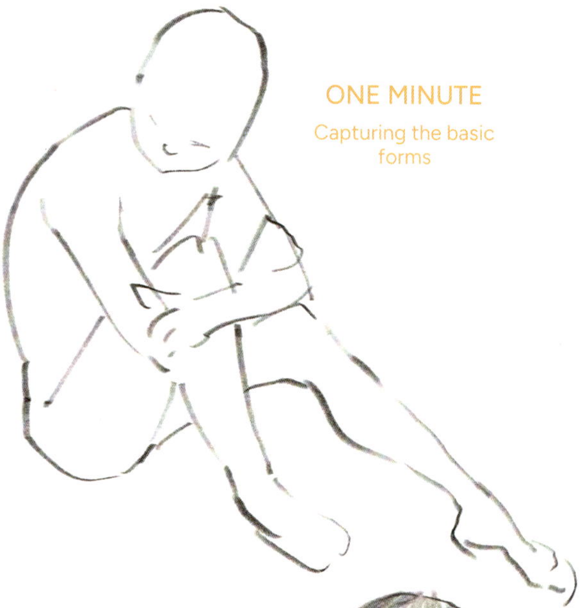

ONE MINUTE

Capturing the basic forms

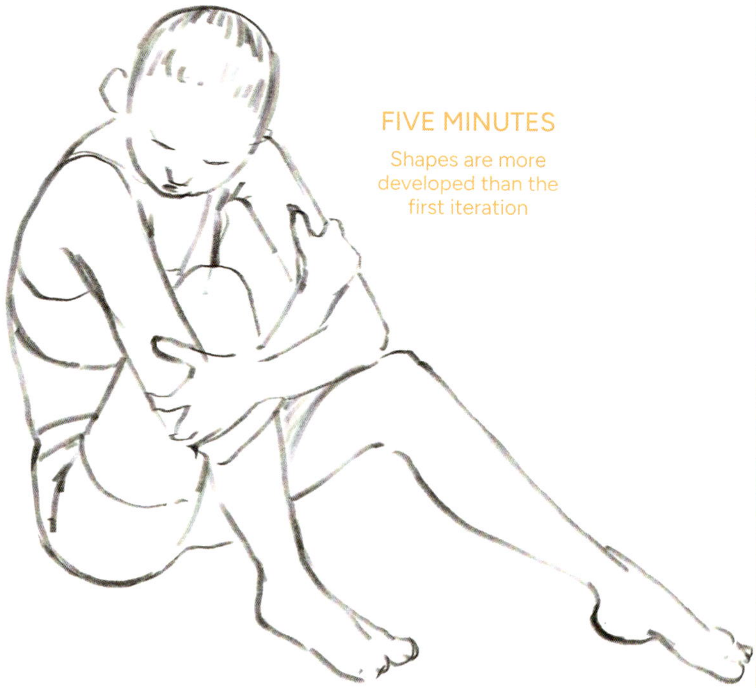

FIVE MINUTES

Shapes are more developed than the first iteration

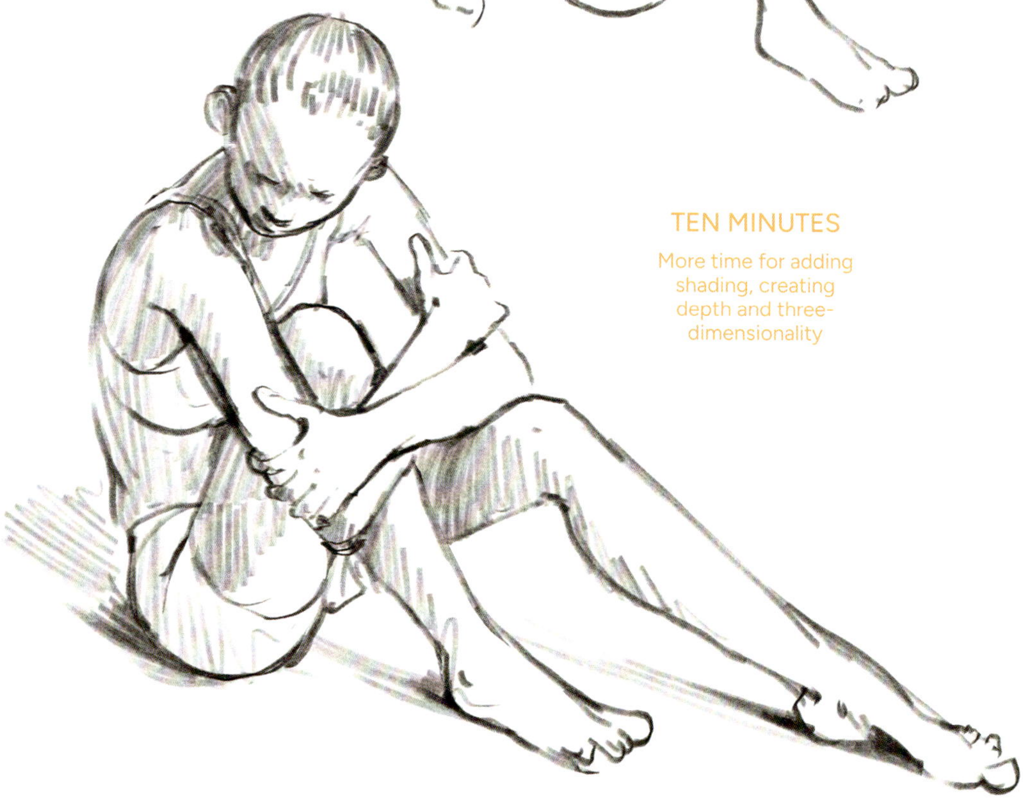

TEN MINUTES

More time for adding shading, creating depth and three-dimensionality

ART: MADI HARPER

BIG, MEDIUM, SMALL

BEGINNER ●

Design an object using only one big shape, one medium shape, and a few small shapes.

This challenge will help you create a design that gives the eye a place to explore and a place to rest. In the example shown, there is one big shape for the body of the washing machine, a medium shape for the door, and a few smaller shapes for the buttons, drawer, and display. The same shape set-up has been used for the detergent containers on top!

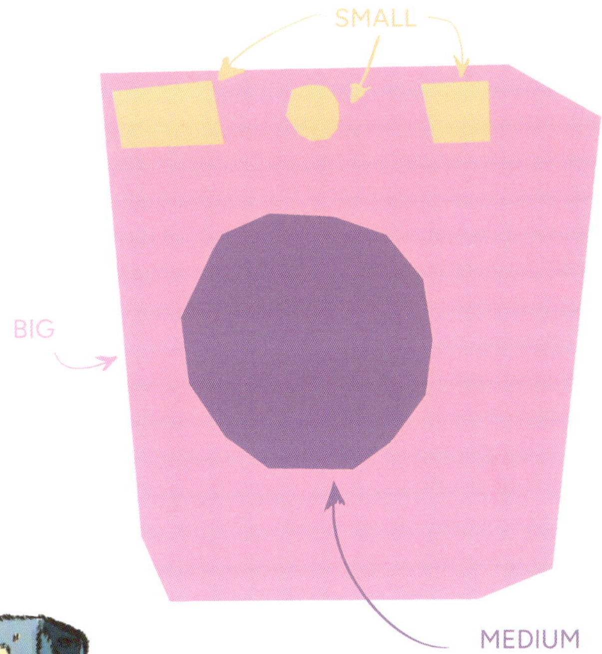

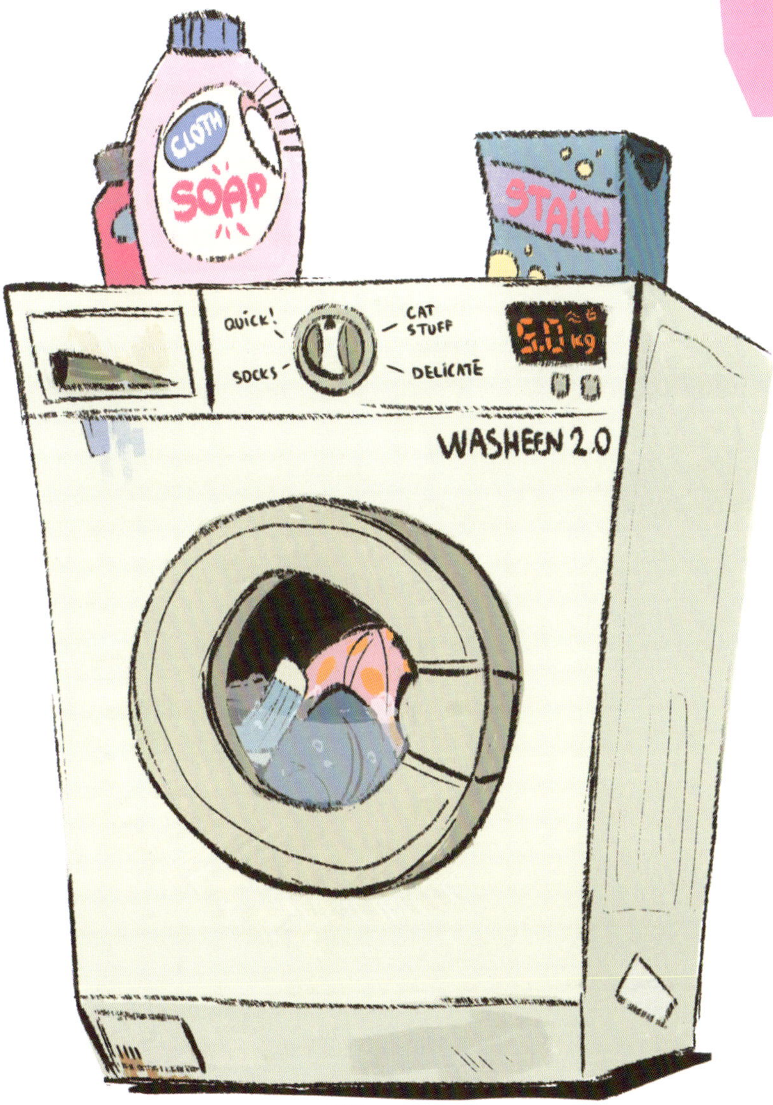

ART: MAGDALENA DIANOVA

LEARNING YOUR LINES

BEGINNER ●

First, draw a subject using a single line weight with no variation, then draw the same subject again using varying line thickness.

This challenge will help you discover the line-work style that suits you best. Line weight can be used to suggest depth – for example, thin lines in the background and thicker lines for the foreground. A thicker line can also be used to convey shadow.

ONE CONSISTENT LINE WEIGHT

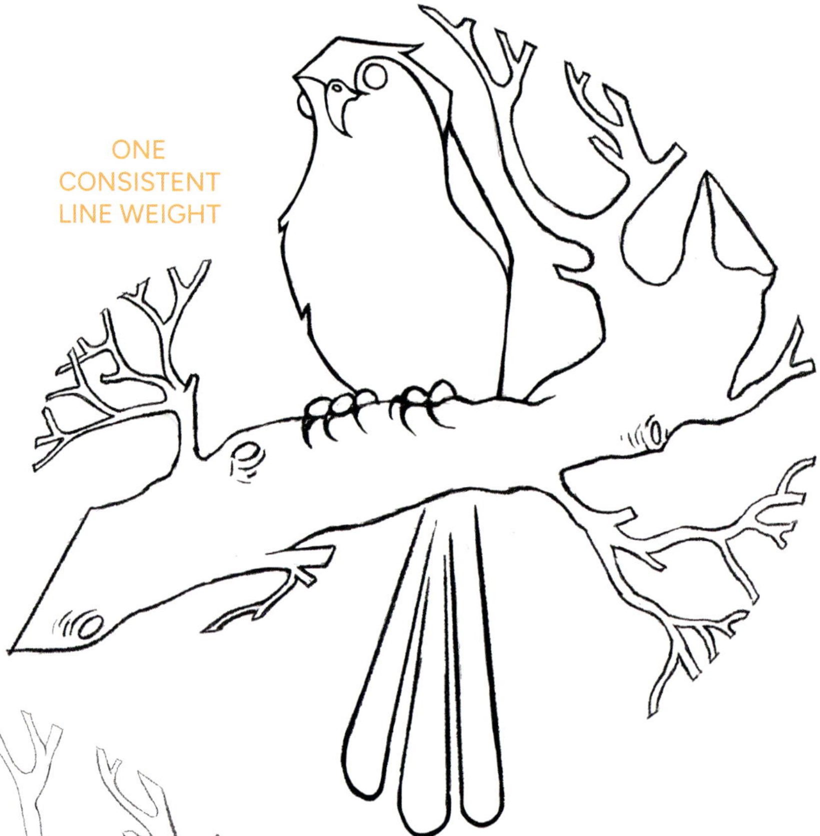

VARIOUS LINE WEIGHTS

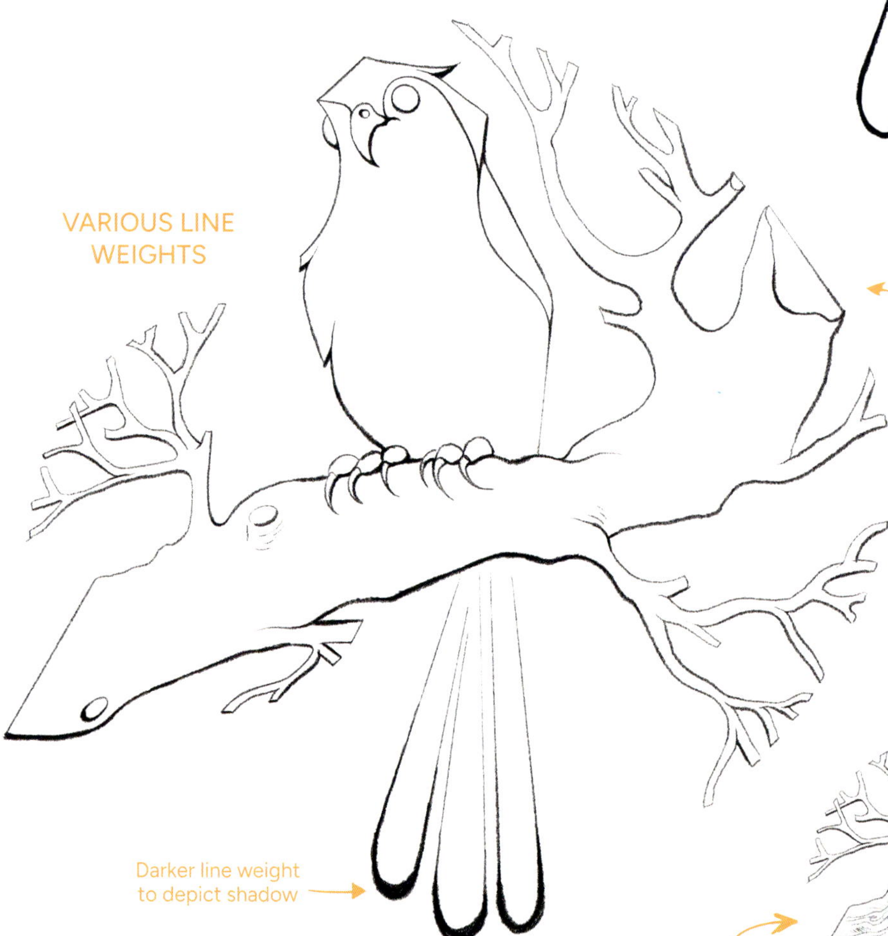

Lighter line weight for elements further back in the image

Darker line weight to depict shadow

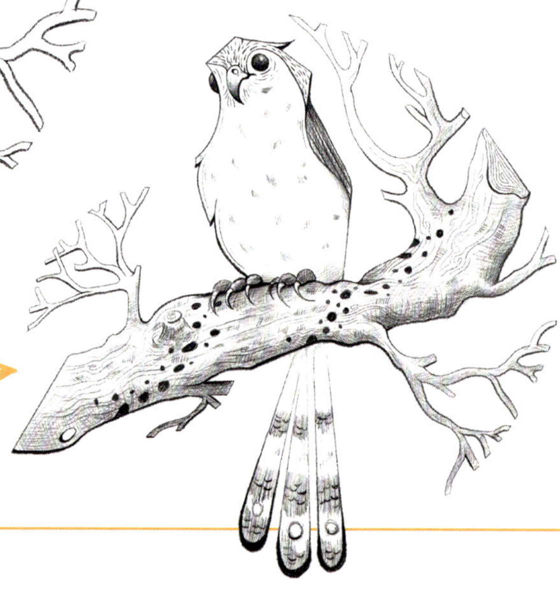

Developing the line work further to add interest and detail

ART: LANDER STRIJBOL

SHAPELY SELFIES

INTERMEDIATE ●●

Create three simple self-portraits – the first using only circular shapes, the second using only triangular shapes, and the third using only rectangular shapes.

Experimenting with shape in this way encourages you to push and stylize a design in ways you may not have previously done. Which do you prefer?

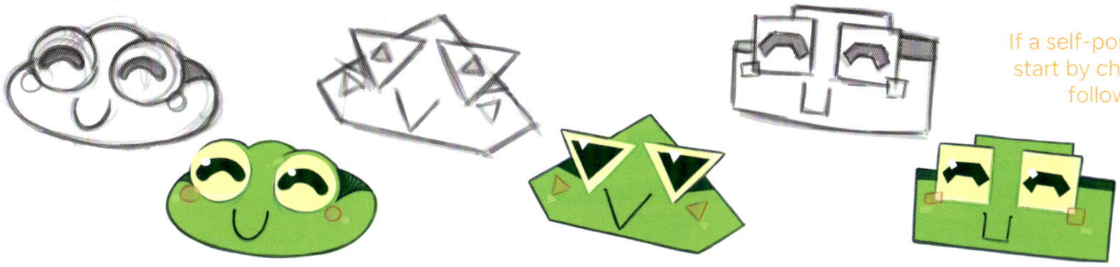

If a self-portrait seems too daunting, start by choosing an animal instead, following the same rules!

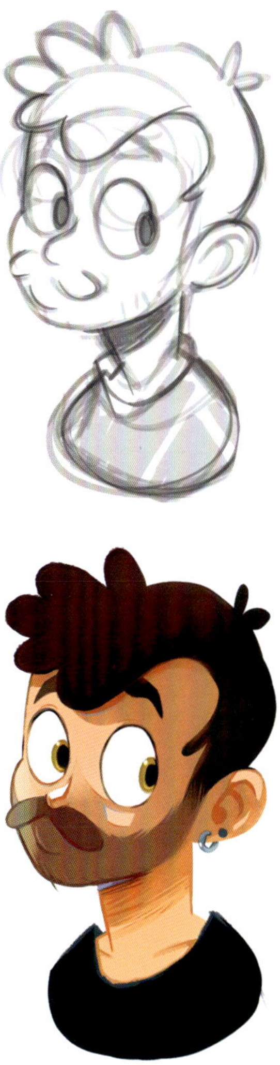

CIRCULAR SHAPES

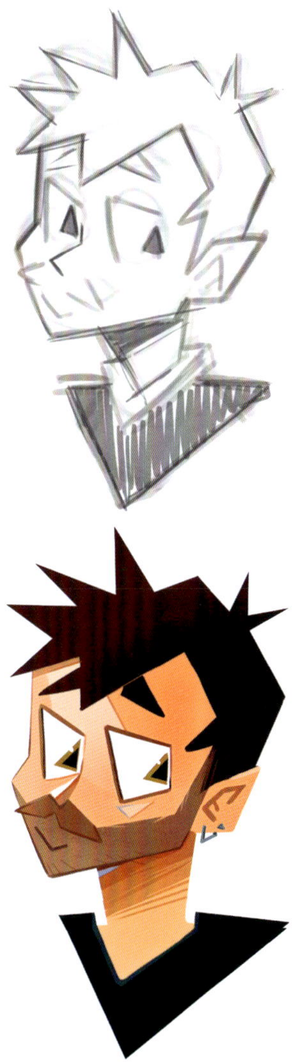

TRIANGULAR SHAPES

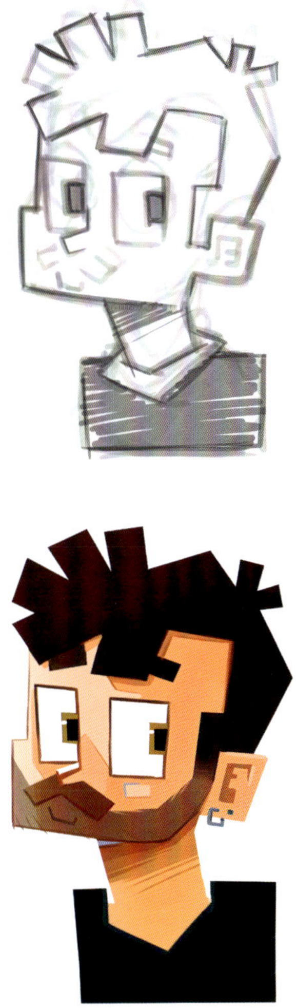

RECTANGULAR SHAPES

ART: LOBON LEAL

SHOPPING FOR SHAPES

INTERMEDIATE ●●

Draw a shopping bag (containing whatever you like) with soft, rounded shapes, then draw it again with more angular shapes.

Shape can change the overall mood and feel of an image. Using softer, curved lines can give an object a friendlier, cuter, and more welcoming look. Sharp edges and harsh angles have the opposite effect, creating an edgier, more severe feeling. Shape language can play a big part in defining your artistic style, so experiment with all kinds of lines and shapes to find what sparks your creativity.

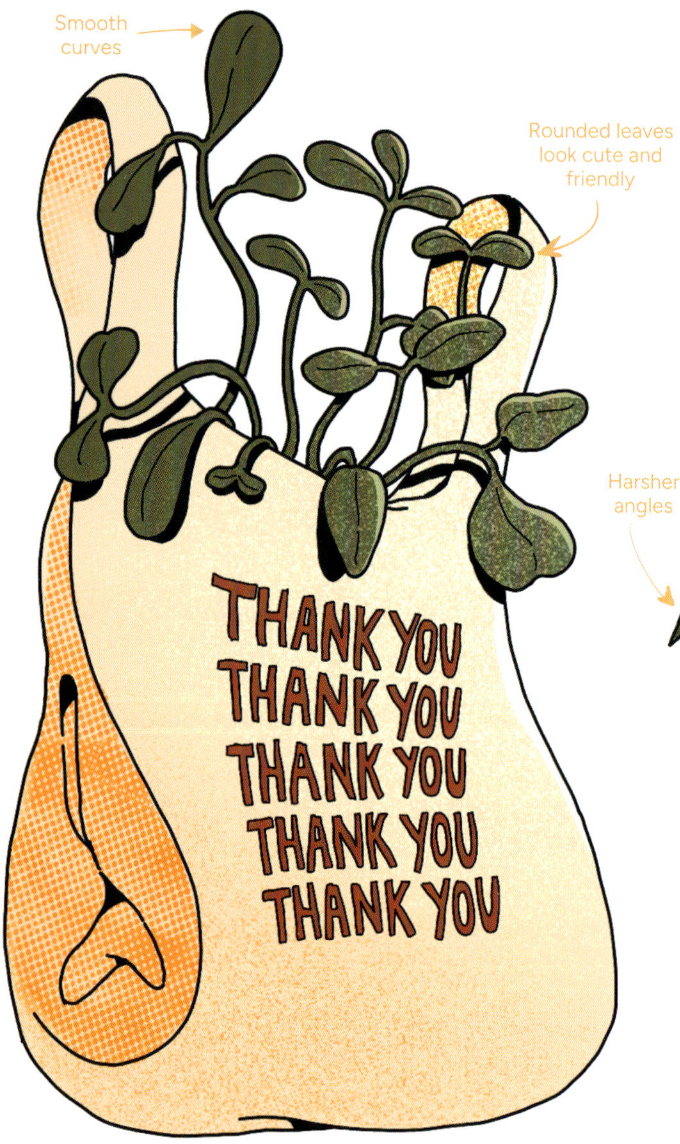

ROUND SHAPE LANGUAGE

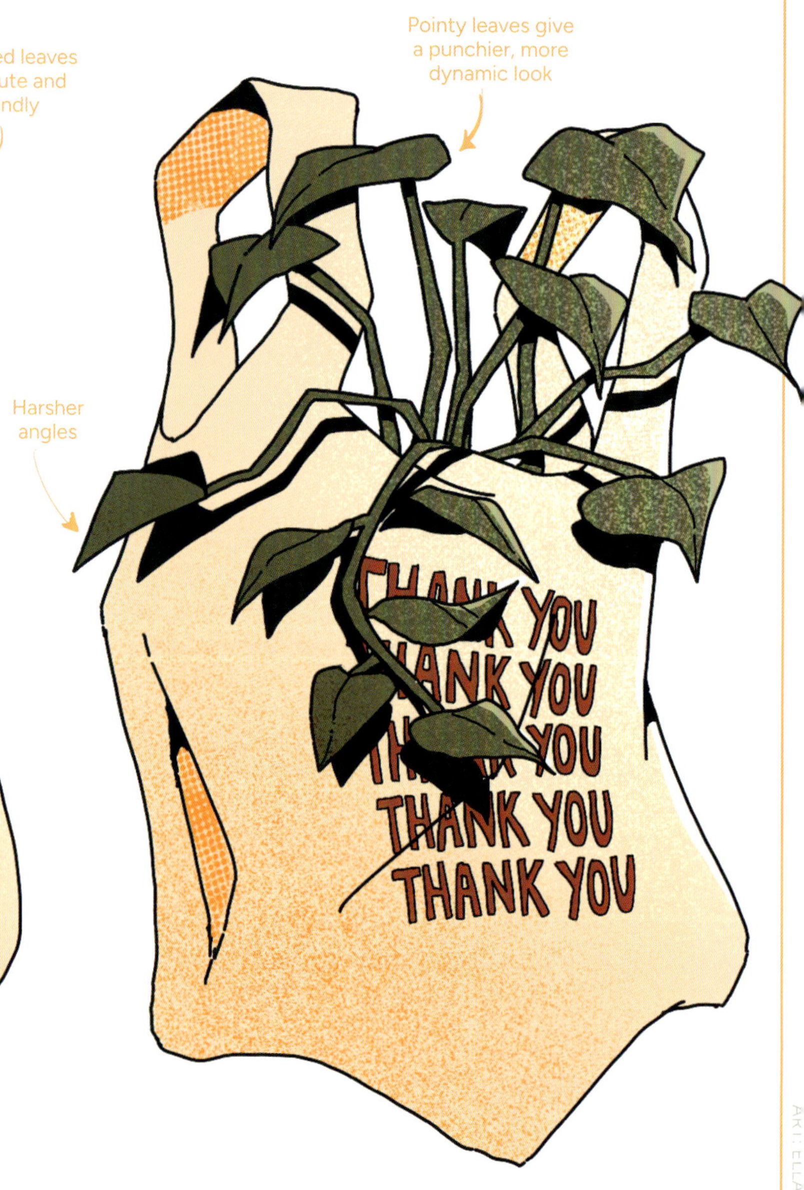

ANGULAR SHAPE LANGUAGE

A SHADOWY SCENE

ADVANCED ●●●

Paint a picture featuring a building and scenery that's only seen in black silhouette, with only the background or characters in colour.

Your image may appear confusing and ambiguous at first, so exaggerate and transform the shapes to ensure the silhouettes are recognizable. Ask yourself what elements are necessary to convey the story you wish to tell. This challenge will force you to consider the form of the elements you include and make them as clear as possible in your own style.

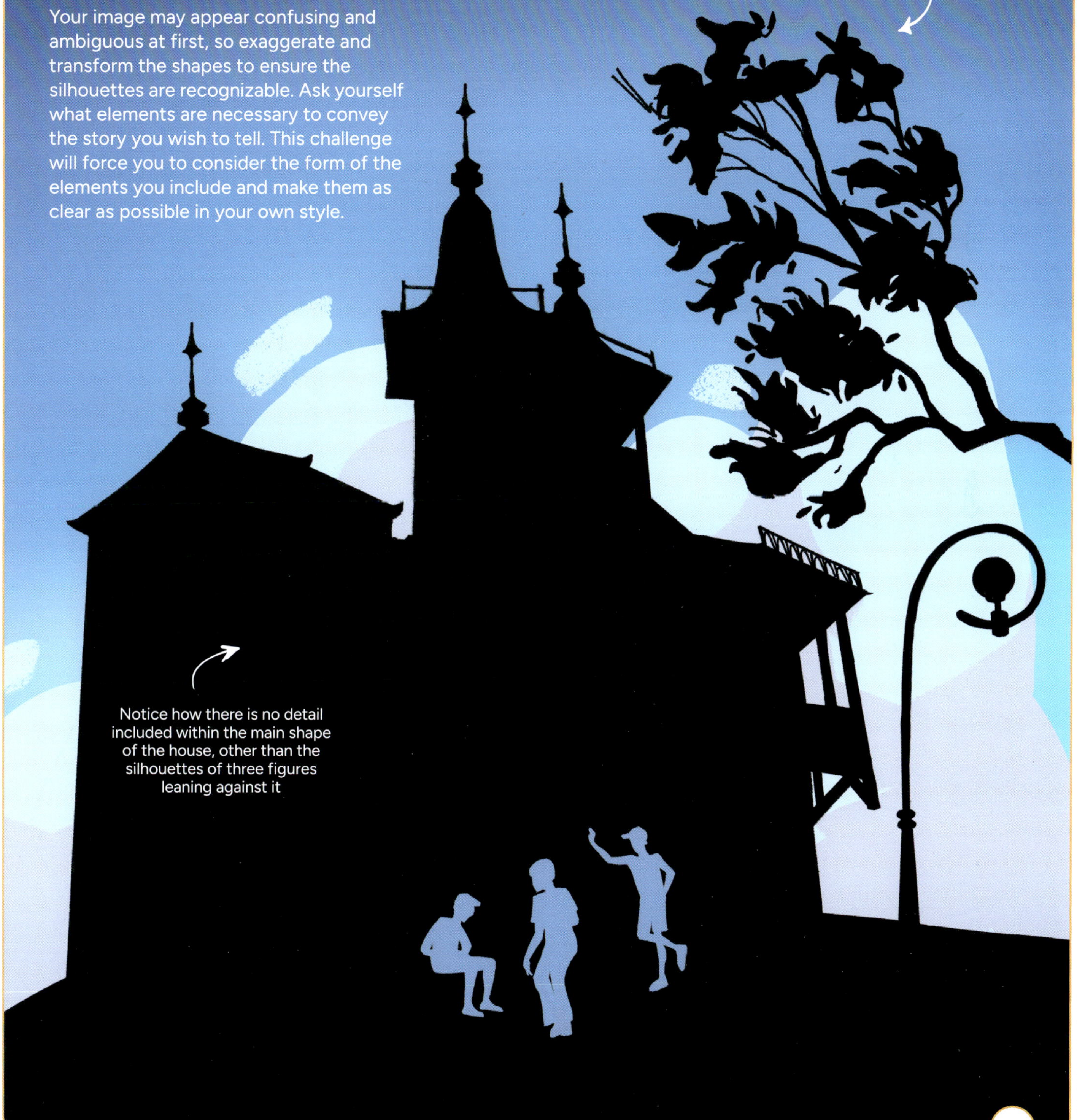

The silhouettes are recognizable as an old house, a lamp post, and a tree

Notice how there is no detail included within the main shape of the house, other than the silhouettes of three figures leaning against it

ART: MARIANA NORONHA

COLOUR, VALUE & LIGHT

Step-by-step challenges:

One-page challenges:

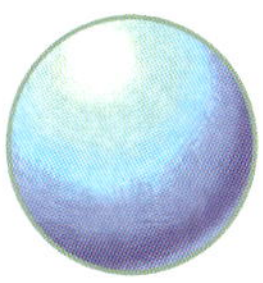

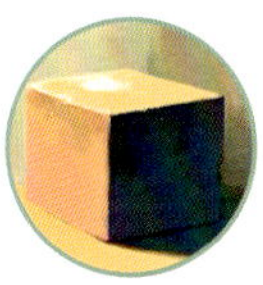

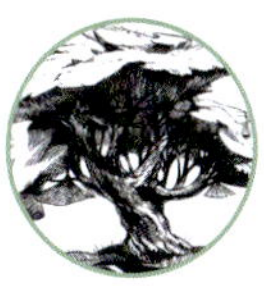

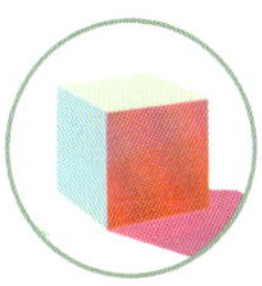

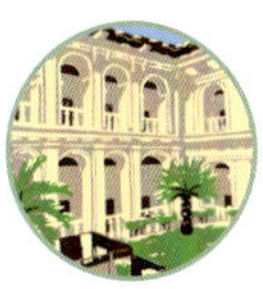

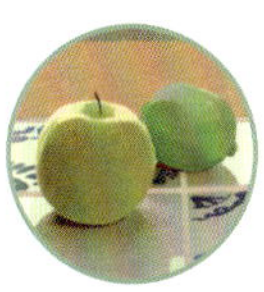

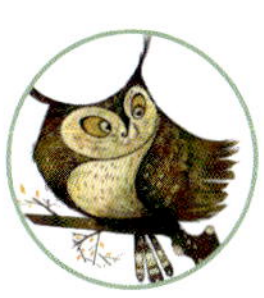

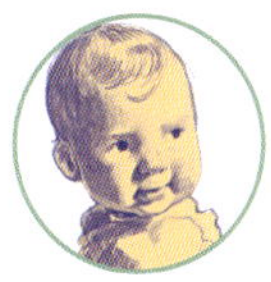

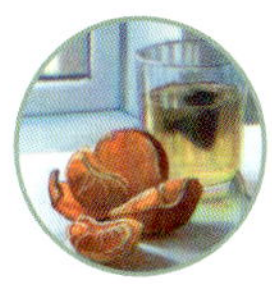

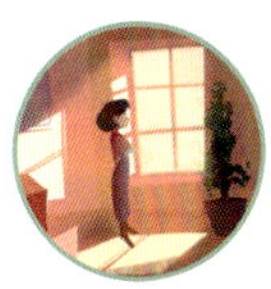

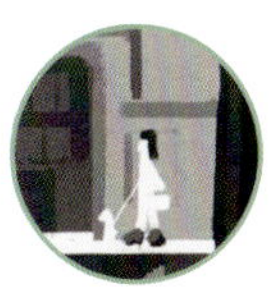

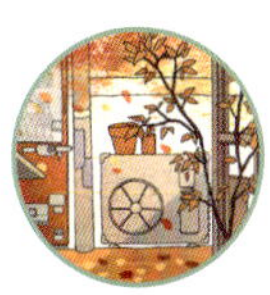

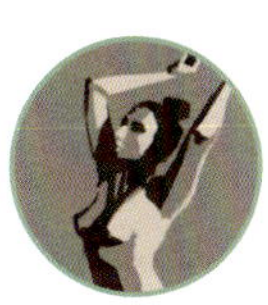

A LIMITED PALETTE

BEGINNER ●

Create an image using no more than three base colours.

The aim of this challenge is to remove the pressure of colour choice and encourage you to be creative, as you're not able to rely on the colours you would normally use. Over time, a limited colour palette could form a recognizable part of your artistic style. In this example, the work is done with digital-painting software, but the same challenge can be adapted to any colour medium.

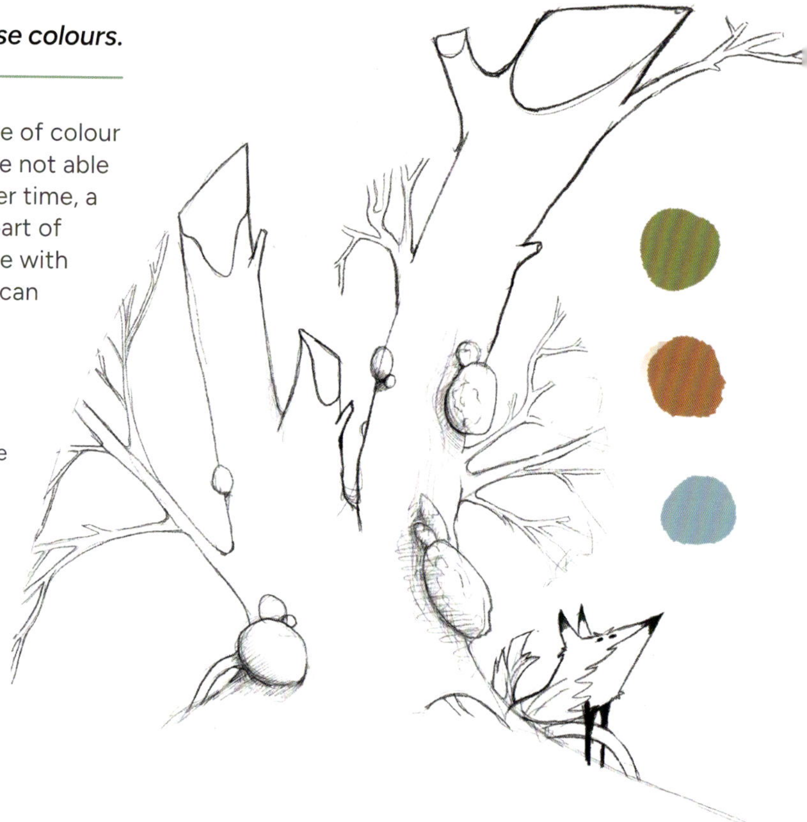

01 Start by drawing a loose sketch, then choose your three base colour swatches.

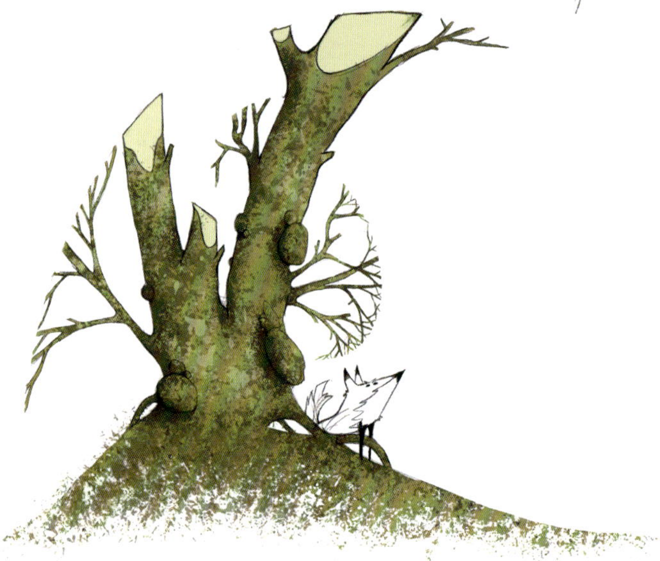

02 Begin to add colour to your sketch by picking from the swatches. Tweak the values to add contrast and texture, staying within the same hue.

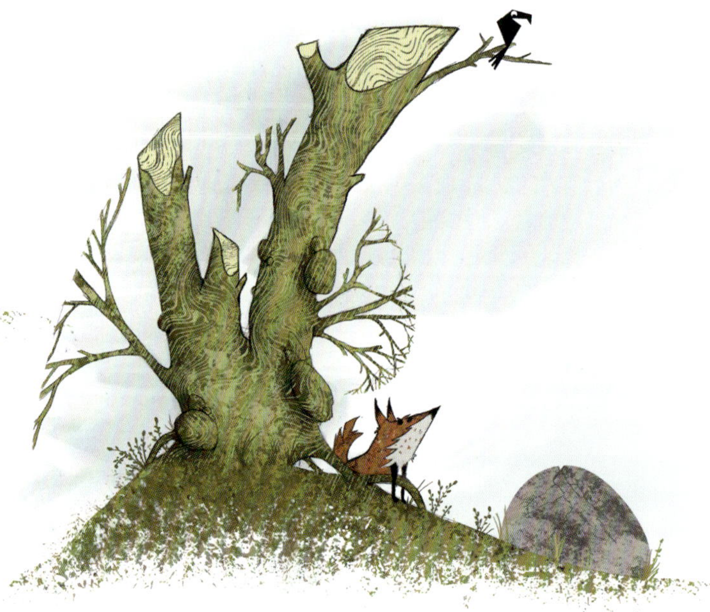

03 Keep adding colour, using only your chosen three. Here, green is used for the tree and ground, orange for the fox, and blue for the sky and rock.

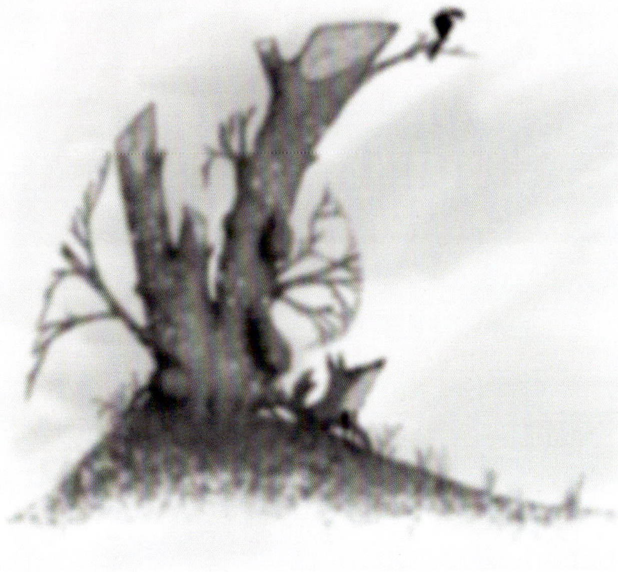

04 When your illustration is almost finished, switch to black and white then squint your eyes or blur the image. This will help you to check the values are working.

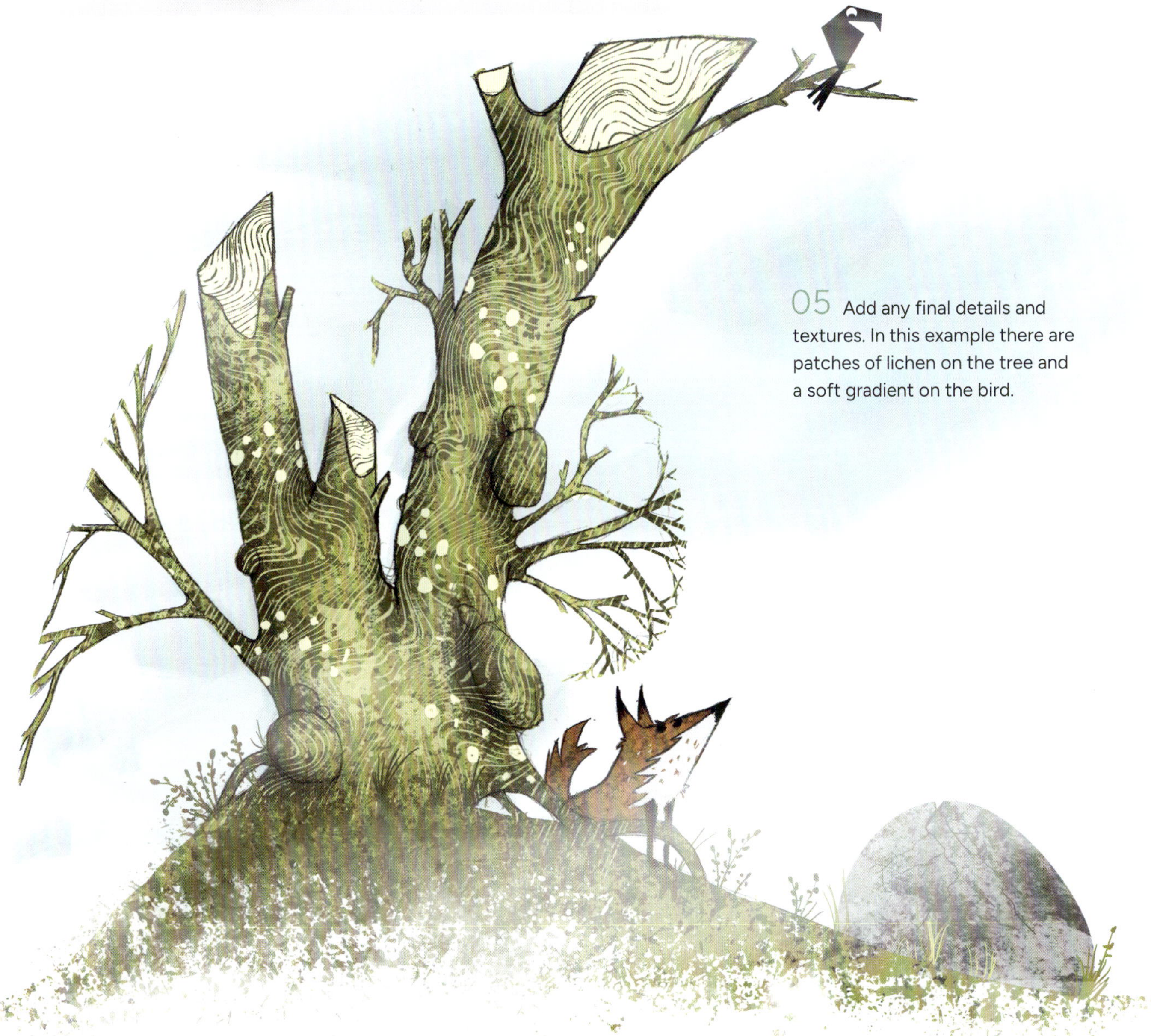

05 Add any final details and textures. In this example there are patches of lichen on the tree and a soft gradient on the bird.

ART: LANDER STRIJBOL

THREE-COLOUR LANDSCAPE

BEGINNER ●

Create a study of a landscape using only red, yellow, and blue.

To make extra colours, layer the primary colours over each other. Be bold and don't confine yourself to 'natural' colours. This challenge is designed to make you think of colour in an entirely new way, encouraging you to break out of your comfort zone and add new depth to your use of colour.

01 Start by sketching the entire landscape in red and begin to fill in some of the shadows. Consider where you want to leave space for the other two colours.

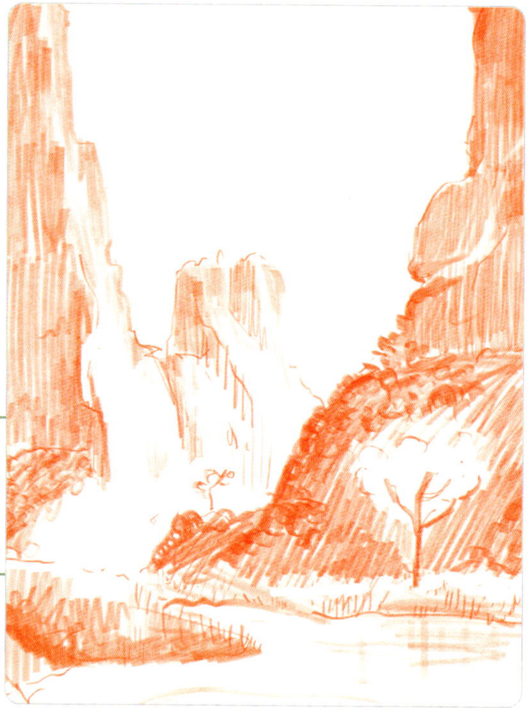

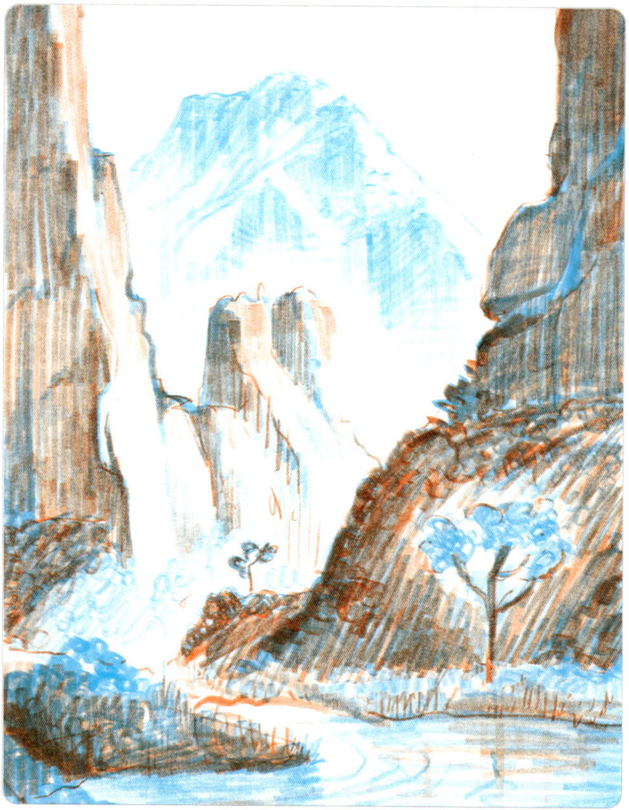

02 Now add blue on a new layer, covering the red to create dark purples for the shadows in the foreground. Use blue for the background, as elements that are further away will always appear cooler.

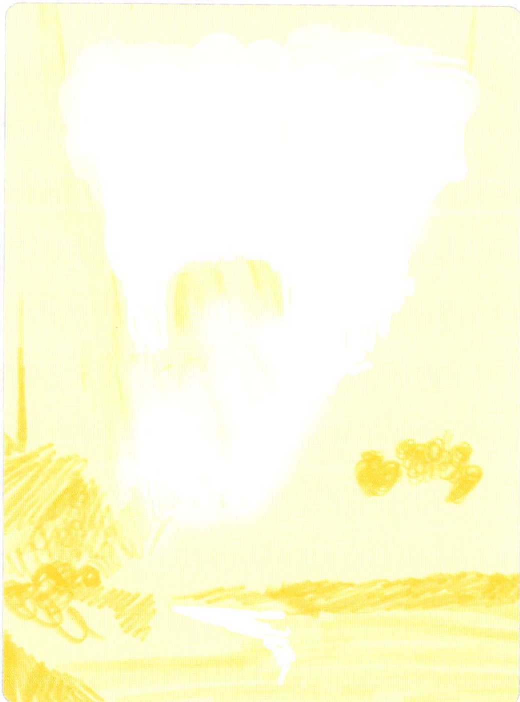

03 Finally, sketch in yellow on a new layer, creating a glow of light across your landscape.

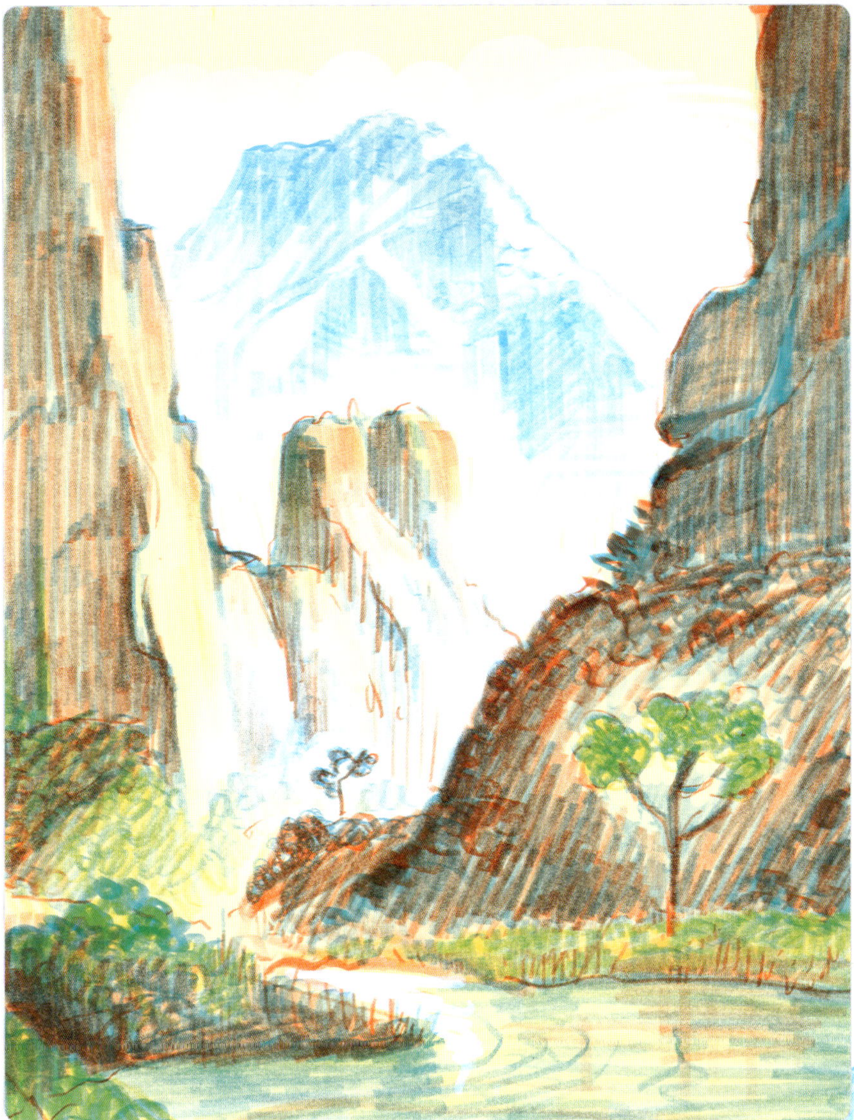

04 Once you have all three colours done, set each layer to Multiply to create an interesting layered effect and lots of new colours.

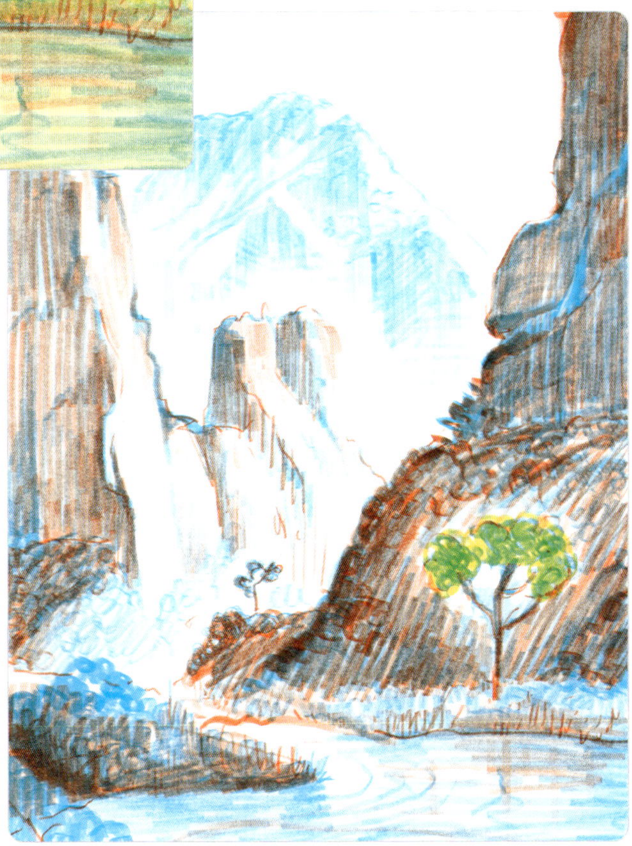

05 Alternatively, you could add the yellow just over the tree to create a single area of green. Use this challenge to explore the use of colour to create different stories and styles.

THE COLOURS OF NATURE

INTERMEDIATE ●●

Go somewhere outdoors and collect a natural object, such as a leaf or pebble, then create a painting of the place you've visited using only colours from the object.

Your artwork is naturally influenced by the world around you, and developing your artistic style can be easier when you use your own experiences rather than photo references from the internet. When you visit this outdoor space, take in the mood and feel of the place to reflect in your illustration.

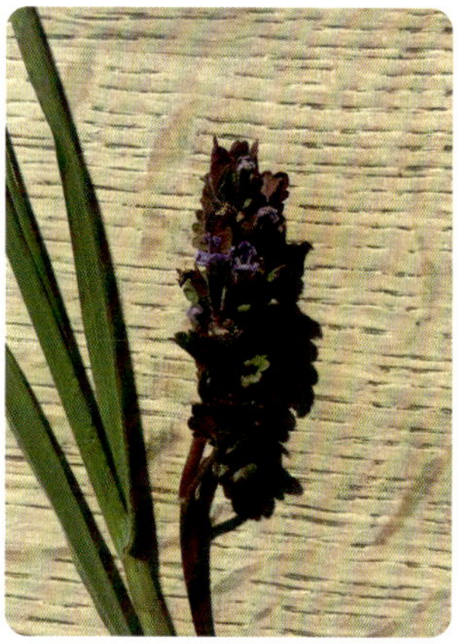

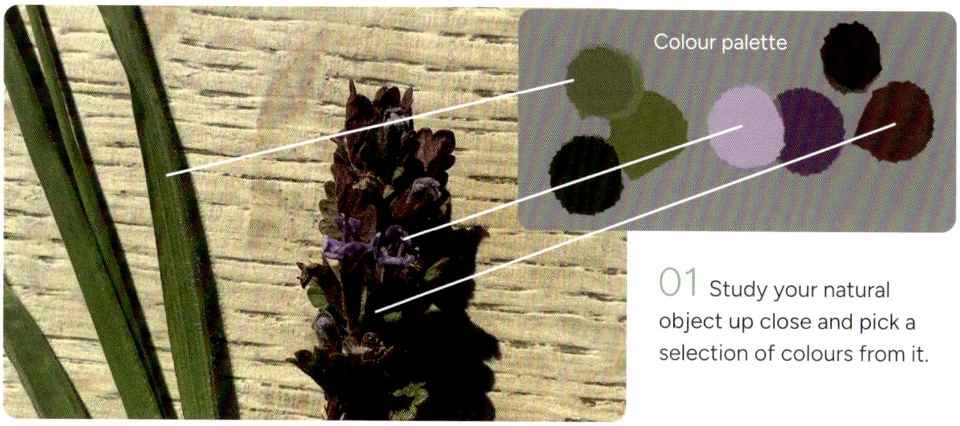

01 Study your natural object up close and pick a selection of colours from it.

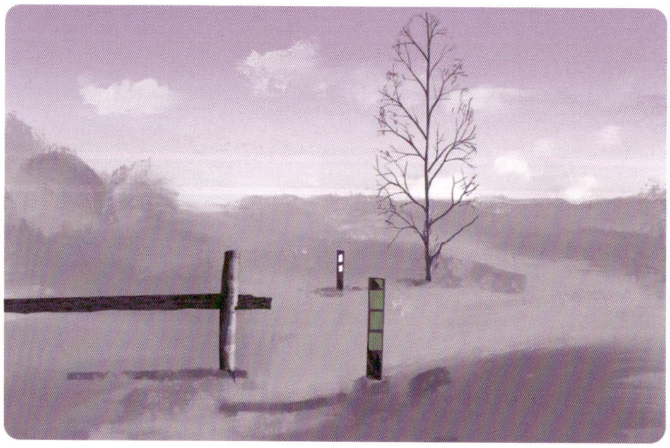

02 Create a rough underpainting of the landscape, sketching in the main elements using one of the colours from your palette.

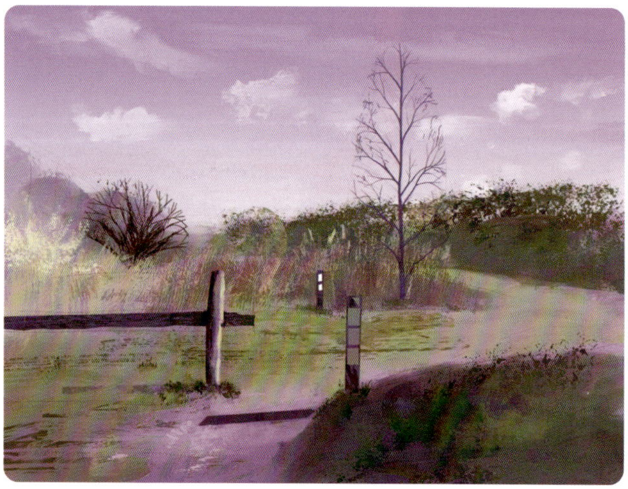

03 Use the other colours in your palette to paint over the sketch and add more detail. This task is about being creative with colour and recreating your own stylized impression of the landscape, rather than achieving realism.

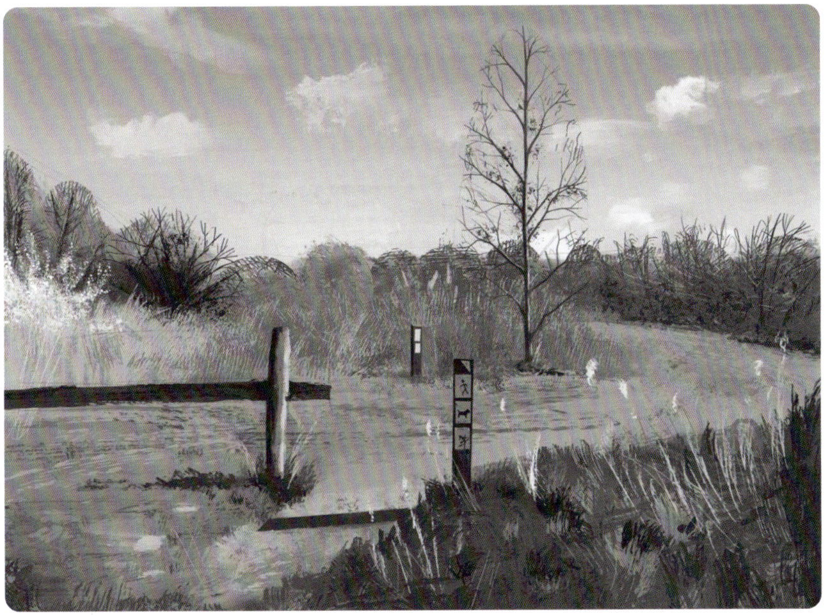

04 View your work in greyscale to check the values are working, and adjust them as needed.

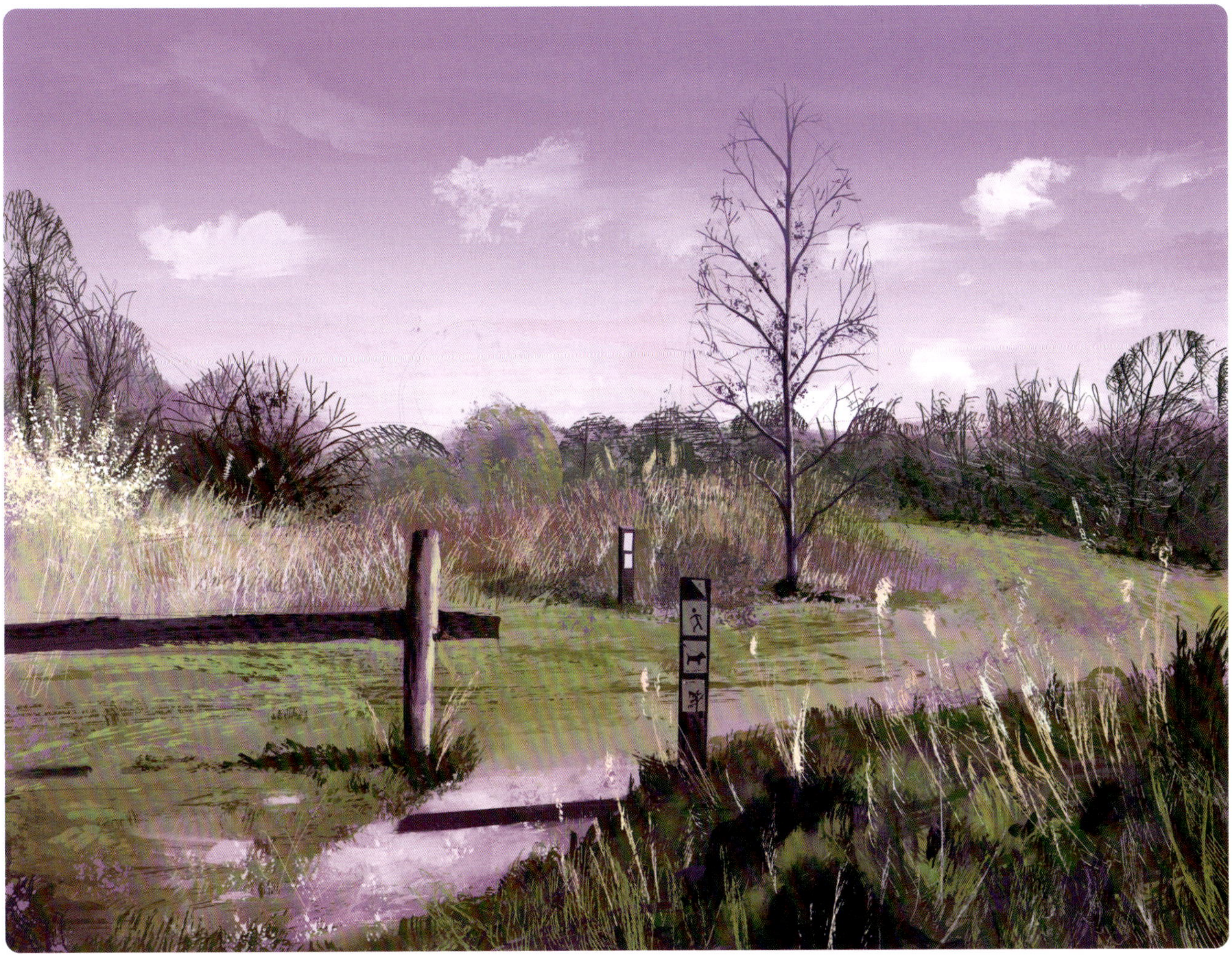

05 Add final details and textures to finish the painting. Are these colours you would have usually chosen to work with?

RENDERING TECH

INTERMEDIATE ●●

Paint a simple item of technology in three different rendering styles.

Start with a sketch then try a style with no lines, a style with lines for shadows only, and a style with non-black lines. Use this as a jumping-off point to experiment with and consider the quality, colour, and thickness of your line work. How might you communicate shadows? How flat or painterly do you want your style to be?

01 Start by creating a simple line sketch, focusing on the main shapes that make up the object. Then add colour to distinguish each element. This will form the foundation for all three renderings.

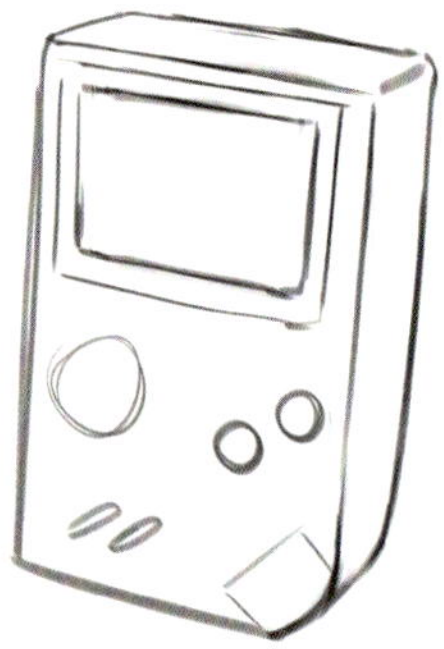

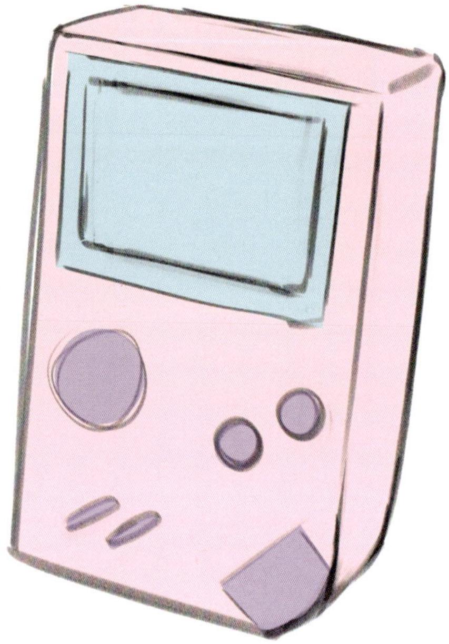

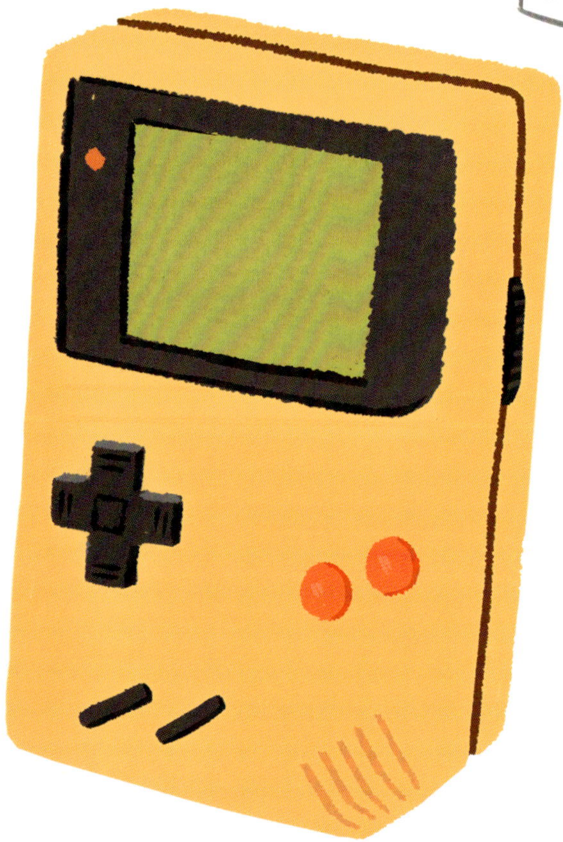

LINE-FREE STYLE

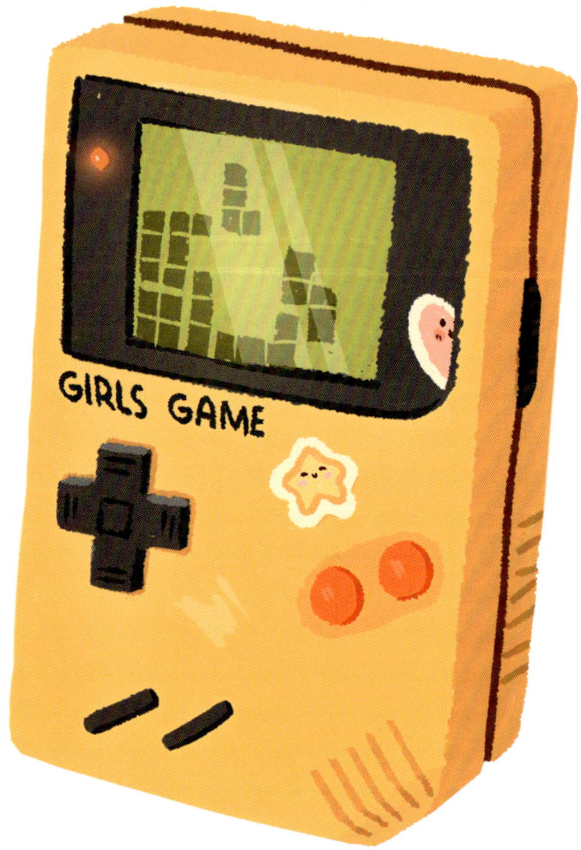

02 For the first version, challenge yourself to create a line-free style, separating the volumes through hard shadows and contrast alone.

SHADOW LINES

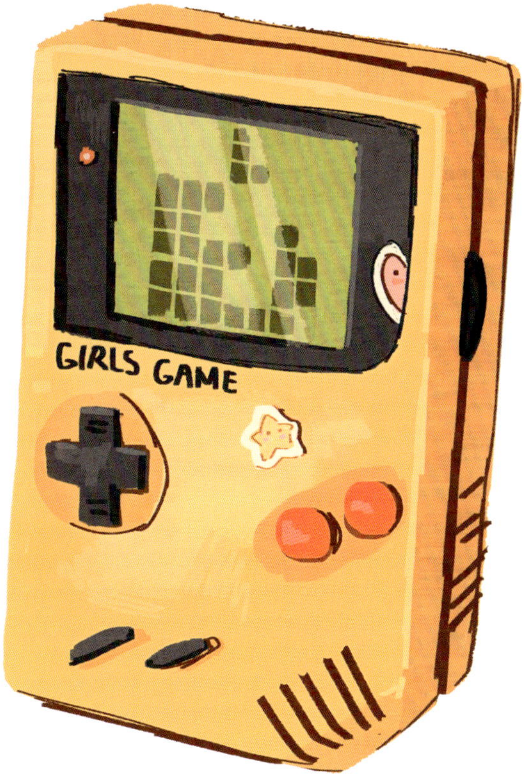

03 For the second style, try adding line work – but only in the shadows.

NON-BLACK LINE WORK

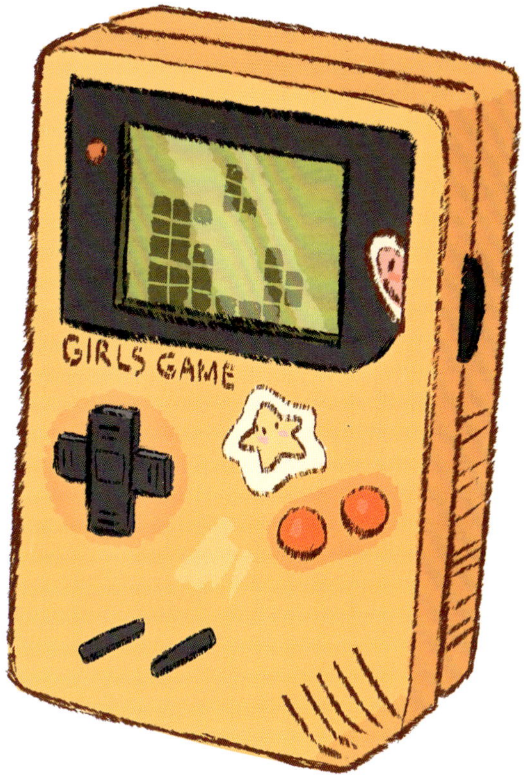

04 For the third version, play around with coloured line work – this example shows lines in brown.

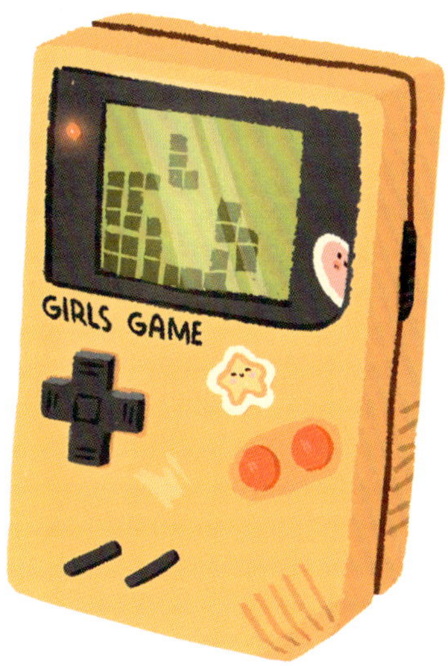

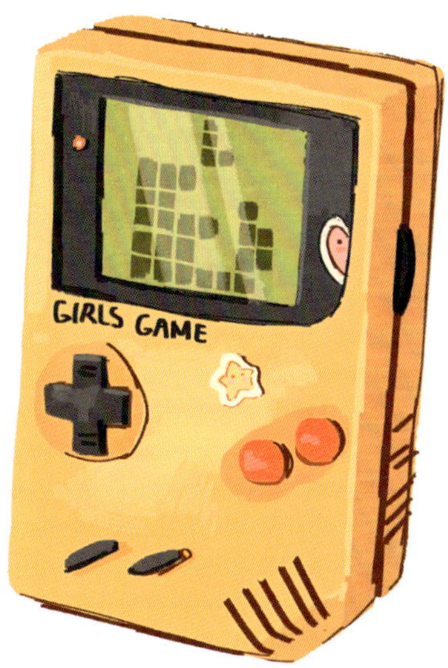

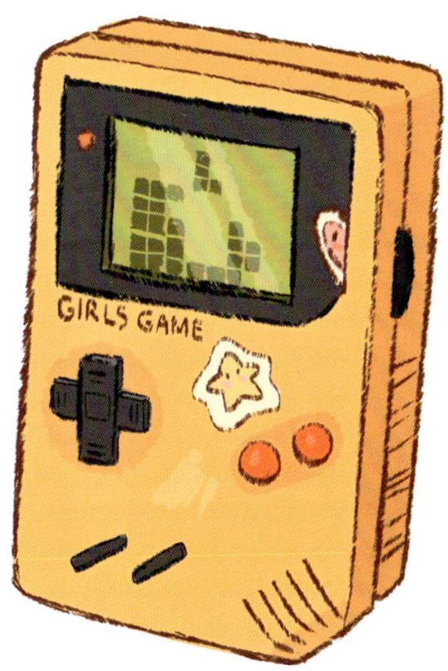

05 Compare the three rendering styles. How does the colour, thickness, or absence of line work change the overall look? How does the level of shadow and contrast alter the appearance of the object?

ART: MAGDALINA DIANOVA

FINDING YOUR VALUE

INTERMEDIATE ●●

Choose a classic painting and create three value studies of it: the first in greyscale (using all values from black to white), the second in three tones (black, a single shade of grey, and white), and the third in only black and white.

This challenge gives you a chance to study how the original artist used light and shade. It will also help you find your own preferred style when creating values.

01 Create a rough sketch of your chosen reference painting, focusing on the main shapes and key elements. This will act as a base on which to create the value studies. Don't worry if it's not completely accurate – you can fill in details as you paint.

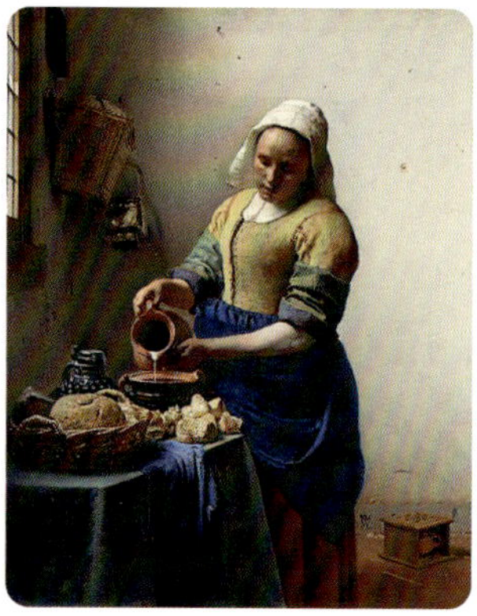

THE MILKMAID BY JOHANNES VERMEER, C. 1657–1658

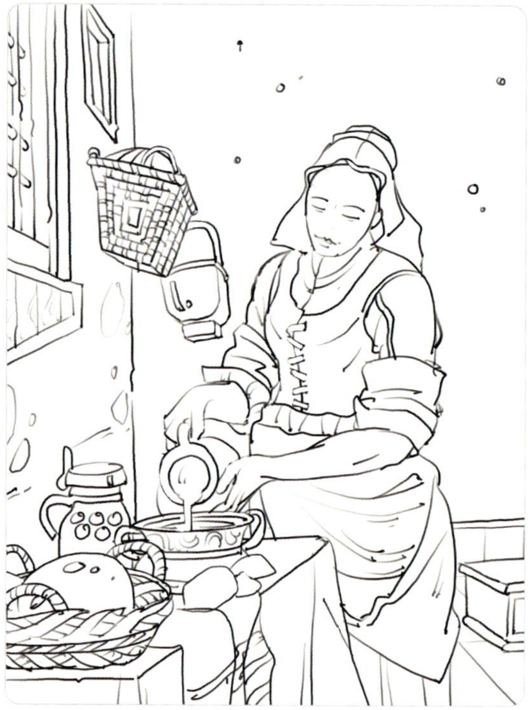

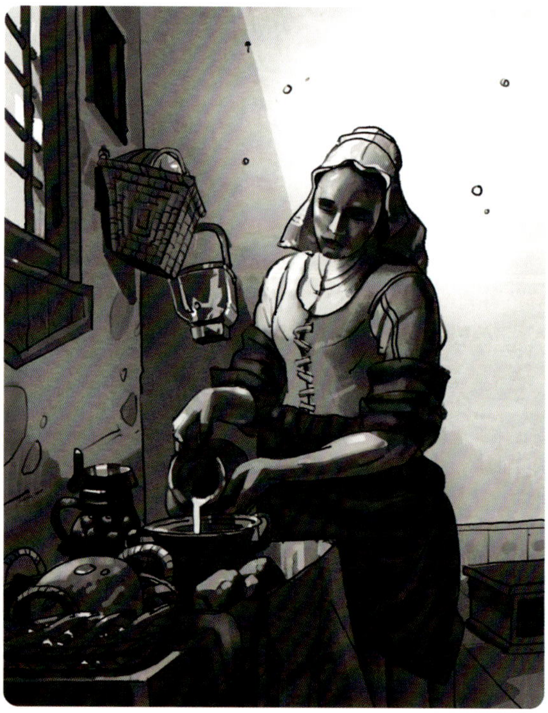

02 Paint a greyscale study including all of the values, from darker to lighter tones, plus everything in between.

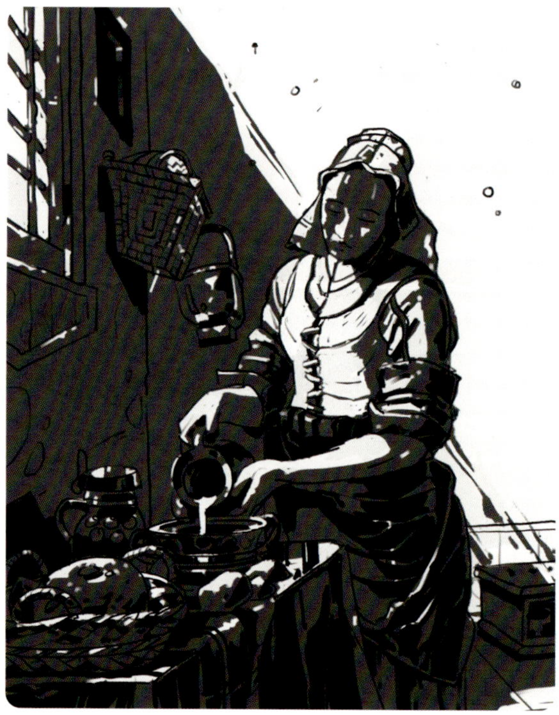

03 For the second study, limit yourself to using only black, white, and grey tones. Identify the darker and lighter areas in the painting, then paint the brightest areas white, medium areas grey, and darker areas black.

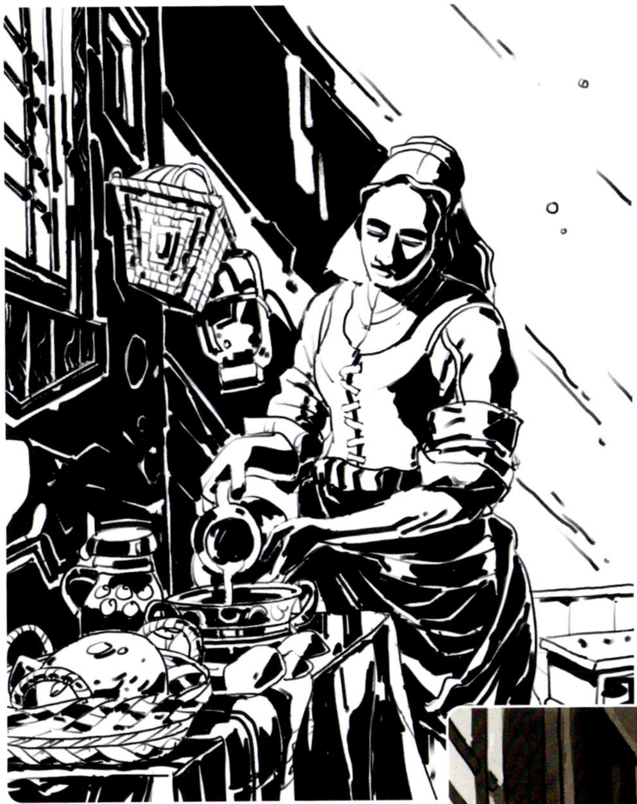

04 For the third study, restrict yourself to using only black and white to capture the values. Imagine you're using black ink to paint the image on white paper. Omit any subtle variations and finer details.

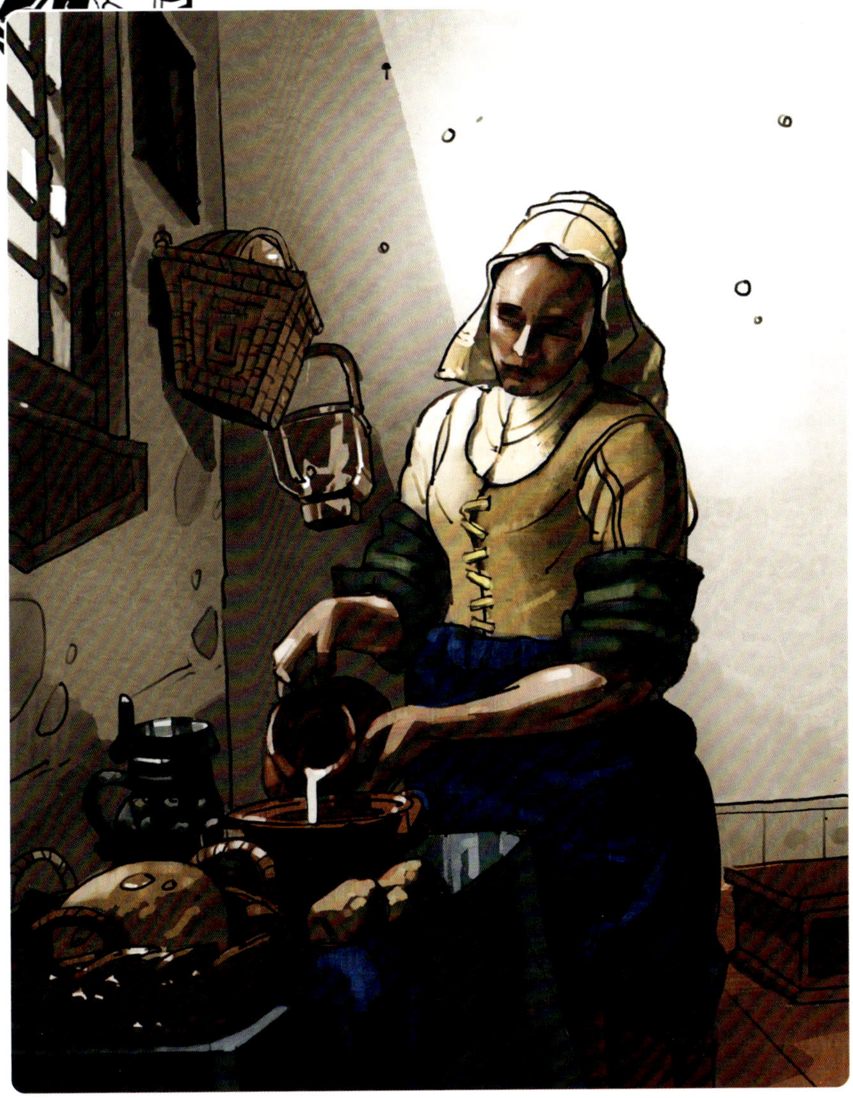

05 Use one of the value studies as a guide to add colour to the image. Do you see your own artistic style showing in your final version?

ART: ALFRED FERNANDES

SIMPLIFYING TEXTURE

INTERMEDIATE ●●

Find an image of an area of interesting texture – such as grass, wildflowers, or carpet – and create a simplified painting of it.

Textures can be complex to paint, but simplifying and grouping the elements makes the process much easier. Look for areas of high contrast, where the value, colour, or detail changes noticably, then divide the elements into groups or planes based on this information. How an artist chooses to group elements can form a key part of their artistic style. What is your favourite part of the subject? What do you want people to look at first?

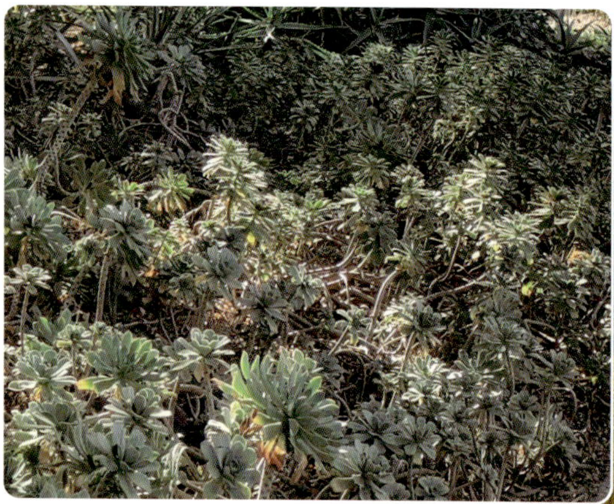

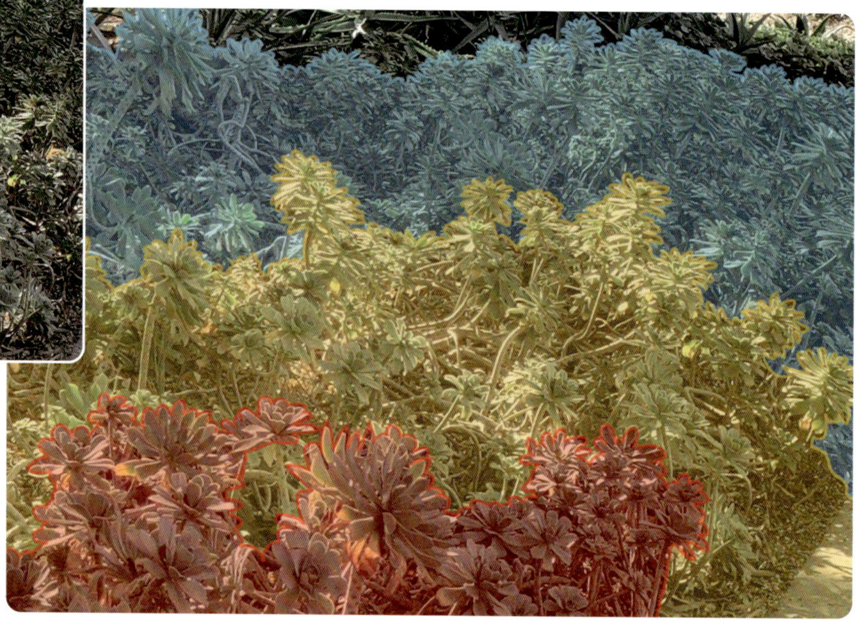

01 Look for areas of high contrast in your reference image and use this information to divide it into three planes: the foreground, middle ground, and background.

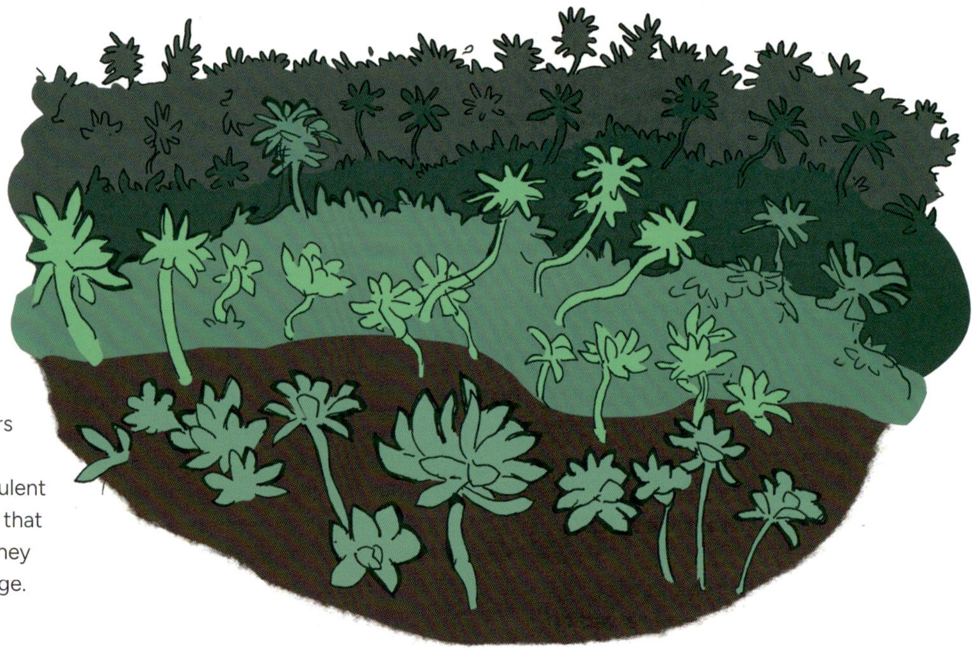

02 Now sketch the image as clearly as possible, adding flat colours to differentiate your planes. In this example, the silhouettes of the succulent plants are more detailed in the areas that overlap the planes, as this is where they are most visible in the reference image.

03 Use shadows and light to separate the planes further. See here how the top of the middle ground is illuminated by sunlight while the lower parts of the background are in shadow. Increasing the contrast of overlapping elements like this creates a sense of depth.

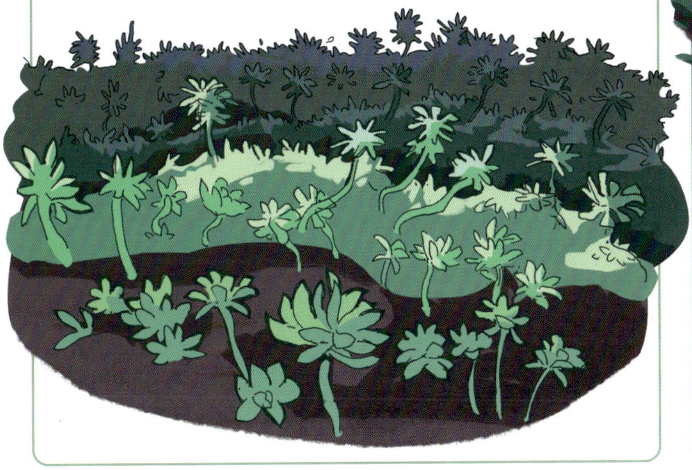

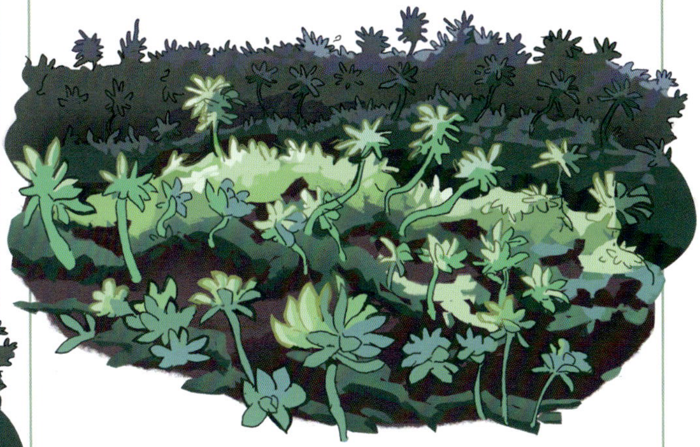

04 Progressively add detail by dividing the planes further, creating different areas of light and shadow or warmth and coolness.

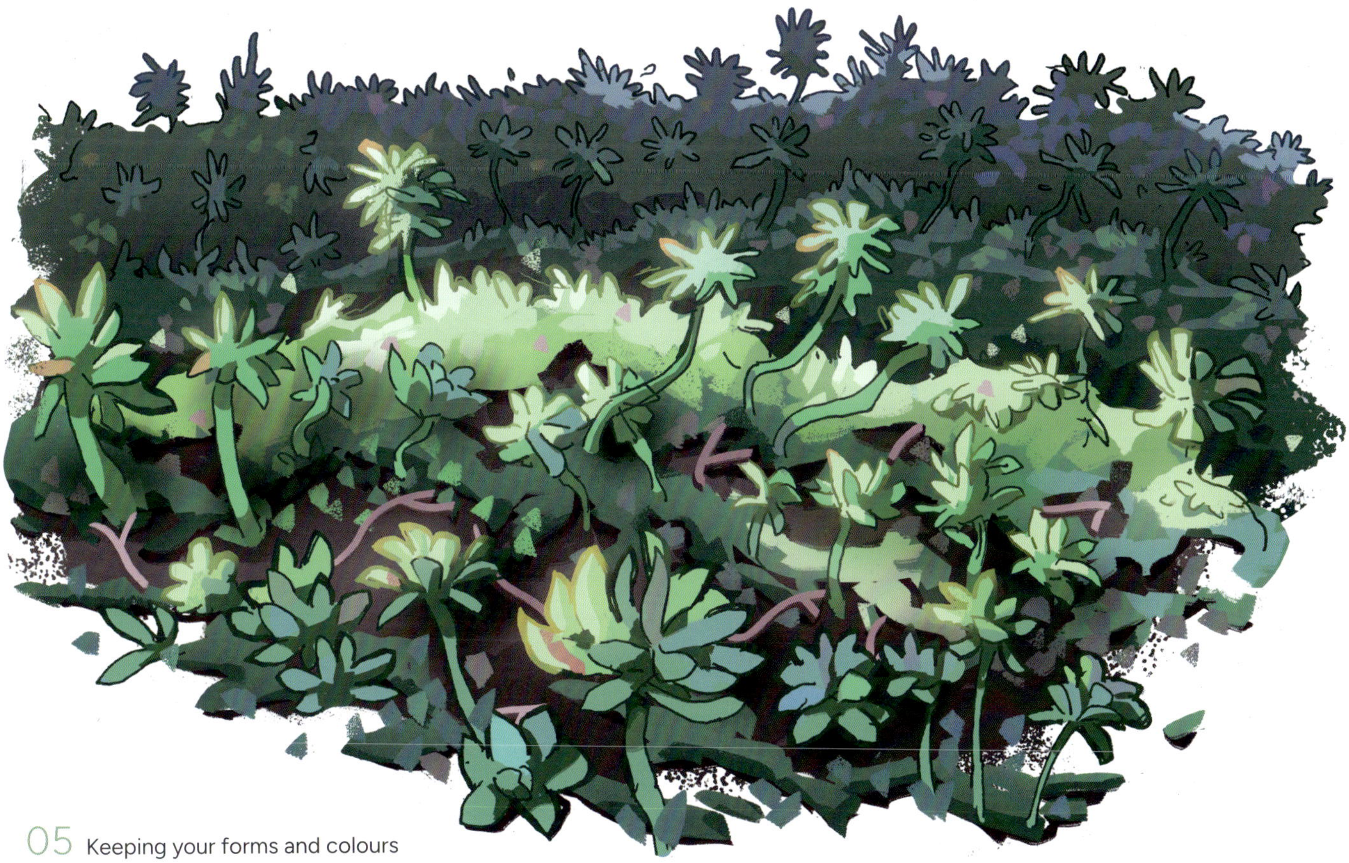

05 Keeping your forms and colours simple, add final details in your high-contrast areas, leaving breathing space in areas of lower contrast.

ART: MARIANA NORONHA

BY THE LIGHT OF DAY

INTERMEDIATE ●●

Paint an object in neutral lighting, then at three different times of day: dawn, midday, and late evening.

How does the direction and strength of the light source (the sun) affect the shadows and highlights? Look up reference imagery for guidance, or set the object on a windowsill and paint from life at the various times of the day.

NEUTRAL LIGHTING

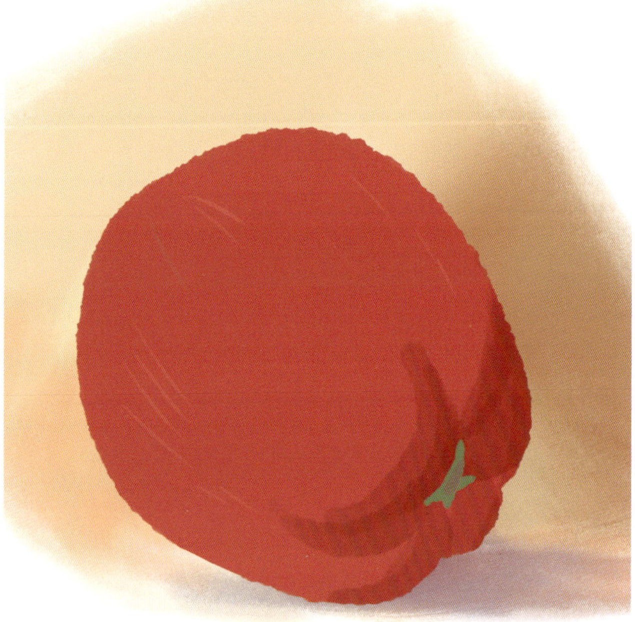

01 Start by painting the object in neutral lighting (no specific direction or tone). This version will lack of strong shadows or highlights.

DAWN LIGHTING

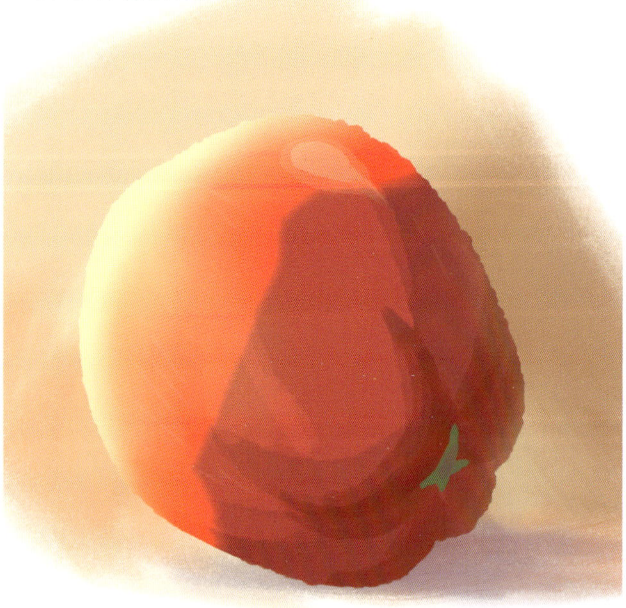

02 Next, paint the object with soft dawn light. See how the light on the apple is warm, while the shadows have semi-cool tones.

MIDDAY LIGHTING

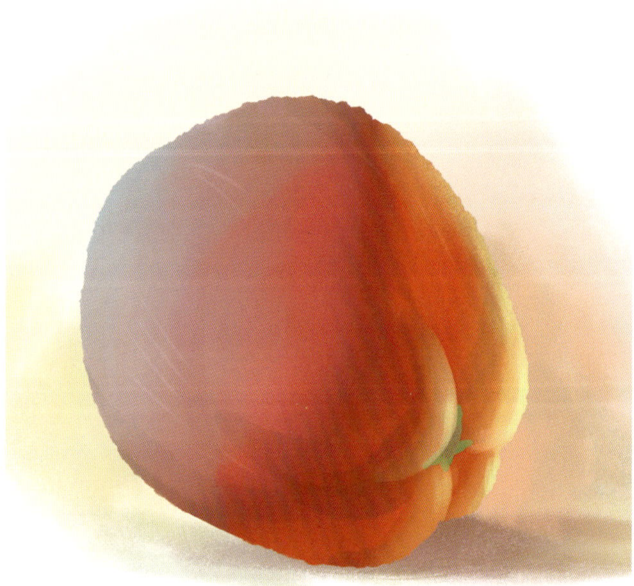

03 Paint the object at midday, when the sun is overhead. The highlights will become slightly cooler as they reflect the light from the sky, while the shadows include bounced light from surrounding surfaces.

EVENING LIGHTING

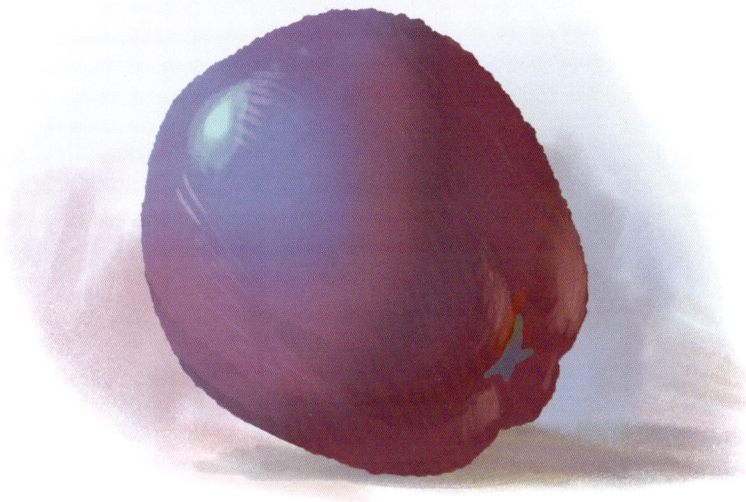

04 Finally, paint the object in late evening light. As the sun is low in the sky, the highlights and shadows will have cooler tones.

05 Finally, compare all three lighting options side by side. Which one appeals to you the most? Which did you most enjoy creating? Lighting can be a big point of difference in your artistic style.

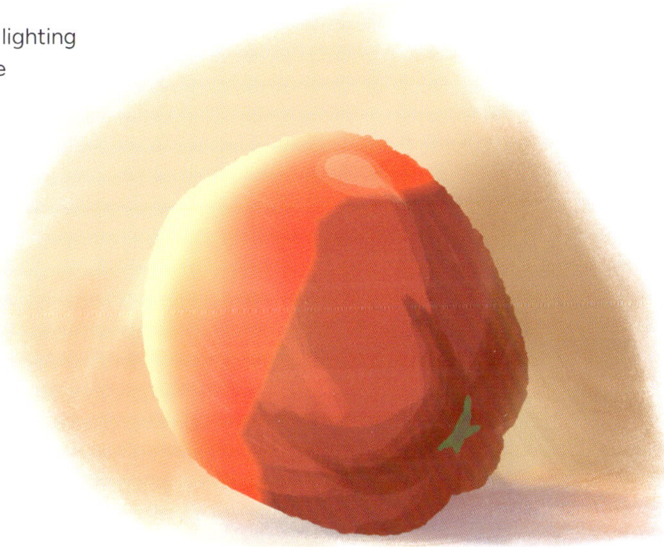

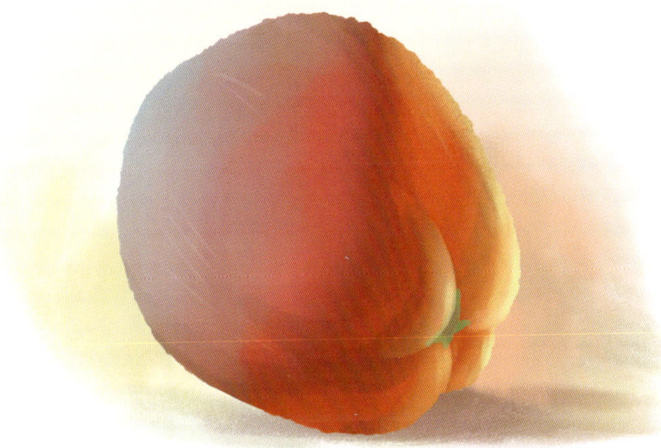

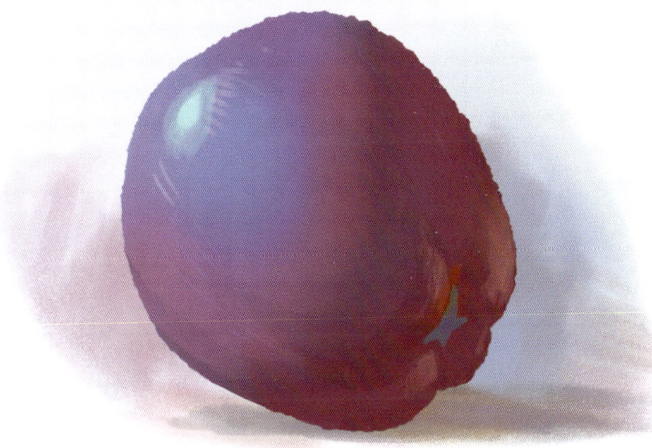

ART: JULIAN DEL REY

ATTENTION GRABBING

ADVANCED ●●●

Paint a scene that uses colour saturation to guide the viewer's eye.

Experiment with complementary colours to create one or more focal points that immediately draw attention, and consider how painting the background or surrounding elements with more muted tones can further direct the viewer's gaze. This challenge will help you to understand how saturation and hue can be powerful tools when used with intention and skill. It also serves as a way to hone your own approach to directing a viewer's gaze in your work.

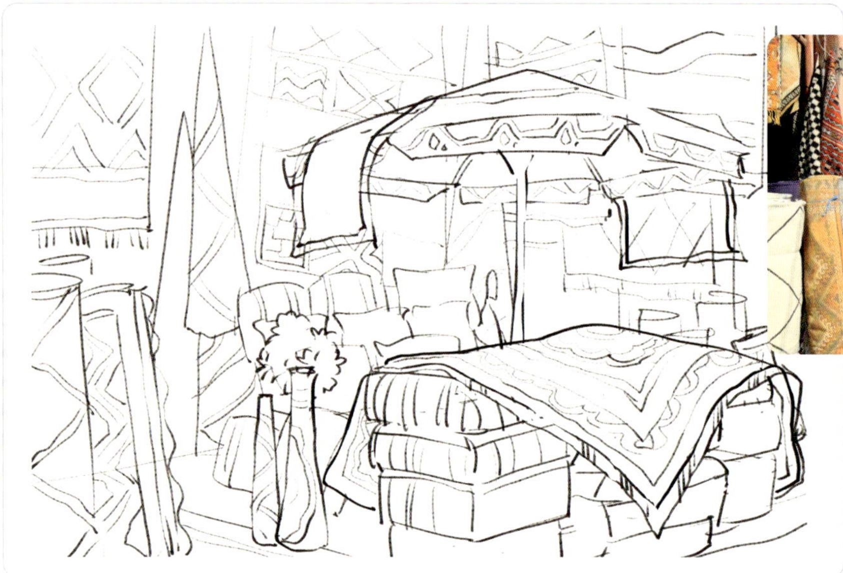

PHOTO BY JENNIFER YUNG ON UNSPLASH

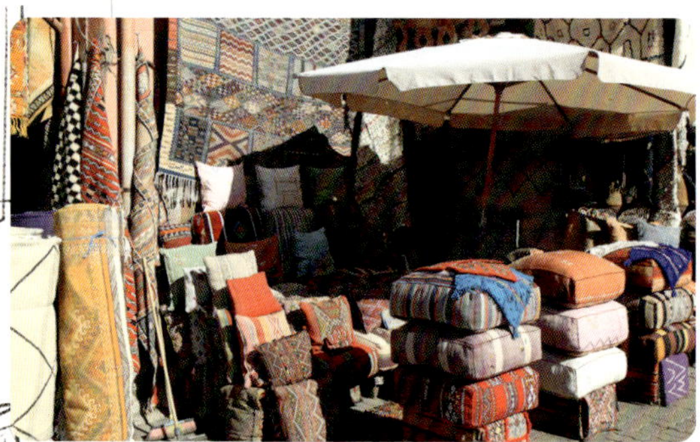

01 Choose a colourful reference photo and draw a rough sketch. Feel free to tweak the composition and add your own elements as you decide which area will form the focal point.

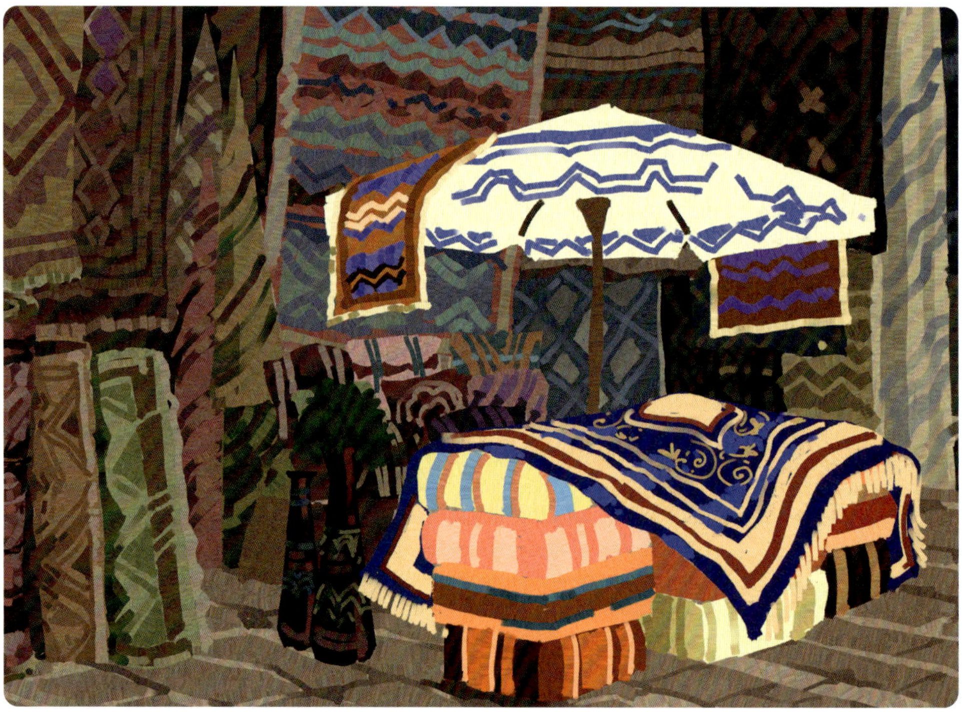

02 Add the base colours, using highly saturated colours for areas of focus and more muted tones for the background. Notice how this background features a lot of natural, earthy reds and browns, whereas the market stall has more vibrant colours, such as bright blues, to pull in the viewer's gaze.

03 Shadow and light can help to create greater contrast between foreground and background. If working digitally, introduce soft purple shadows using a Multiply layer. If you want to add more contrast, simply make the shadows darker.

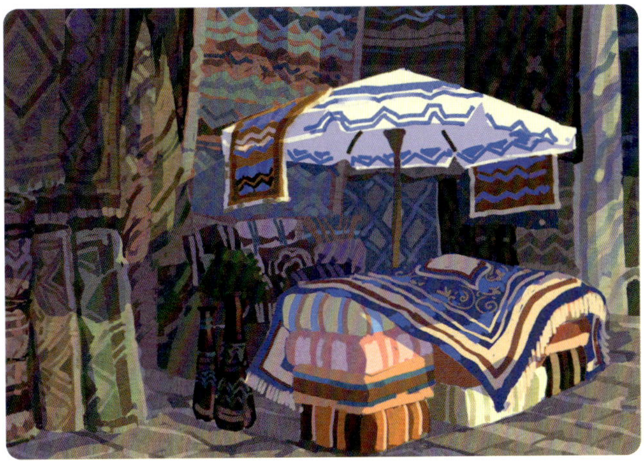

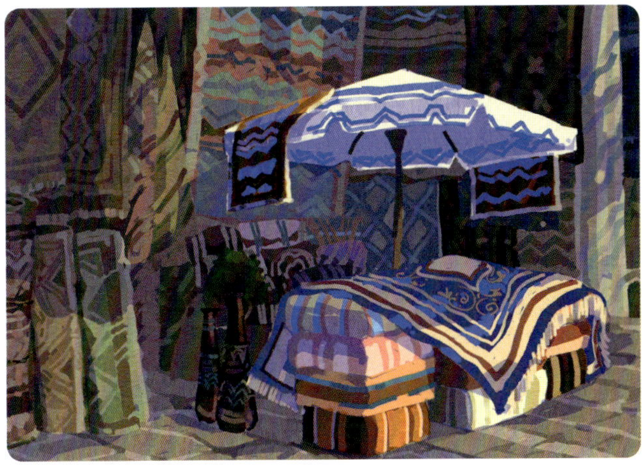

04 Paint areas of bright sunlight on an Overlay layer, such as on top of the parasol. These will work in tandem with the saturated colours to direct the viewer's eye to the market stall.

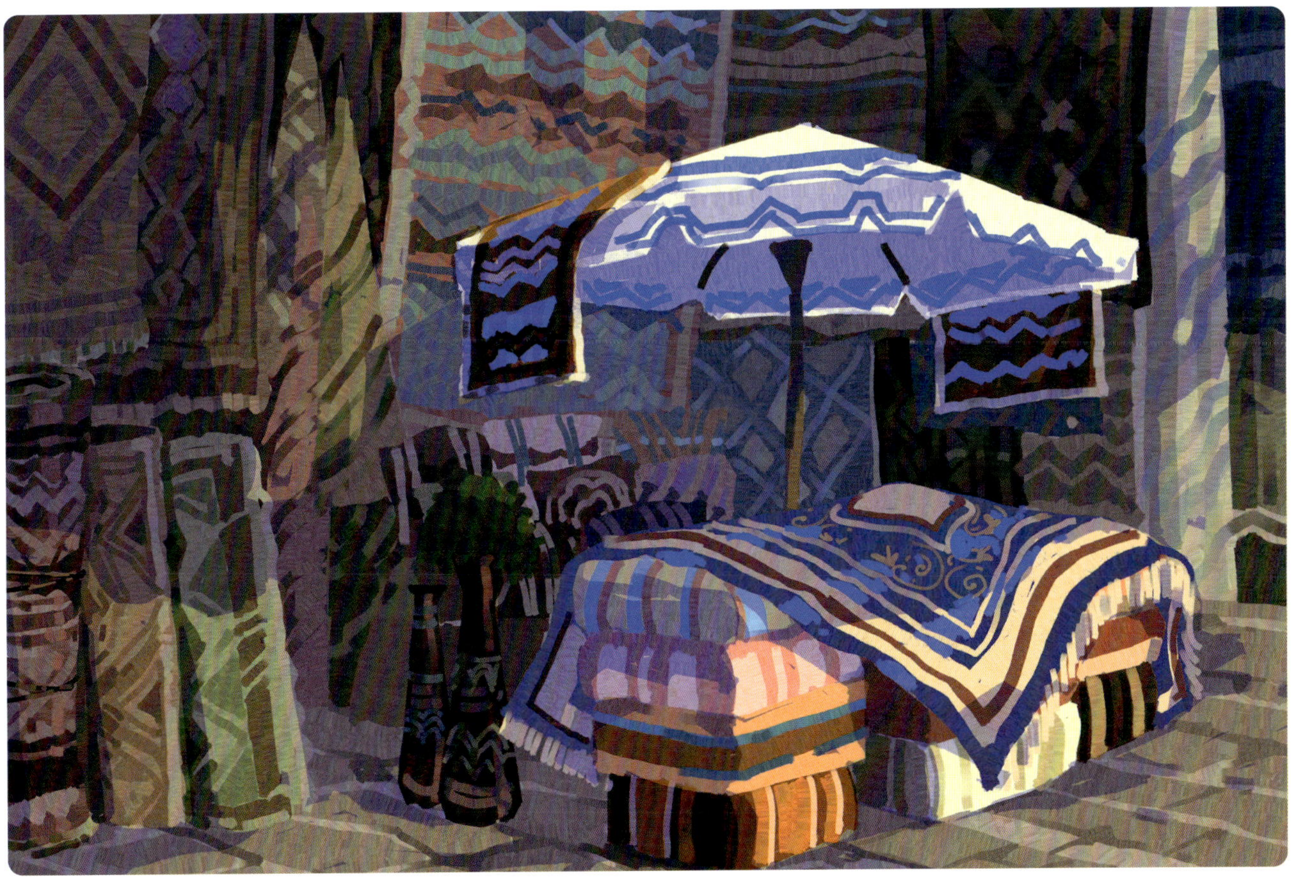

05 Finish by painting in any last areas of light and shadow, increasing the level of saturation to ensure your focal point really does grab attention. Is this level of saturation contrast something you could incorporate into your personal style?

ART: ALFRED FERNANDES

A ROOM WITH A VIEW

ADVANCED ●●●

Paint the view from your window in three different lighting scenarios – perhaps an overcast morning, in bright midday sun, and at sunset.

These should be thirty-minute thumbnails. Use a big blocky brush with high opacity to avoid blending the colours too much. You may wish to include interior elements in the composition to create an opportunity to study the contrast between the indoor and outdoor colours.

01 Take photographs of the same view from a window at three different times of day.

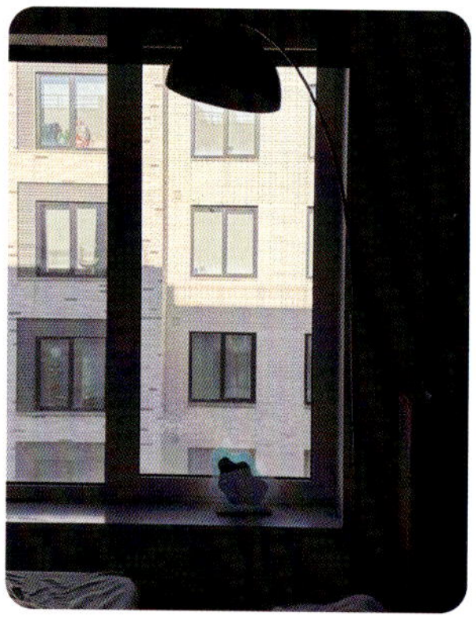

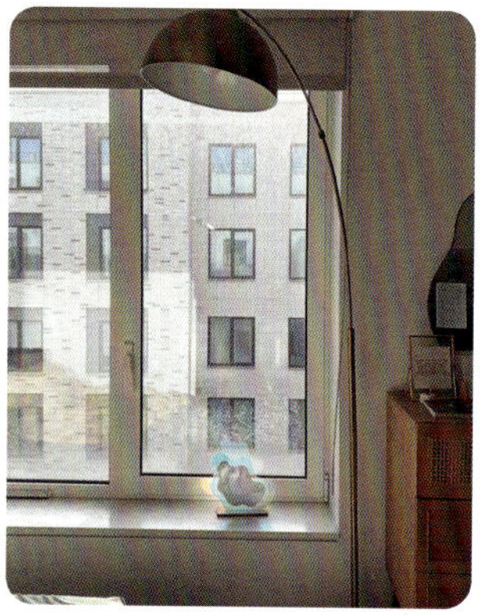

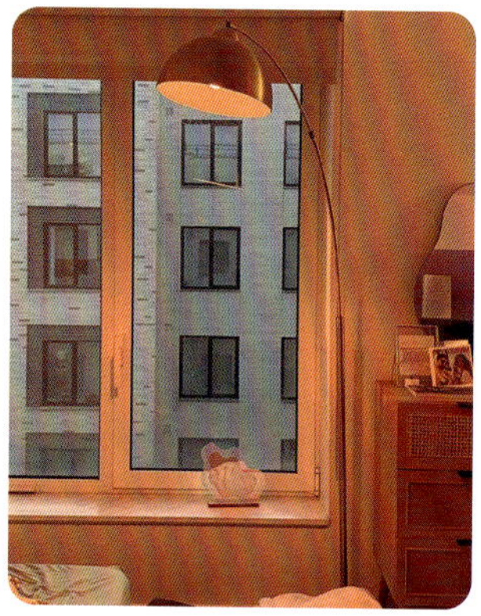

02 Sketch a rough line drawing of the scene. This will be used as a basis for all three paintings.

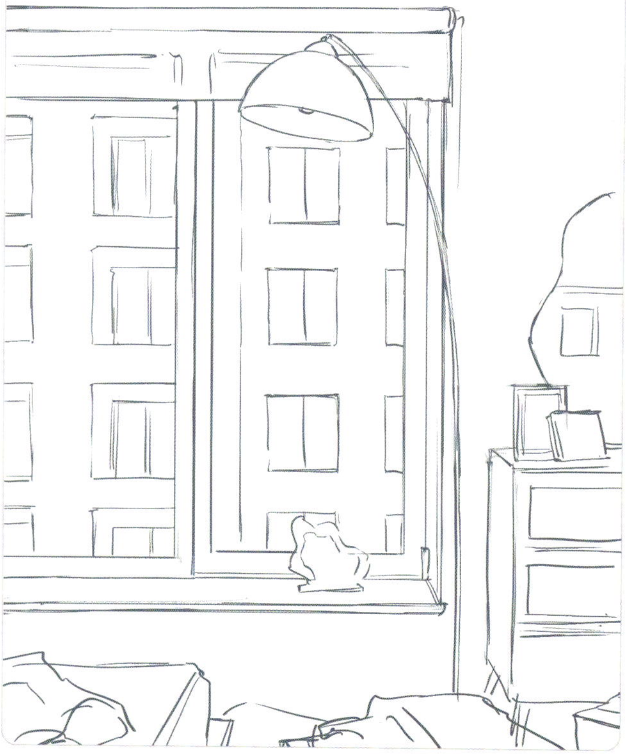

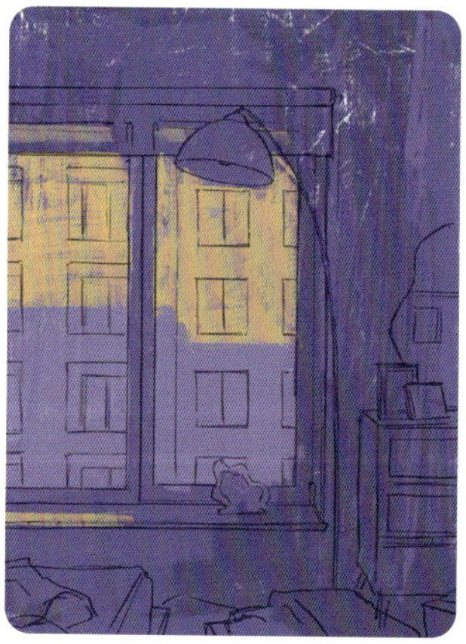

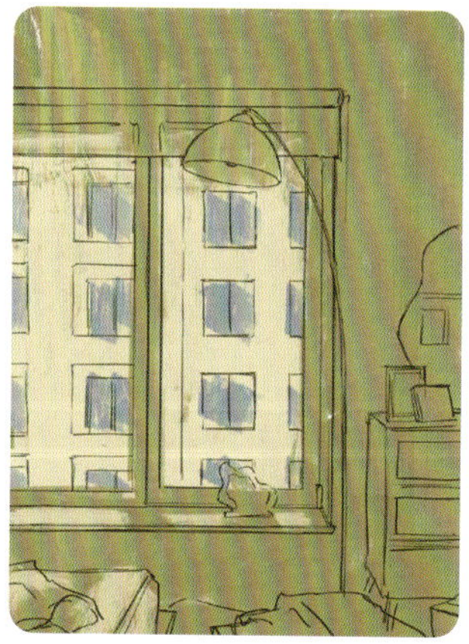

03 Use a big textured brush to block in the main colour scheme of the three lighting scenarios. Note how the early morning scene is mostly a cool purple, the midday scene is a warm olive, and the evening scene contrasts a warm orange interior against a cool blue for the outside.

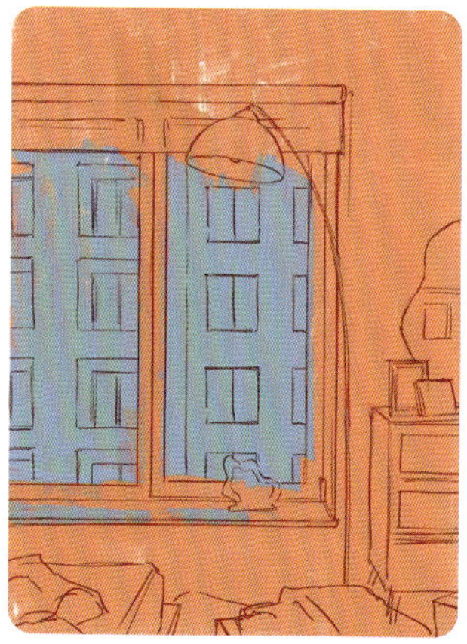

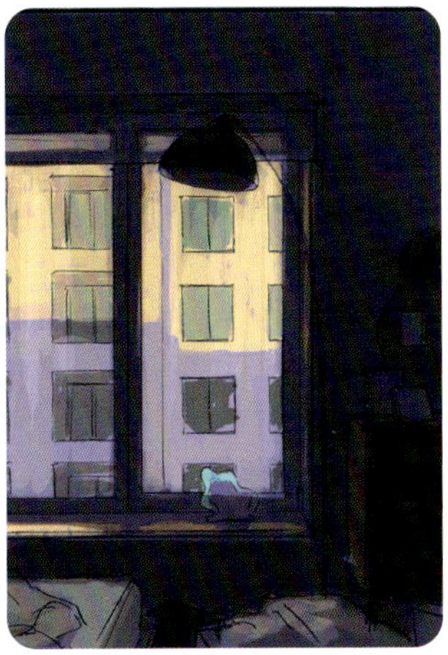

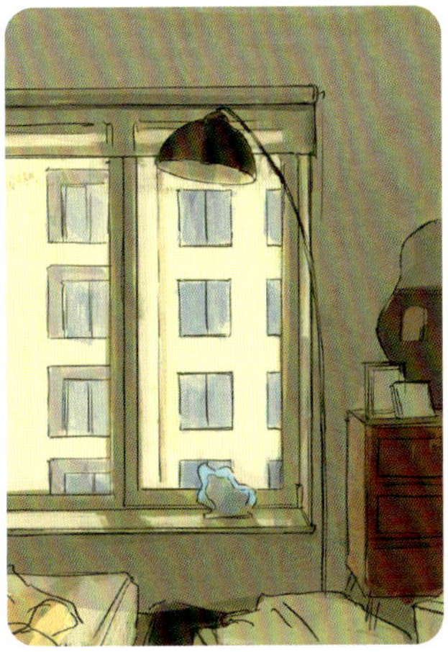

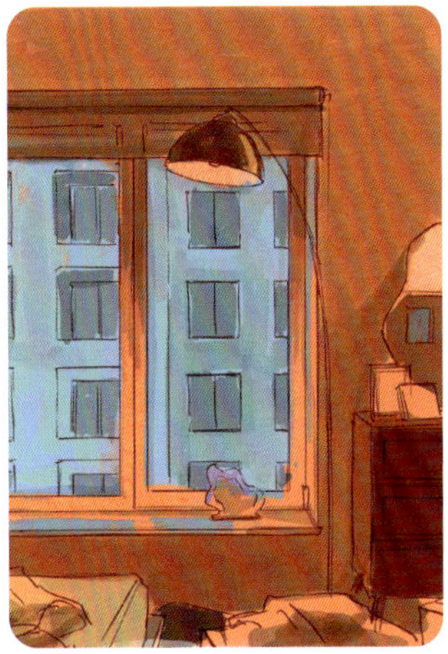

04 Add more detail, focusing on defining the edges and using big blocky colours. Aim to capture the essence of each photo, rather than creating a hyper-realistic copy.

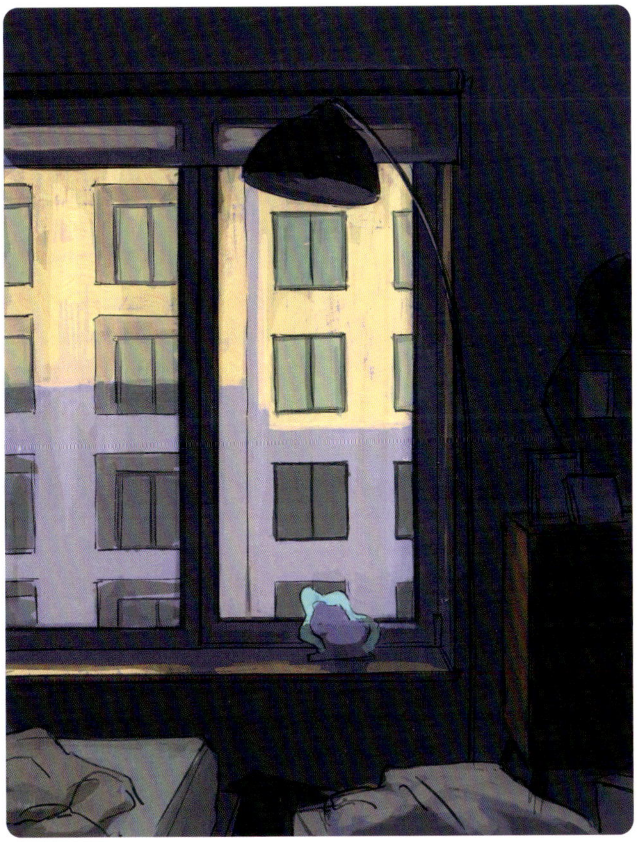

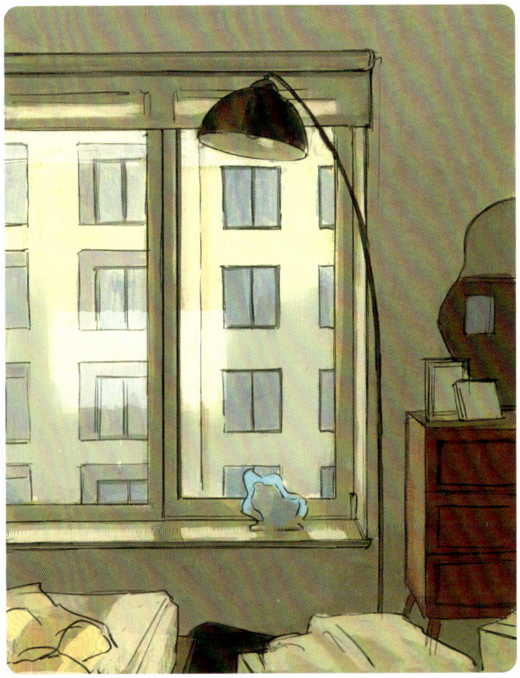

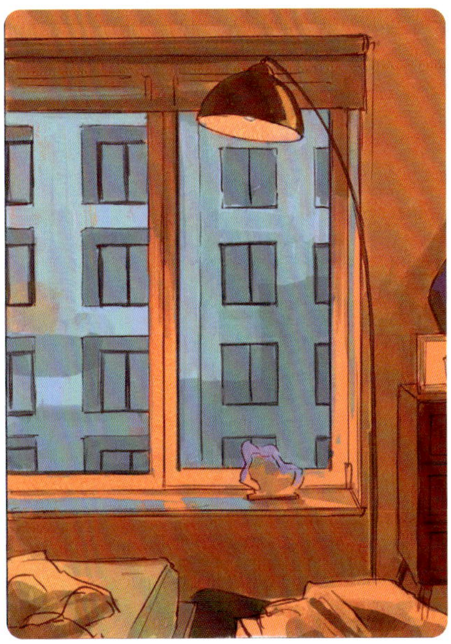

05 Paint in final details, then compare the three images. How does the lighting scenario change the overall look and mood of the scene?

A SCENE OF VALUE

ADVANCED ●●●

Create a scene using only values – play with the balance of light and dark to bring the subject to life.

This is a useful exercise for focusing on the essence of light, shadow, and form without the distraction of colour. It will also help you to sharpen your understanding of contrast and depth, allowing you to emphasize mood and structure. Whether you're aiming for dramatic intensity or soft subtleties, working with value helps to build a strong foundation in any composition.

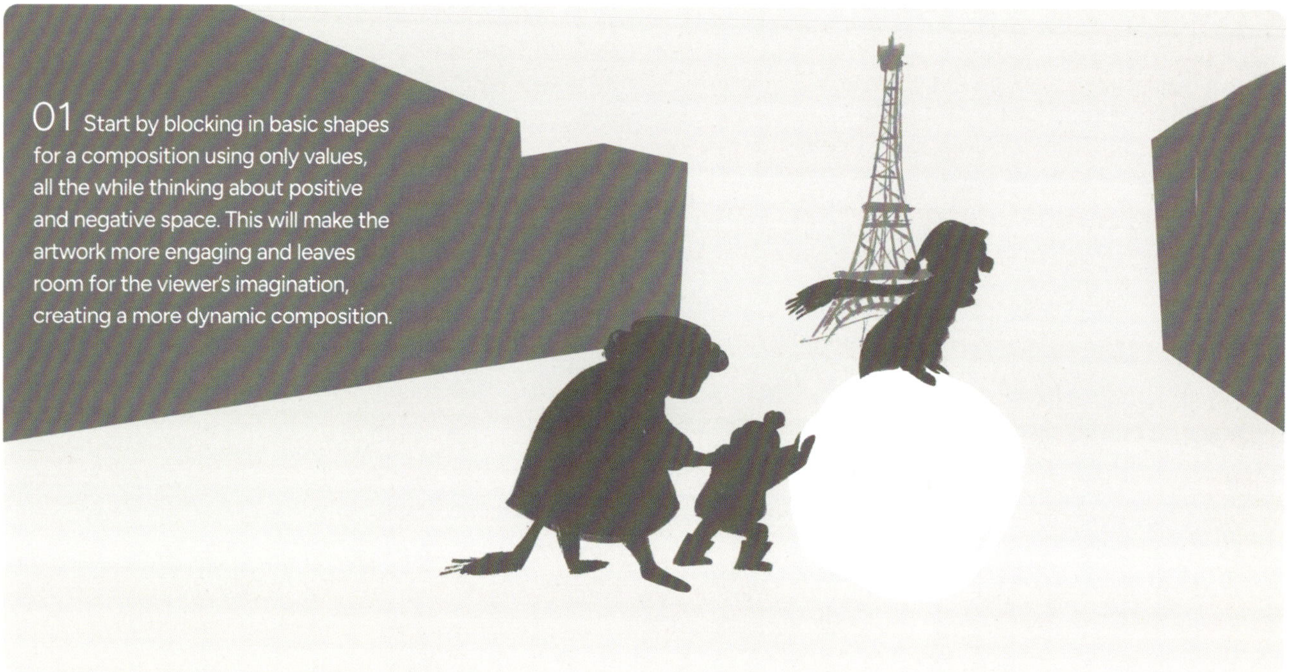

01 Start by blocking in basic shapes for a composition using only values, all the while thinking about positive and negative space. This will make the artwork more engaging and leaves room for the viewer's imagination, creating a more dynamic composition.

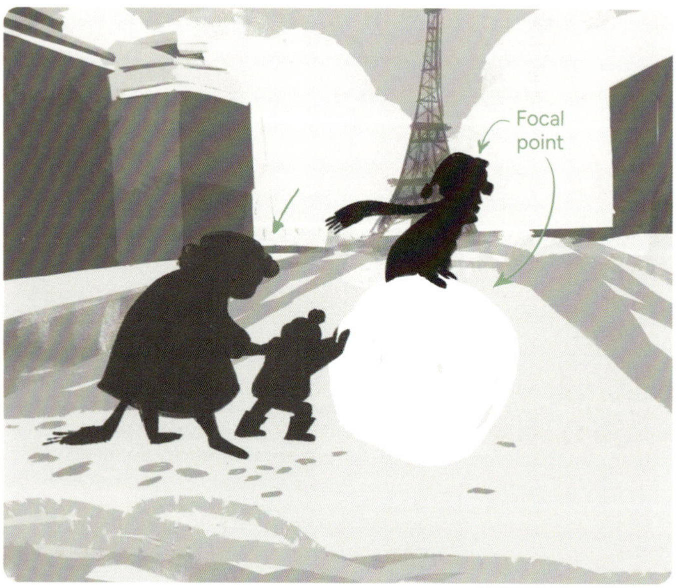

02 Establish a strong focal point. Emphasizing the area where the story unfolds, leaving the rest rough and in a neutral zone, will direct the viewer's eye.

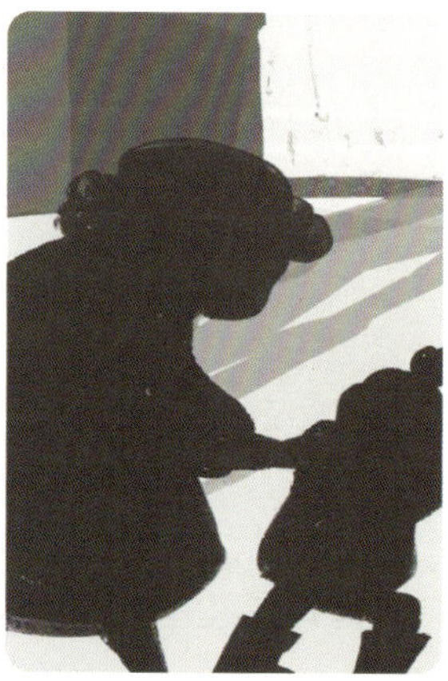

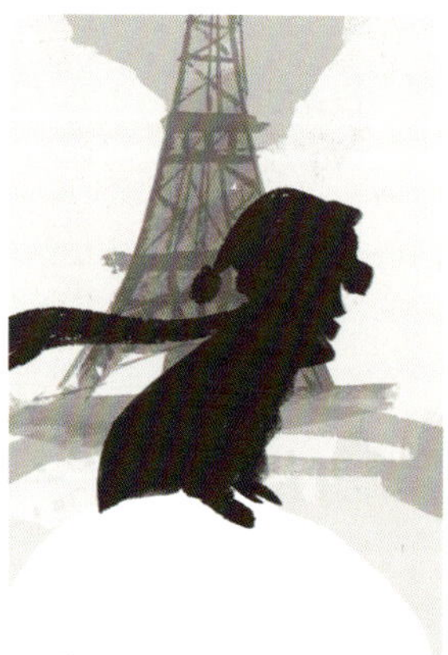

03 Limit your palette, working with only three to five values. This will encourage you to think more carefully about the values you choose.

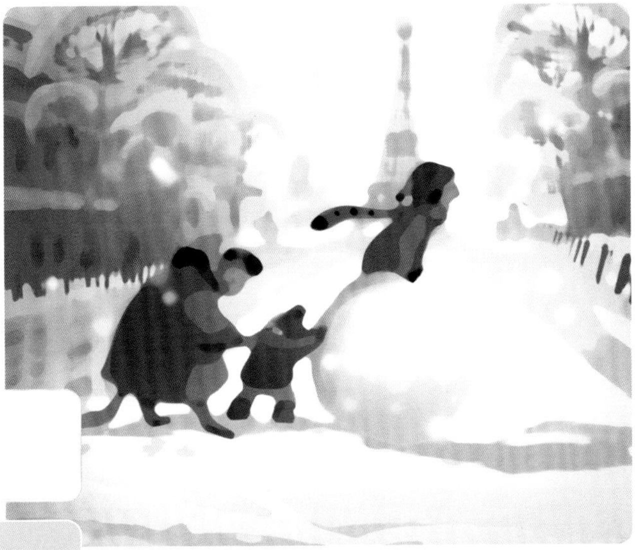

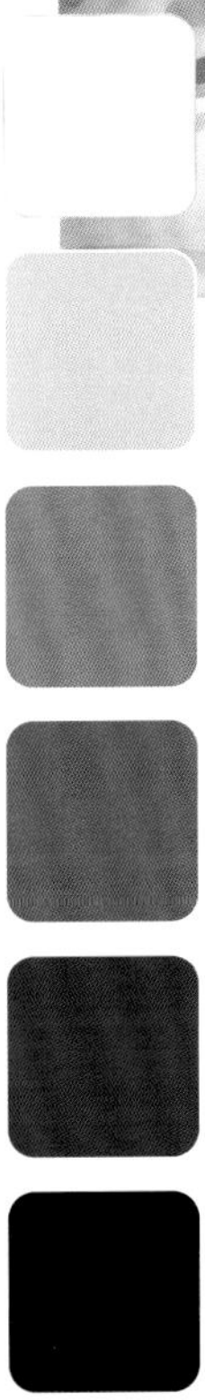

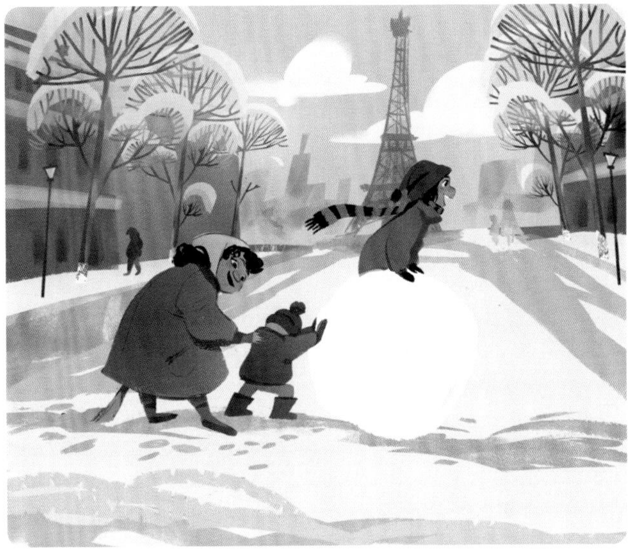

04 Gradually build up the values, starting with light layers before progressively darkening the shadows.

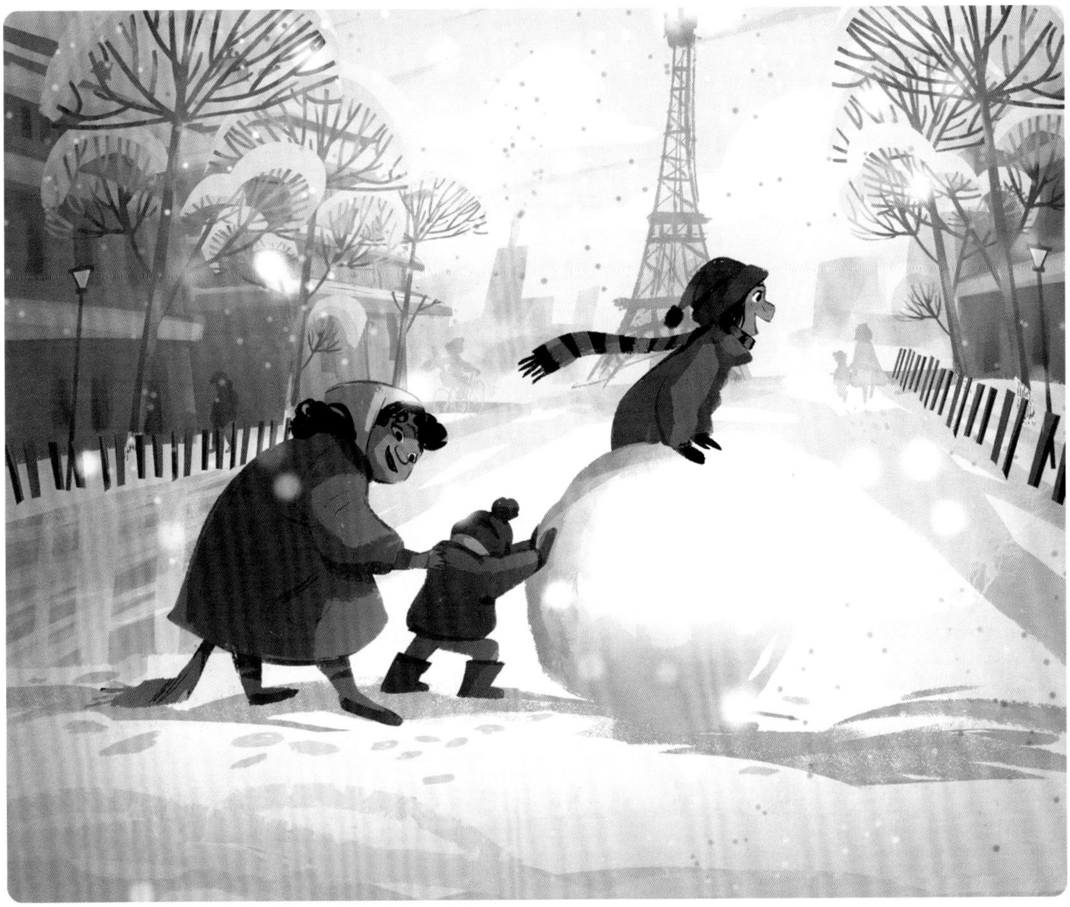

05 Continue to add as many light or shadow layers as needed to create depth and interest.

ART: TARANEH KARIMI

TESTING TEMPERATURES

ADVANCED ●●●

Use digital tools to try out cool and warm colour palettes for the same scene, then combine them.

Start by choosing a strongly lit reference photo featuring direct sunlight or another strong light source. Create a digital greyscale sketch focusing on the light and dark values, then change the shadows to a cool colour and the light to a warm one. Next use blending layers and colour tweaks to create a warm version, then a cool one. Finally, try combining the two palettes for an effective final image.

01 Begin by drawing a greyscale sketch to form a clear idea of where the light and shadow will be.

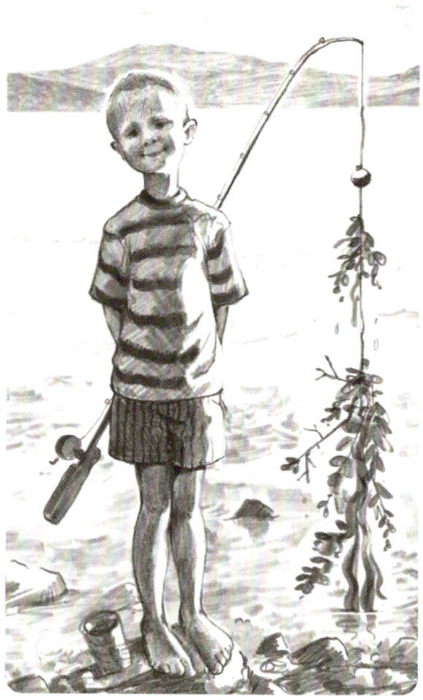

02 Introduce a cool colour for the shadow and a warm colour for the light.

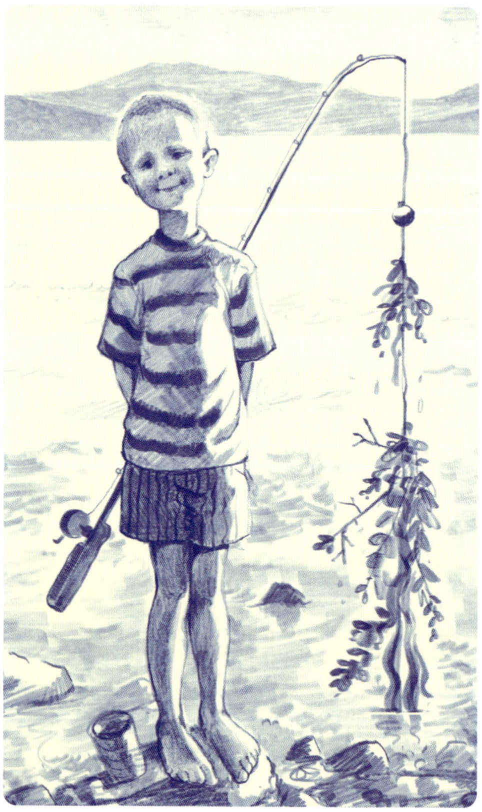

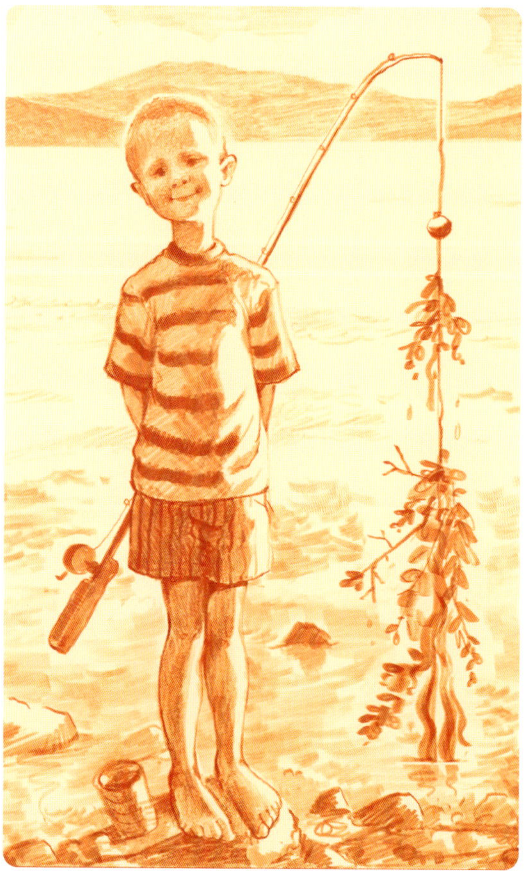

03 Now create a version with a warm palette by experimenting with digital overlays, changing the colour of the line work, and adjusting the colour hues.

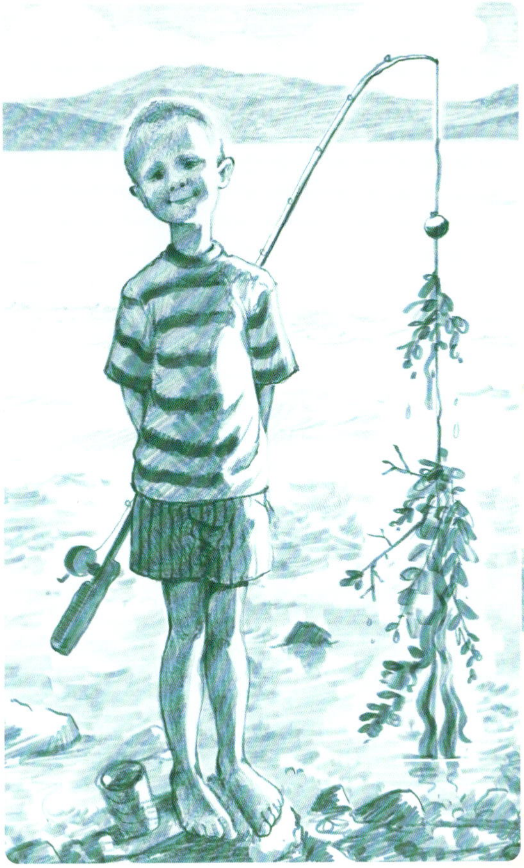

04 Repeat step 03 but this time creating a cool colour palette. How does this change the mood of the scene and the perceived state-of-mind of the character?

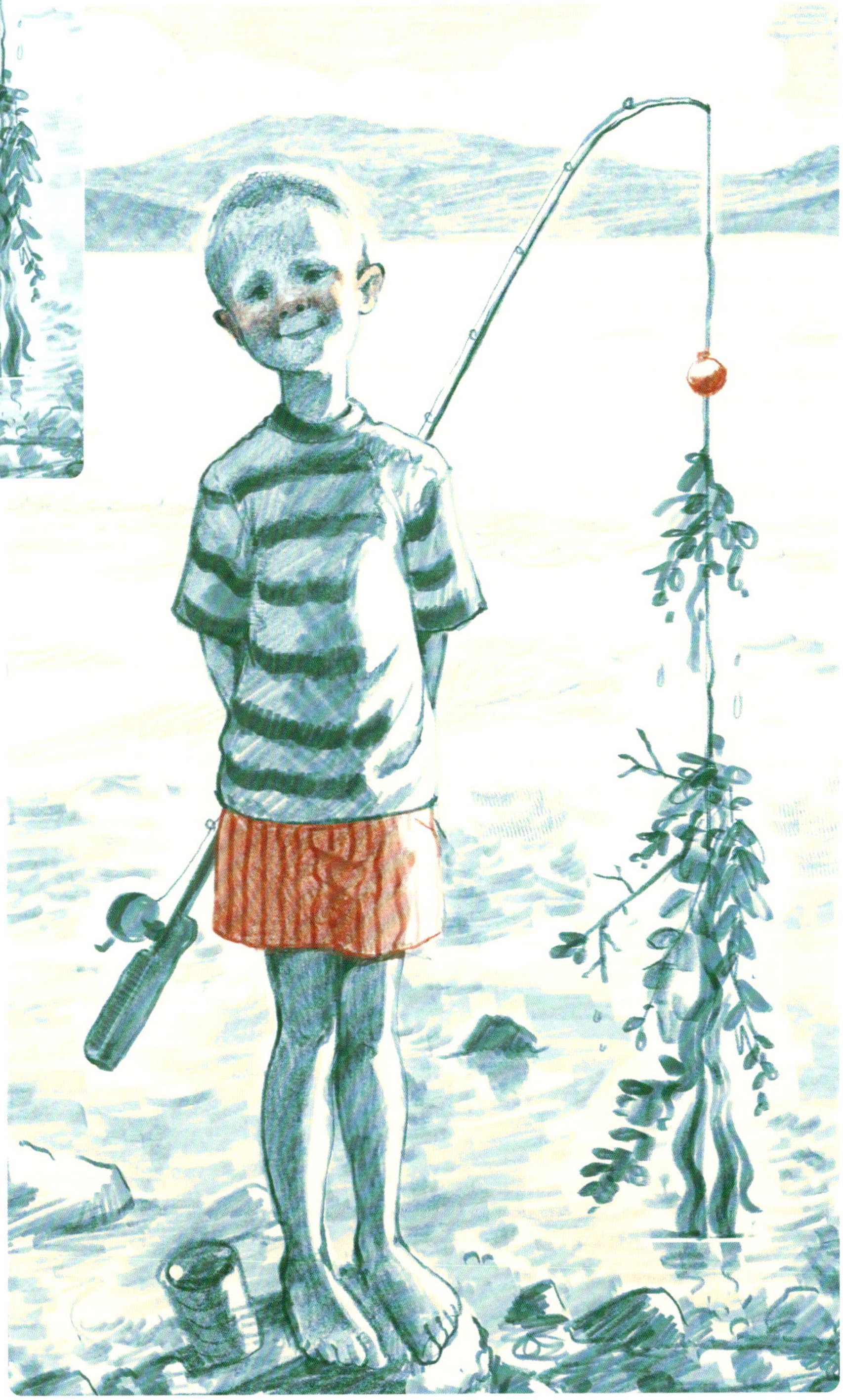

05 As a final step, choose elements from each colour palette to blend together. Here, the warm tones are applied to the background, part of the fishing rod, and the child's face and shorts. The left is rest with the cool palette. Could this kind of palette-mixing technique become part of your personal style?

ART: MADI HARPER

One-page challenges:

BALLS OF COLOUR

BEGINNER ●

Paint three spheres using three different types of colour scheme – analogous, complementary, and triadic.

Start with analogous, where you can clearly separate light from dark. When you venture into the other two more expansive colour palettes, it can become tricky to clearly show light and shadow – such as when using red as a shadow colour, like in the triadic example shown. However, the more complex schemes can make for more interesting illustrations.

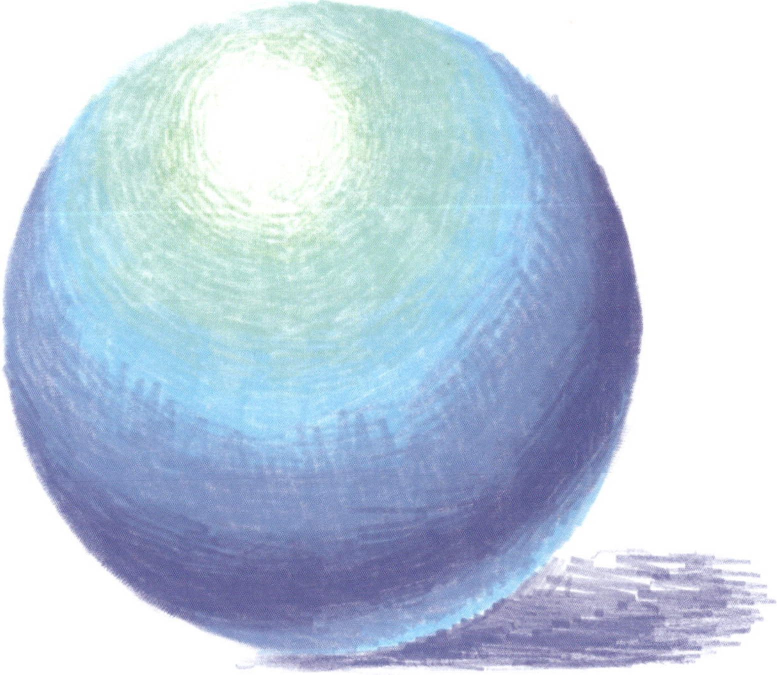

ANALOGOUS

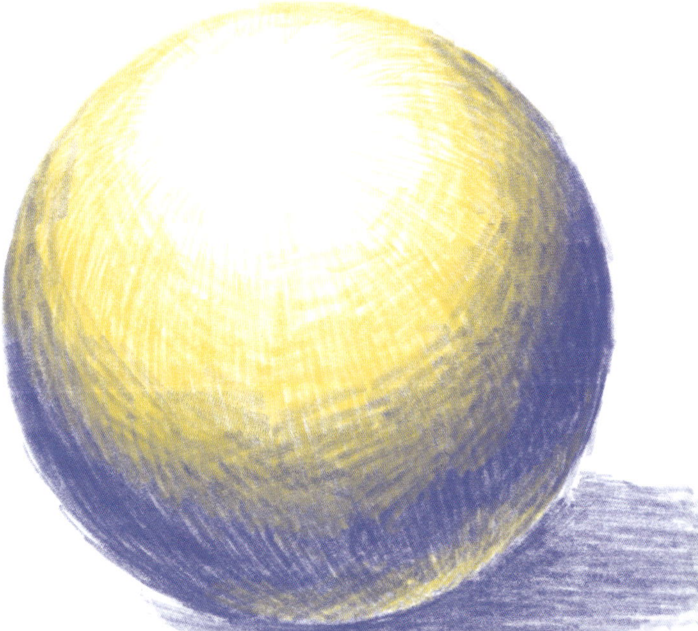

COMPLEMENTARY

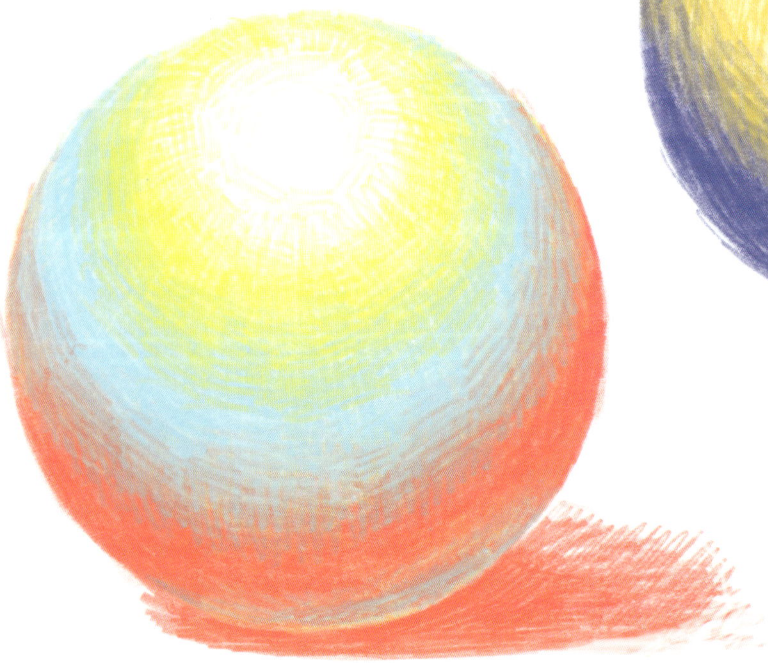

TRIADIC

ART: MADI HARPER

THREE-VALUE CUBE

BEGINNER ●

Draw a cube using only three values.

On a geometric shape, using three tonal values provides a clear way to simplify light and volume without getting lost in the process. Assign one tone to the light, another to the midtone, and another to the shadow. You can then add three more tones within each of these, reaching nine different values, all subordinate to the primary values. Redraw the cube with a reimagined light source using the same three values. Then redraw the cube again with a different light source. Studying still-life shapes is essential for practising and understanding form and light.

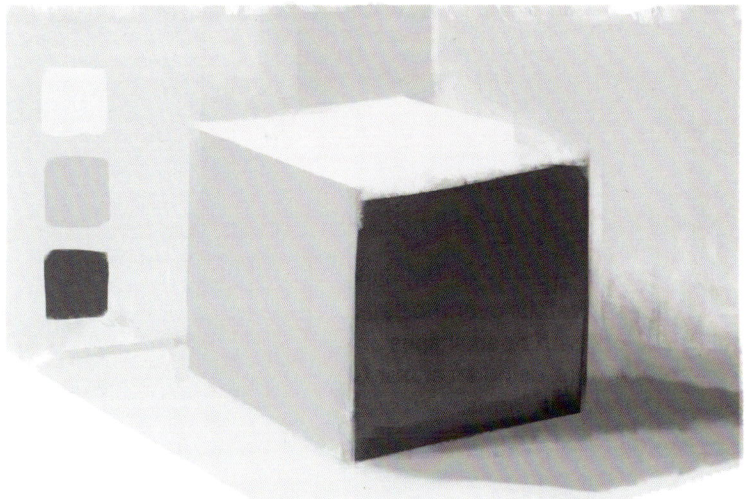

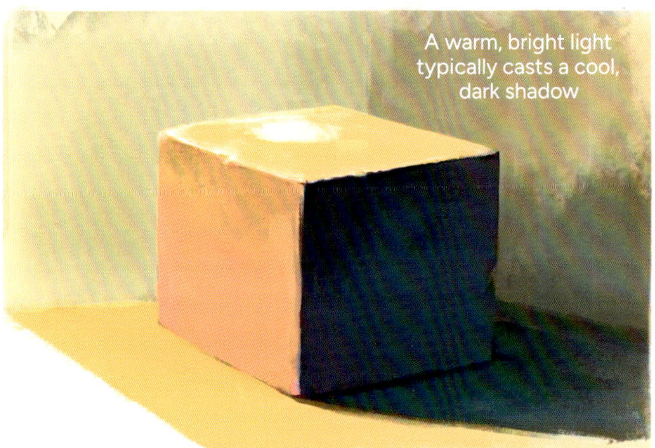

A warm, bright light typically casts a cool, dark shadow

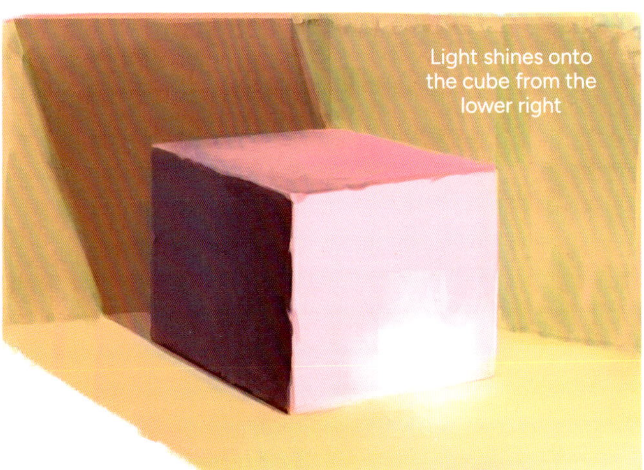

Light shines onto the cube from the lower right

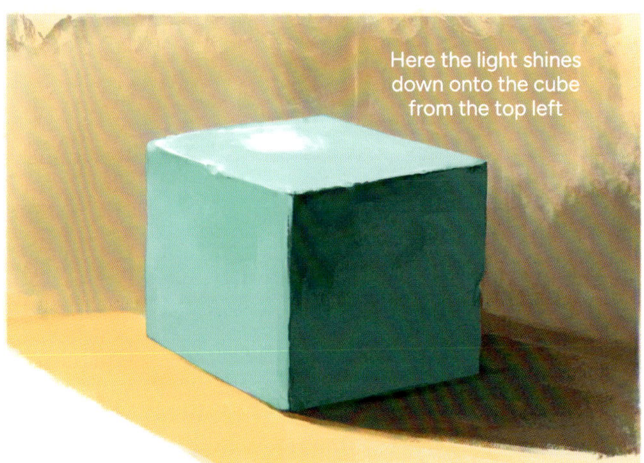

Here the light shines down onto the cube from the top left

ART: LORON LEAL

ONE-PEN TREE

BEGINNER ●

Use a fine-tipped black pen to draw a study of a tree.

Capture the shadows and different values by hatching and layering with the same pen, rather than switching to a thicker or darker pen. Start by visualizing the volumes and parts that make up the form. Simplify the silhouettes, then mark the dark areas, adding details over the basic shapes. Work with open shapes and broken contours, using an eraser to define the various forms.

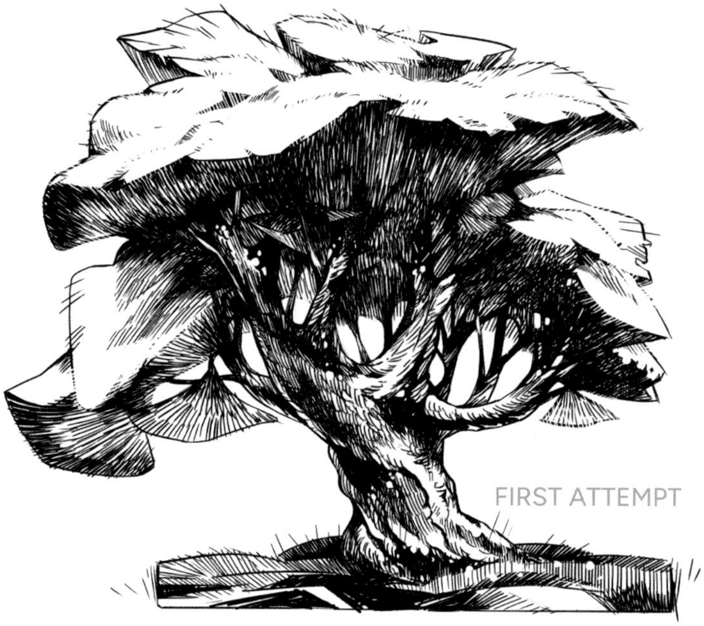

FIRST ATTEMPT

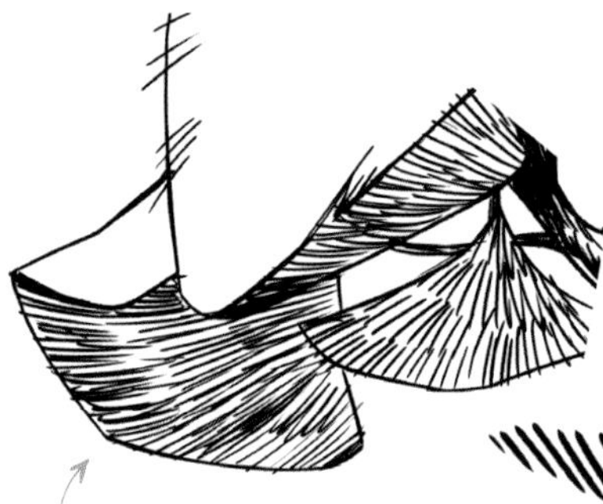

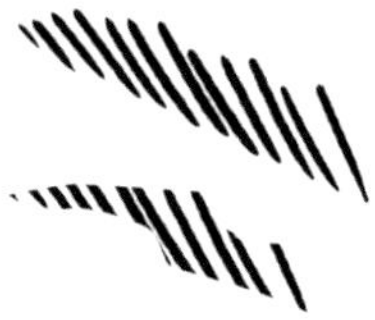

Experiment with various styles of hatching

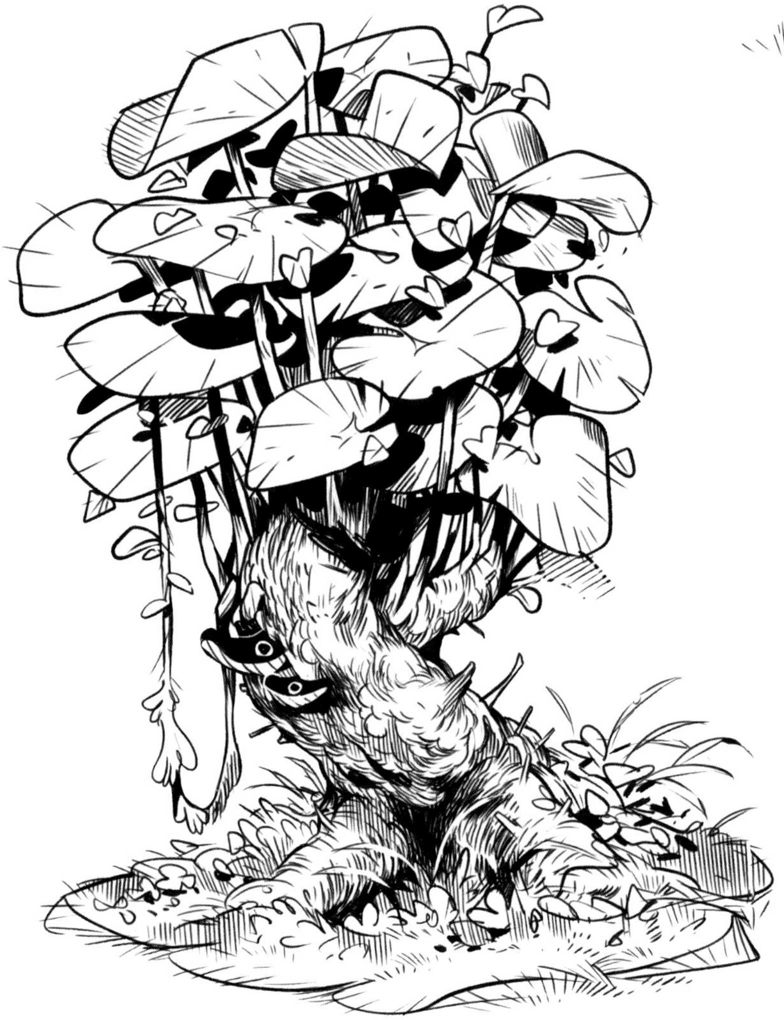

SECOND, MORE STYLIZED VERSION

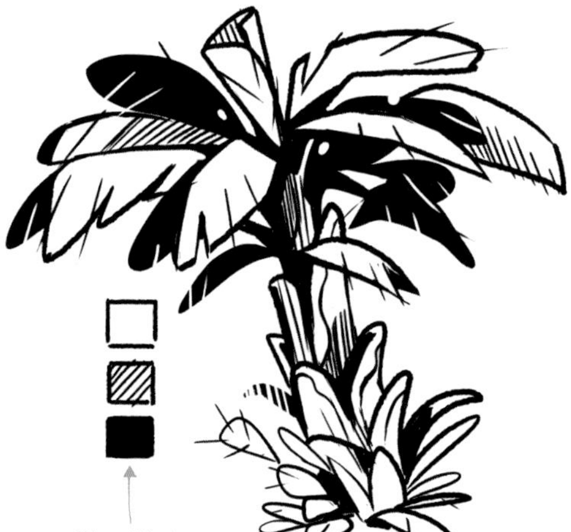

Simplify in three tones

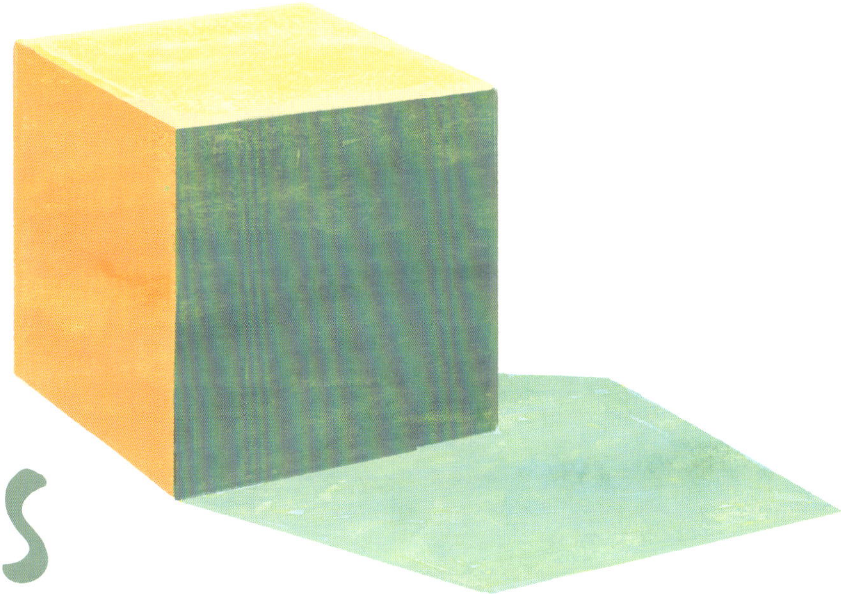

BRIGHT SHADOWS

BEGINNER ●

Paint a cube three times using a different bold, unusual shadow colour for each.

Compare the three and examine how the shadow colour changes the mood or feel of each painting. This challenge is a fun way to experiment with colour and mood on a simple object, before progressing to paint a more detailed or complex image.

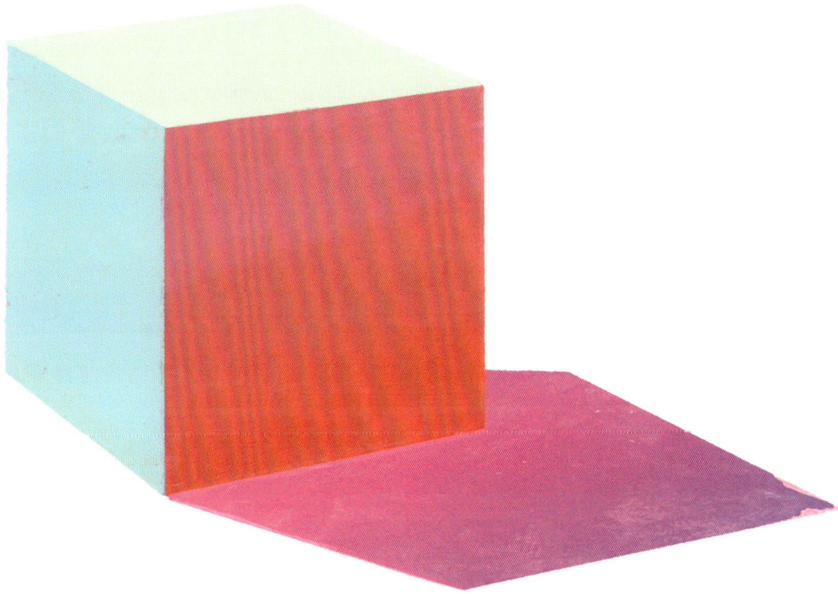

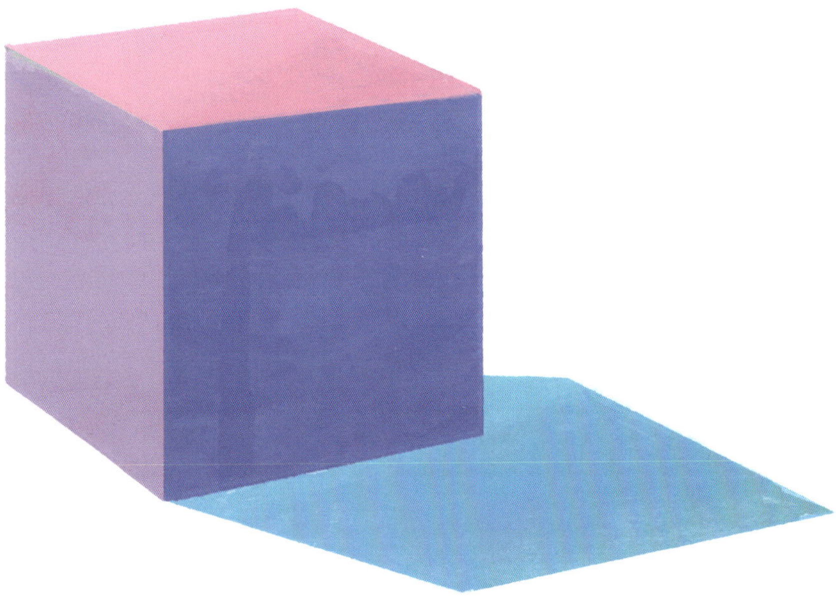

ART: CHAVOOM (HITOMI TAMURA)

COLOUR BLOCKS

INTERMEDIATE ●●

Select a reference photo and simplify it into three to five colour blocks.

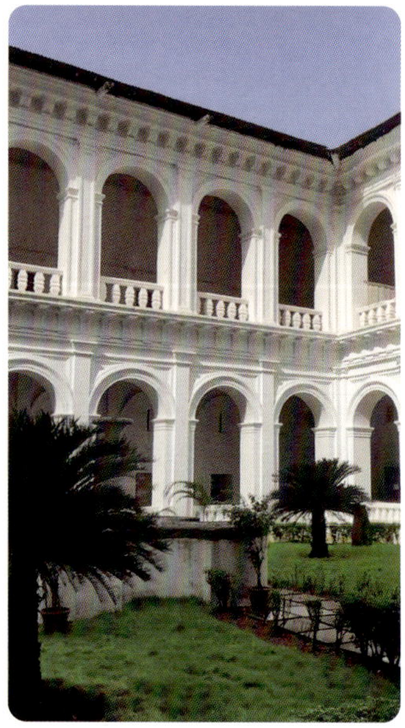

Dividing up colours and simplifying objects in this way provides a solid foundation to build on. Start by identifying the main colours and areas of light and shade in the reference photo. Here, the image is divided into five key colours: blue for the sky, light brown for the building, green for plants, dark brown for shade, and yellow for light. Avoid getting distracted by detail and don't worry about recreating the scene perfectly.

1

2

3

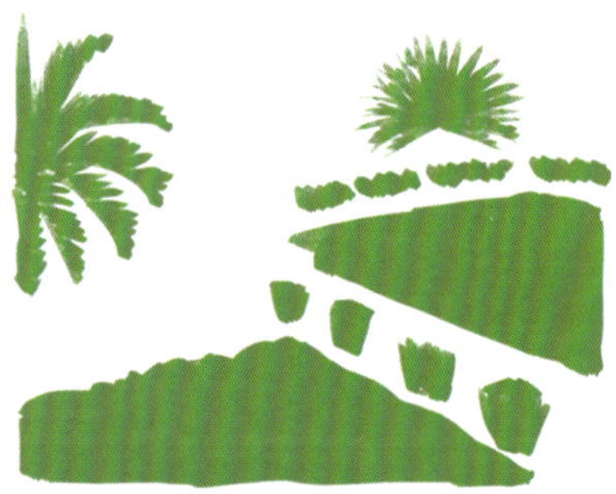

4

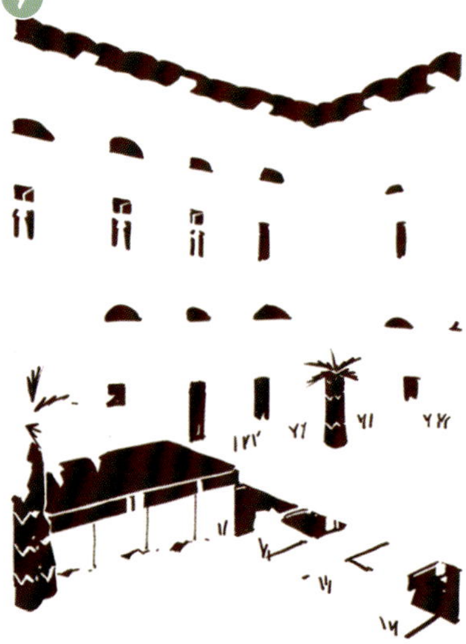

5

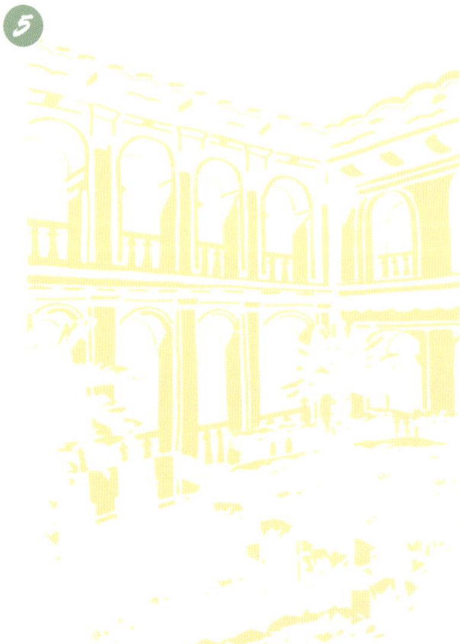

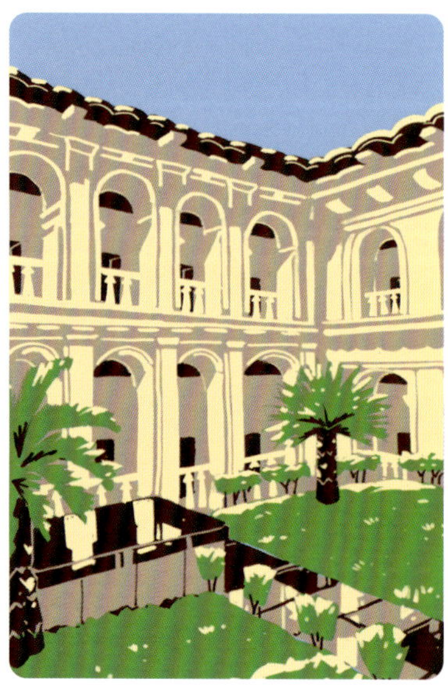

ART: ALFRED FERNANDES

FRUITFUL LIGHT

INTERMEDIATE ●●

Paint a piece of fruit from life, taking time to analyse the light sources.

It's useful to think about colours as relative, as opposed to absolute. Shadows can feel darker if surrounded by lighter tones. Objects can seem warmer if enveloped by cooler notes. Familiarizing yourself with colour properties – such as hue, saturation, and value – in relation to each other will help you to capture subtleties that will make your artwork look more lifelike. For example, while the lime appears green, it actually consists of multiple hues with slightly different temperatures and shades that work together to push its vibrancy. This is something that can be exaggerated for a more stylized look.

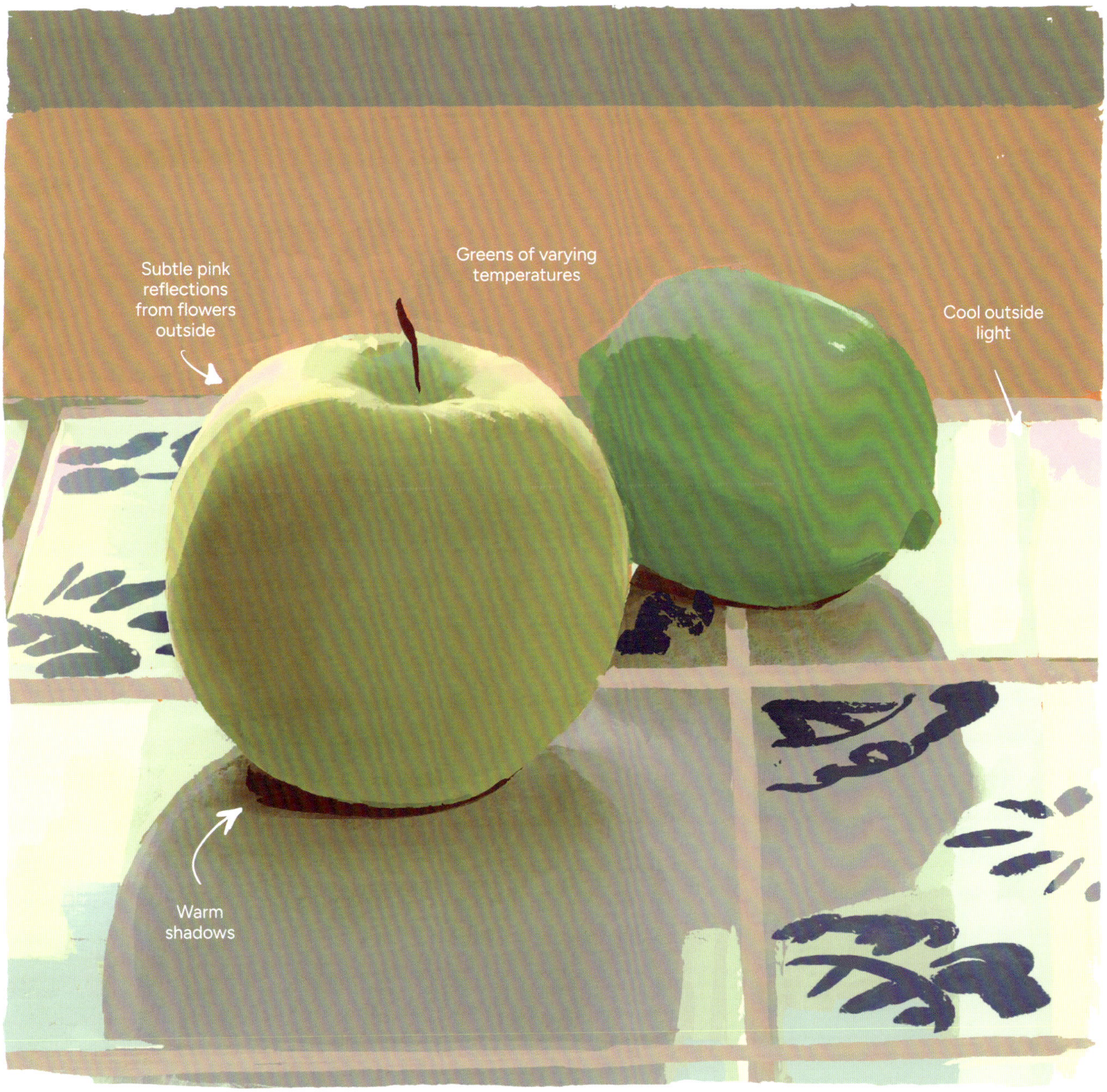

Painted outside on a cloudy day, the light areas are less intense and more desaturated

ART: MICHELLE CHENG

ONE-COLOUR CREATURE

INTERMEDIATE ●●

Colour a creature using only shades from a single colour hue, using saturation and value to direct the eye to the focal points.

When creating a design with a single hue, you must use saturation and value to create contrast. These are two important, and often overlooked, design elements. An area with increased saturation will draw the eye when surrounded by more desaturated colours. In the example shown, the ochre area surrounding the owl's eyes has more contrast than the rest of its body.

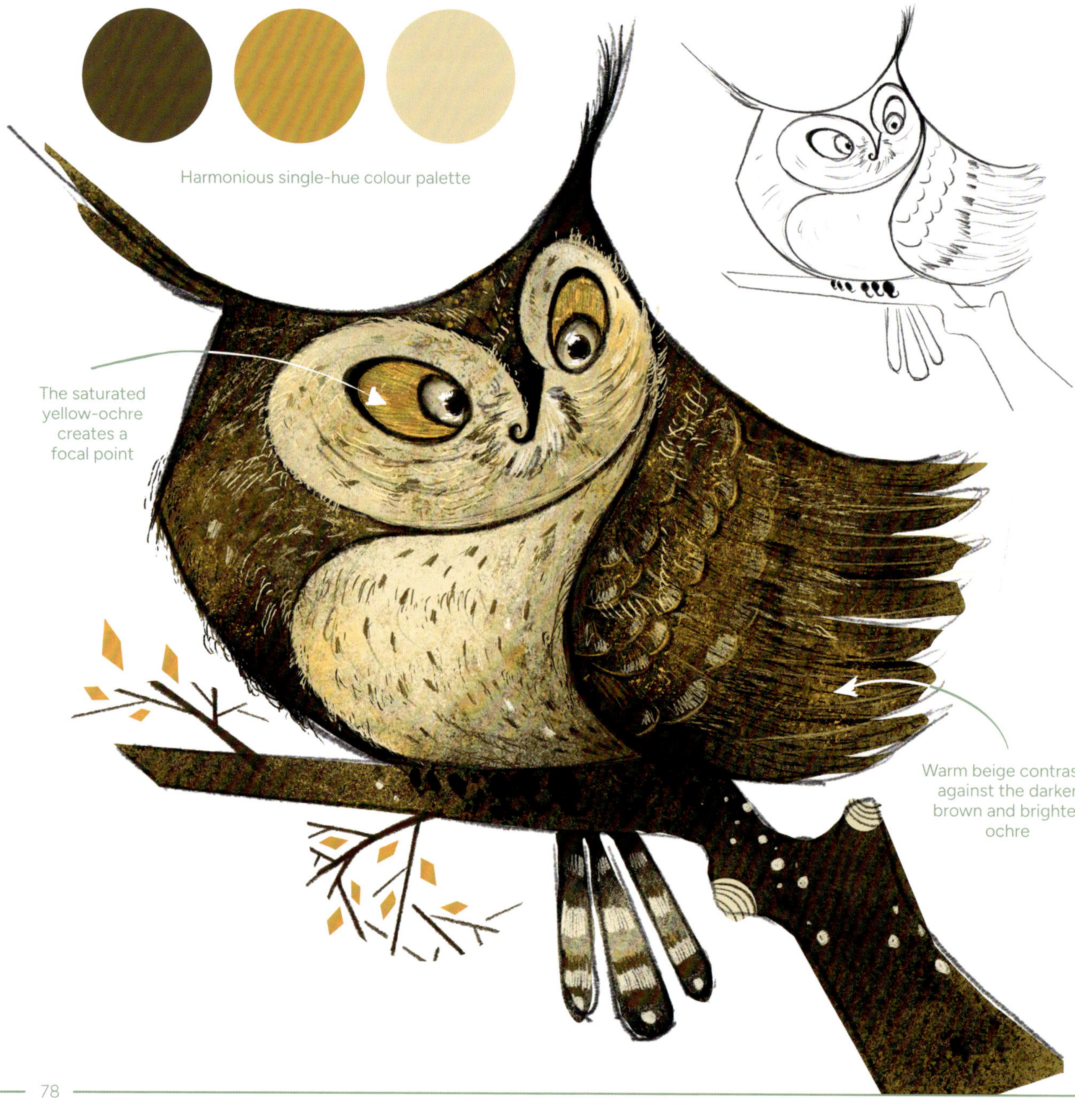

Harmonious single-hue colour palette

The saturated yellow-ochre creates a focal point

Warm beige contrasts against the darker brown and brighter ochre

ART: LANDER STRIJBOL

TWO-COLOUR PORTRAIT

INTERMEDIATE ●●

Create a simple portrait using only two complementary colours: one colour as the light and the other as the shadow.

The trick is to use a reference photo with distinct lighting, such as direct sunlight, to clearly see where the light and dark hit. This challenge will help you to practise painting the bounce and reflections of light. After painting a light base, block in the darks on top, then paint in softer lighting. Alternatively, you could try blocking in light on top of a dark base.

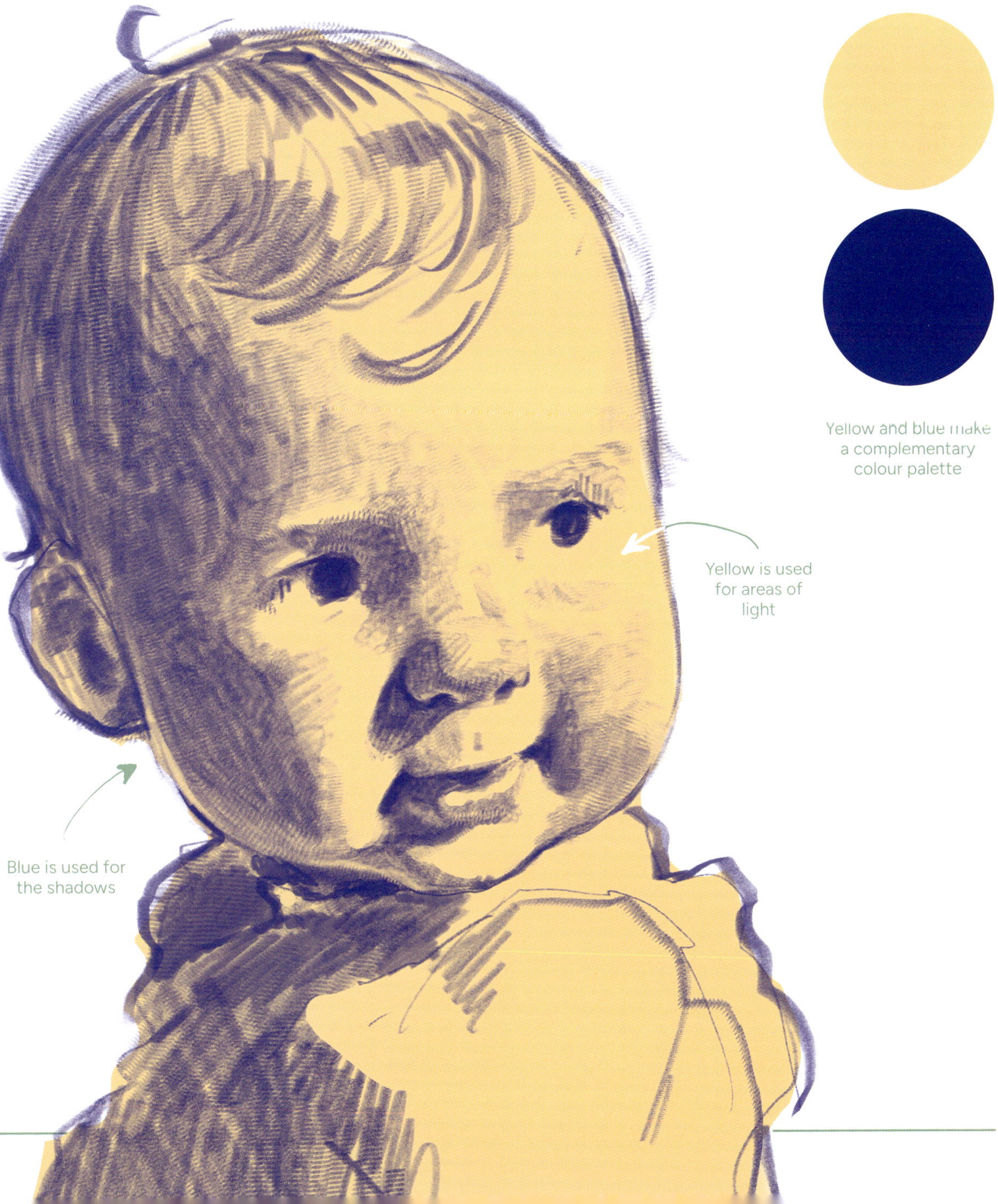

ART: MADI HARPER

BACKGROUND MOODS

INTERMEDIATE ●●

Create two paintings of the same still-life scene with different background colours – one analogous and one complementary.

Which version yields more interesting results? What kind of mood or feeling does each create?

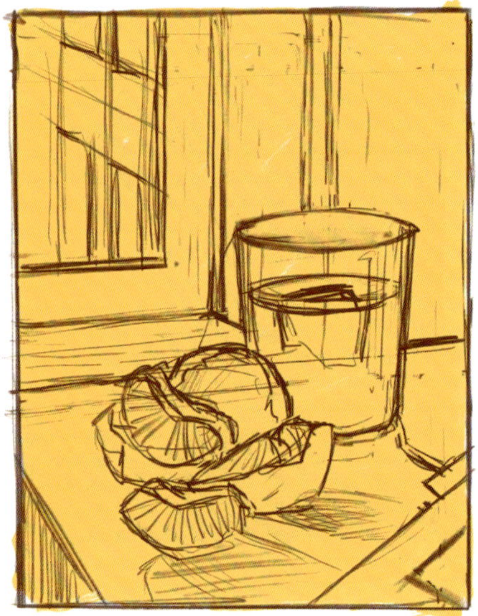

Yellow sits next to orange on the colour wheel, making it analogous with the main objects in the scene

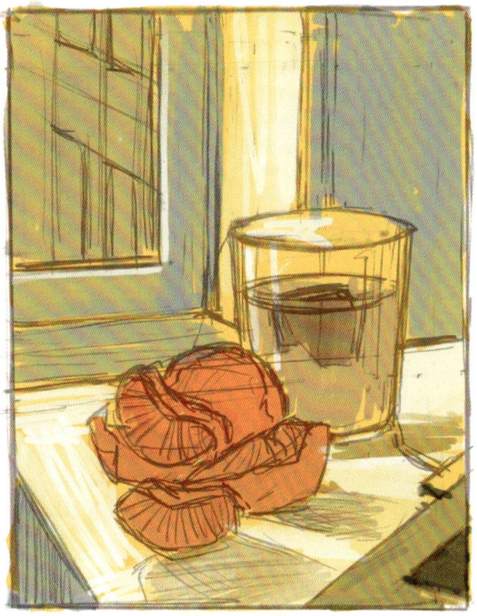

A paler yellow is used for the light in the scene, and grey for the shadows

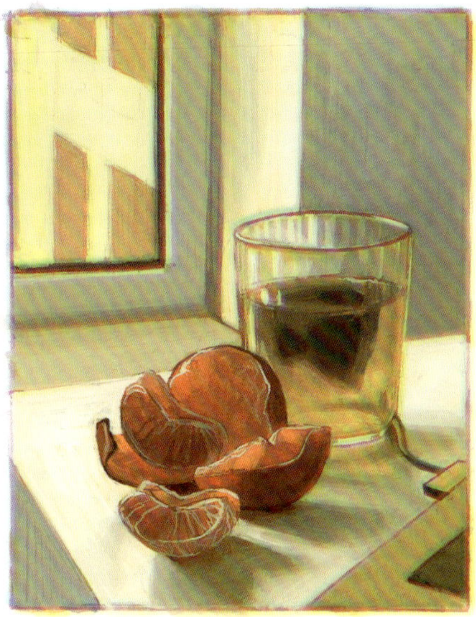

This version results in a warm, harmonious final illustration

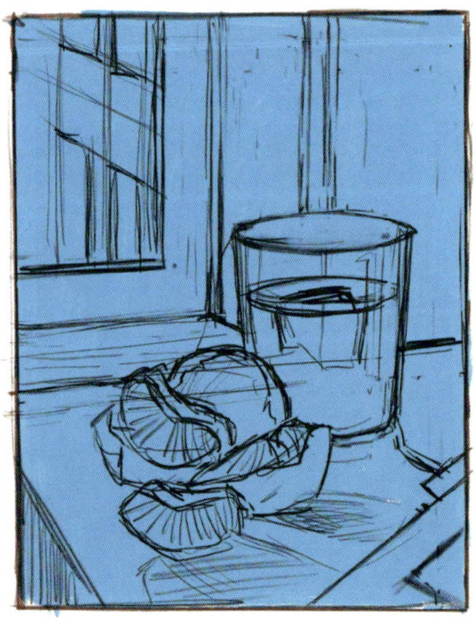

Blue sits opposite to orange and yellow on the colour wheel, making it a complementary colour

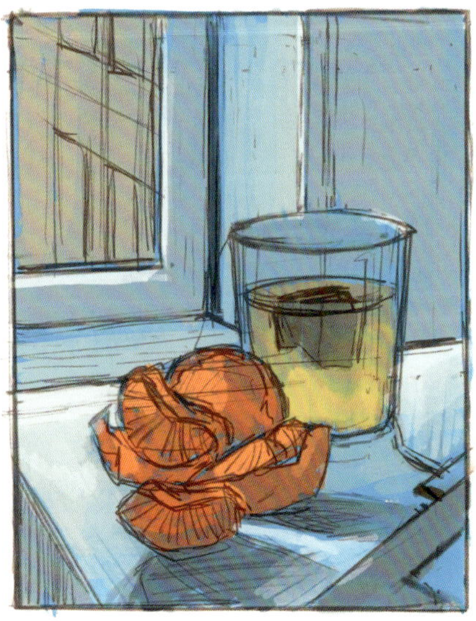

Pale and dark blue are used for light and shadow

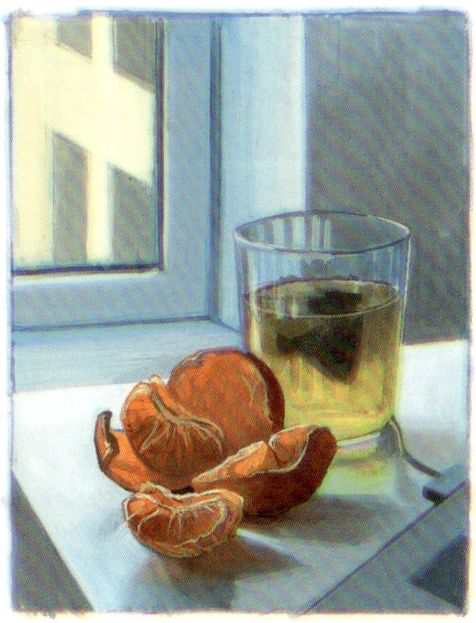

The objects now stand out against the background, but the overall image has a colder feel

SOFT OR SATURATED

INTERMEDIATE ●●

Paint an object twice, using two different colour palettes. Select soft, pastel colours for the first version and saturated, contrasting colours for the second, then compare them.

How does the colour palette change the mood of the image or the appearance of the object? Experimenting with colour in this way can create different styles of illustration and can help you to form your own artistic style, identity, and signature palette.

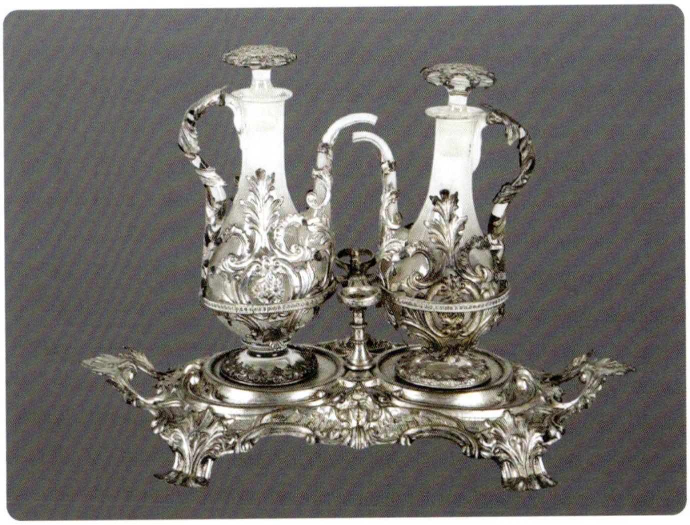

PHOTOGRAPH OF [illegible] BY ANTONIO CUNHA, UNDER THE COMMISSION OF THE CALOUSTE GULBENKIAN FOUNDATION © MUSEUM OF CHRISTIAN ART, GOA

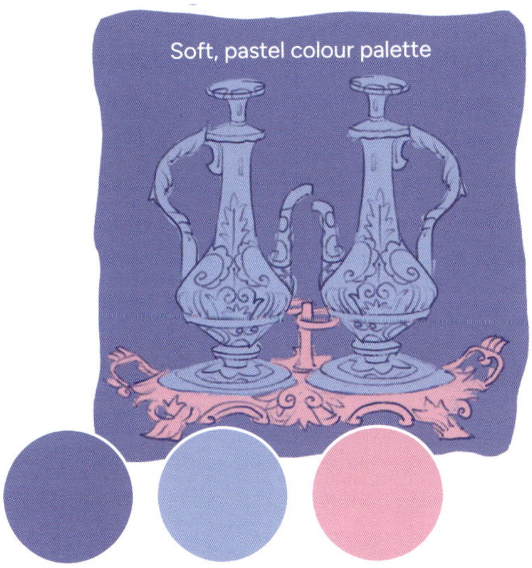

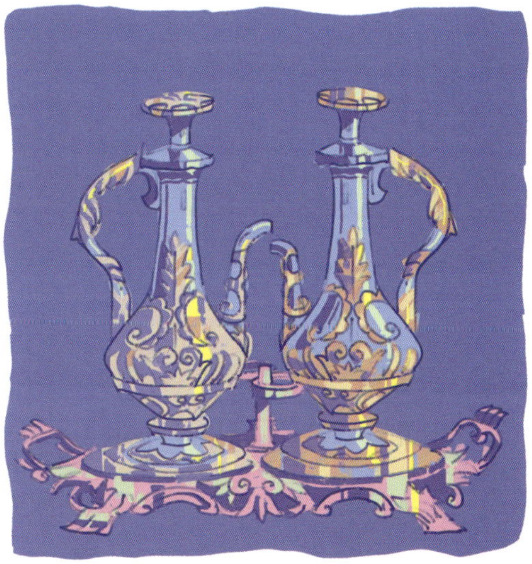

Lighter pastel colours make the objects appear cute and whimsical

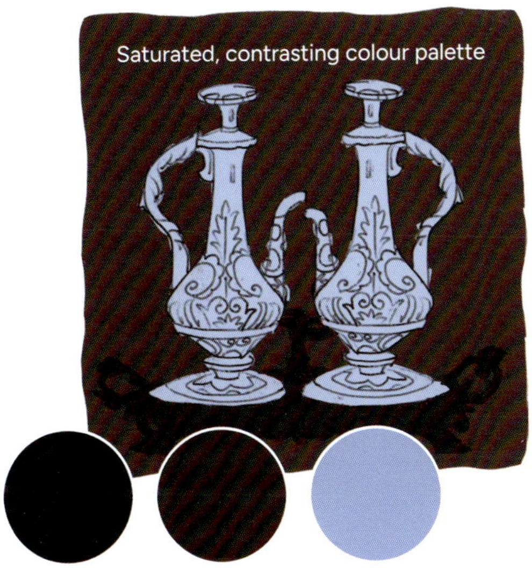

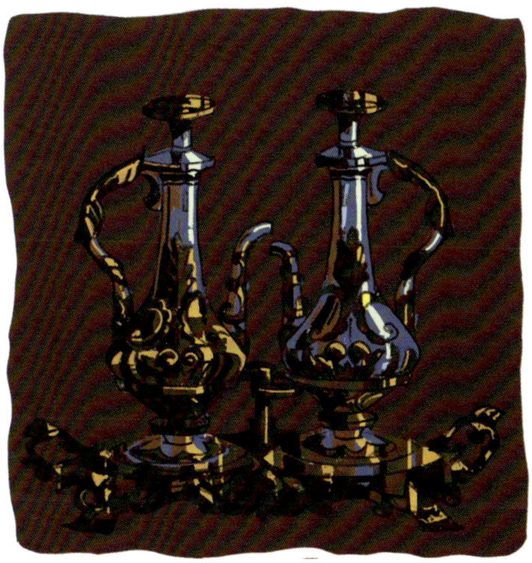

Deeper, richer colours make the objects seem more ornate and mysterious

MOODY COLOURS

INTERMEDIATE ●●

Paint a character in a scene and try out three different colour palettes, each conveying a different mood.

Start by deciding the three moods you want to create, then use your knowledge of colour theory to consider how you can reflect those feelings through colour. Even a simple environment with minimal objects can be made to feel entirely different just by changing the colour palette. Adjusting the amount and direction of light can also create new focal points that enhance the storytelling – using different times of the day is a perfect tool for this.

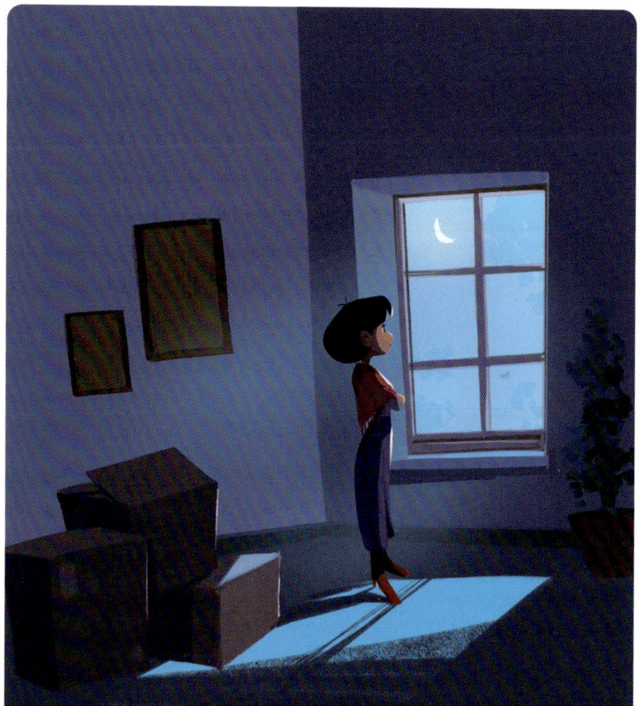

MELANCHOLY
A cool, late evening colour palette symbolizes sadness and the end of an era

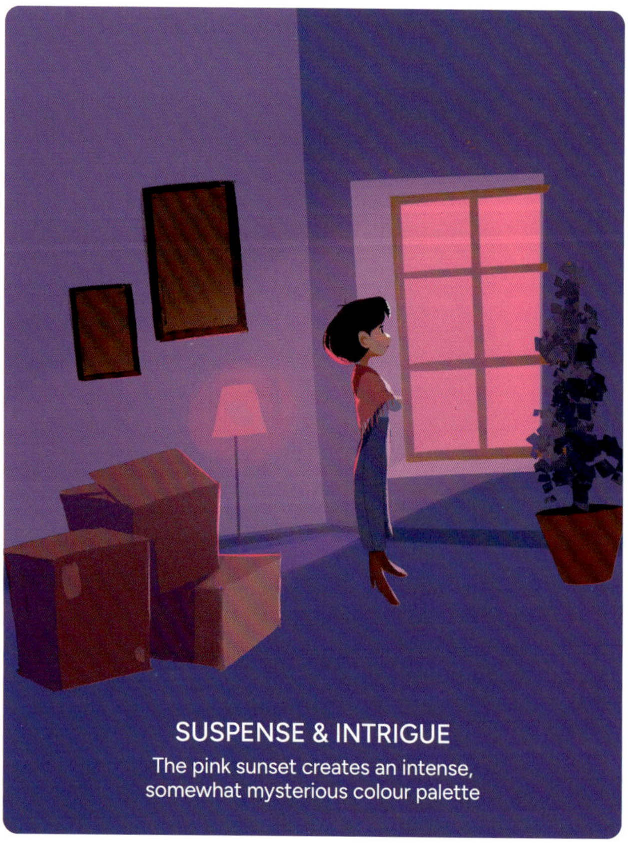

SUSPENSE & INTRIGUE
The pink sunset creates an intense, somewhat mysterious colour palette

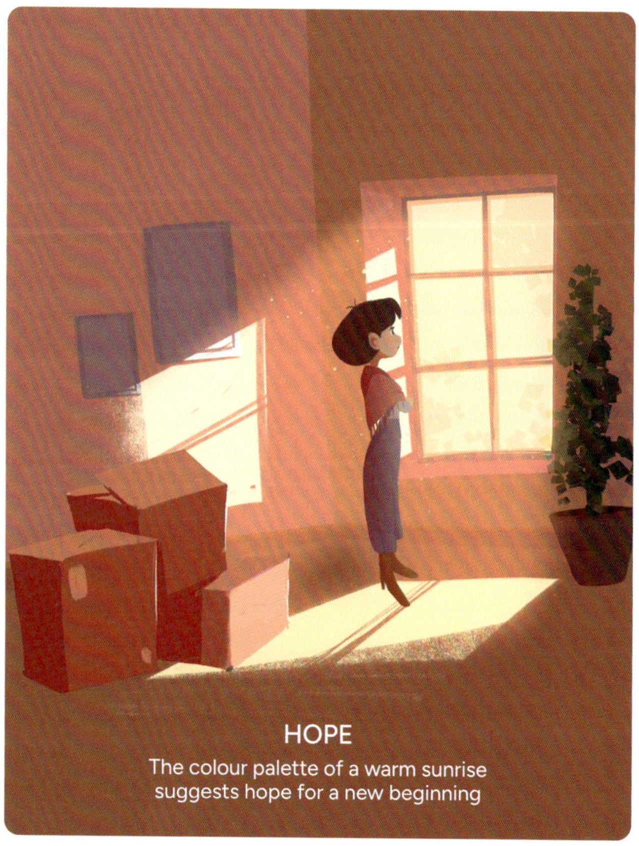

HOPE
The colour palette of a warm sunrise suggests hope for a new beginning

THIRTY-MINUTE SCENE

ADVANCED ●●●

Using a photograph for reference, create a three-value study of an outdoor scene in no more than thirty minutes.

Restricting the time allowed for a task can train you to focus on what's important right away. It can also help you to see your strengths and weaknesses more clearly. Use a light, medium, and dark value and separate the reference into three parts: foreground, middle ground, and background. Omit small details and focus on the biggest shapes and elements, grouping values together.

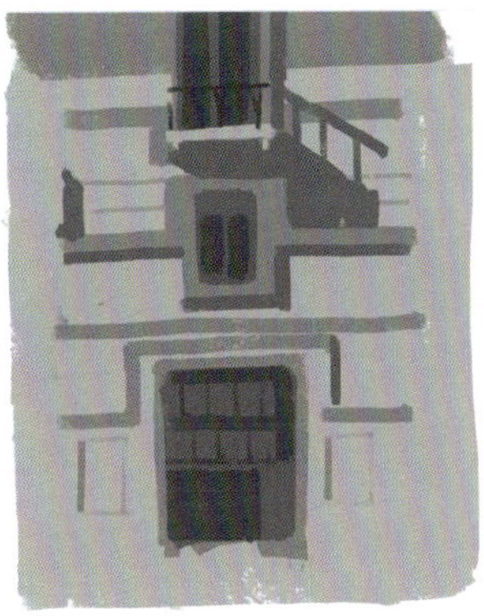

BACKGROUND

MIDDLE GROUND

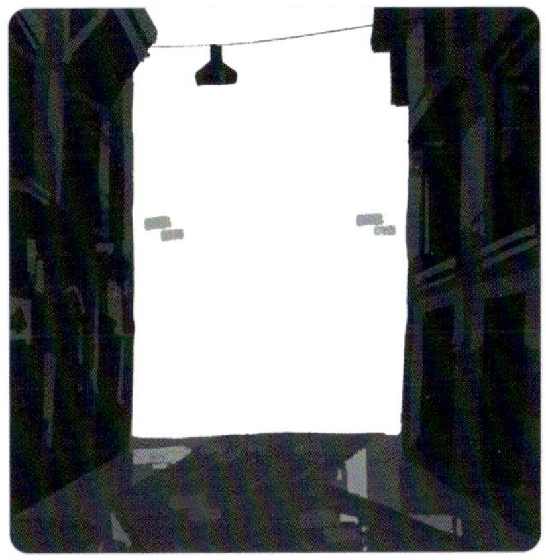

FOREGROUND

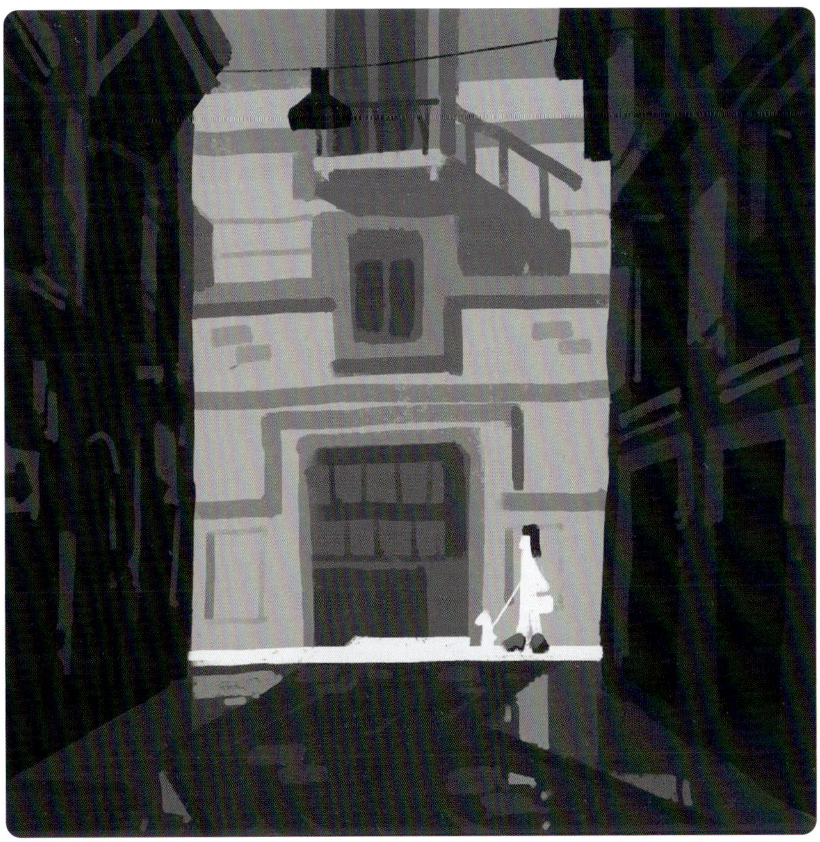

RESULT AT THIRTY MINUTES

FOUR SEASONS

ADVANCED ●●●

Choose a reference photo of a window, then paint it in spring, summer, autumn, and winter.

Start by selecting a palette of three to five colours for each season. Consider how the position of the sun changes through the year and how this might affect light and shadow. Give the lighting the same hue and gradient as the colour palette to fully encapsulate the feel of each season. Finally, consider what extra details you could add, such as fallen leaves or snow.

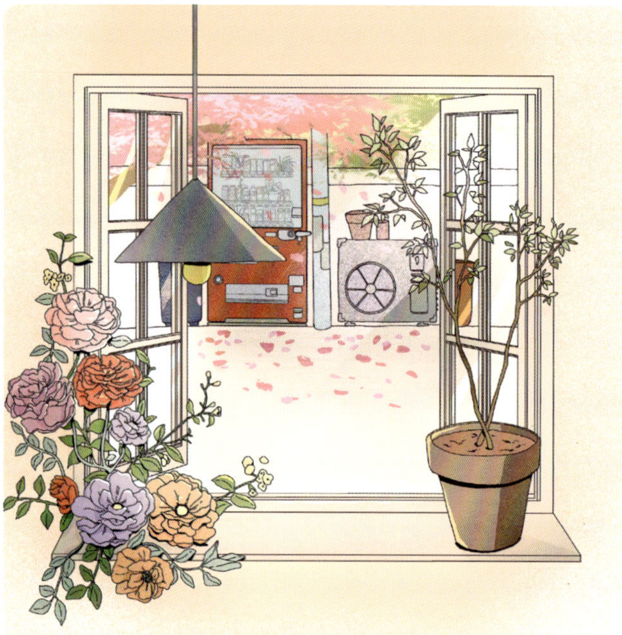

SPRING

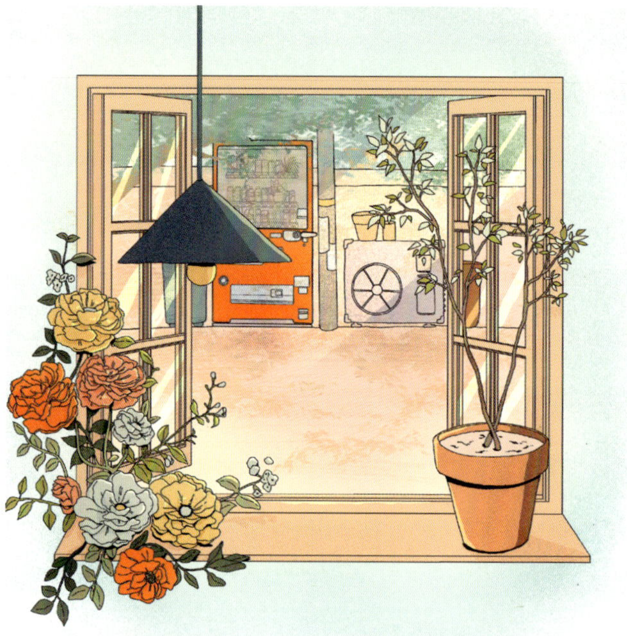

SUMMER

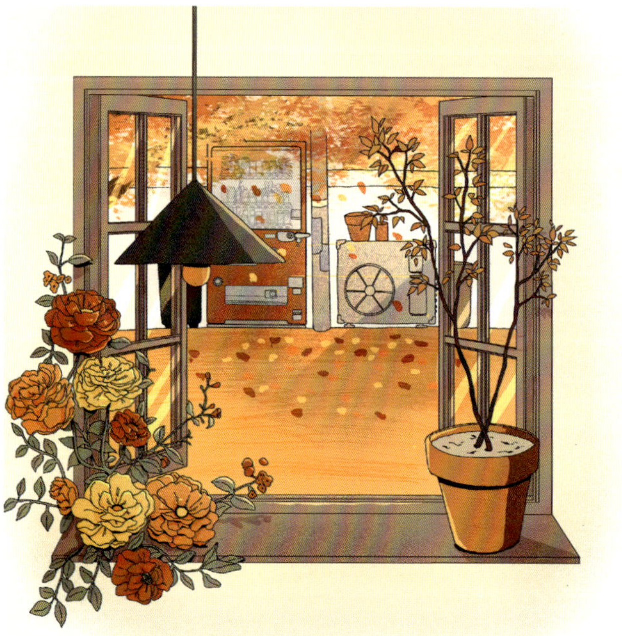

AUTUMN

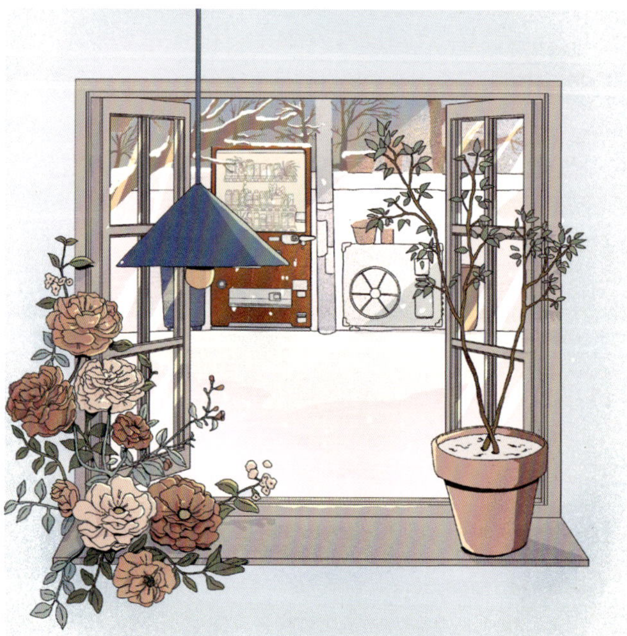

WINTER

ARIELLA OHWELLADAYS

FIGURE LIGHTING

ADVANCED ●●●

Capture a series of poses by painting in the areas of shadow and highlight only, using the background as the midtone.

Start by choosing a midtone background, a dark colour for shadow, and a light colour for highlight, then set your brush at 100% opacity. Squint your eyes as you analyse your reference image – this will help you to focus on the big shapes and essential forms.

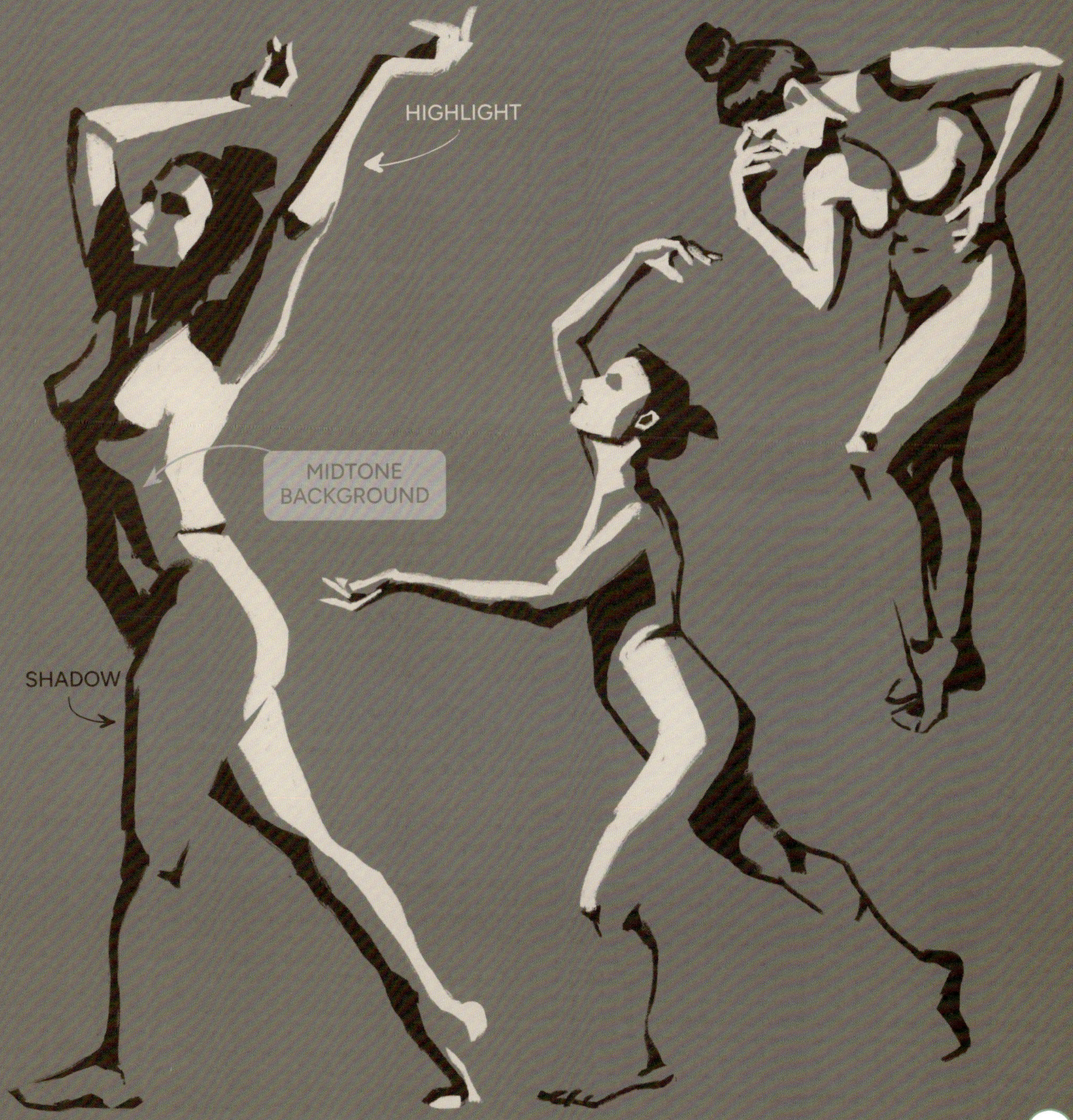

ART: MARIANA NORONHA

COMPOSITION, FRAMING & PERSPECTIVE

Step-by-step challenges:

One-page challenges:

THREE-LINE LANDSCAPE

BEGINNER ●

Create a landscape composition using only three lines (one straight, one circle, and one wavy).

Think about how these elements could overlap to create depth and dimension. This challenge is a great way to come up with new compositional ideas and shapes.

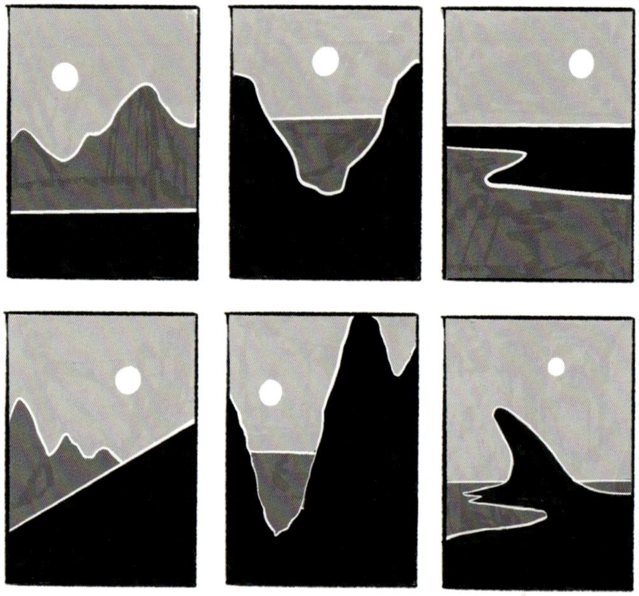

01 Start by sketching six basic compositions using different configurations of the three types of line: straight, circle, and wavy. Feel free to add some tone to make the shapes clearer.

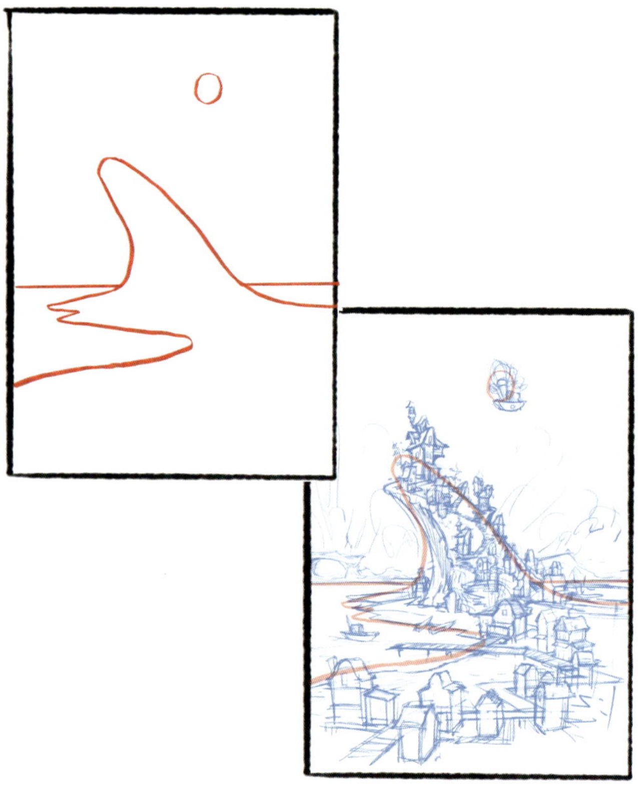

02 Choose the most interesting composition and decrease the opacity of the lines. Draw a light pencil sketch over the top, adding environmental details to turn it into an illustration.

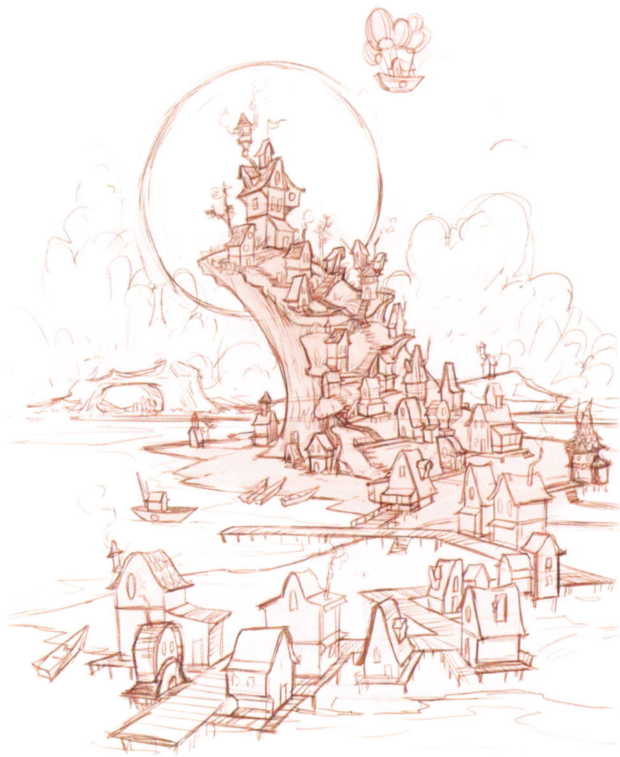

03 Clean up the sketch to aid clarity. Consider how added elements affect the overall composition.

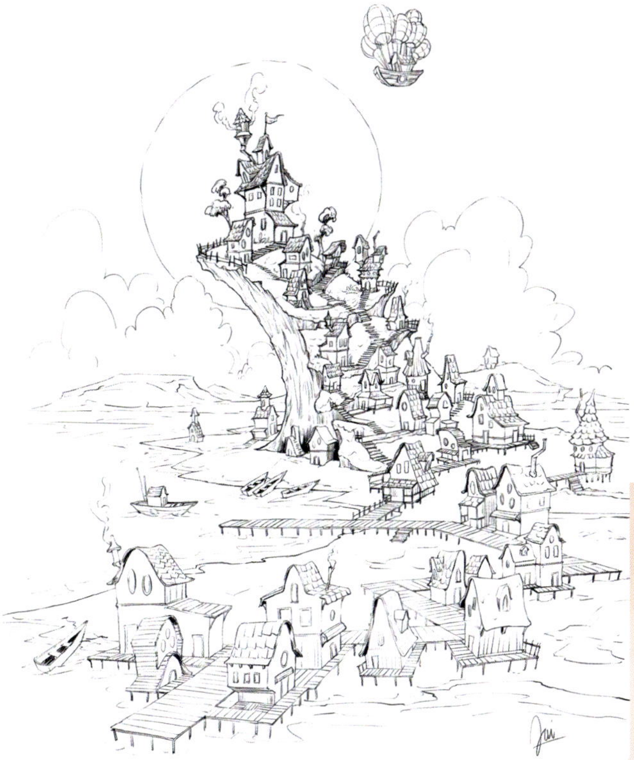

04 Once you're happy with the sketch, decrease its opacity then use a hard brush to refine the lines.

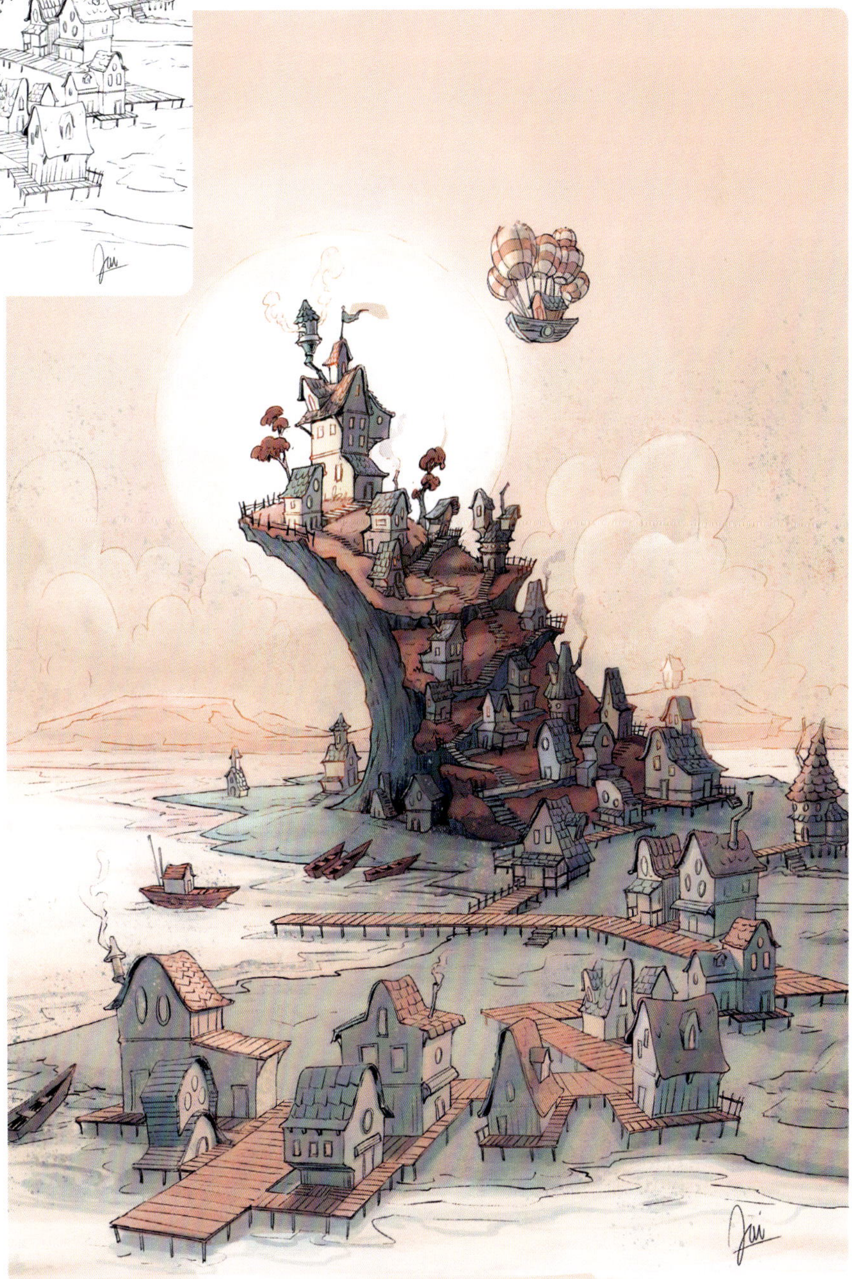

05 Finish by adding colour to bring the illustration to life. Does the final image differ from the type of compositions you usually draw? How might this task inform how you compose a landscape going forwards?

ART: JUI TALUKDER

FOCUS ON THE FRUIT

BEGINNER ●

Set a piece of fruit on a table and draw it, making it the focal point of the composition.

Include other objects in the scene, but ensure they all direct the viewer's eye towards the piece of fruit. Experiment with how you can use other artistic elements, such as lighting, to draw attention to the fruit too. This challenge will help you to practise your composition and focus on the ways you direct attention in your artwork.

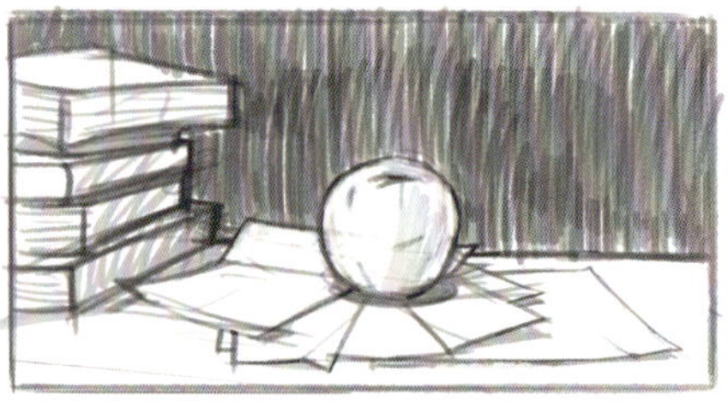

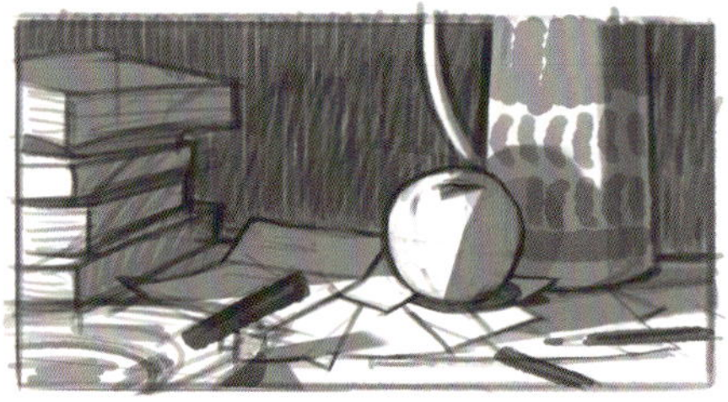

01 First, create a series of sketches exploring different compositions. The golden spiral is a handy rule to use here, to ensure you position things in the most effective way.

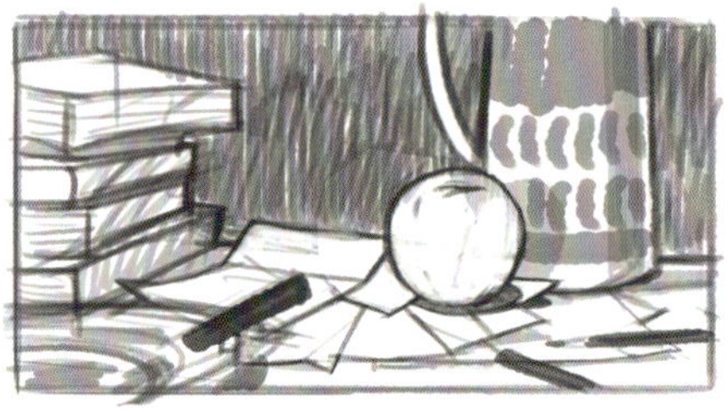

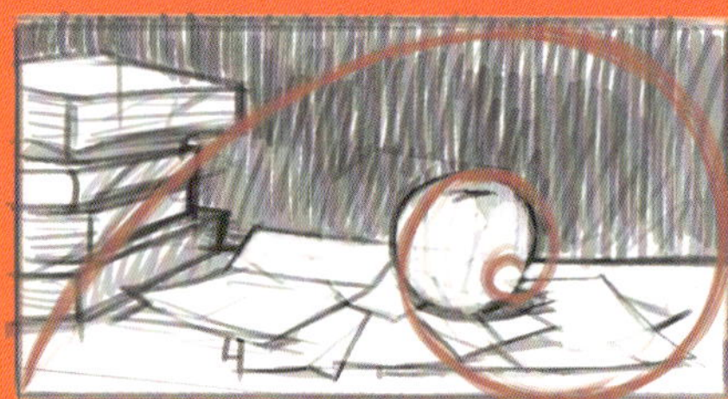

GOLDEN SPIRAL

A compositional guide that allows you to organize visual elements in a harmonious and balanced way, directing the viewer's gaze.

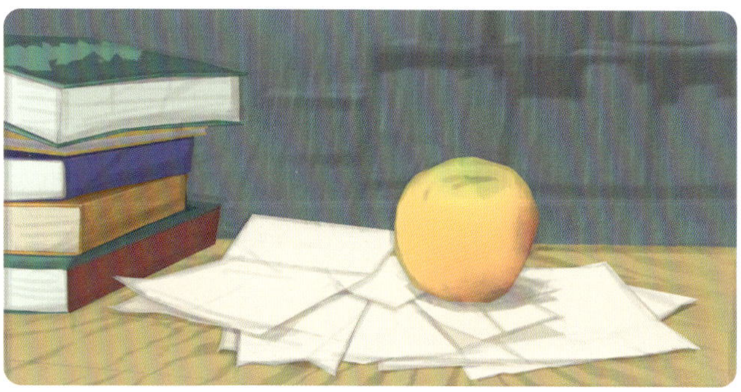

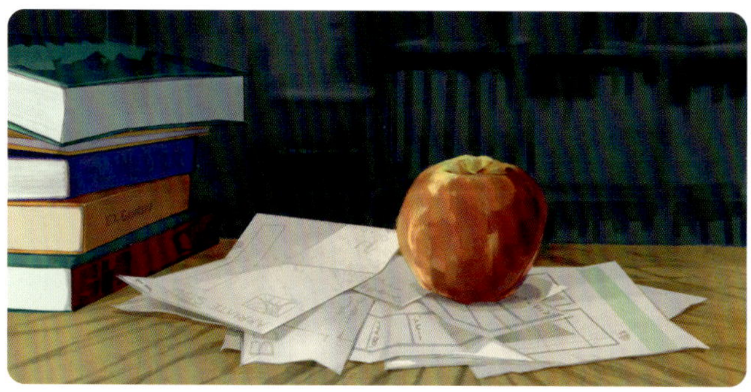

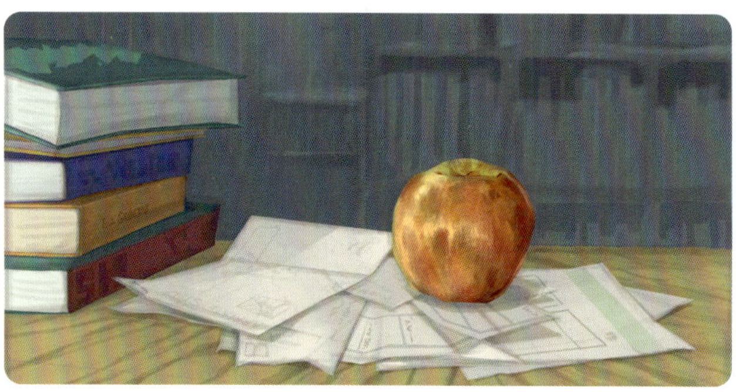

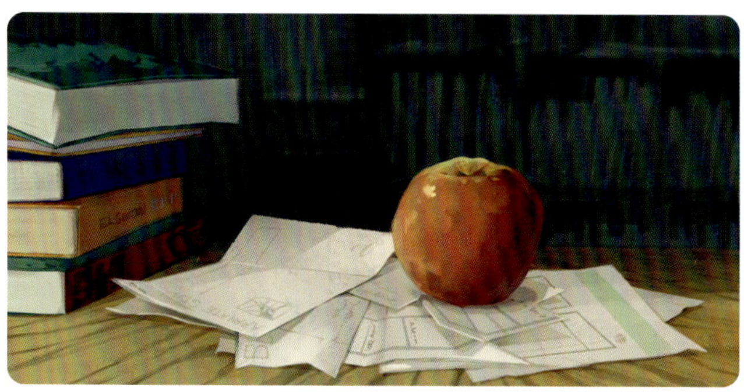

02 Choose one composition to develop further, then add colour, working from lighter to darker tones.

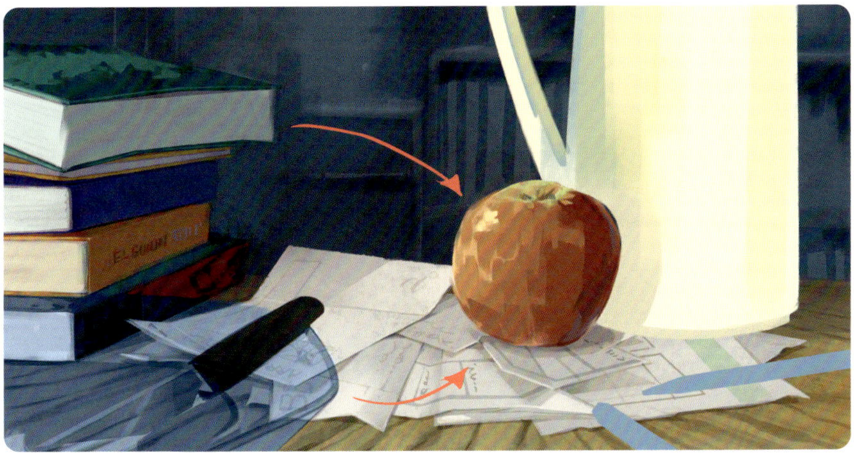

03 Introduce additional elements that reinforce the focal point, using lines created by the arrangement of objects to guide the viewer's eye.

04 Add additional details, all leading attention to the piece of fruit. Adjust the lighting to accentuate the visual focus too.

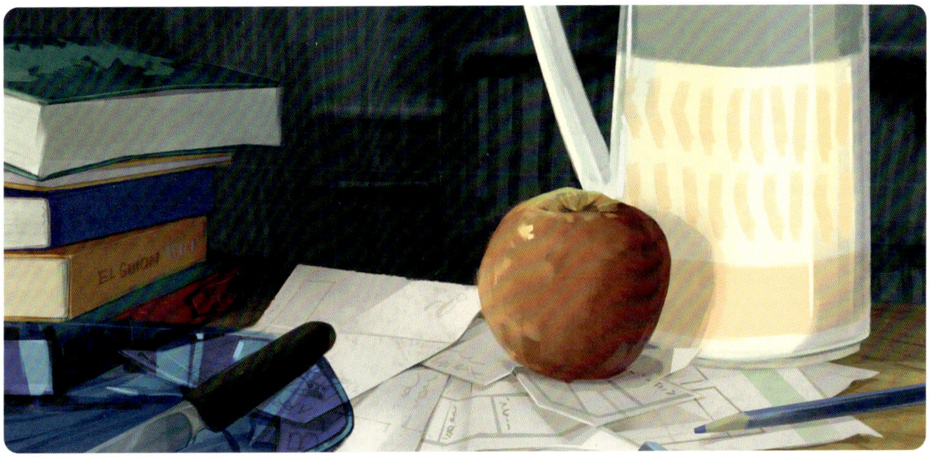

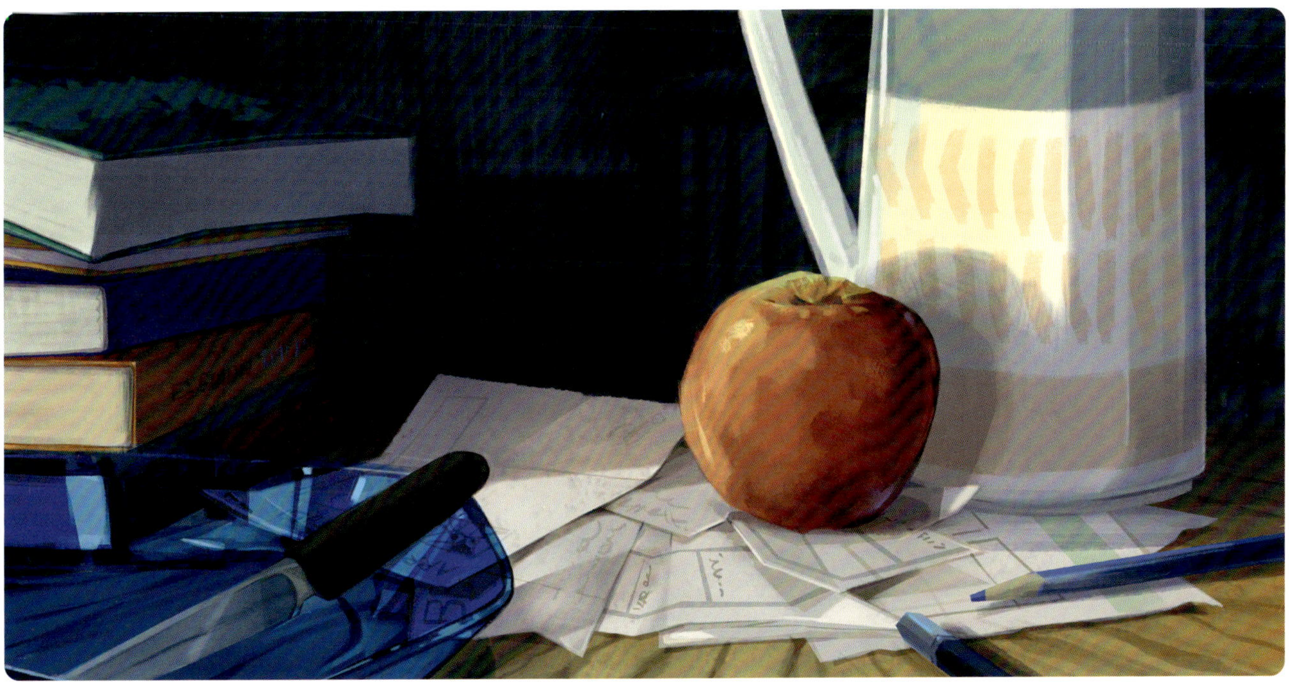

05 Your final painting should place the fruit in full focus, with other elements acting as background support.

BACK-TO-FRONT PAINTING

INTERMEDIATE ●●

Paint a scene starting with the background elements, then introduce the middle ground, and finally the foreground.

Experimenting with how you order and layer these planes can alter the end result. As you work from back to front, explore how this influences your design choices and affects the style of the final image.

01 Start by painting the background, making sure to keep it simple.

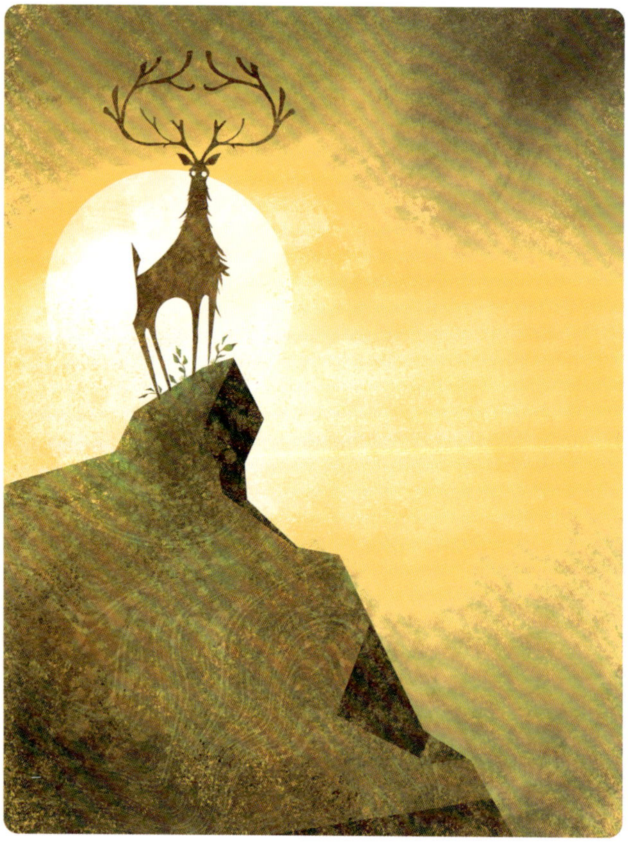

02 Paint in the middle ground, introducing a character or point of interest.

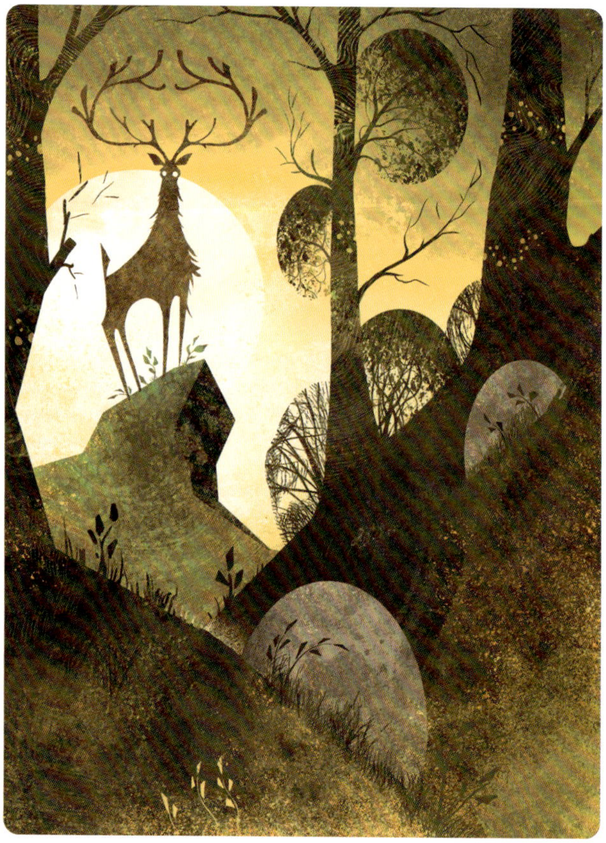

03 Next, add in foreground elements, using them to frame your point of interest.

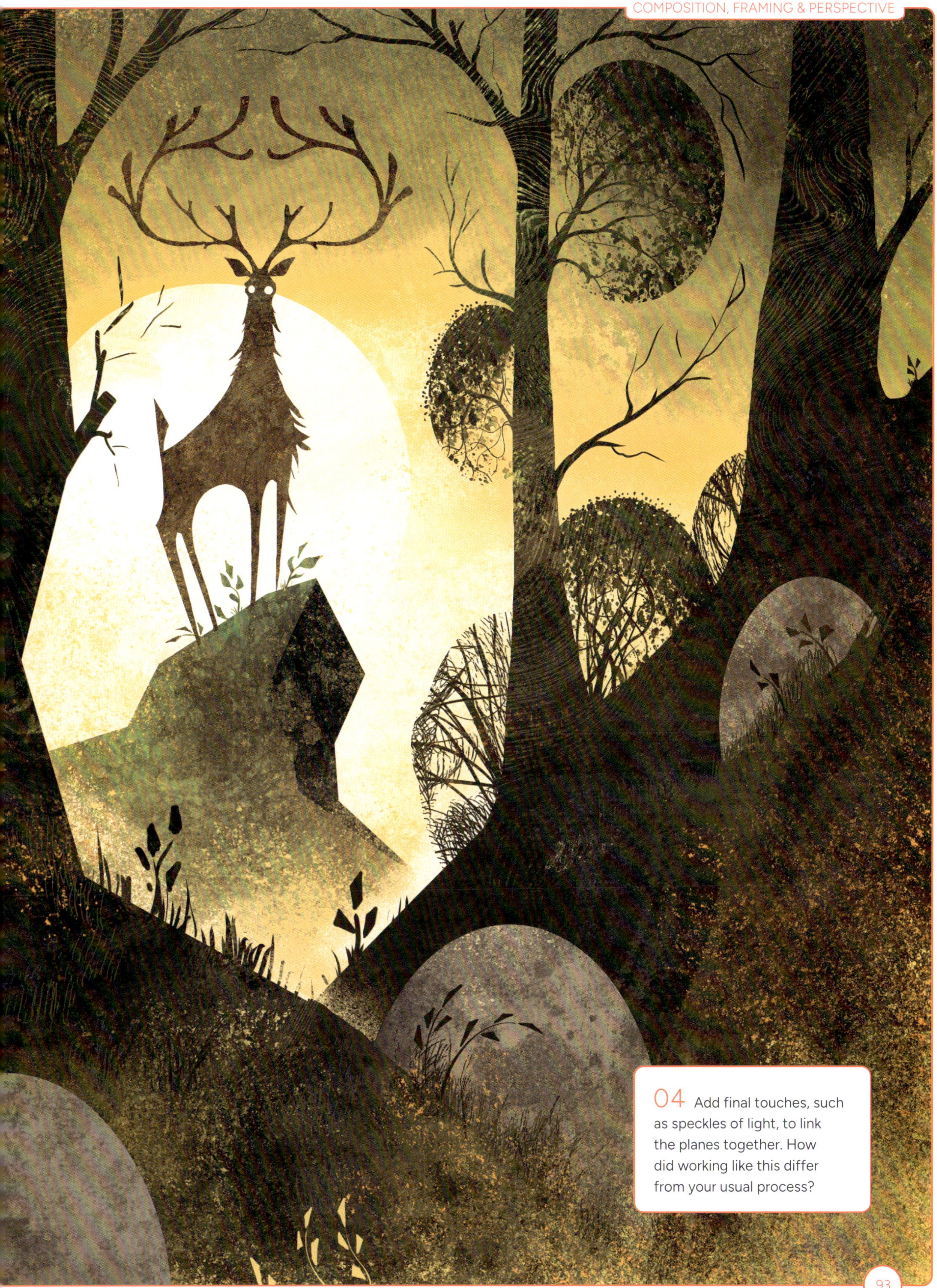

04 Add final touches, such as speckles of light, to link the planes together. How did working like this differ from your usual process?

ART: LANDER STRIJBOL

FRONT-TO-BACK PAINTING

INTERMEDIATE ●●

Paint a scene starting with the foreground elements, then add the middle-ground elements (including a character), and finally the background.

Identify different planes and group elements together to make the image easier to read, paying attention to how different groupings create different moods and effects. Defining a scene like this helps to guide the viewer's eye and takes away any guesswork. Clearly defining the front, middle, and background elements can also help when it comes to colouring and shading. There are many ways to push objects forwards and backwards in a plane of sight, all of which can enhance the believability of your drawing.

01 Start by sketching out rough ideas, exploring which elements will sit on which plane. This example will depict a young boy playing with a town he's built out of toys.

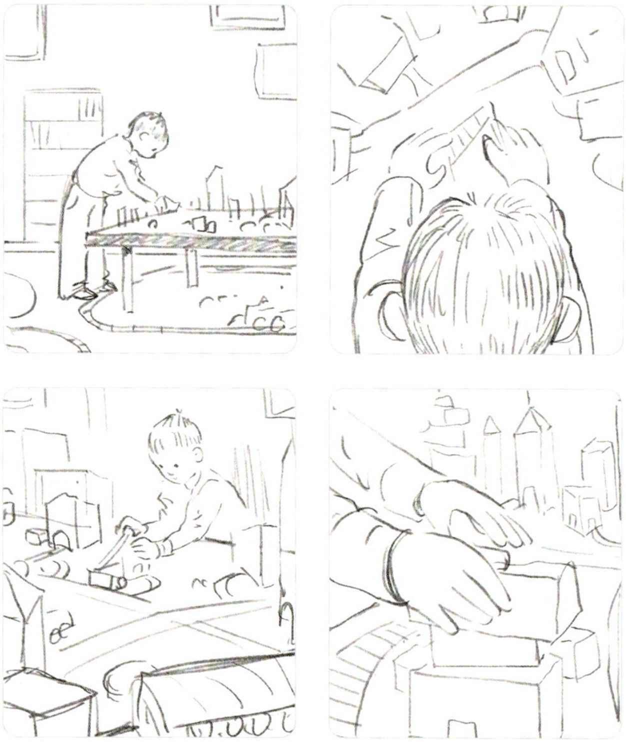

02 Choose one of the rough sketches to continue with, then begin drawing in the foreground elements. These are important elements, but not the focus of the scene.

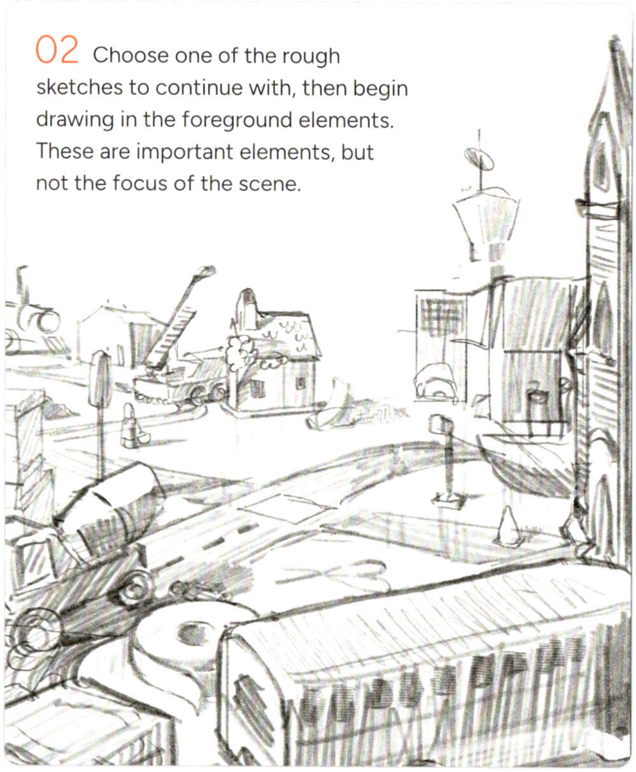

03 Sketch the character in the middle ground. Avoid tangents, where objects on different planes accidently line up with each other, as this can create confusion in the composition as the clearly defined front, middle, and background are lost.

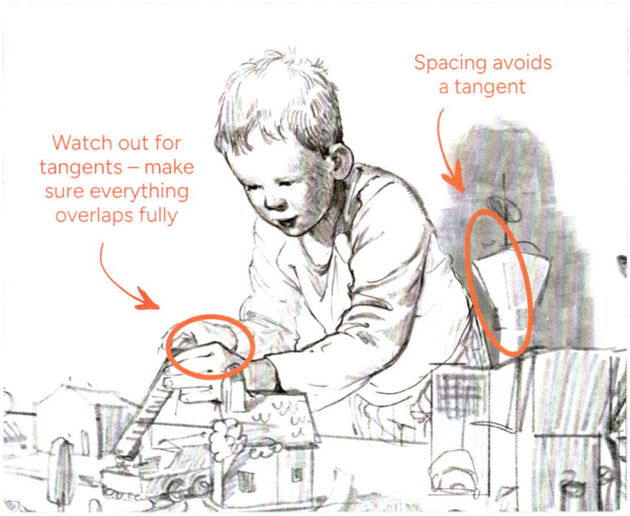

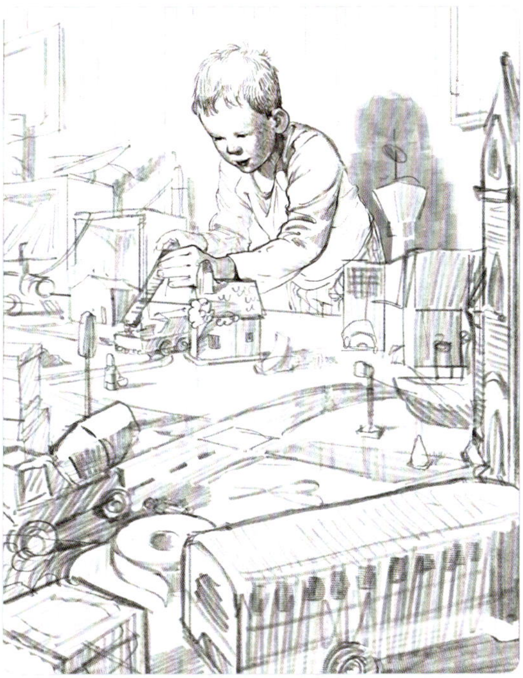

04 Finally, sketch in a background. This grounds the image and provides stability, telling the viewer where it ends. Use the background to frame the focal point, using objects that lead the eye back towards the centre.

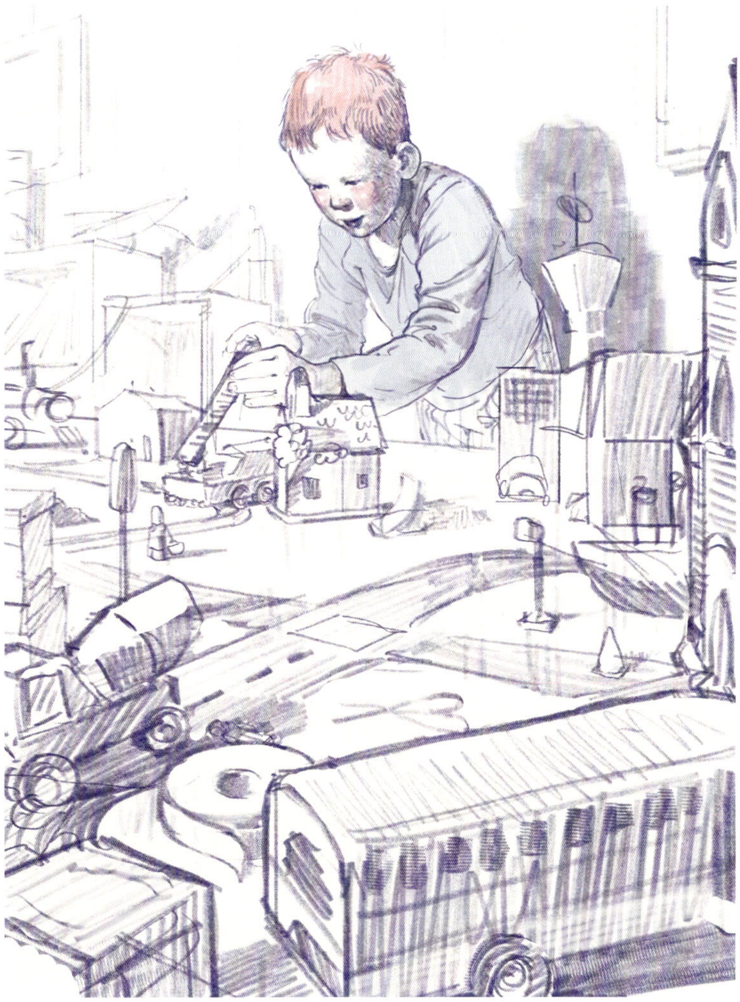

05 To finish, you could change the colour of the line work and add some pops of colour to take the illustration to the next level. How does working front to back affect the style of your art?

MODERN RECREATION

INTERMEDIATE ●●

Recreate a classic artwork with added modern elements, keeping enough of the original composition to ensure it's recognizable.

Studying the composition and framing of classic paintings is a great way to discover new techniques and learn how to apply them to your own way of working.

01 Create a sketch of the original artwork, capturing the overall composition and main shapes.

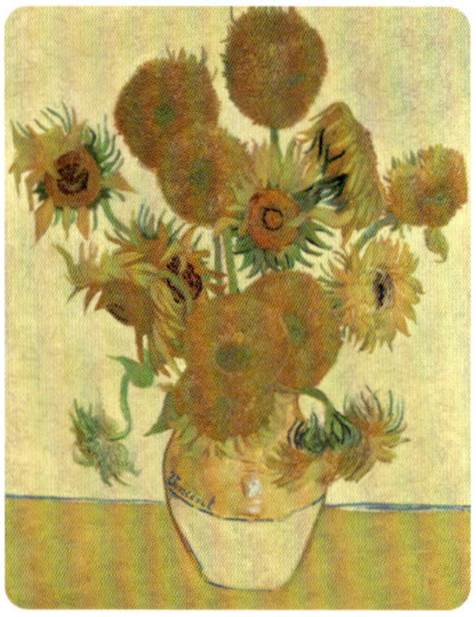

SUNFLOWERS BY VINCENT VAN GOGH, 1889

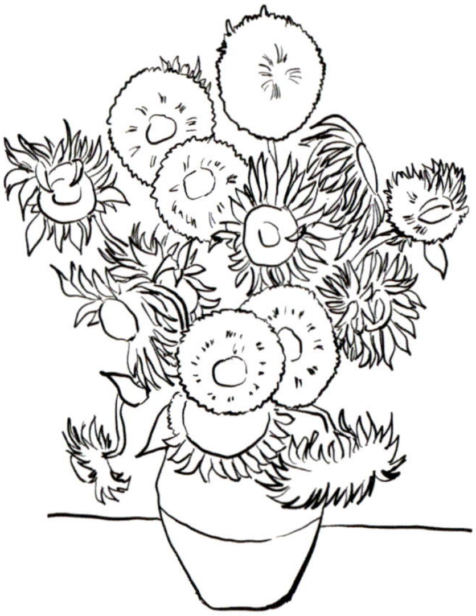

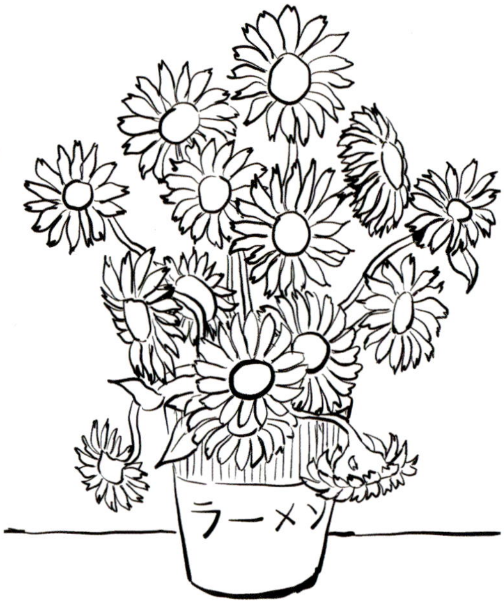

02 Redraw the image and add modern elements while preserving the composition and silhouette of the original. Here, the vase is swapped for an instant-noodle pot!

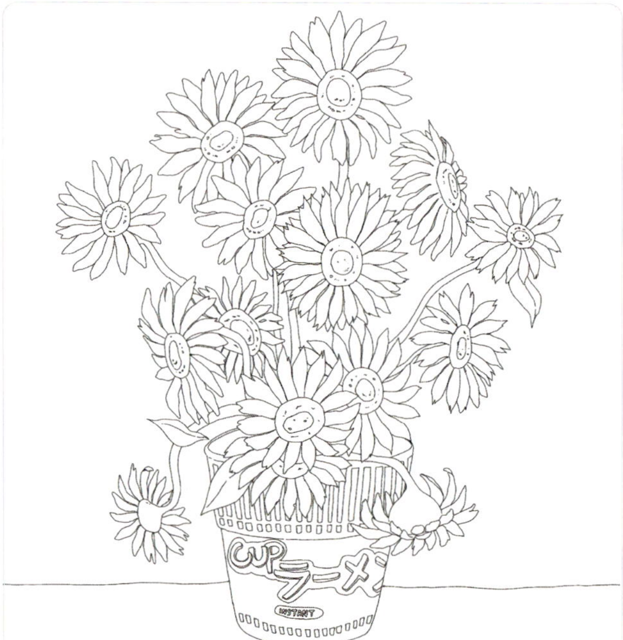

03 Draw neater line art to create your final outline.

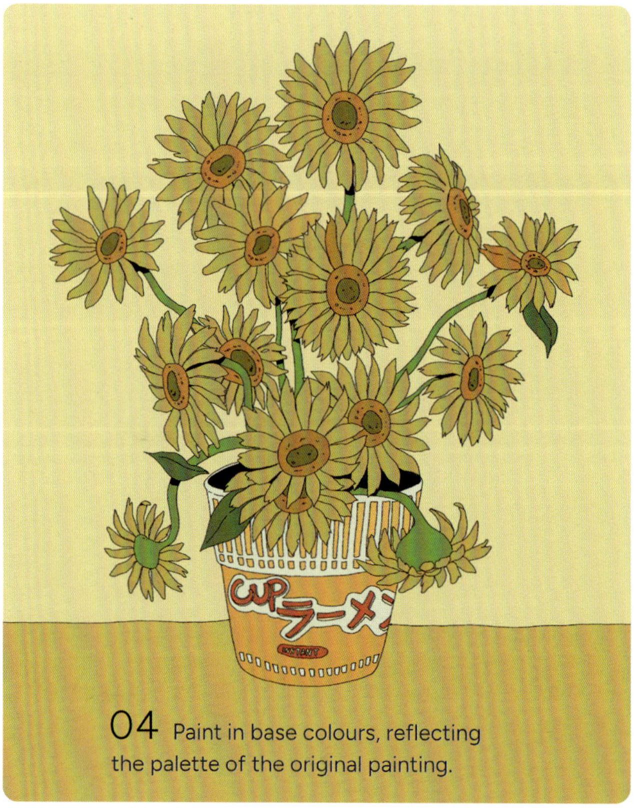

04 Paint in base colours, reflecting the palette of the original painting.

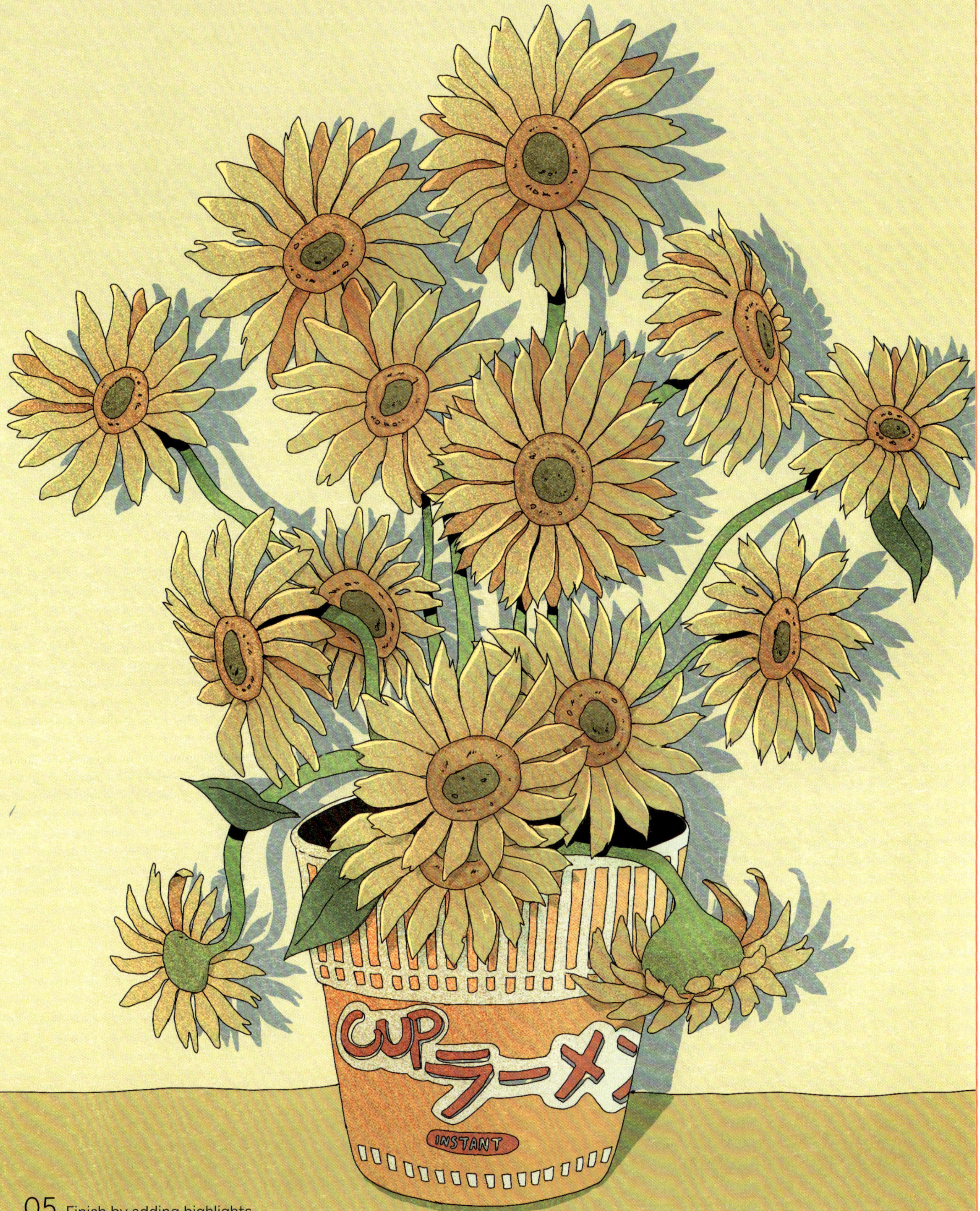

05 Finish by adding highlights, shading, and texture, continually referring back to the original for inspiration.

IN THE DEPTH OF THE WOODS

PHOTO BY BABI PUTU ON UNSPLASH

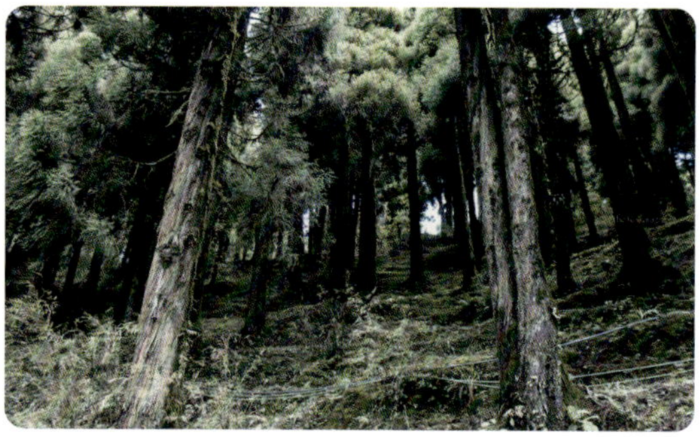

ADVANCED ●●●

Sketch a woodland scene, then separate your drawing's elements into different planes: background, middle ground, and foreground.

This challenge will help you practise grouping and dividing elements into different depth planes in your artwork, which is a useful skill when creating a simplified version of a scene. Take care to create clear layering to ensure the image is easily readable, and review how this process affects the style of your work.

01 Select a reference photo and sketch it. Draw detailed recognizable elements, such as branches and leaves, in the foreground, then fewer details in the distance. The viewer's eye will automatically fill in any gaps in detail as the planes recede.

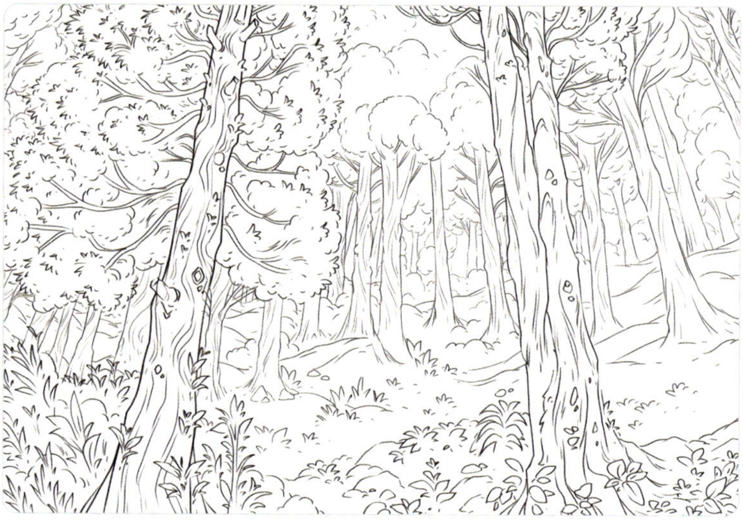

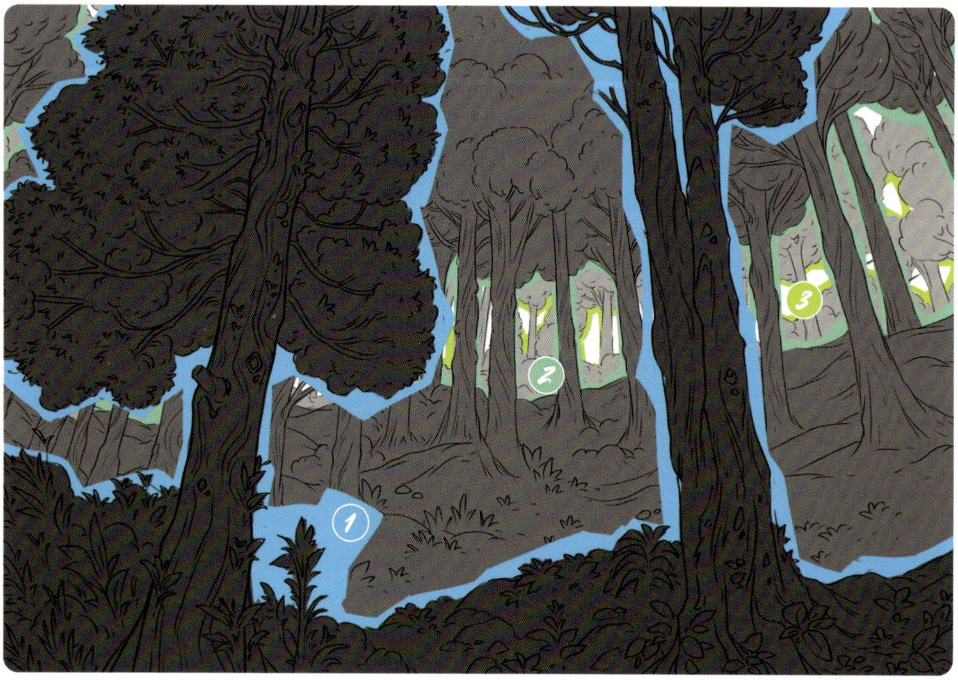

02 Now identify the foreground, middle ground, and background, and fill each with a different value tone, so you can see the clear division of planes.

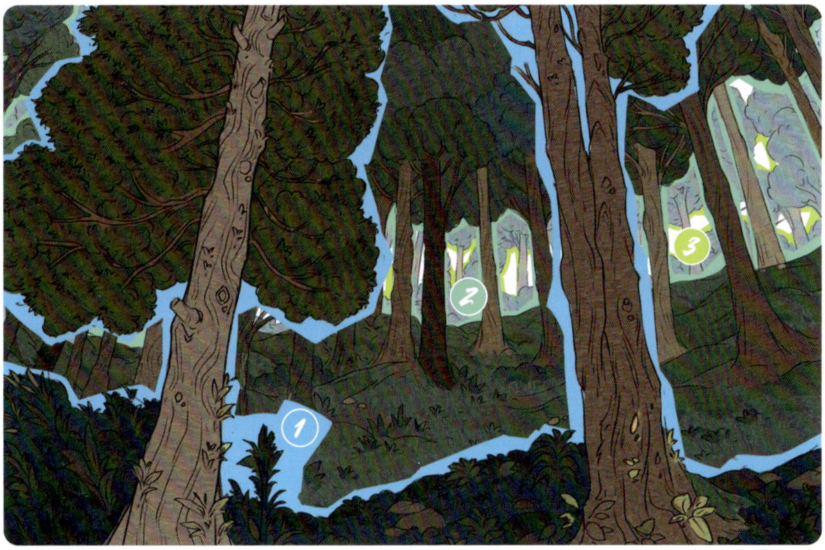

03 Colour each plane in turn, using darker tones for the foreground, midtones for the middle ground, and lighter tones in the distant background. Try to maintain the values introduced in the previous step.

04 Add more detail and make use of atmospheric effects – such as mist, dappled sunlight, or glow – to enhance the sense of depth.

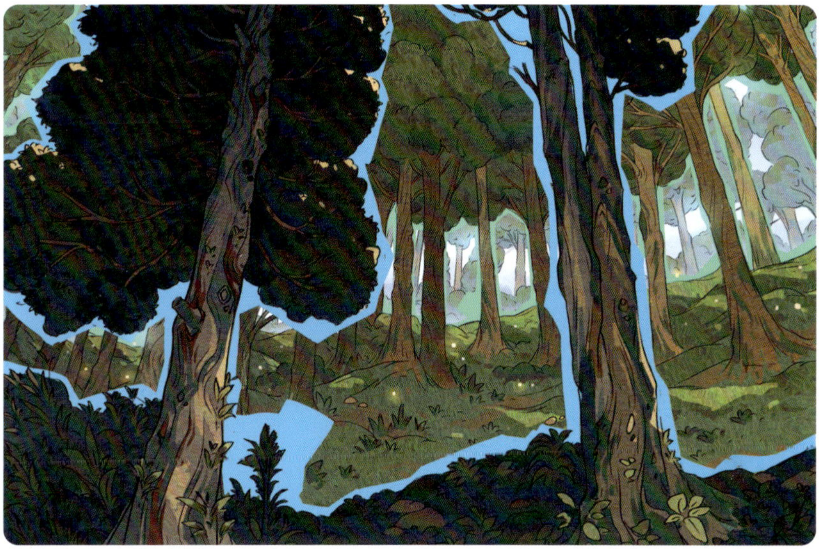

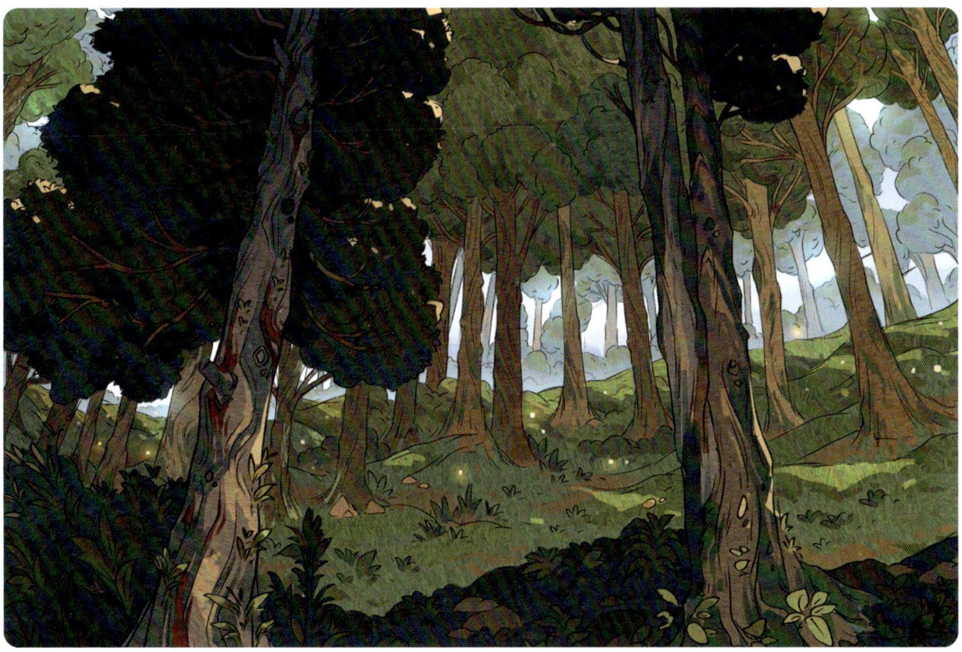

05 Your finished piece should show a clear sense of depth across three visual planes.

ART: ALFRED FERNANDES

CHANGING PERSPECTIVES

ADVANCED ●●●

Draw the same building three times – with one vanishing point, then two, then three.

Explore how this change in perspective affects the visual language of the image and the style of the artwork. The mood of the story you want to tell can be immediately conveyed by the point of view in a scene.

ONE-POINT PERSPECTIVE

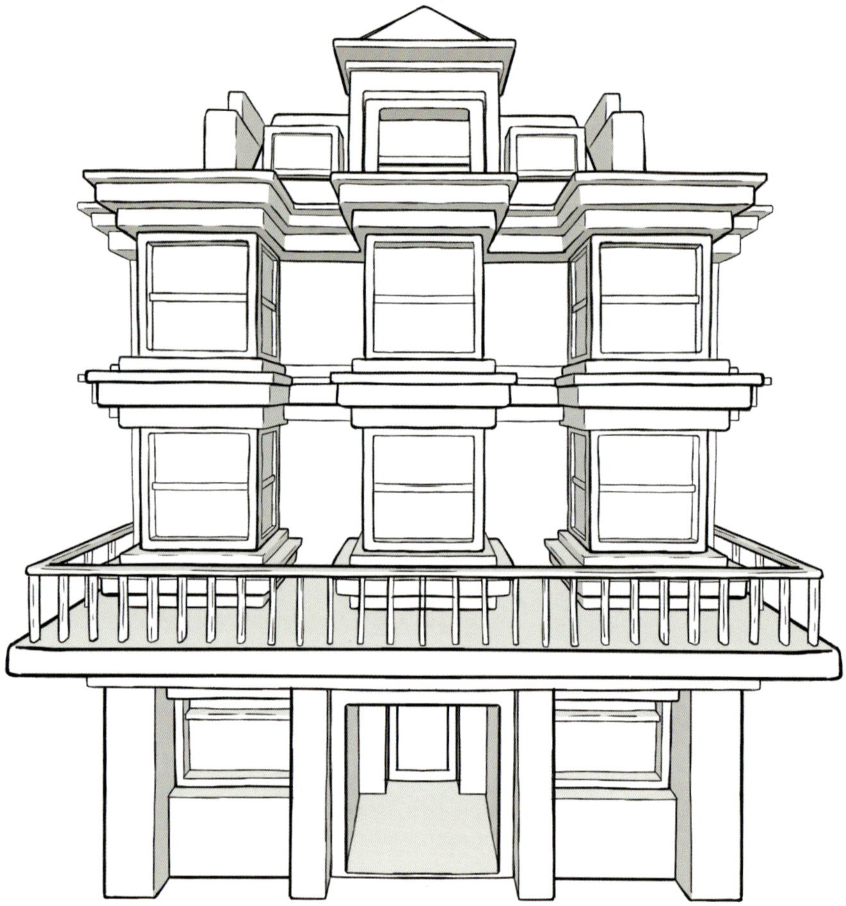

01 In one-point perspective, the lines of the building converge towards a central vanishing point on the horizon. This perspective can make the viewer feel physically close to the building, as if about to step inside.

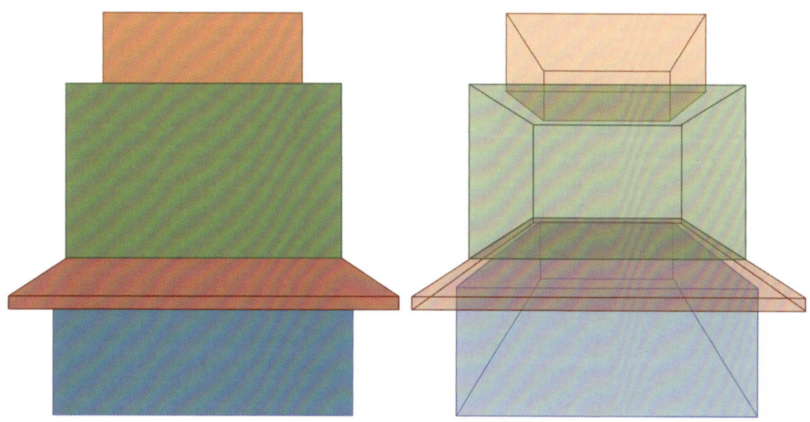

DRAWING THROUGH THE OBJECT

In the rough stages of drawing, make sure to include the hidden lines of the building as well as the visible lines. This is called drawing through the object and ensures finer line accuracy.

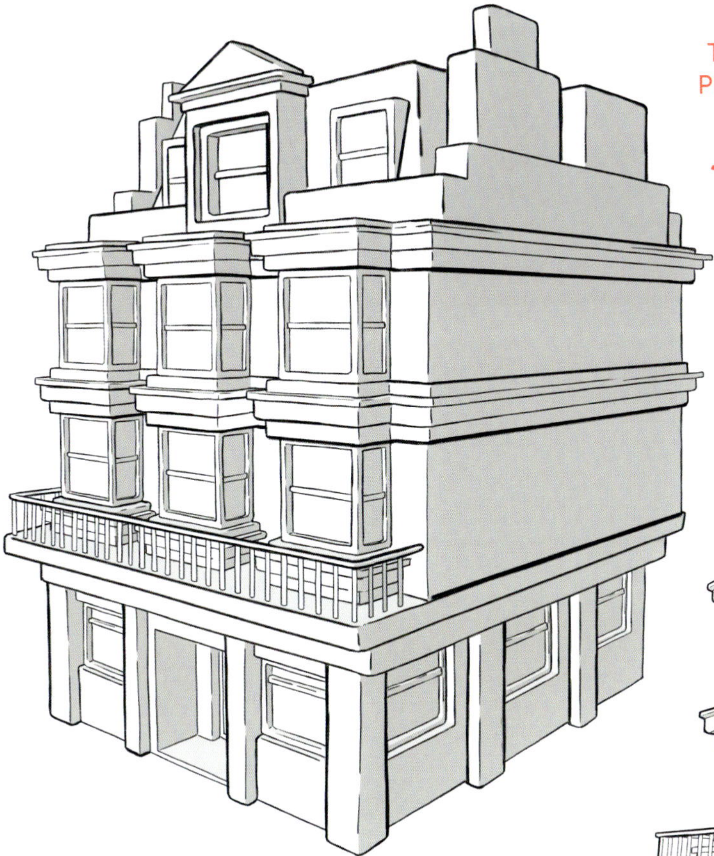

TWO-POINT PERSPECTIVE

02 Using two vanishing points, one either side of the building on the horizon line, means the corner of the building faces the viewer. This gives more of a distant viewpoint, or a graphic-art feel.

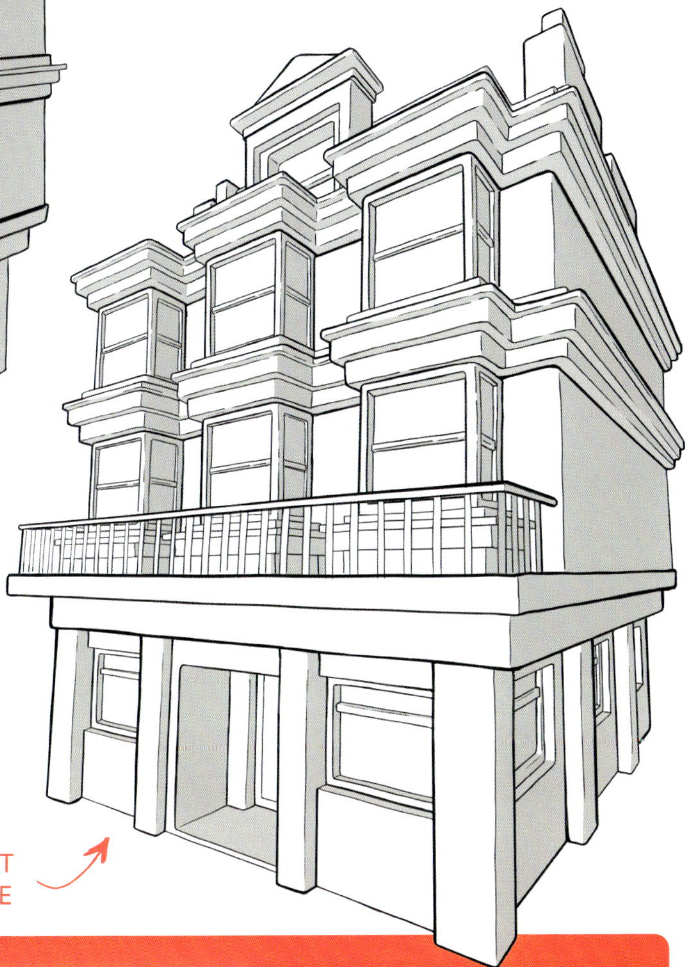

03 With a third vanishing point added above the buidling, the viewpoint is close to the corner and angled upwards, which creates a more dramatic look. The vertical lines converge, which adds to the theatrical feel.

THREE-POINT PERSPECTIVE

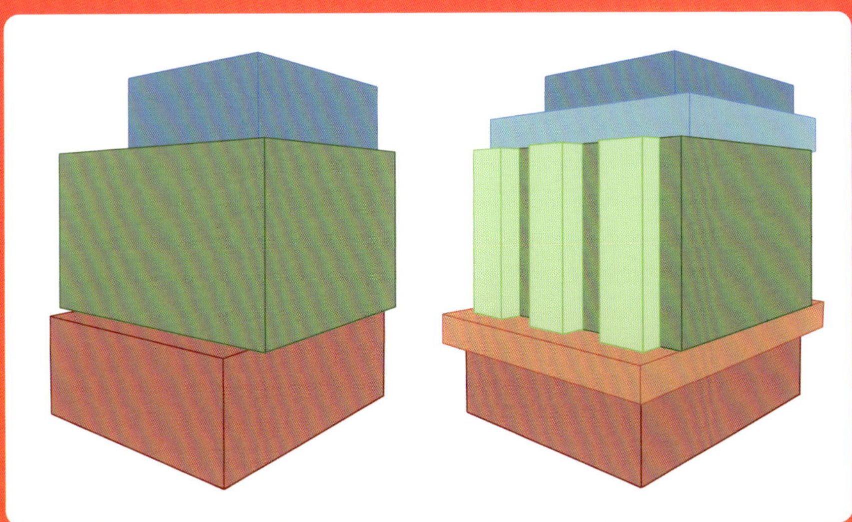

PRIMITIVE SHAPES

When drawing a complex building, start by simplifying it into big primitive shapes. Put these solids in perspective, then add and subtract smaller solids to make up the building's features.

ART: MARIANA NORONHA

DRAW A CORNER BUILDING

ADVANCED ●●●

Find or take a photograph of a corner building and identify the two vanishing points, then draw or paint your own version.

The perspective used in an image will greatly affect the overall mood of the scene, so deciding on the location of vanishing points is an important step. This challenge encourages you to practise identifying the perspective used in a reference image, or in the image in your head. You may ultimately stick to similar perspectives across your work – this could become part of your artistic style.

01 Study your chosen reference photo and draw perspective guidelines over the top to locate the vanishing points (which are likely to be somewhere outside of the frame). Pay attention to the angles of the building – this one has a cut-off corner.

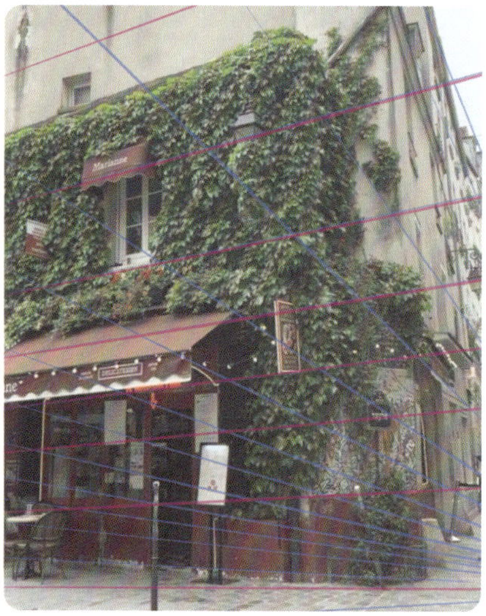

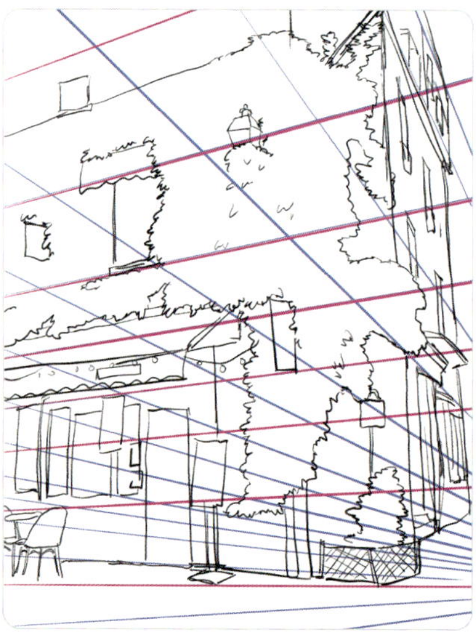

02 Now create an outline sketch of the building. Lay down the foundational shapes and main subjects of the composition, following the perspective guidelines to inform your choices.

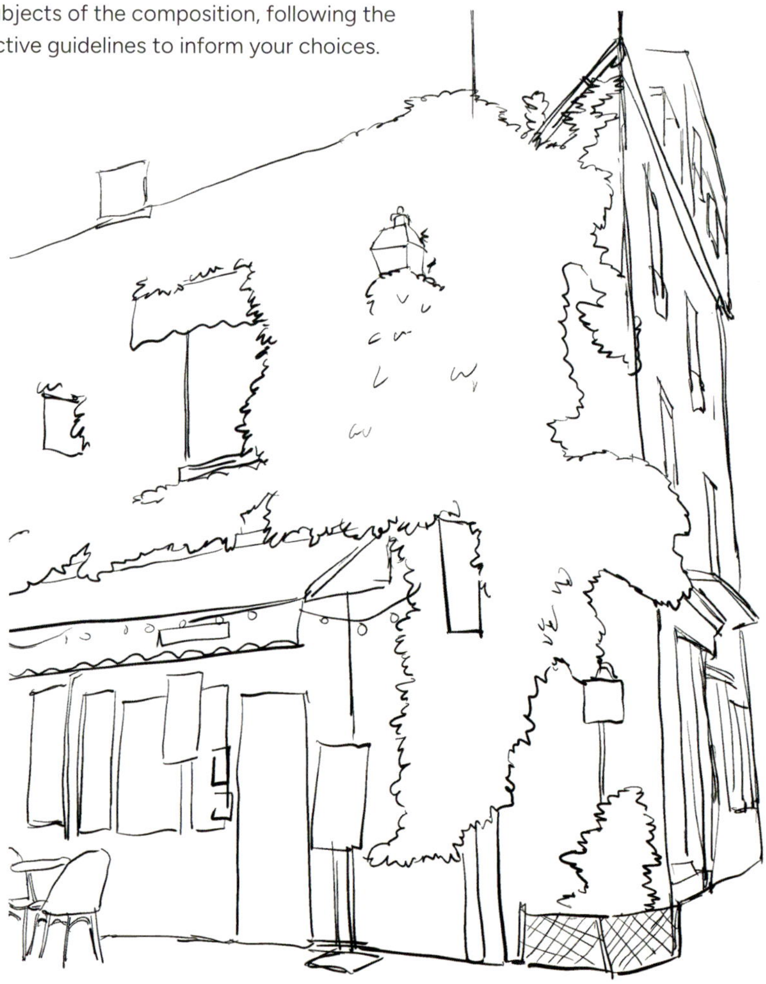

03 Next draw neater line work, capturing finer details from the reference photo. Simplify details to prevent distraction and remove any objects that clash with the composition or obstruct the sense of perspective.

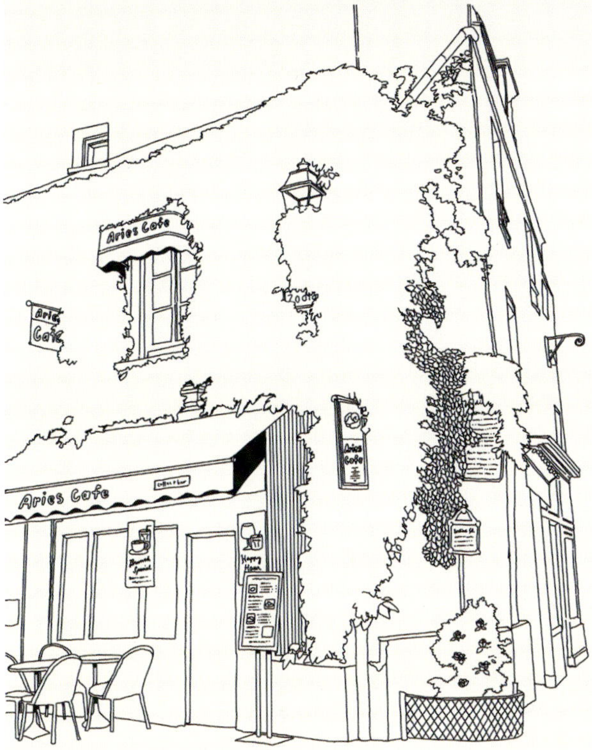

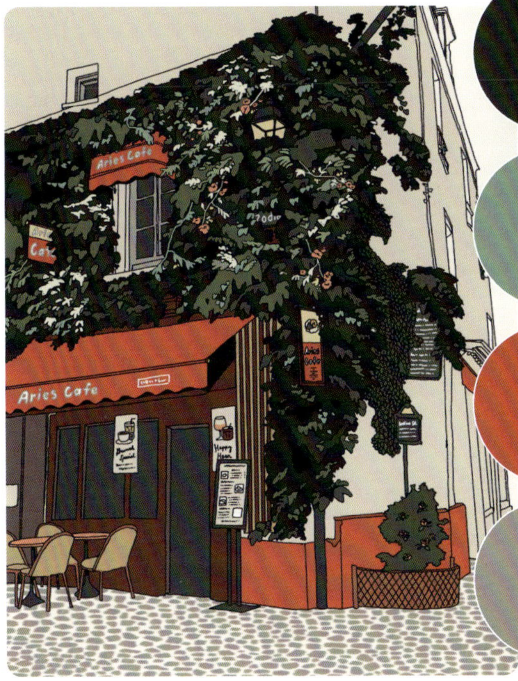

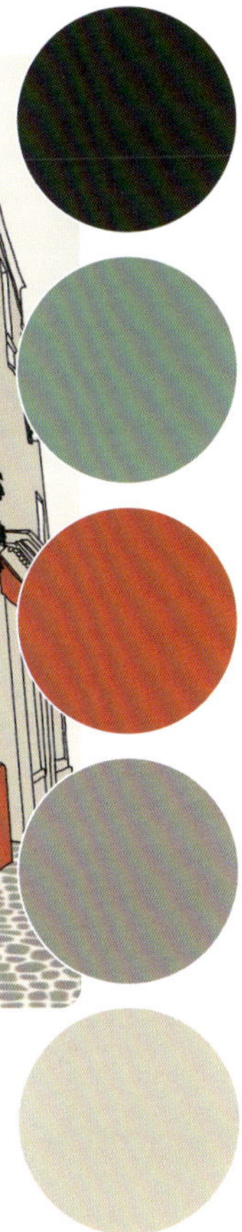

04 Choose a colour palette that conveys your intended mood for the scene, then paint in the base colours.

05 Finish by introducing shadows and highlights to create depth and ambience.

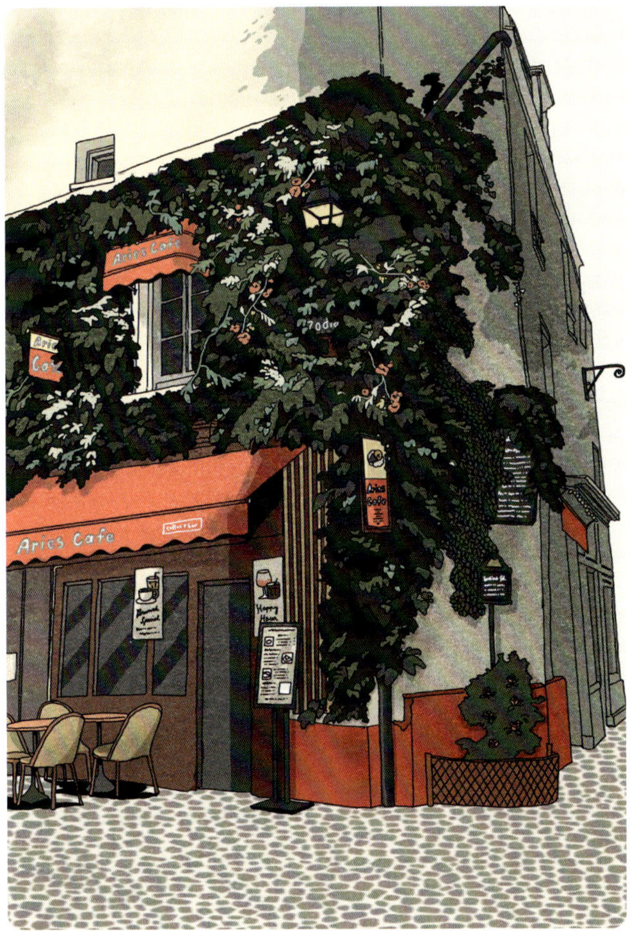

THE SPACING OF VANISHING POINTS

The position of vanishing points can make a huge difference to an image. When the points are far apart, like the example on this page, the image is calm, orderly, and natural-looking. If the vanishing points were brought closer together, it would create a more impressionistic, stylized look.

ART: ELLA OHWELLADAYS

One-page challenges:

GO WITH THE FLOW

BEGINNER ●

Draw three small thumbnail sketches with clear compositions that lead the viewer's eye to a main point of interest.

Use repeated shapes, contrast, and directional lines to create a harmonious flow that directs the gaze. Practising constructing compositions with simple shapes, without worrying about detail, will help when progressing to bigger, more complex scenes. It's a useful and important step for building strong, appealing compositions in your artwork.

The trees frame the path and focal point

The zigzag lines of the path direct the gaze to the horse and rider

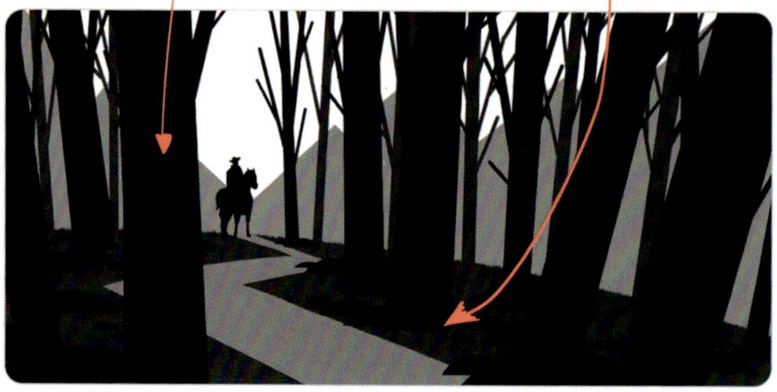

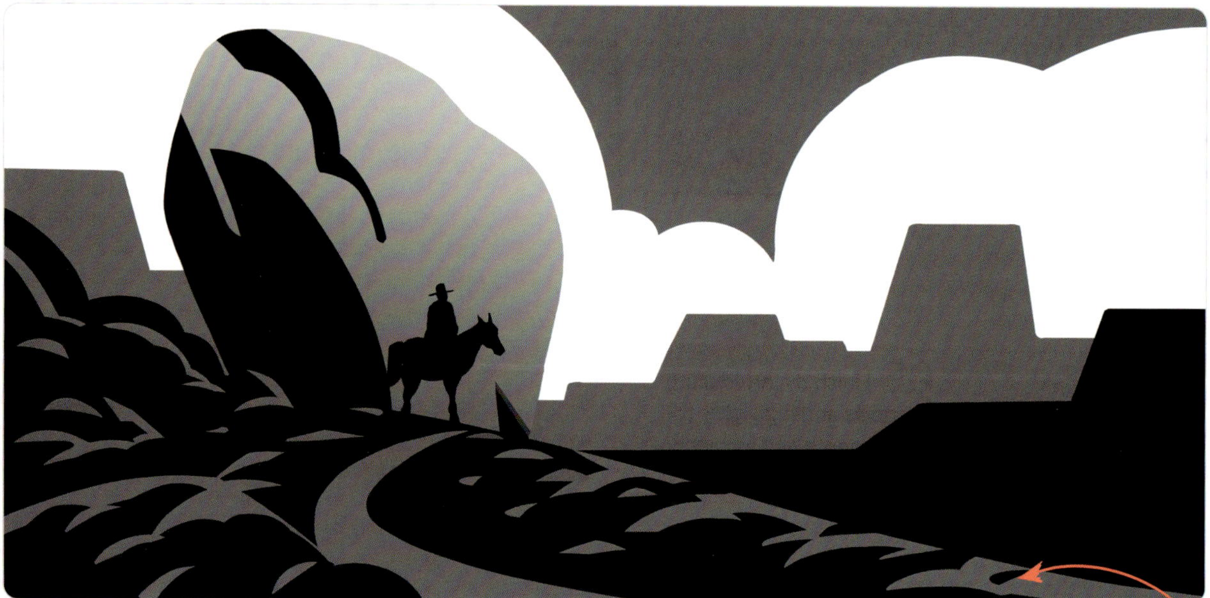

The eye follows the sweeping curve of the path to the horse and rider

The cave walls frame the scene

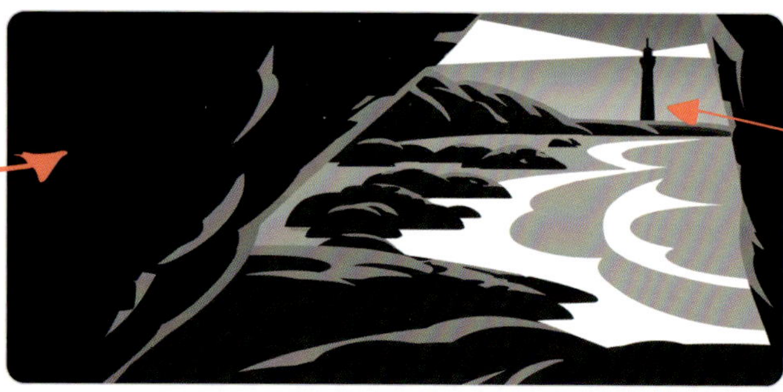

The pattern and contrast of the waves direct the gaze to the lighthouse in the distance

ART: CHAVOOMI (HITOMI TAMURA)

SKETCH A SHOPFRONT

BEGINNER ●

Visit your favourite shop and make an ink sketch of the shopfront, without making any corrections.

This challenge will help you to loosen up and be less afraid of making mistakes. Don't aim for perfect perspective. Try to make your image look believable, but embrace any imperfections and don't be afraid of wobbly lines. Simplify the shapes and details, especially towards the edges of the canvas.

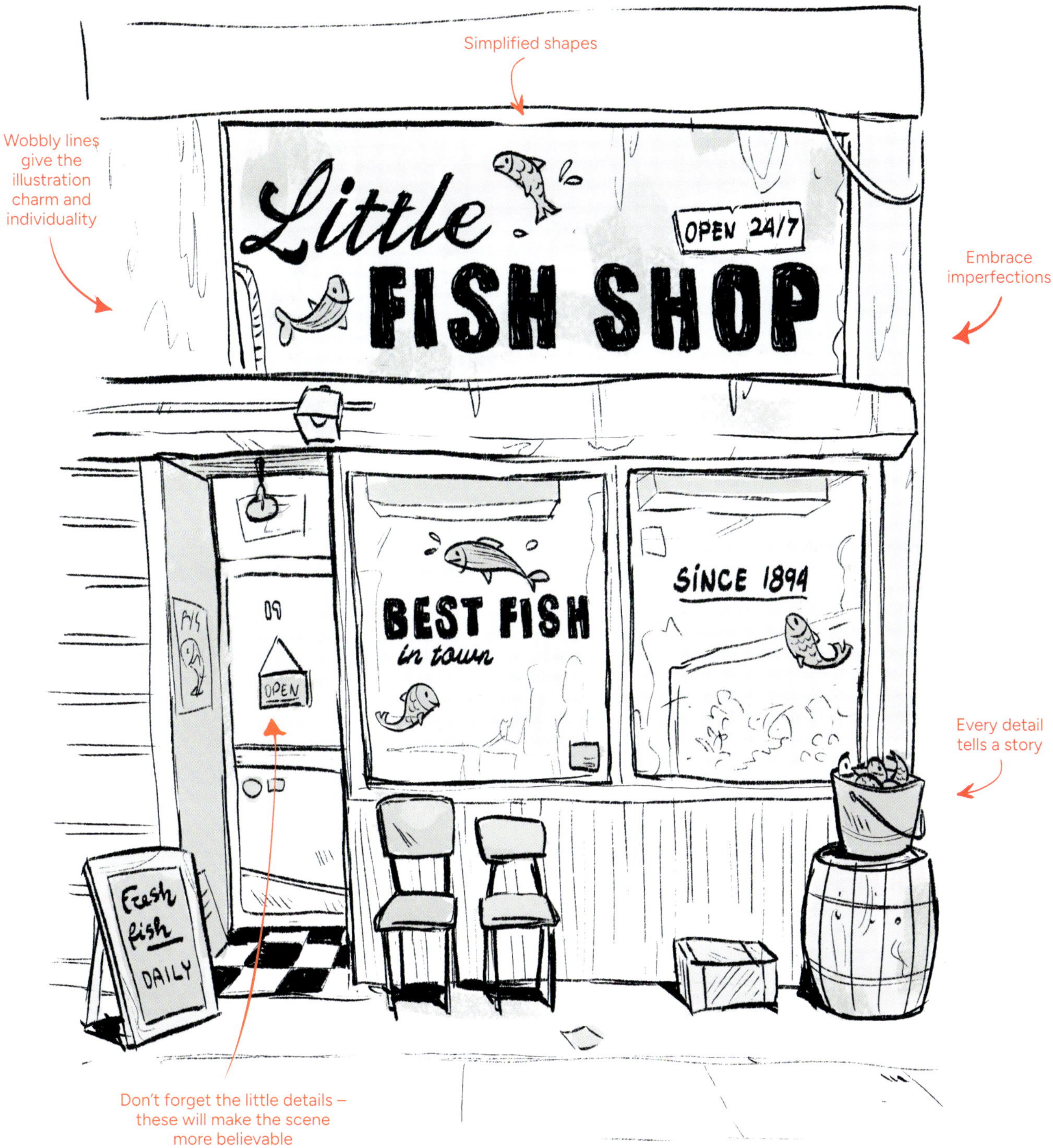

ART MAGDALINA DIANOVA

SWITCHING VIEWPOINT

BEGINNER ●

Sketch four greyscale thumbnails of the same landscape from different viewpoints.

This could be a famous landscape or one from your imagination. The example on this page uses an observatory with a balcony as the setting. Think of the camera as a character: positioning it at eye level can make a scene feel more intimate, whereas placing it overhead can convey a colder, more objective feeling. As you create your compositions, consider how you can use foreground, middle ground, and background to push the feeling of depth.

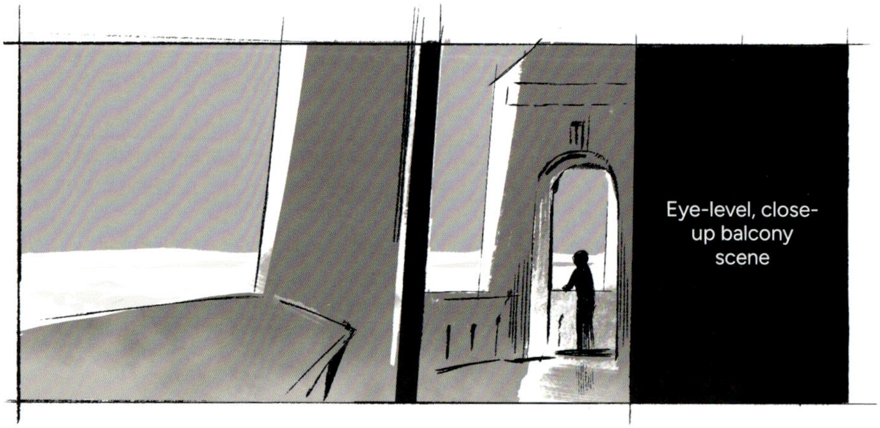

Eye-level, close-up balcony scene

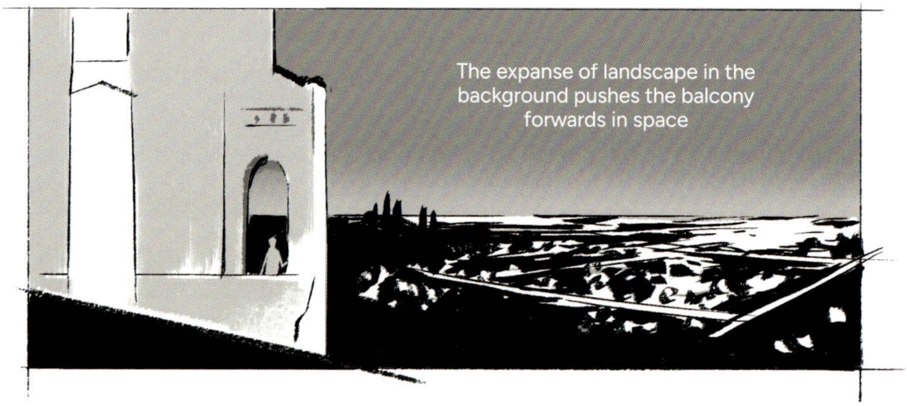

The expanse of landscape in the background pushes the balcony forwards in space

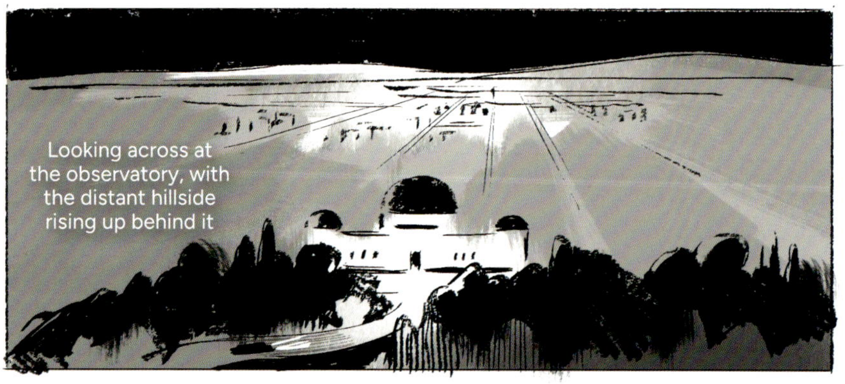

Looking across at the observatory, with the distant hillside rising up behind it

Looking up at the observatory from below, the night sky above

ART: MICHELLE CHENG

SILENCE & NOISE

INTERMEDIATE ●●

Sketch a street scene from life, grouping elements together to create areas of silence and areas of noise.

In this example, notice how the heavily detailed elements – such as the characters, architecture, and cobbled street – are concentrated in the lower third of the image, while the upper two thirds show an unobstructed view of the sky. Balance areas of complexity and simplicity to guide the viewer's eye and create a sense of harmony.

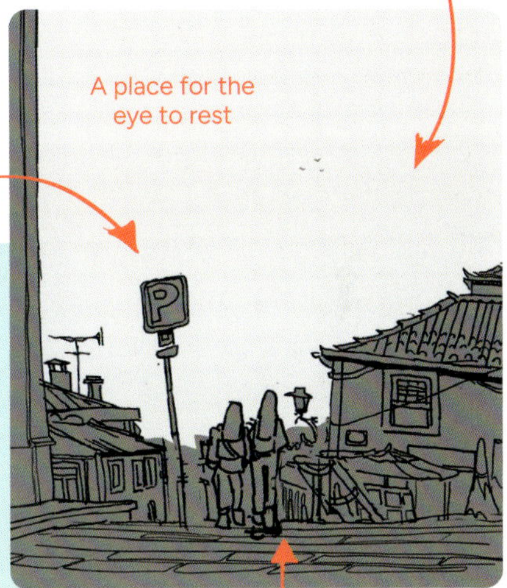

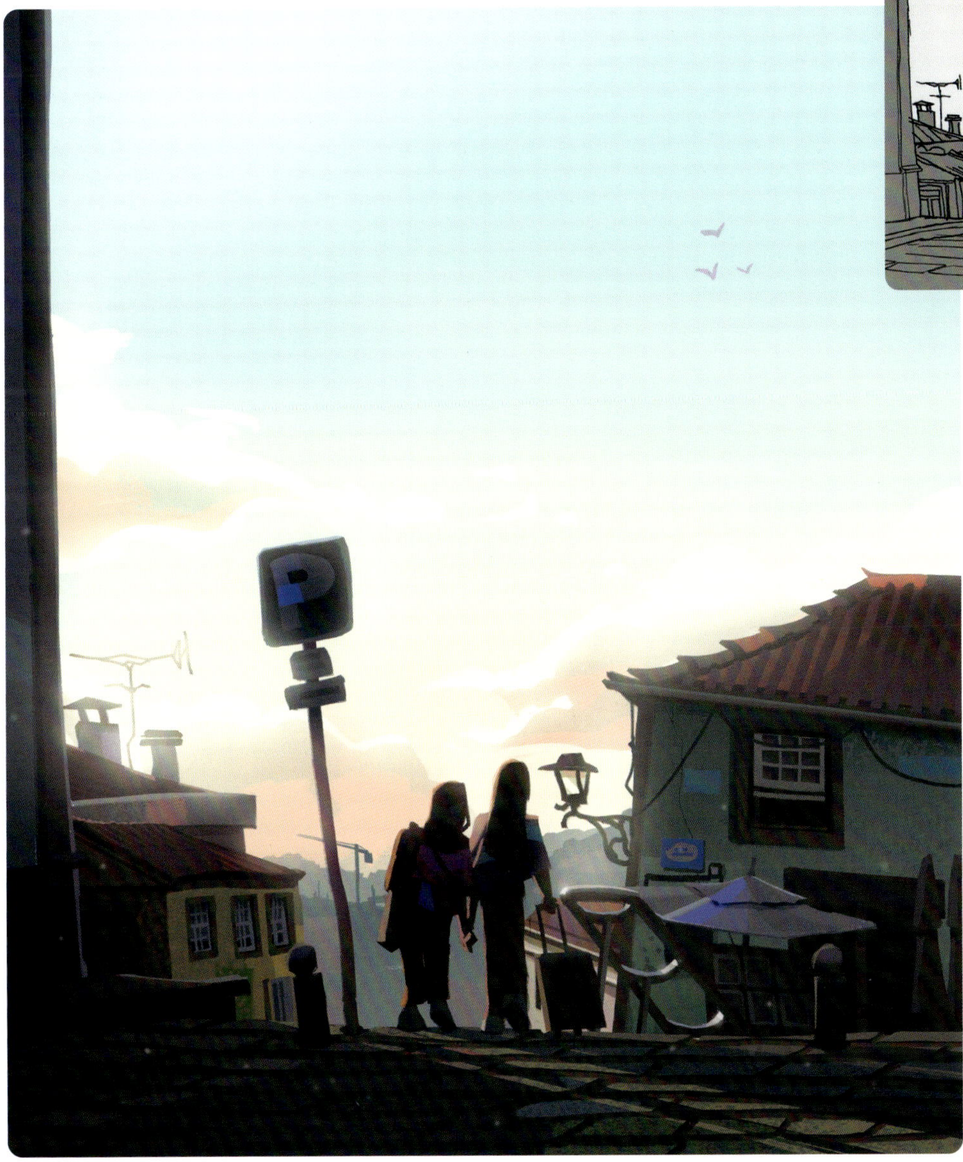

ART: MARIANA NORONHA

TWO-POINT INTERIOR

INTERMEDIATE ●●

Draw the interior of a room in two-point perspective.

Position two vanishing points, then draw a perspective grid. Make a rough sketch, following the perspective lines to depict every object at the correct size – larger in the foreground and smaller further away. Next, clean up the sketch and add greyscale tones to understand the light sources and the way light hits everything in the room. Finally, add colour to complete the illustration. The best way to learn about perspective is to observe the world around you.

The left vanishing point (red) sits on the left of the scene, while the right vanishing point (blue) sits just off canvas

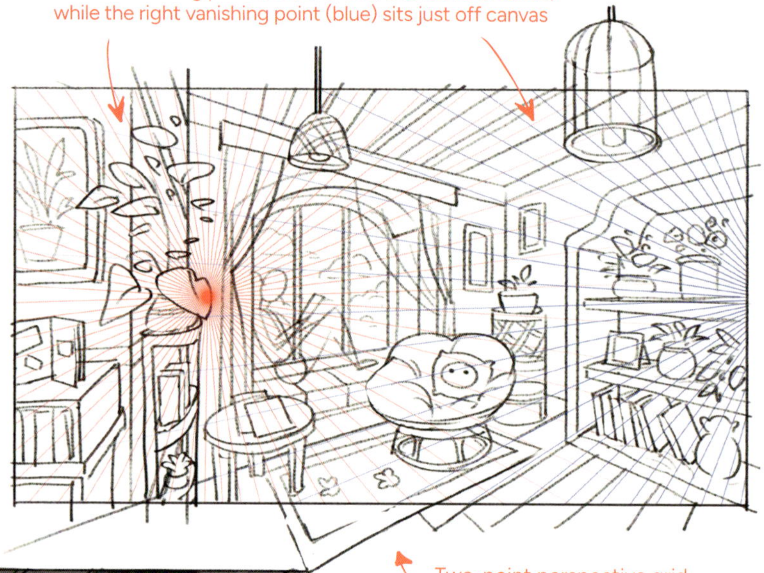

Two-point perspective grid drawn with red and blue lines

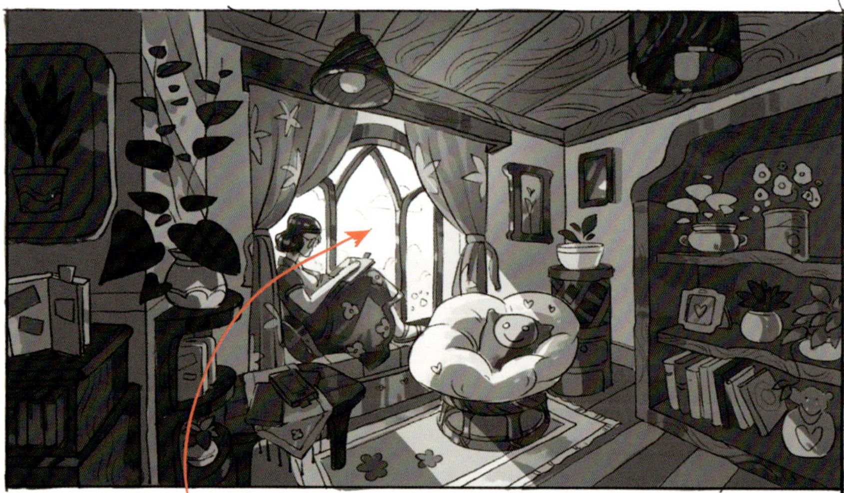

The window is the only light source in this scene

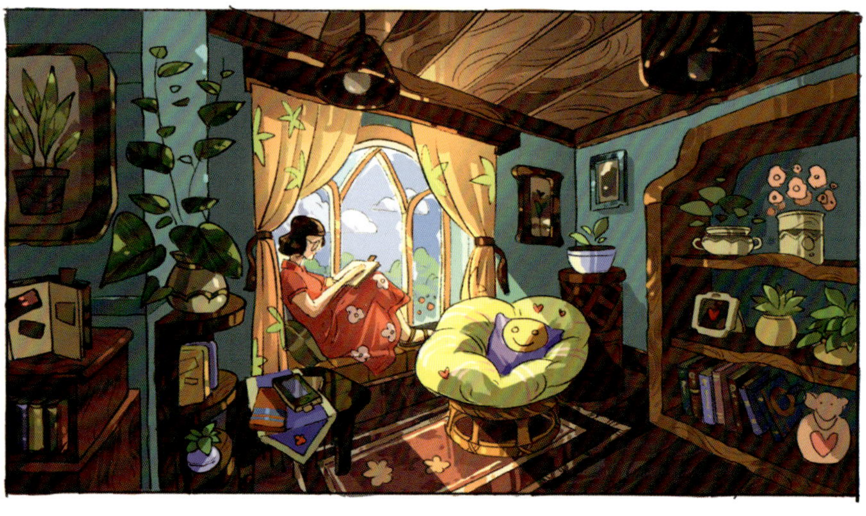

ART: ALINE FERNANDES

PERFECT FRAMING

INTERMEDIATE ●●

Create a painting of the view through a window, including the frame in the foreground.

Not only will this create an interesting composition, but it will also give the painting more story. A scene viewed through a window could suggest secrecy or apprehension. This challenge will help you think about different methods of framing, and how foreground objects can affect the emotional tone and composition of an image, adding context and atmosphere.

The window frame, curtains, and lamp work together to frame the scene

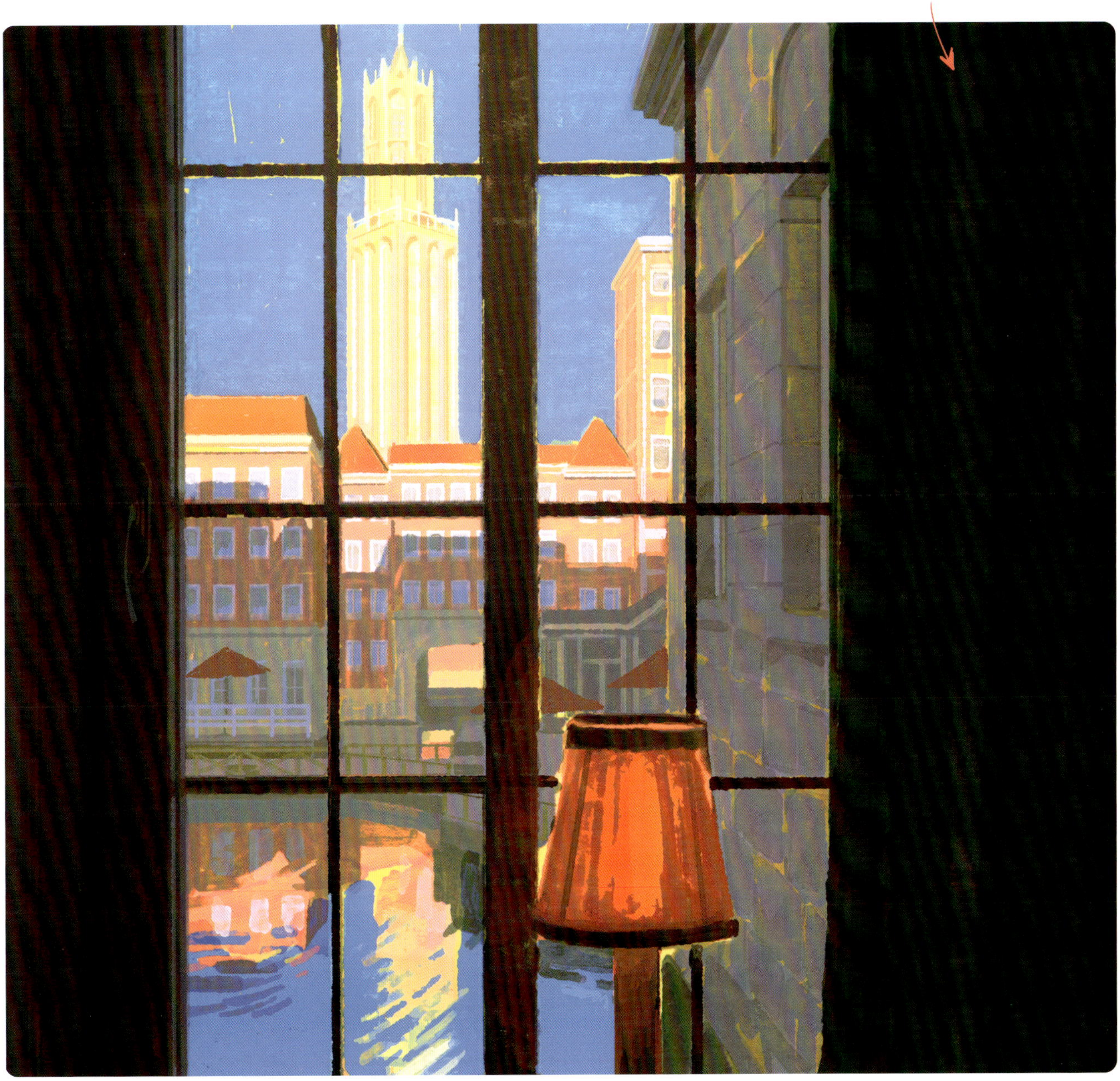

The framing creates a sense of observation – is the person in the window taking in the view, casually people-watching, or spying on someone in particular?

ART CHAVOOM (HITOMI TAMURA)

STRIKE A POSE

ADVANCED ●●●

Draw a character from three different angles – in three-quarter view, from above, and from below.

Adding a subtle twist to part of a character's body can add a lot of intrigue to a pose. As well as making sure the character's volumes work in perspective, consider your line quality to improve dimensionality – the way two lines meet can do a lot to suggest the overlap of forms. Similarly, use line thickness to suggest if an object is closer or further away from the viewer.

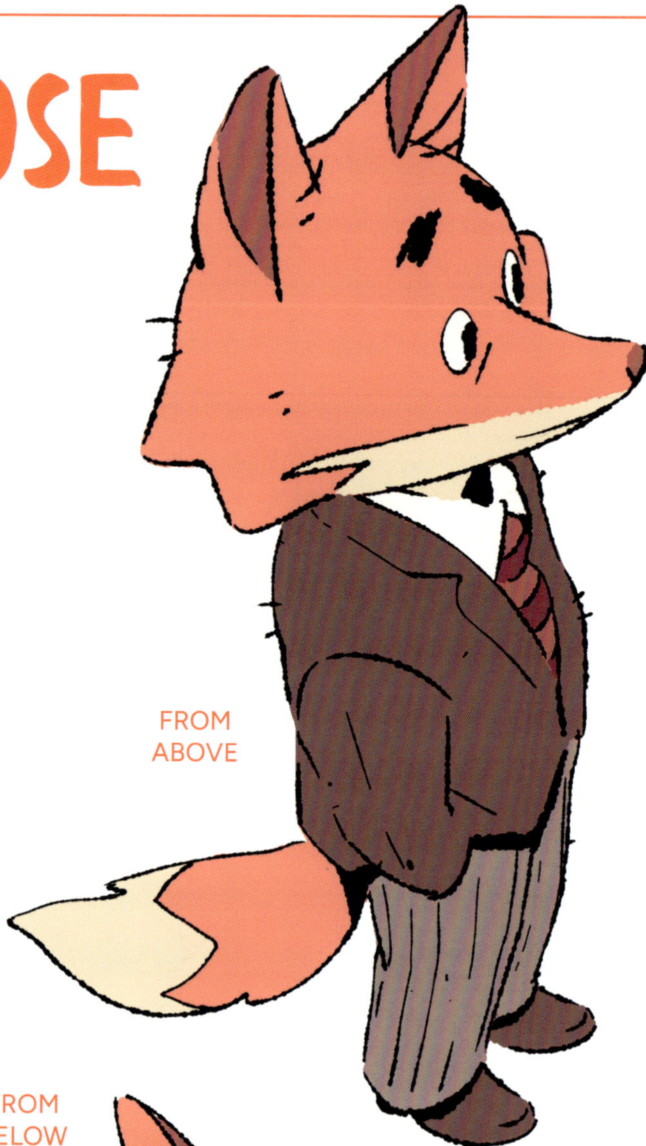

FROM ABOVE

THREE-QUARTER VIEW

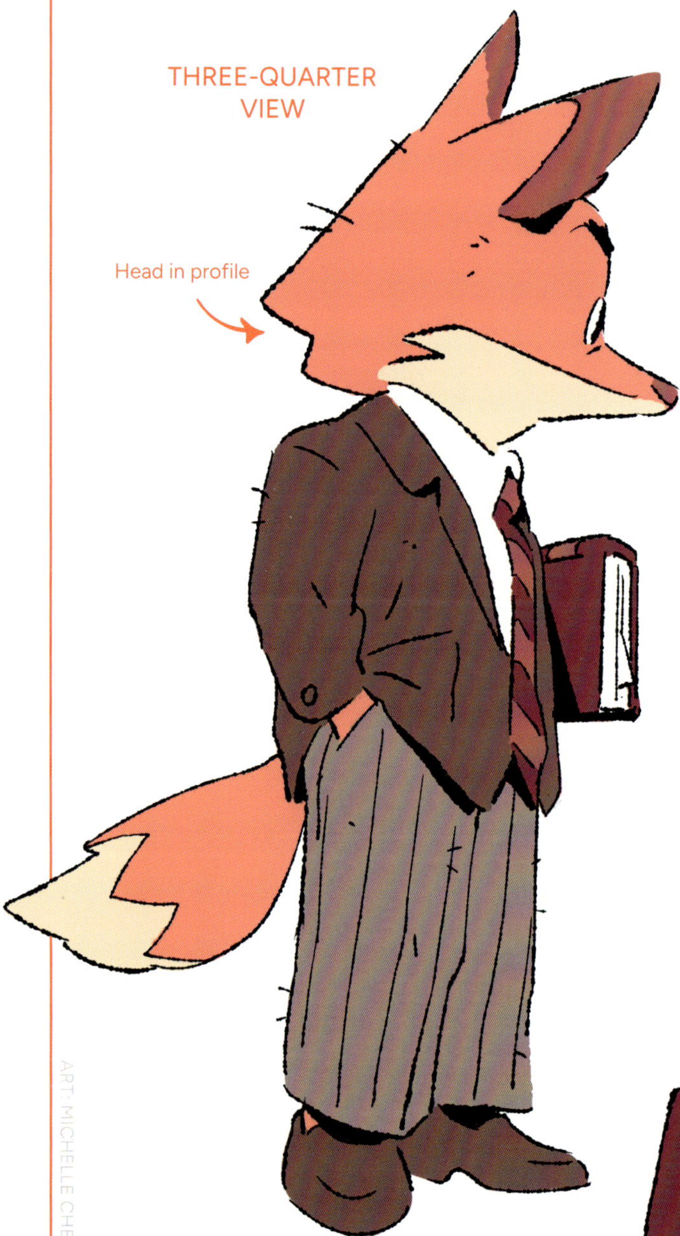

FROM BELOW

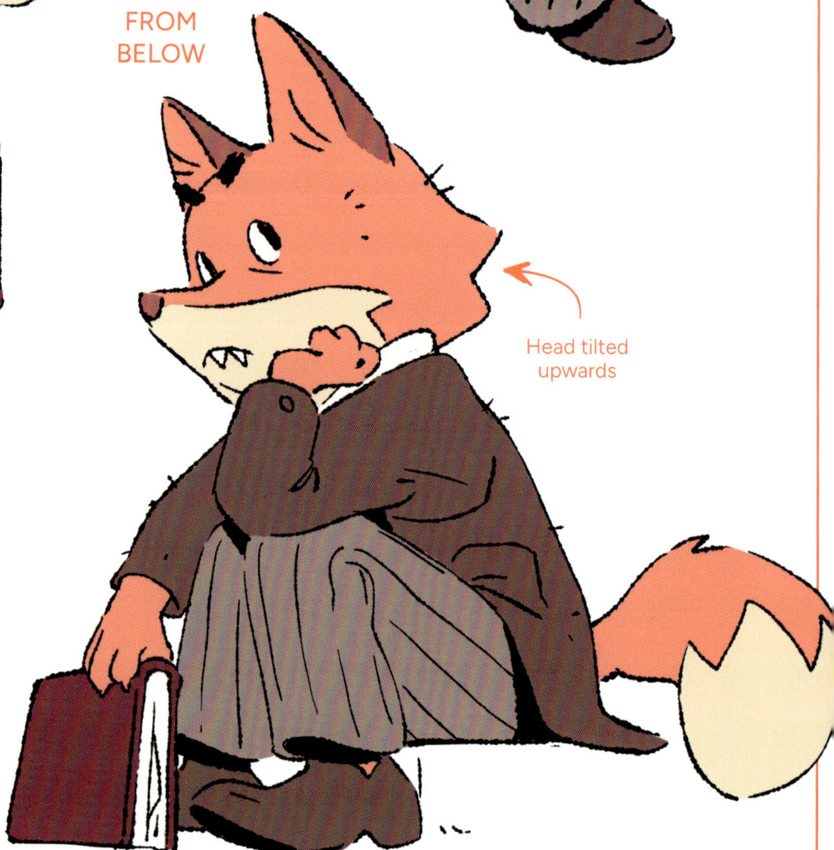

ART: MICHELLE CHENG

ALTERING COMPOSITION

ADVANCED ●●●

Recreate a famous painting in your own style, sticking to a similar composition while adding your own elements.

Examine the existing composition and consider how you could put your own stamp on it. For example, if you like drawing nature, add more plants and trees, or add a character if that's your thing. How does using inspiration from a classic painting affect your framing style?

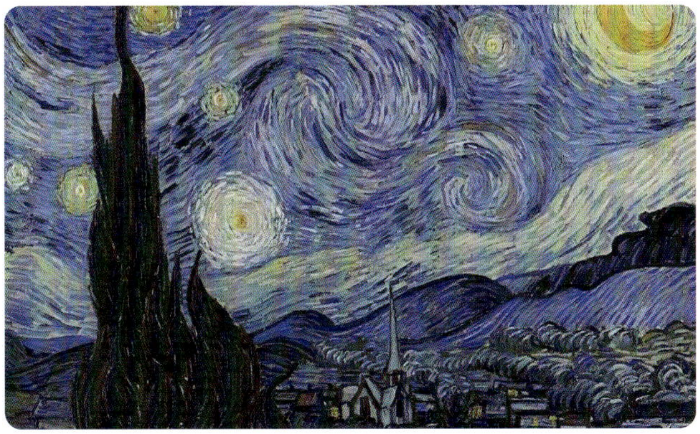

THE STARRY NIGHT BY VINCENT VAN GOGH, 1889

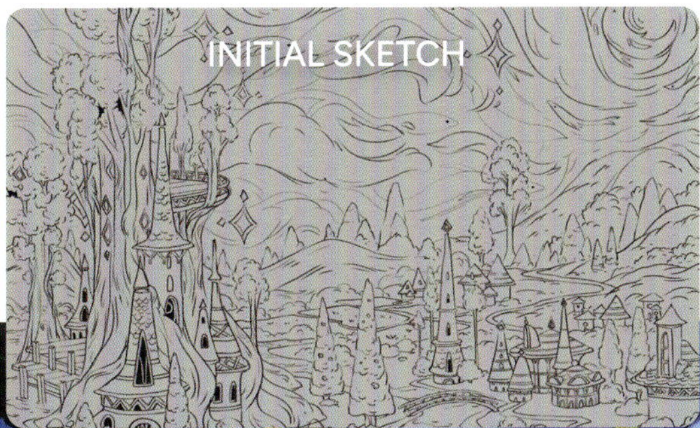

INITIAL SKETCH

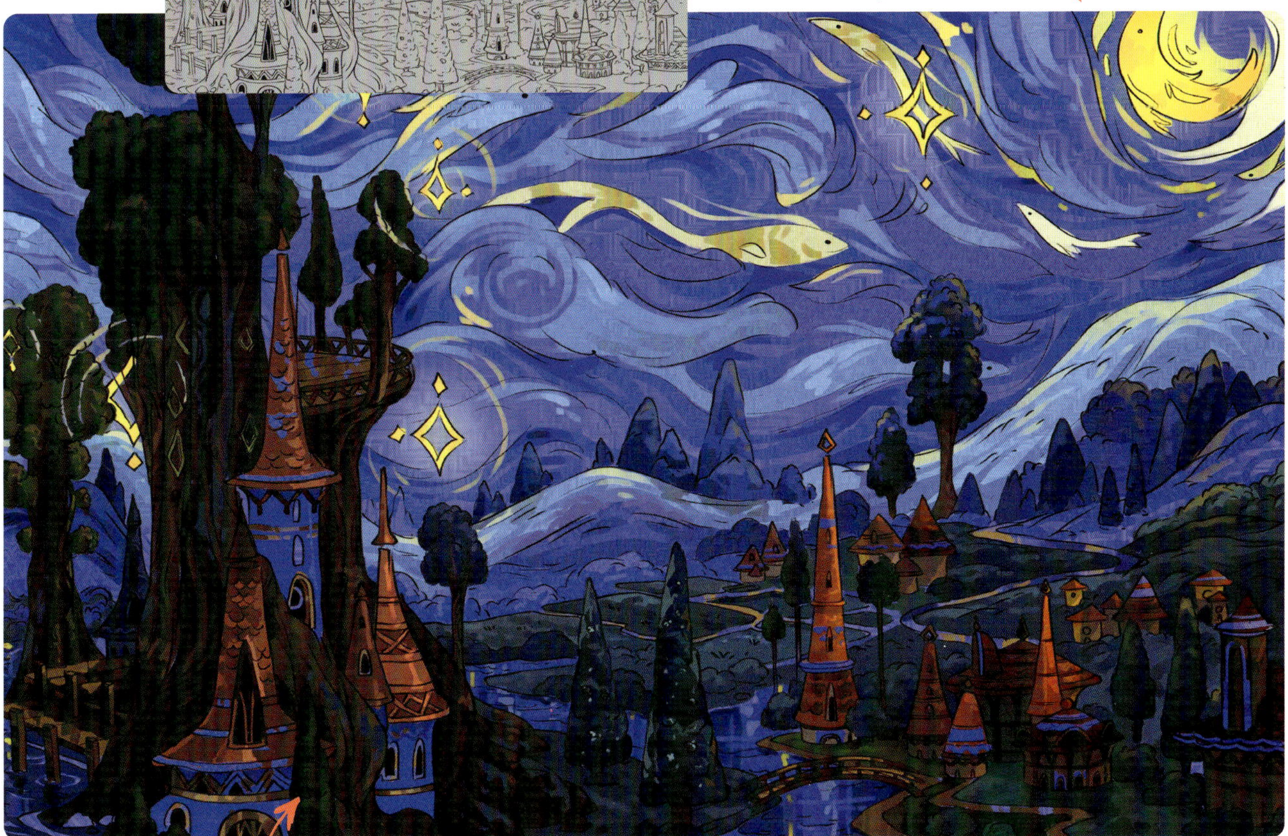

Magical sky creatures addded!

As the overall composition remains the same, the new painting is still recognizable as a recreation of the original

Develop and push existing elements into fully formed buildings or trees

ART: ALFRED FERNANDES

COMPOSITION INSPIRATION

ADVANCED ●●●

Study* The Great Wave off Kanagawa *by Japanese artist Hokusai, then use the same composition elements – such as movement, proportions, planes of depth – to create a drawing of a landscape in your hometown.

The finished piece should bear a resemblance to the original in its movement and composition, despite depicting a different scene.

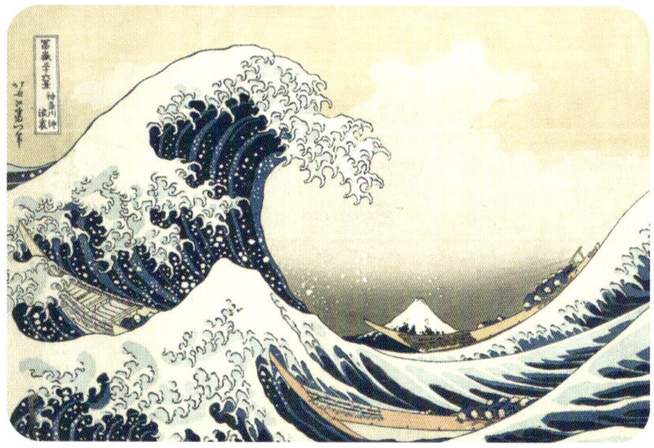

THE GREAT WAVE OFF KANAGAWA BY HOKUSAI, 1831

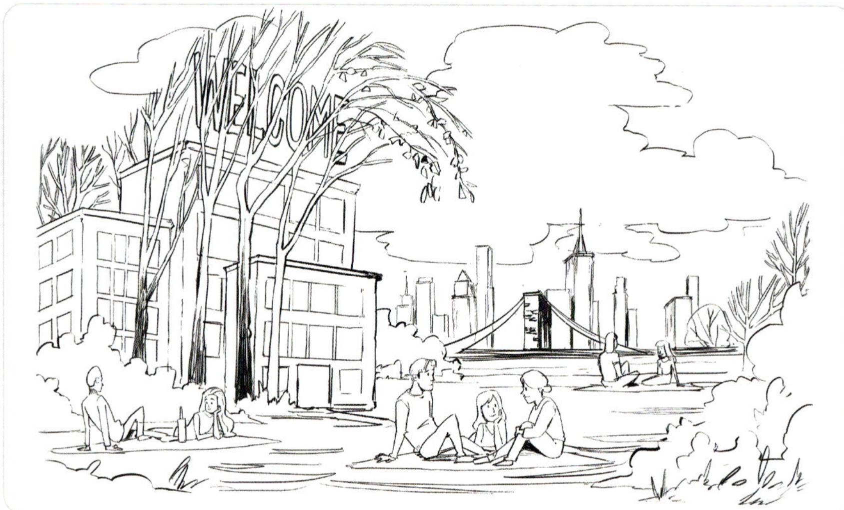

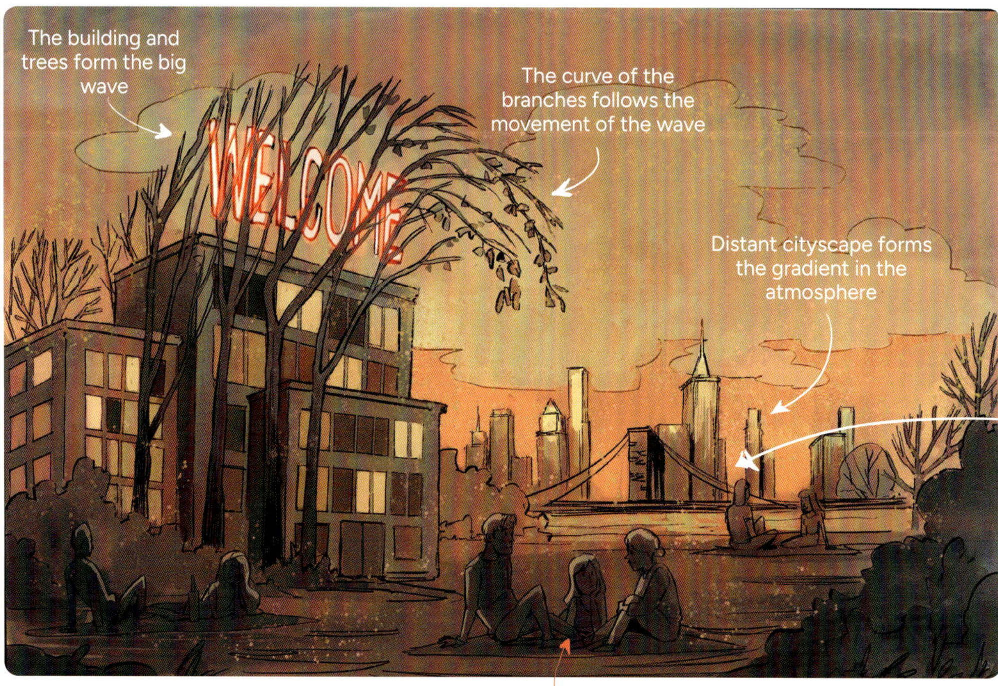

FOCUS ON THE NEGATIVES

ADVANCED ●●●

Draw three objects, but rather than drawing the objects themselves, draw the space around them instead.

The objects could be household items, buildings, or even characters. It may seem strange at first, but understanding negative space will help you to see shape and composition from a whole new angle. This exercise is especially useful when working on framing and perspective.

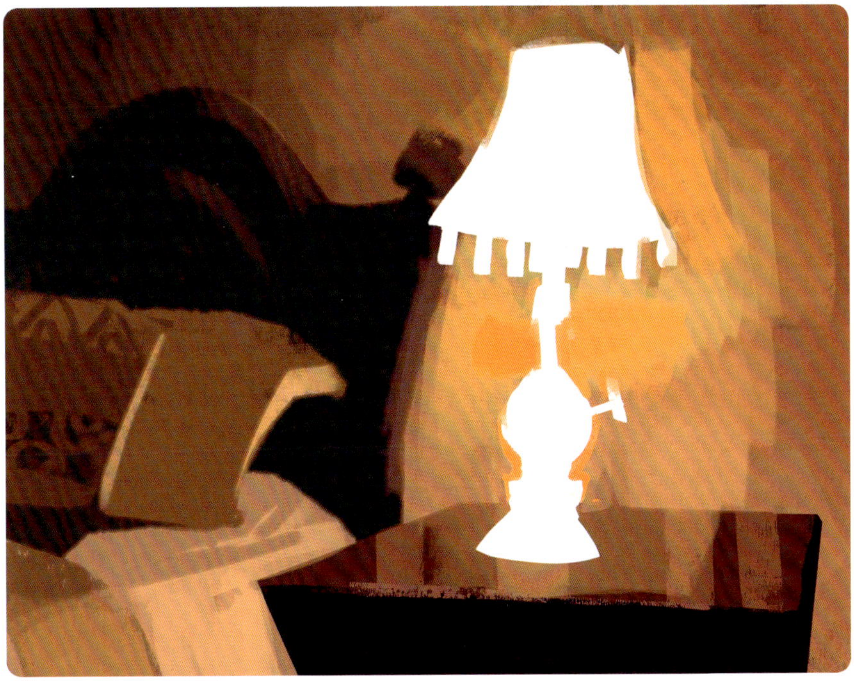

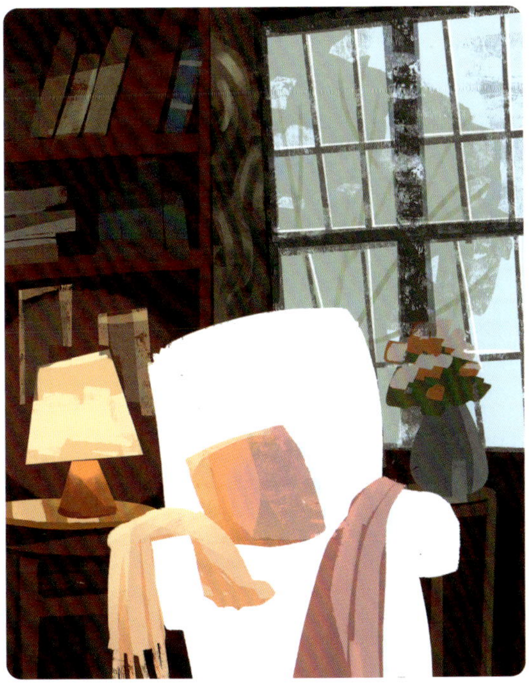

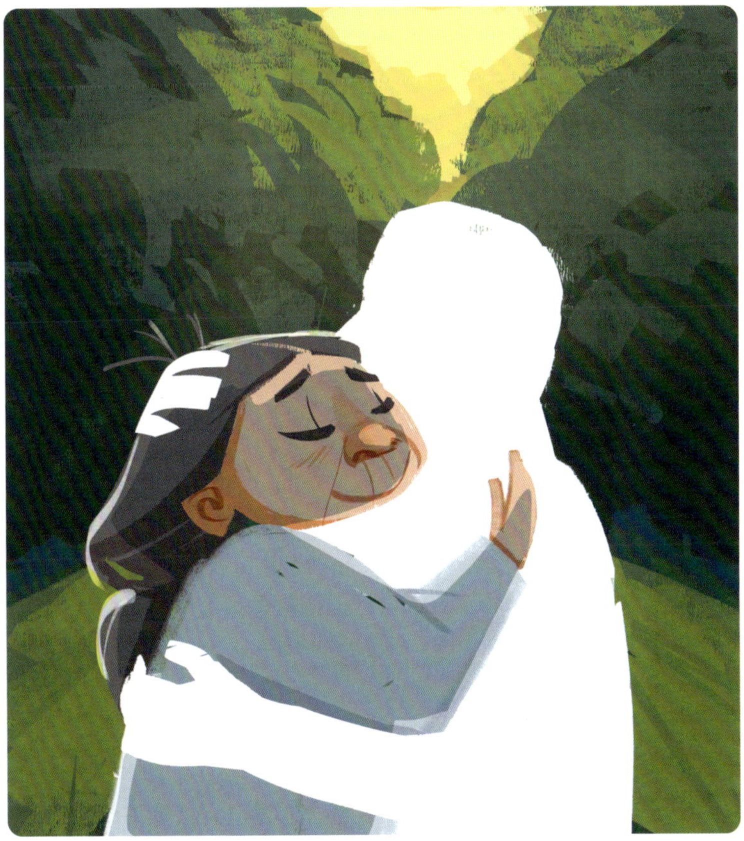

ART TARANEH KARIMI

CHARACTERS & CREATURES

Step-by-step challenges:

One-page challenges:

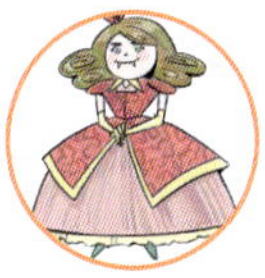

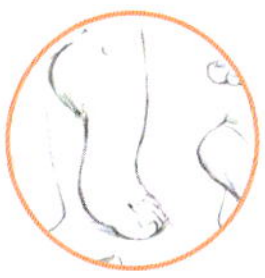

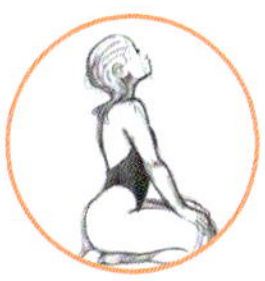

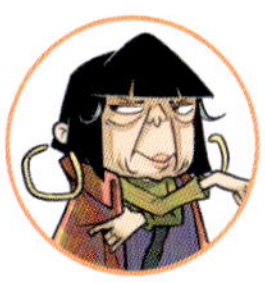

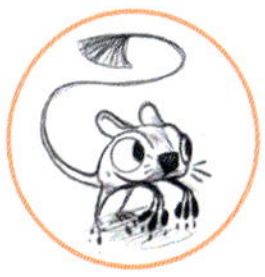

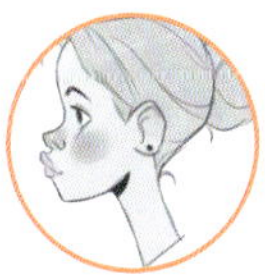

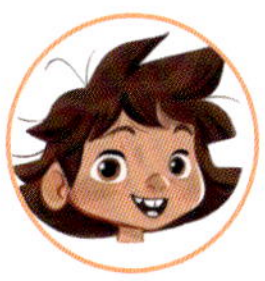

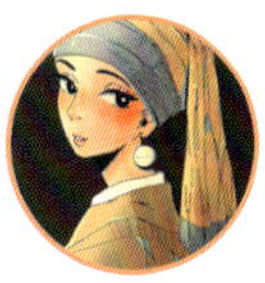

MIX & MATCH FACIAL FEATURES

BEGINNER

Draw an assortment of facial features, then mix and match them to create different faces.

This exercise will help you break out of your usual character-design habits and show you how each feature can impact the overall personality, pushing you to boldly experiment with expression and style.

01 Begin by sketching three pairs of eyes and eyebrows, three noses, and three mouths. Vary the shape and size, but don't combine them just yet.

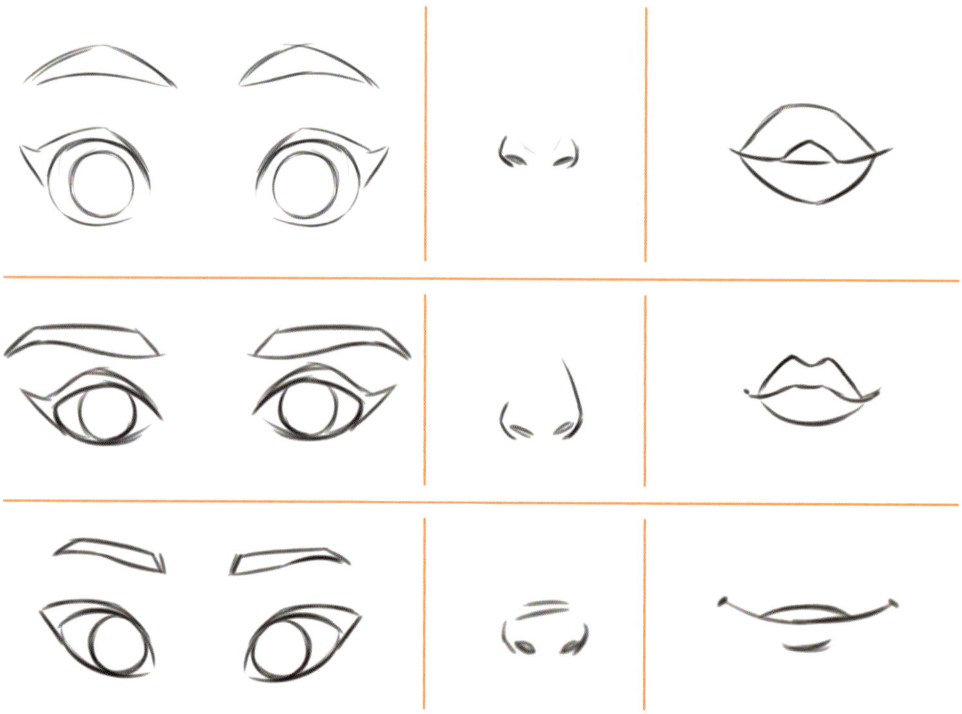

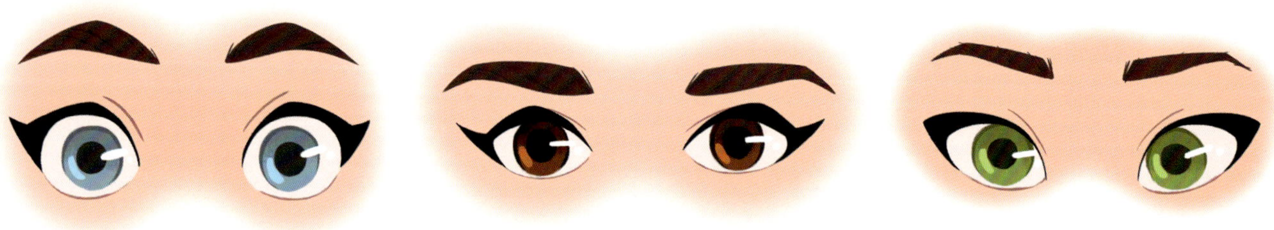

02 Give each set of eyes a different colour, but maintain a consistent skin tone.

03 Add colour to the noses, using the same style and skin tone as you did for the eyes.

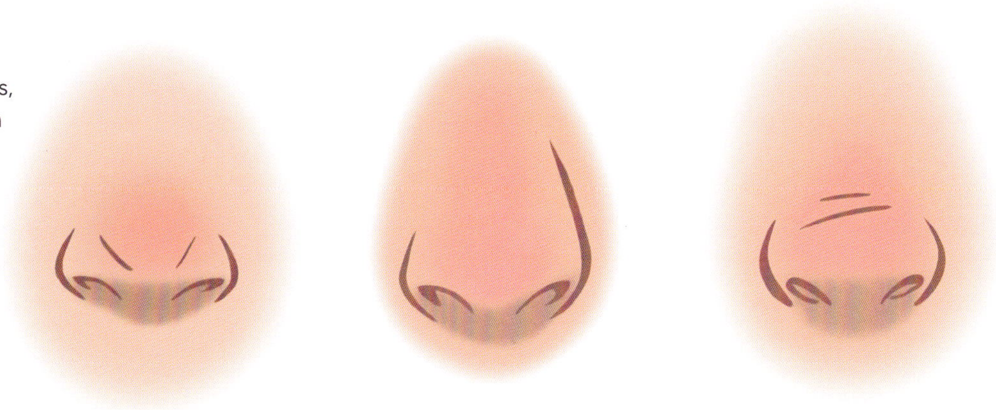

04 Now colour the lips, experimenting with different lip shades.

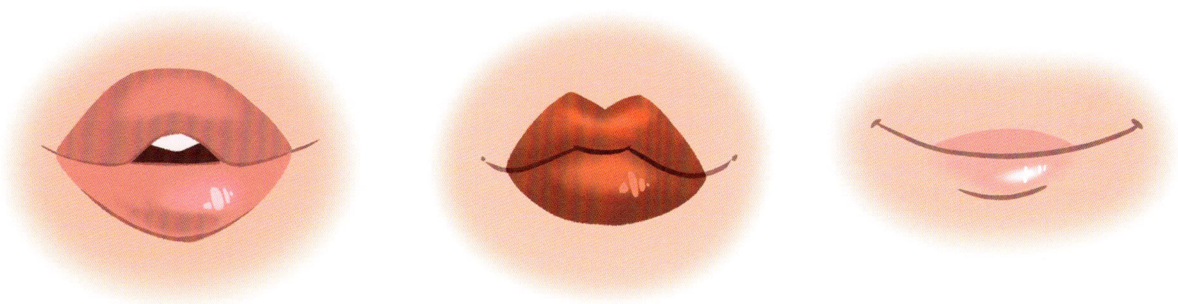

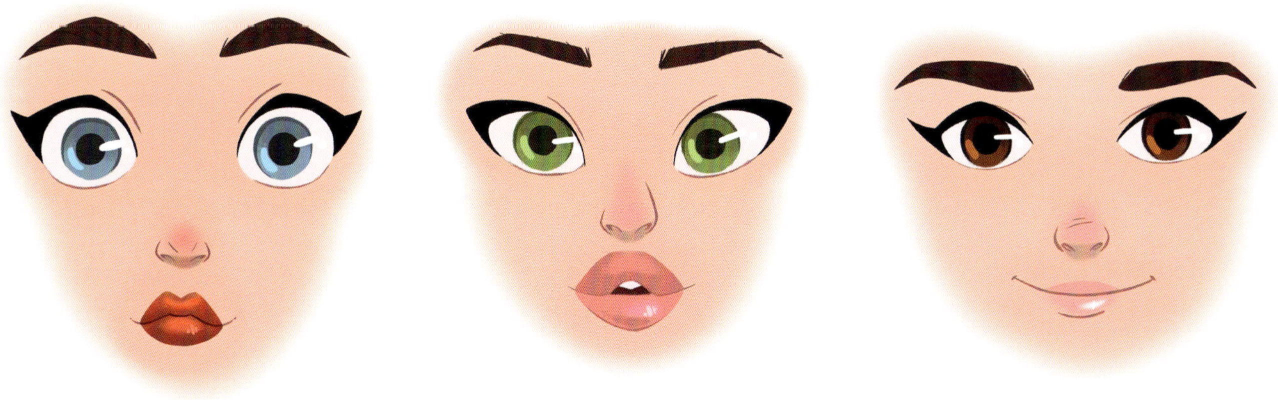

05 Finally, mix the different eyes, noses, and mouths together to discover new character expressions!

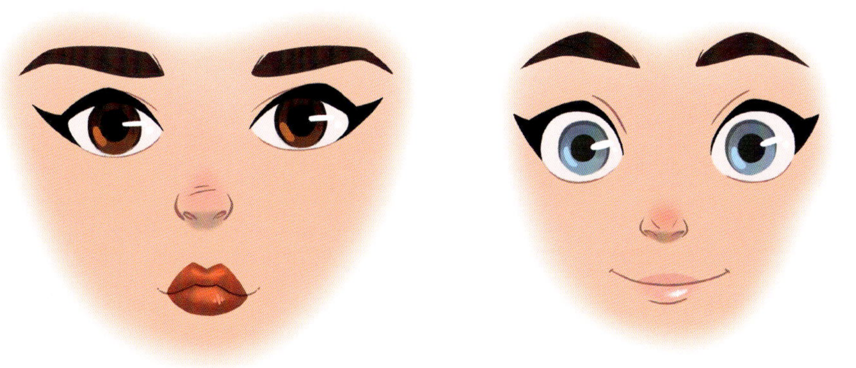

ART PERNILLE ØRUM

PLAYING WITH PROPORTIONS

BEGINNER ●

To explore the power of size hierarchy, try redesigning a character with varied proportions.

Dividing the character into three sections (head, torso, and legs) allows you to build different proportion ratios that you can use to create various personalities and art styles. For example, stylized character designs typically feature large heads and thick limbs, while realistic characters tend to have more balanced proportions.

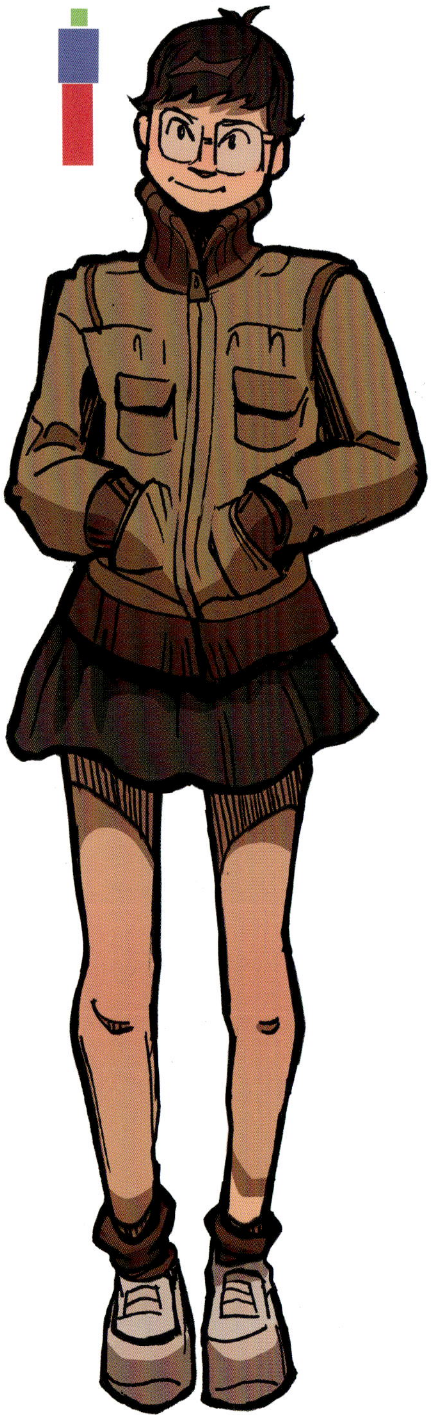

01 Draw a character using realistic, balanced proportions for the head, torso, and legs.

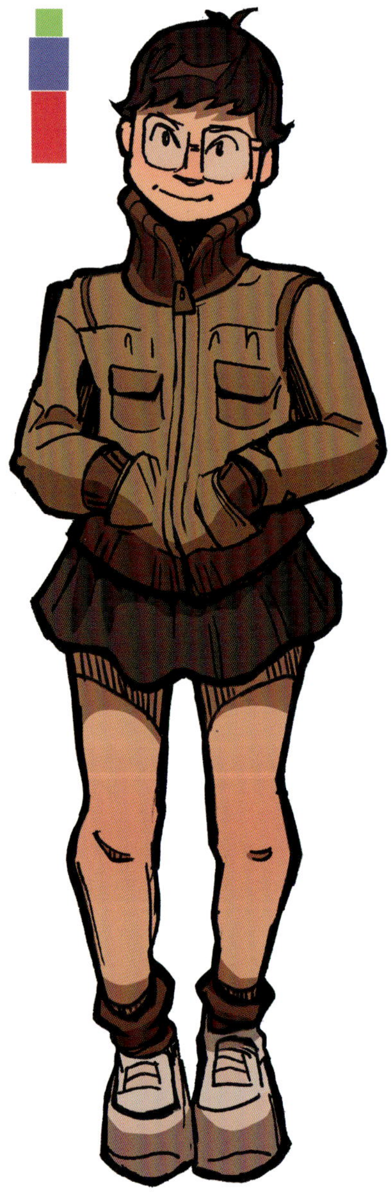

02 To begin stylizing, exaggerate the size of the head, widen the limbs, and slightly shorten the legs. This will immediately make the character appear more approachable.

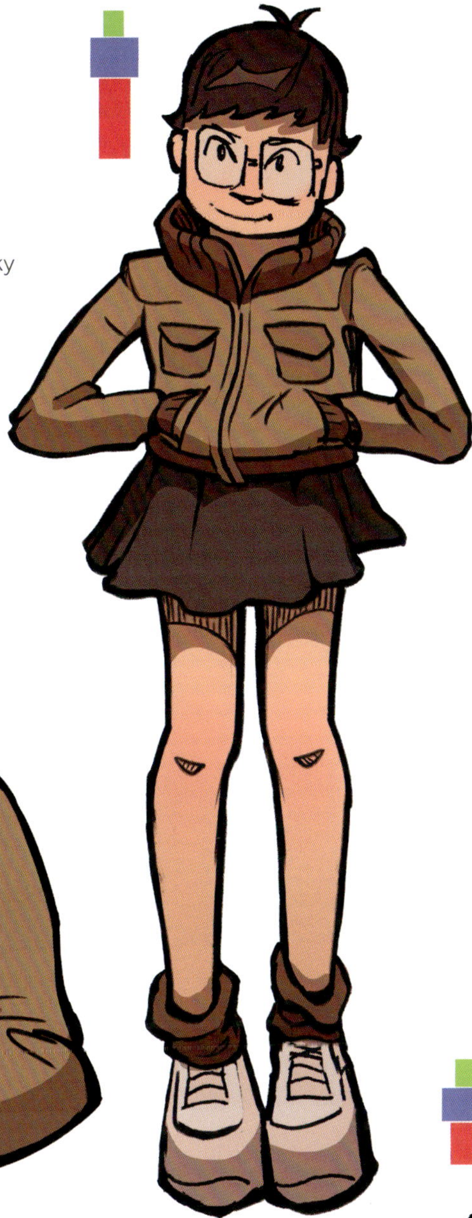

03 Try shortening the torso and elongating the legs this time. A lanky look can symbolize awkwardness, agility, or youthfulness.

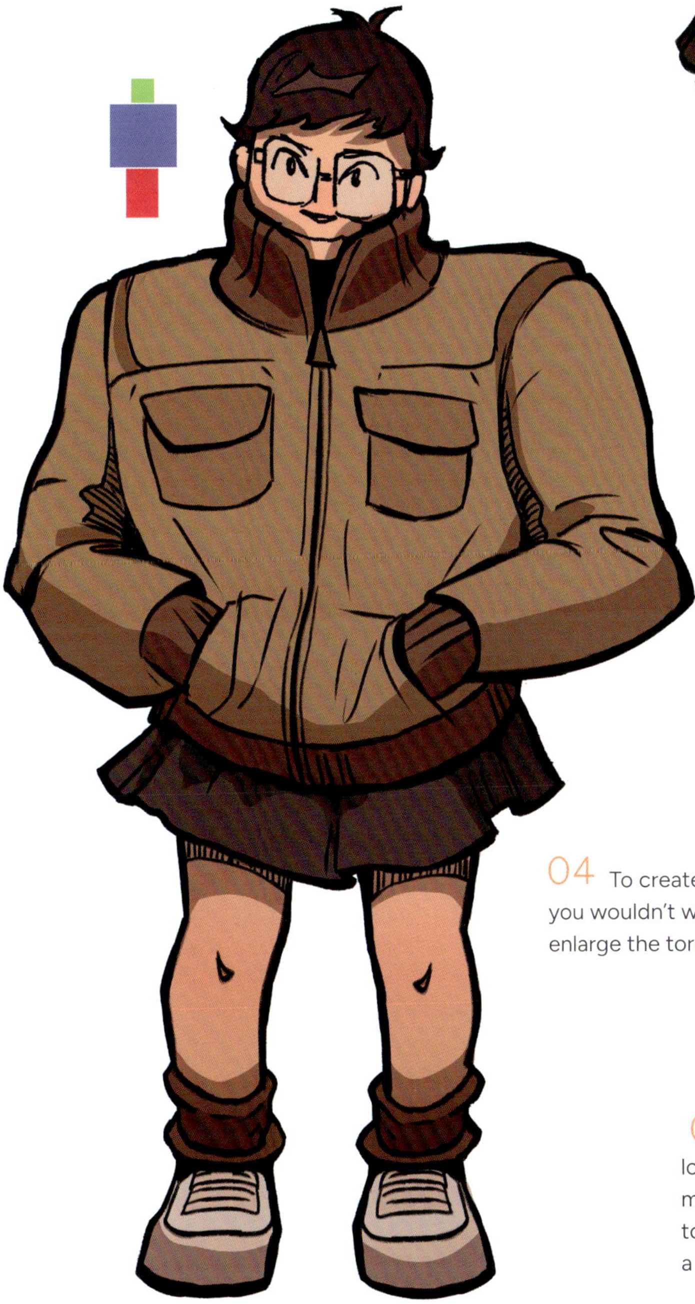

04 To create a tough-looking character you wouldn't want to face in a fight, enlarge the torso and shorten the legs.

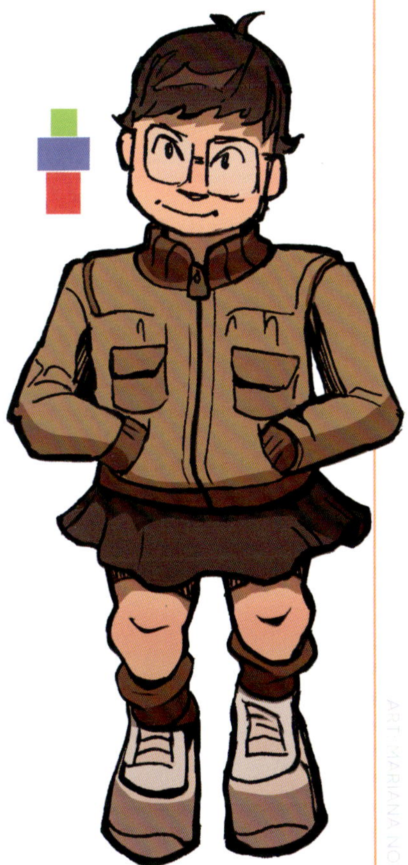

05 To make the character look friendly and cartoon-like, make the head one-third of the total body height. This creates a soft, stylized design.

ART: MARIANA NORONHA

ON THE FLIP SIDE

BEGINNER ●

Think of a character you would normally draw, then draw the complete opposite.

Do you normally design young female characters? Design an old grandpa instead. Normally make noses cute and pointy? Try opting for a larger, bolder shape. It's easy to fall into the habit of making the same design choices, so push outside your comfort zone by exploring new shapes and colour palettes. Mixing things up will help you grow as a character designer.

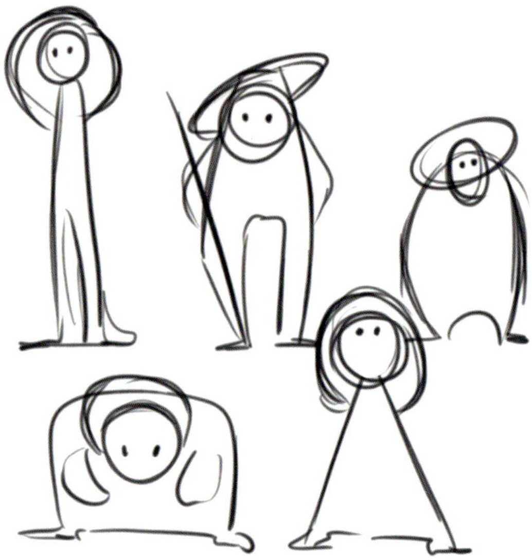

01 Start by loosely sketching different characters, considering how you can stretch, squash, or exaggerate the form.

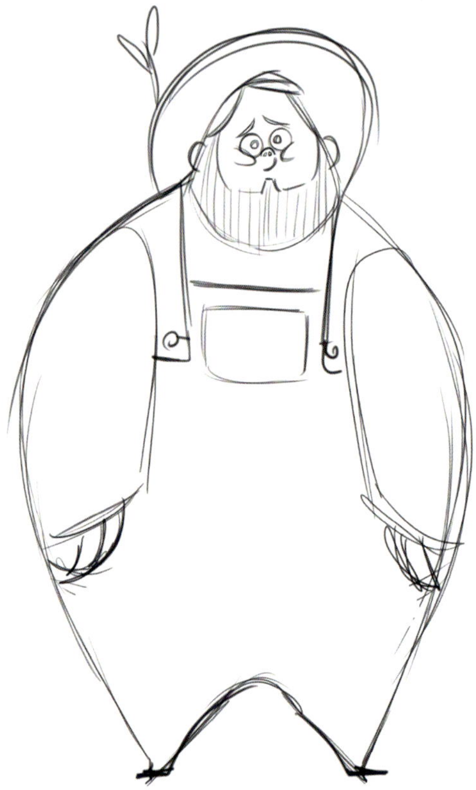

02 Pick a sketch outside your normal comfort zone and start fleshing out your character. Make sure to keep experimenting with shapes and sizes as you add details!

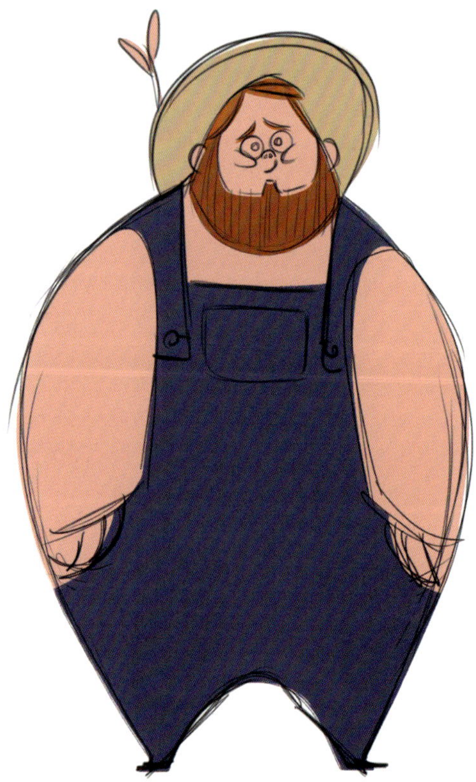

03 What kind of colour palette do you usually lean towards? Choose the opposite for this design. Introduce flat base colours, keeping it simple.

04 What details can you include that you wouldn't typically use? Perhaps it's a certain hairstyle, patterned clothing, or accessories? Or maybe it's a stripey top and big, bushy beard?

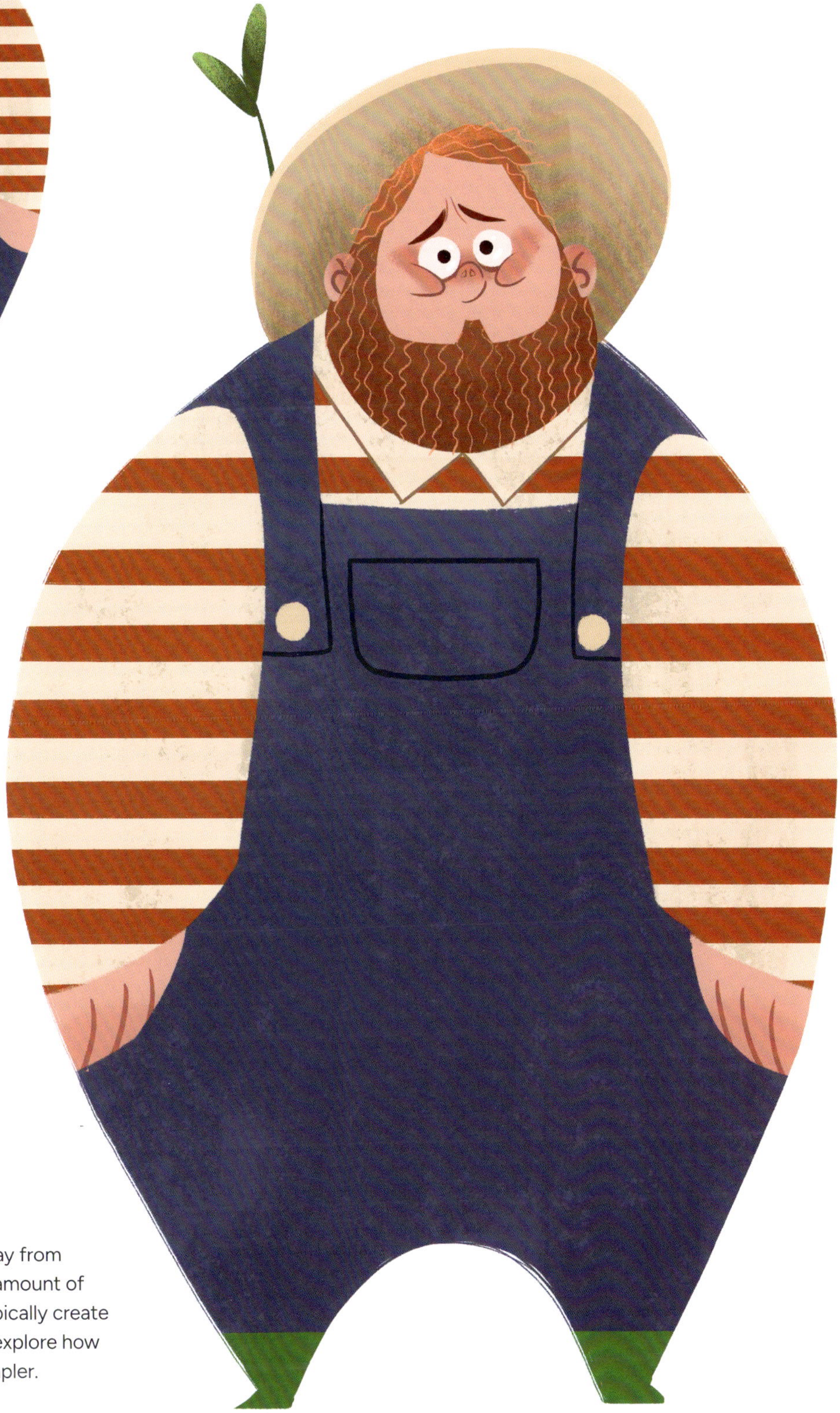

05 If you tend to shy away from busy designs, increase the amount of detail and texture. If you typically create highly detailed characters, explore how you could keep this one simpler.

ART: PERNILLE ØRUM

EDIBLE INSPIRATIONS

INTERMEDIATE ●●

Turn a piece of fruit into a character or creature design.

A pear may lend itself well to a soft, shy character, while a pineapple's bold shape might inspire a spiky, energetic personality. This task provides a fun way to explore unexpected shapes and new possibilities. Using familiar organic forms forces you to think differently about balance, silhouette, and proportions.

01 Start by sketching your chosen fruit, experimenting with how you can push and stylize the shape.

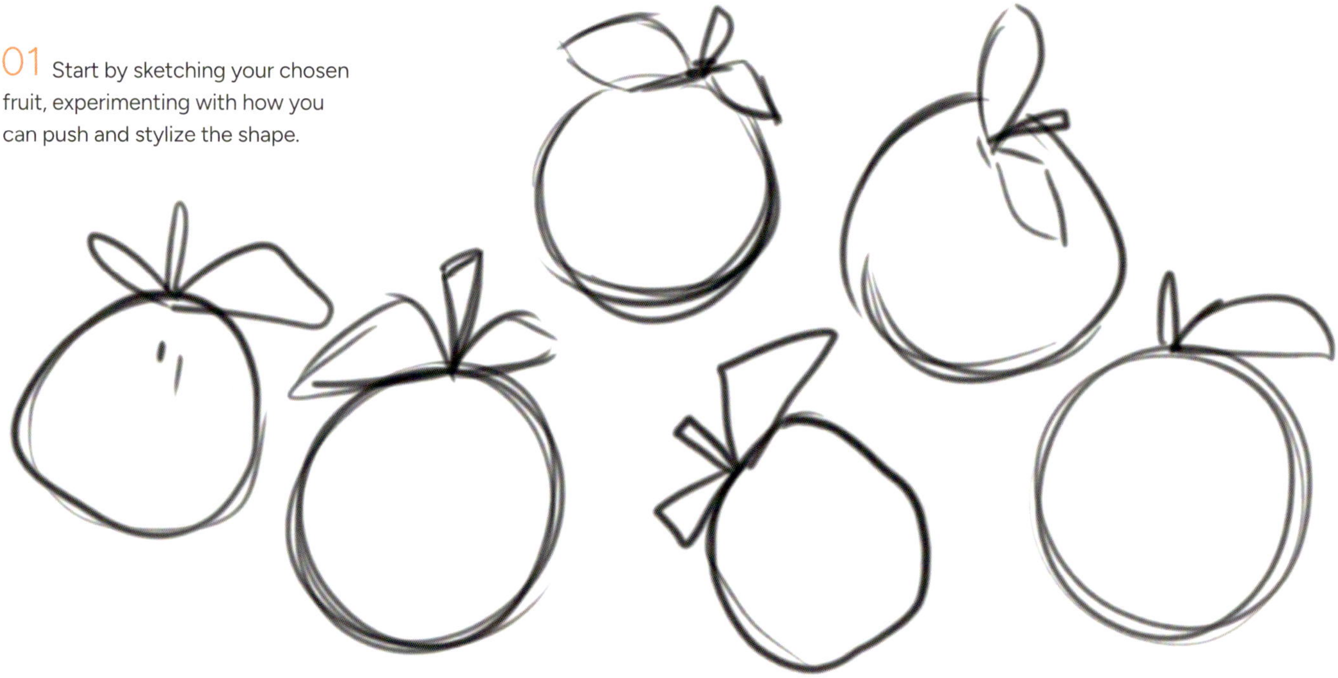

02 Try out different colours, textures, and line weights. How does this alter the look or vibe of each fruit?

03 Select a sketch to develop into a character or creature design.

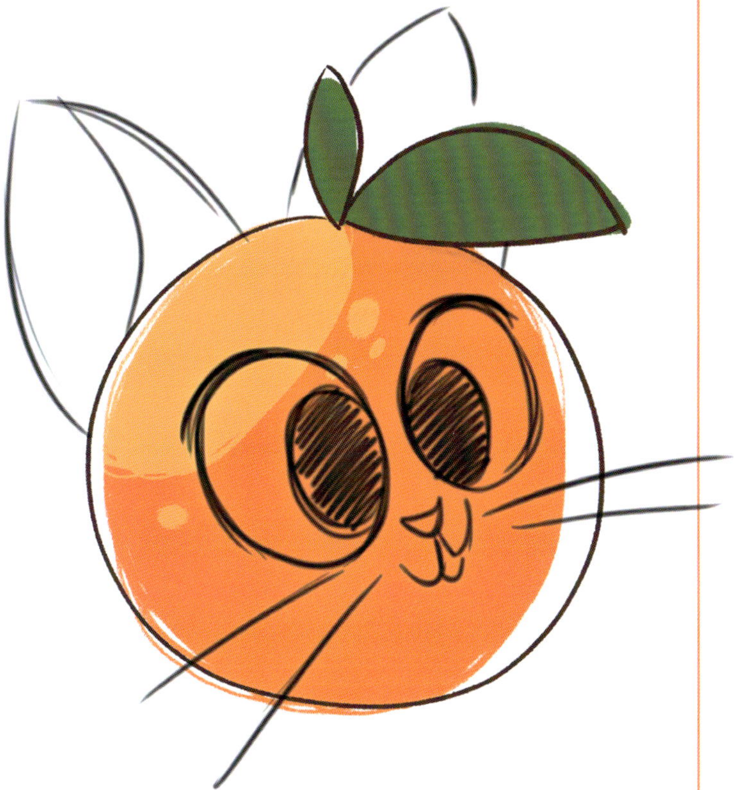

04 Sketch your character using only the features and colours provided by the fruit, while staying within its original shape. The goal is to preserve the personality of the fruit.

CLEMENTINE CAT

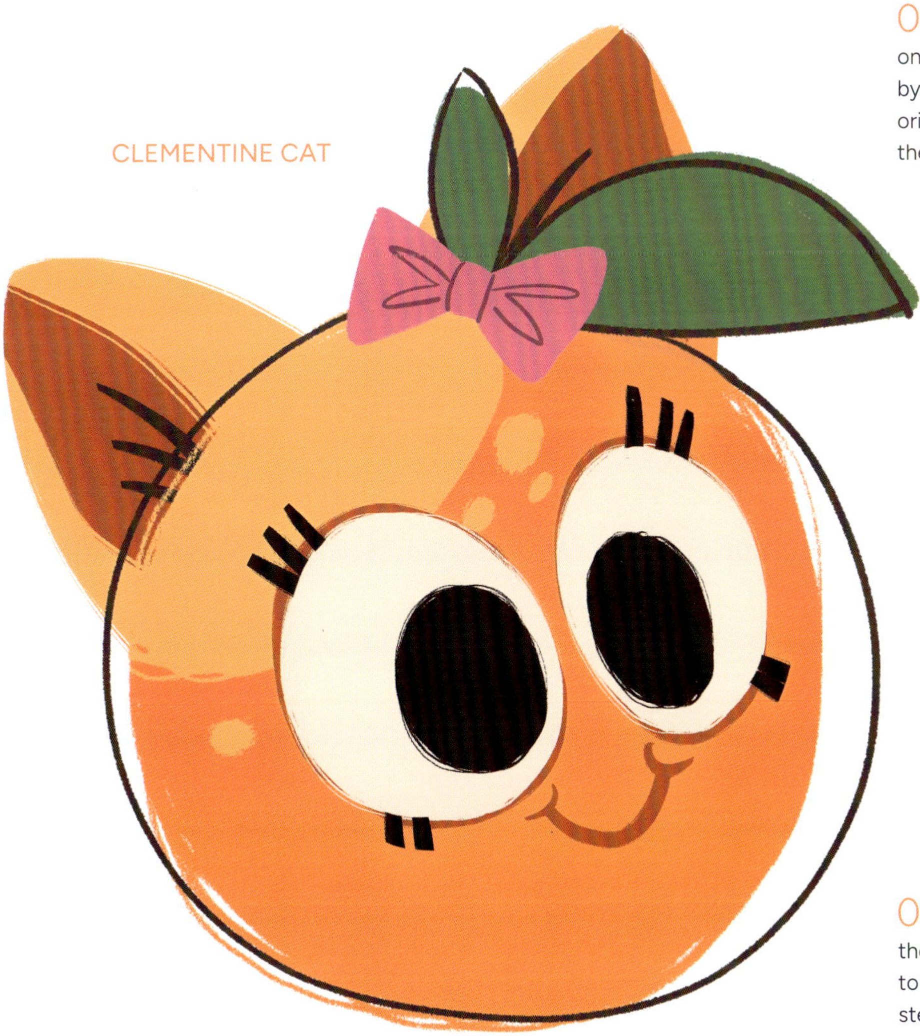

05 Colour in each element, keeping the original palette in mind. Feel free to remove line work from the previous step if it makes things appear too busy.

ART: PERNILLE ØRUM

STRIKE A POSE

INTERMEDIATE ●●

Find a famous cartoon character in five dynamic poses, then replicate those poses for your own character.

This is a great exercise to avoid drawing stiff-looking characters.

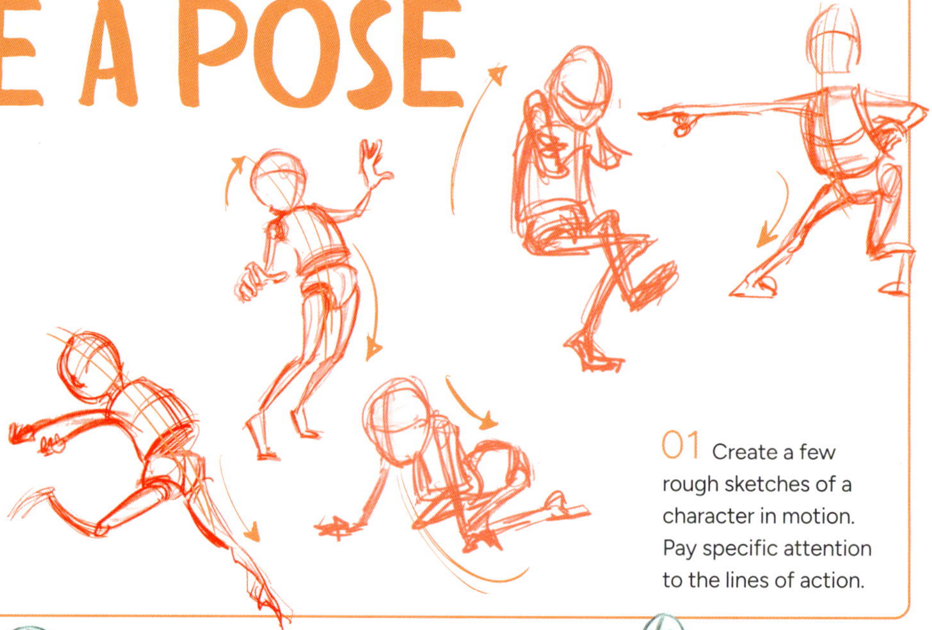

01 Create a few rough sketches of a character in motion. Pay specific attention to the lines of action.

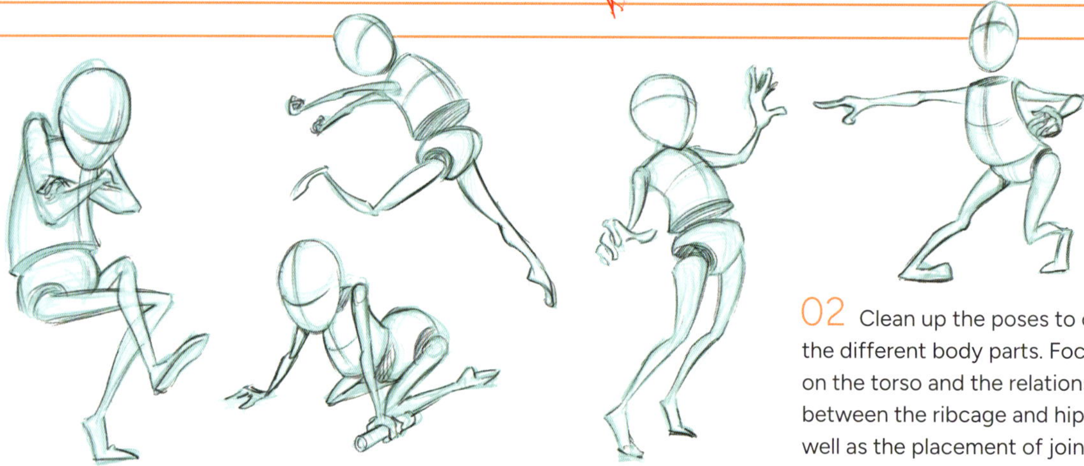

02 Clean up the poses to clarify the different body parts. Focus on the torso and the relationship between the ribcage and hips, as well as the placement of joints.

03 Reduce the opacity of the layer in step 02. Next, create a new layer and roughly sketch your original character on top of the poses. Notice how the joints are positioned to better capture the essence of each pose.

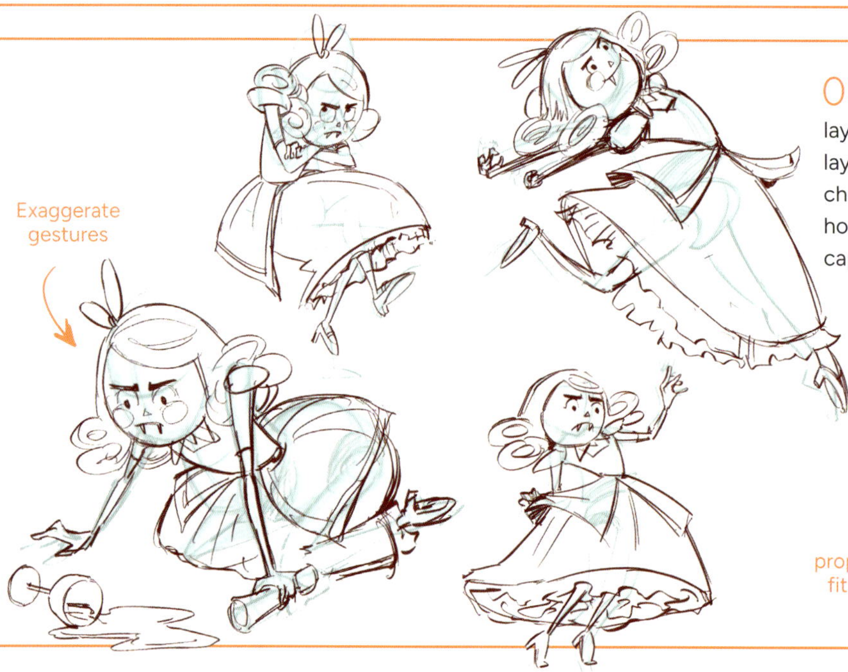

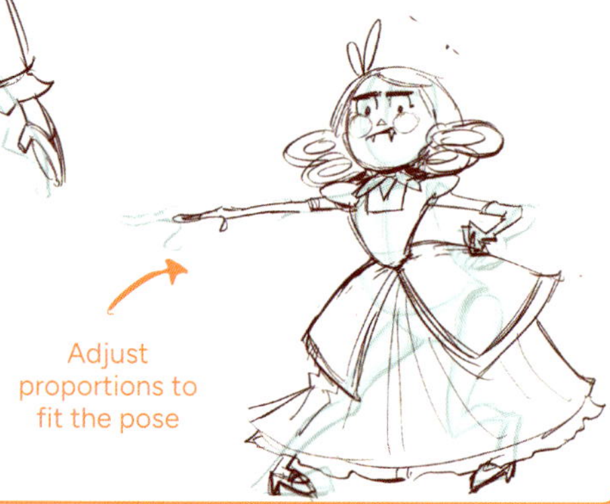

04 Refine the sketches, paying attention to the proportions of your character, as these are likely different from the reference character. Make sure the proportions are consistent across all five designs.

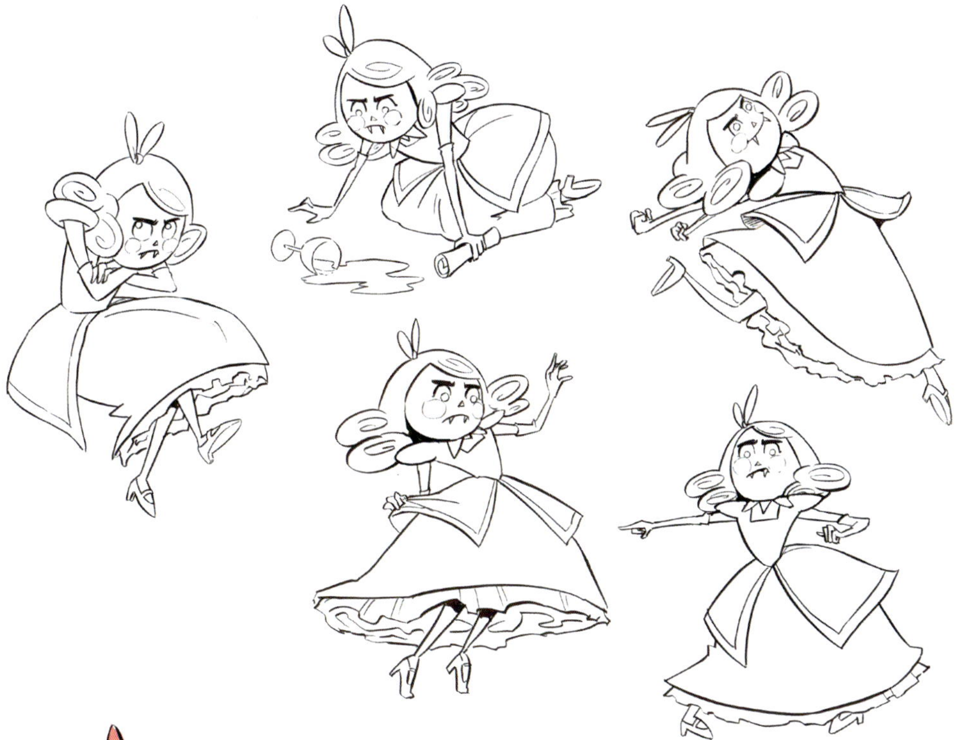

05 Add colour and simple details to finish.

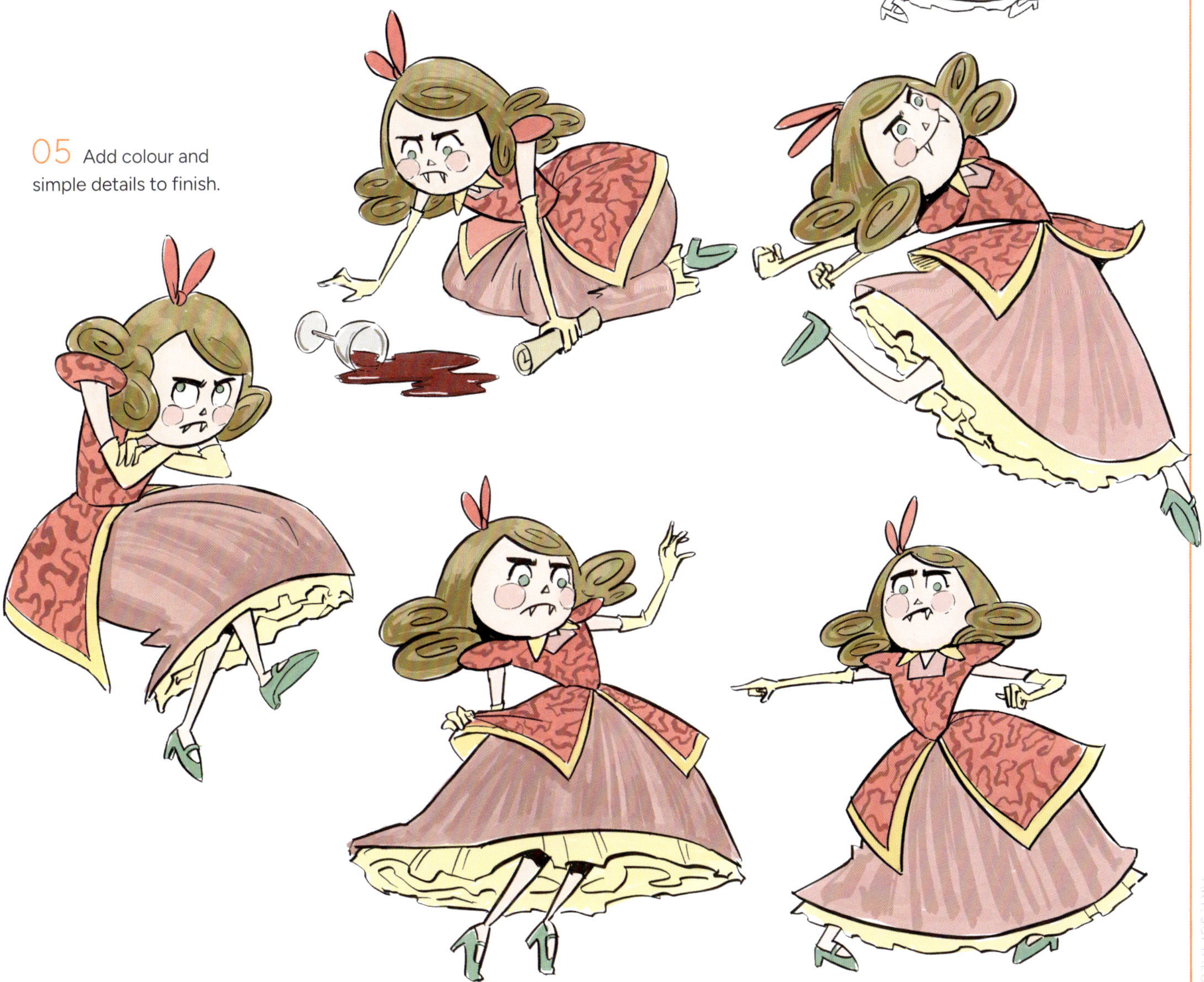

ART: JUI TALUKDER

HUMAN TO CREATURE

INTERMEDIATE ●●

Create a stylized animal by incorporating human elements.

Remember – the creature you design doesn't have to exist in the 'real world'. Let your imagination run wild! This exercise will help you to better understand elements like colour and proportion, while allowing you to flex your creative muscles.

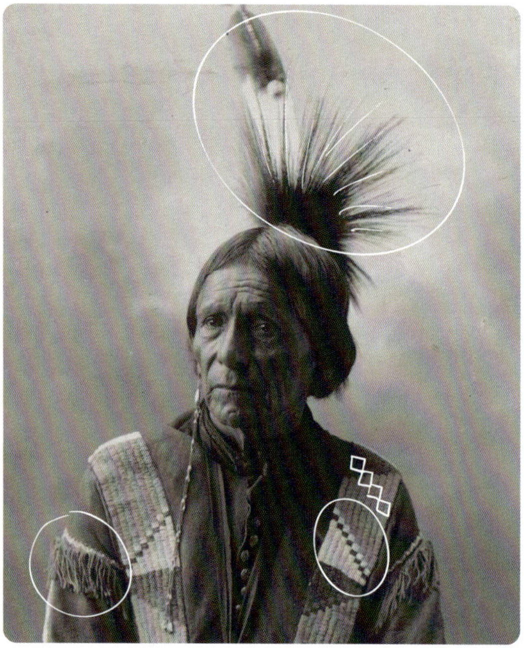

PEATWY TUCK, SAC & FOX, PHOTOGRAPHED BY F. A. RINEHART, C. 1898, ON UNSPLASH

01 Pick two reference images – one human and one animal – and look for shapes, colours, textures, and patterns you can add to your creature design.

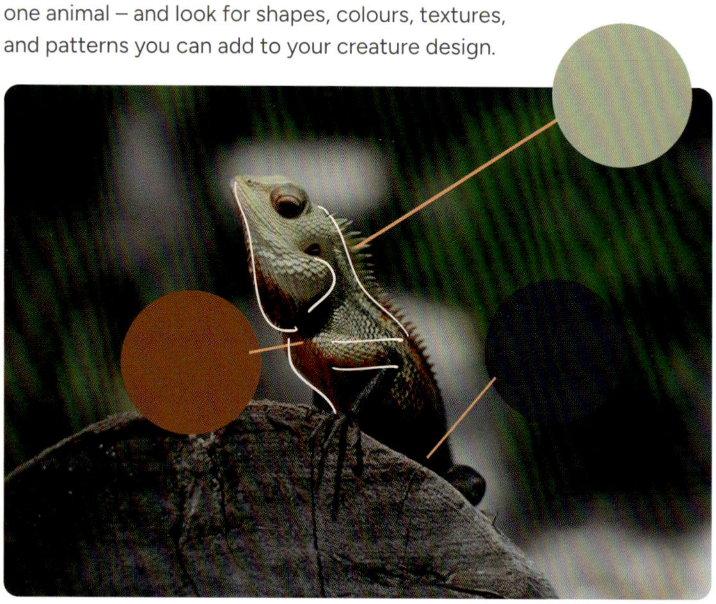

PHOTO BY ALEKSEI ZHIVILOV ON UNSPLASH

02 Sketch your creature using only the animal reference as inspiration. Don't just copy it – explore how you can make the design your own.

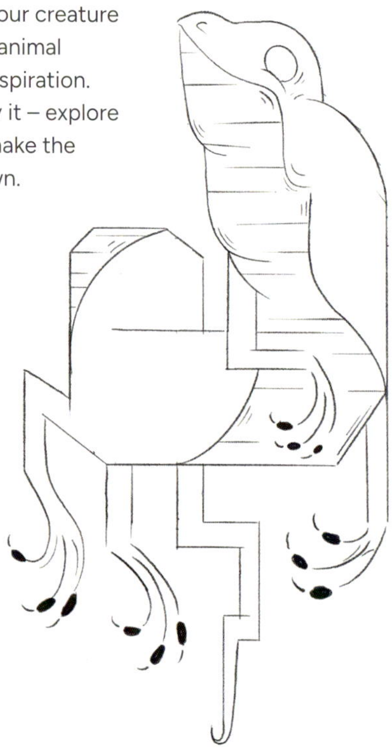

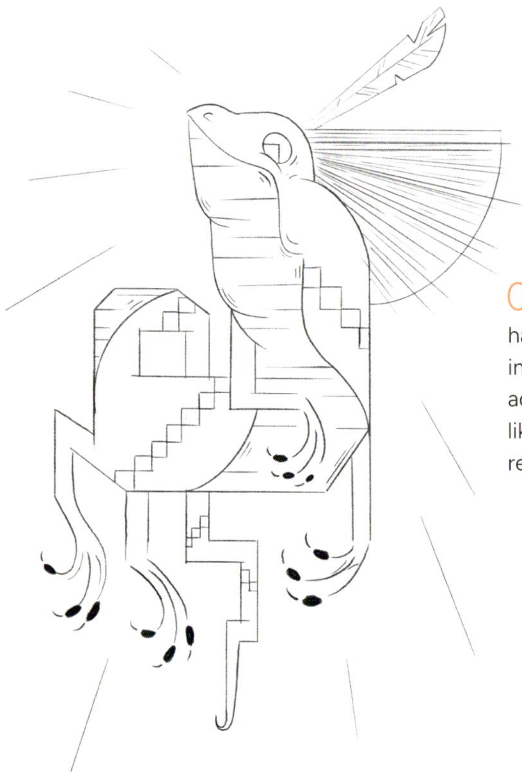

03 Once you're happy with your initial sketch, start adding elements you like from the human reference image.

04 Introduce simple colour to create a silhouette and check the design is clearly readable.

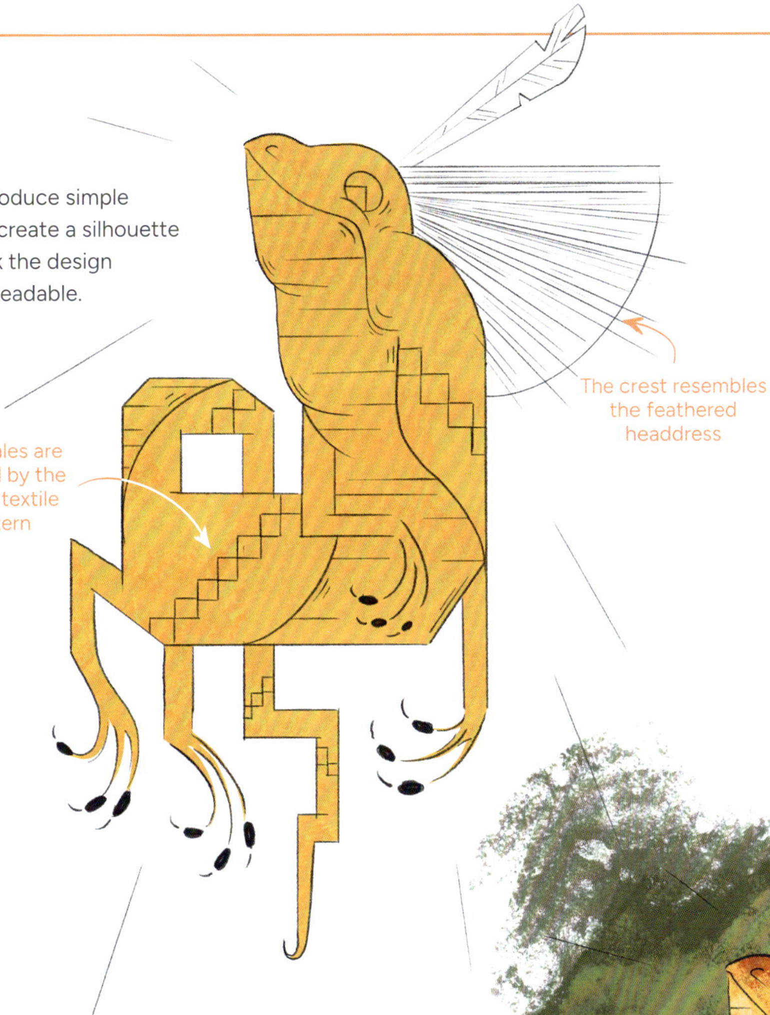

05 Continue to add colour, patterns, and texture, referring back to your reference photos for inspiration.

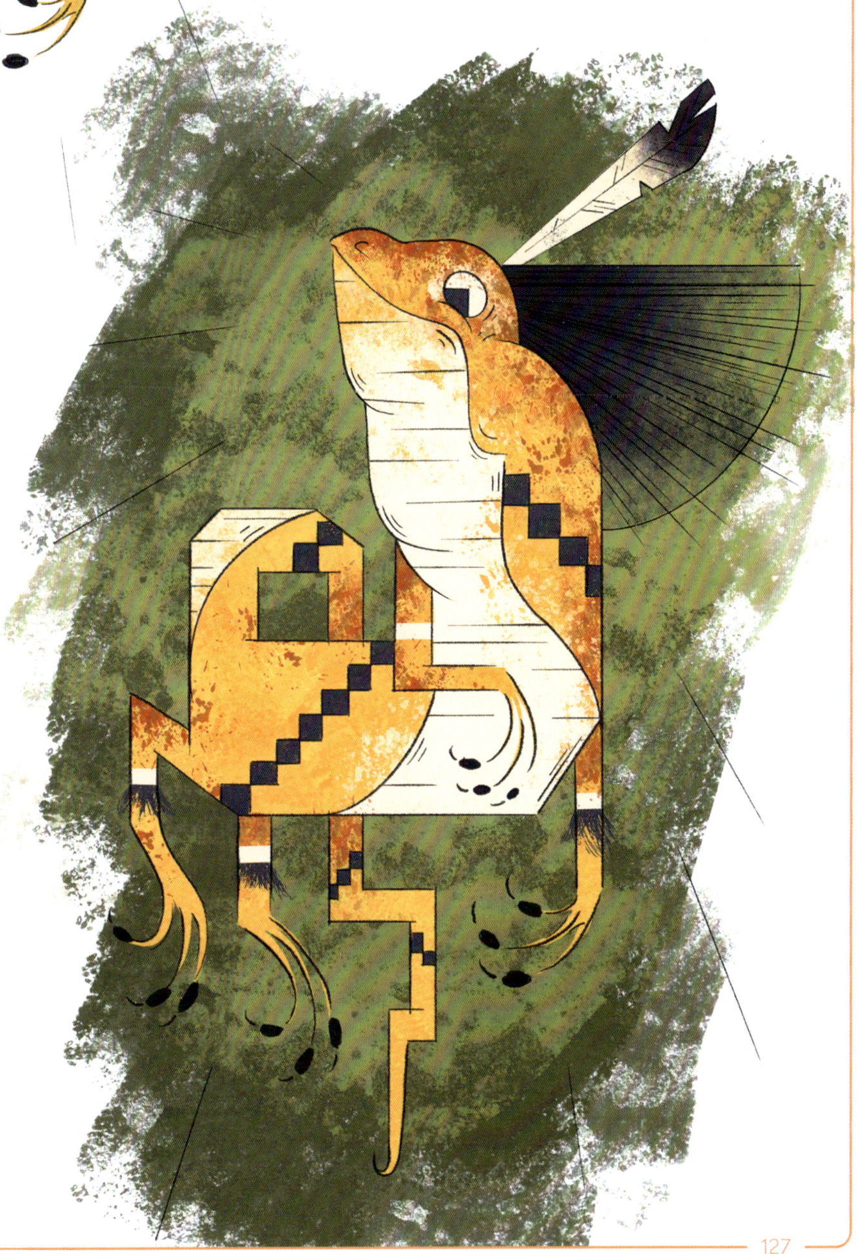

ART: LANDER STRIJBOL

CREATURE TO HUMAN

INTERMEDIATE ●●

Create a stylized human character by incorporating animal-like elements.

Choose a mammal, reptile, bird, or fish and consider which human feature you can expand, contract, or contort to resemble it. For a fun challenge, pick a family member and their favourite animal.

01 Start by creating a sketch of your human reference. Familiarize yourself with the person and don't concern yourself with the final look just yet.

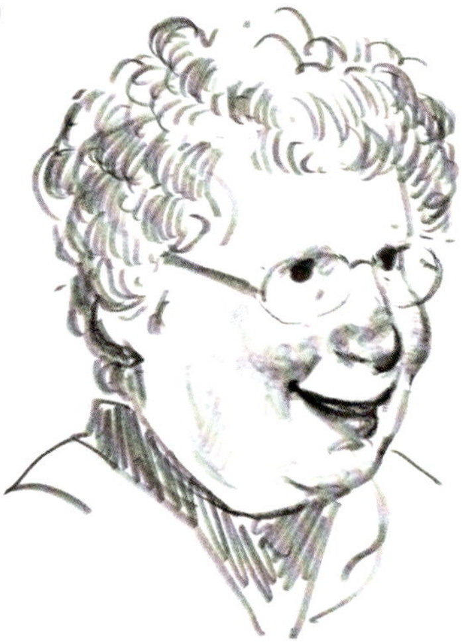

02 Sketch your chosen animal from different angles, studying its features to see how they could translate onto a human character.

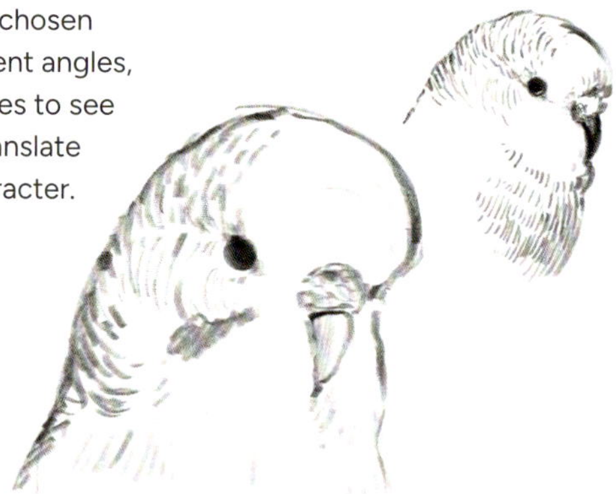

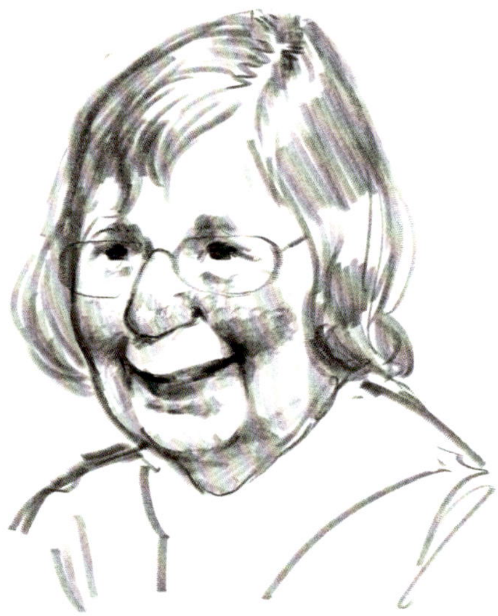

03 Create a second sketch of your human and begin tweaking their features to look like your chosen animal. In the image above, notice how the nose is slightly bigger and the hair looks soft and feather-like.

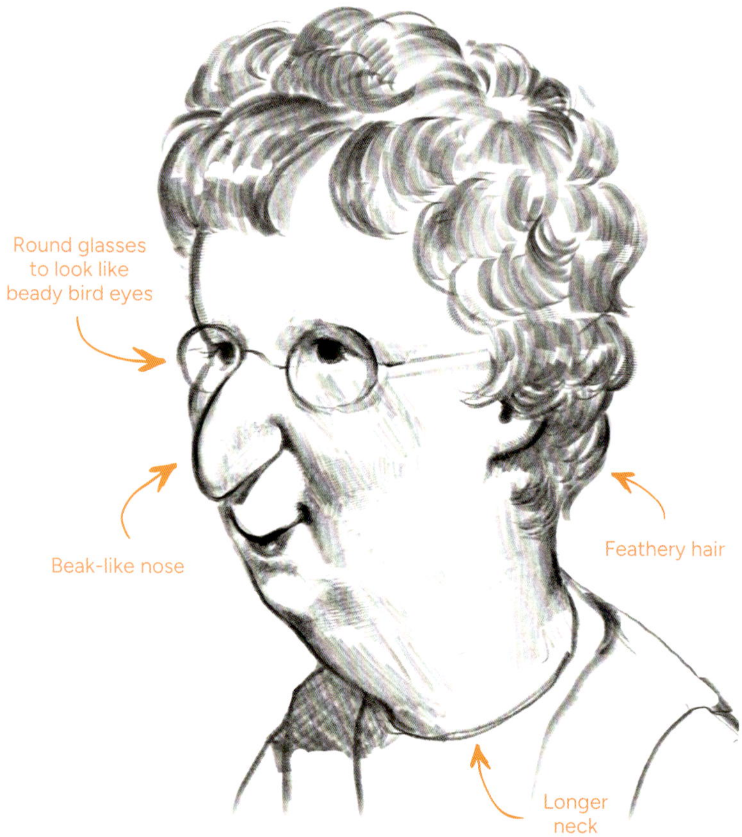

04 Get creative with how you incorporate the animal's features. Here the character's hair is 'puffed up' to resemble budgie feathers, plus circular glasses help to mimic the bird's round eyes.

05 Introduce simple colours to bring the character to life, referring back to your references.

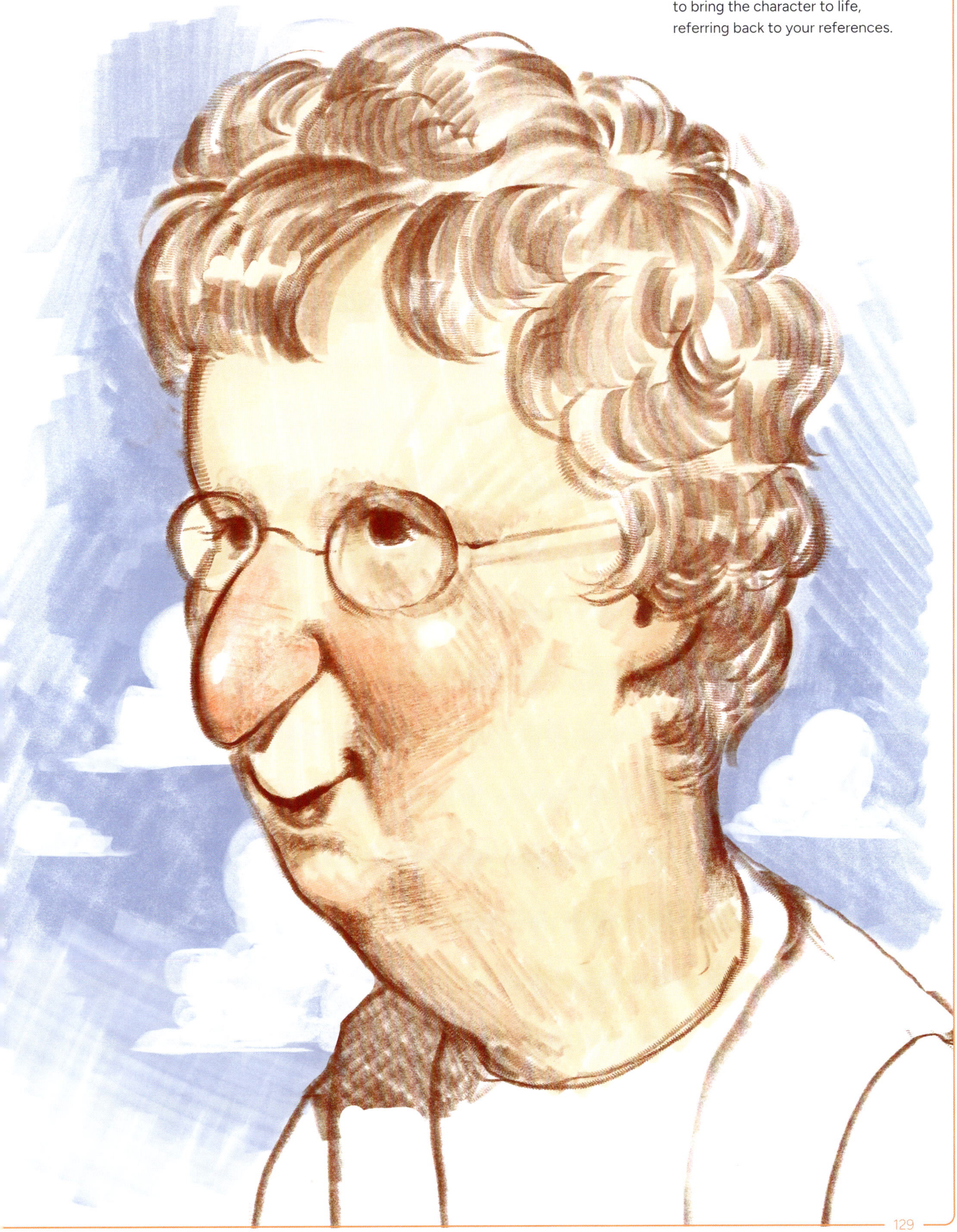

ART: MADI HARPER

COMBINING REFERENCES

INTERMEDIATE ●●

Combine two unrelated references to create a character.

For example, a mermaid and a pomegranate, a top hat and a tiger, or, as in this example, a watering can and a jellyfish. Carefully study the shapes, colours, and textures of each reference and consider how you could fashion these into a character design. This exercise will help you think outside the box and push your creativity.

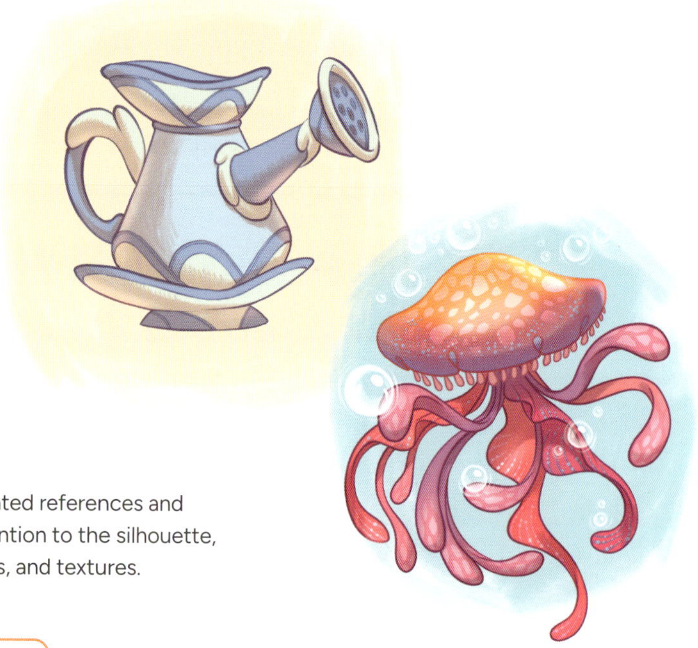

01 Pick two unrelated references and draw them. Pay attention to the silhouette, main shapes, colours, and textures.

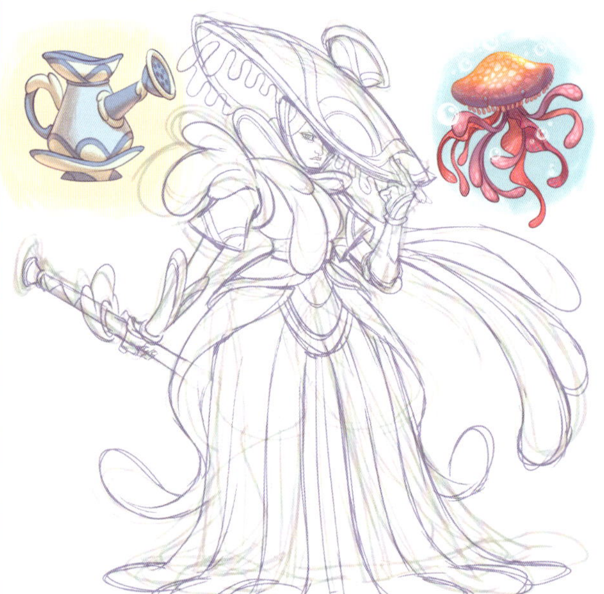

02 Explore which shapes you could use to form different elements of the character's design. See how the jellyfish tentacles inspire the samurai warrior's dress, while the watering can informs her hat and armour. This will create a pleasing contrast between hard and organic materials.

03 Draw neater line work to refine each element. Next, select a colour palette based on the references and add the base colours.

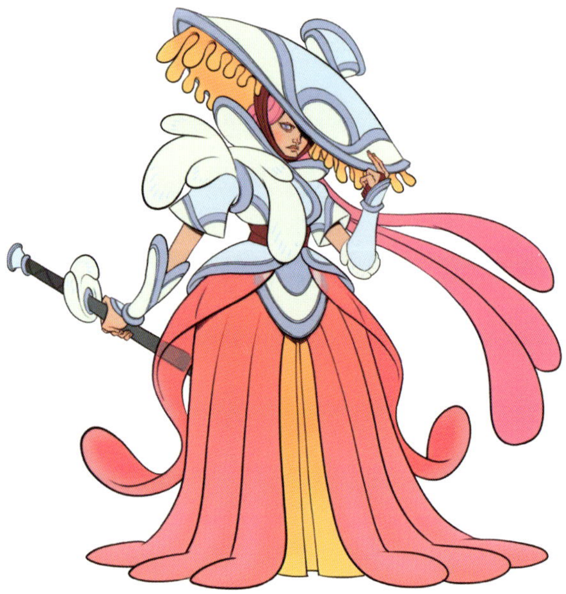

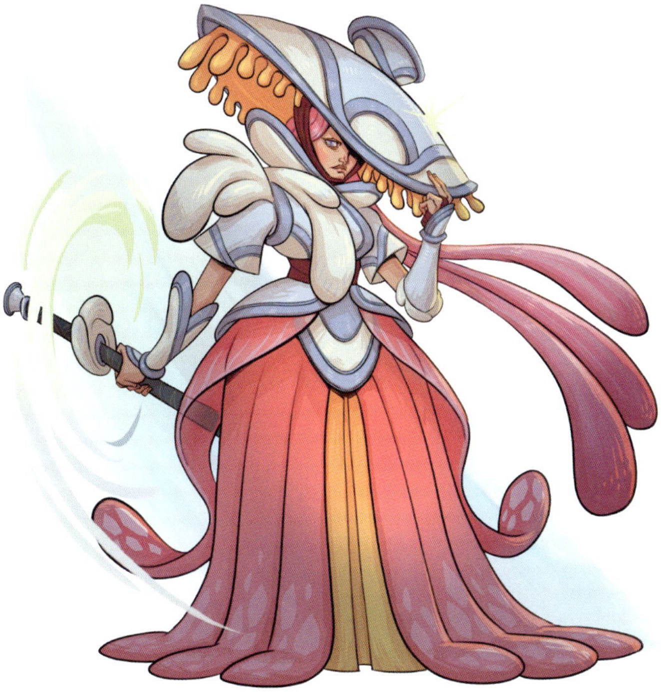

04 Define the various materials and textures, referring back to your references. Here the tentacle-like oral arms are given stinging cells, while the watering-can armour has a smooth reflective sheen.

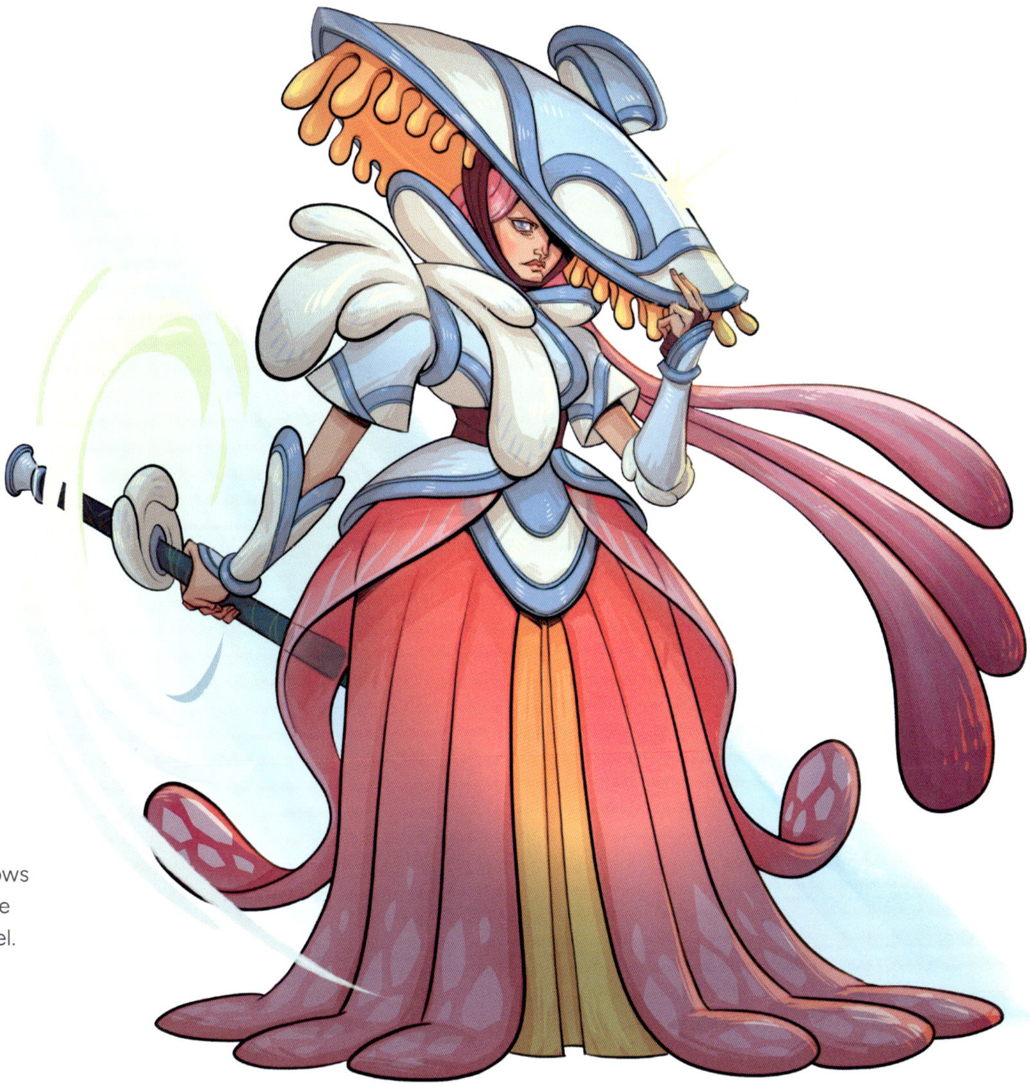

05 Introduce shadows and lighting to take the design to the next level.

SAME CHARACTER, DIFFERENT STYLES

ADVANCED ●●●

Draw the same character or creature in three different art styles.

Pick from manga, surrealist, art deco, comic book, Disney animation ... the choice is yours. This task is a useful and refreshing way to explore other styles and genres. Stepping into a new visual language can open your eyes to different ways of solving design challenges. Manga might exaggerate a character's expressions more than your usual style, while cubism may break down form in a way you've not tried before. It's not about changing who you are as an artist, but expanding your visual toolbox.

01 Select one of your existing character designs and consider different ways you could alter the style.

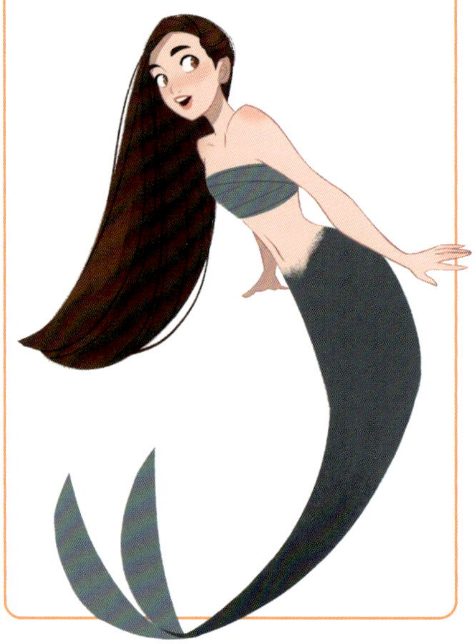

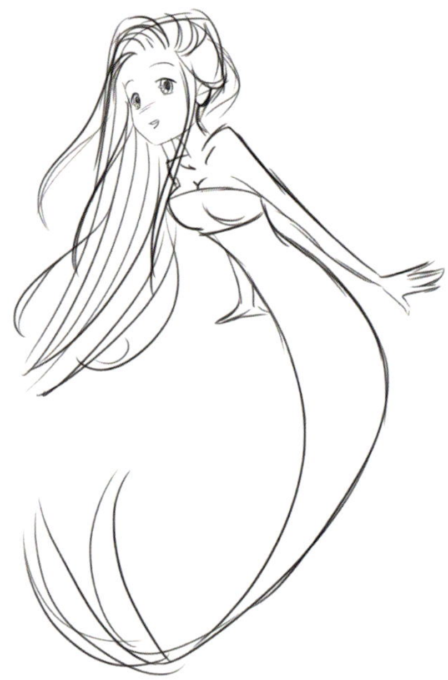

02 To redraw the character in a manga style, sketch the eyes with wide, round irises and a small mouth and nose. Make the chest slightly larger and the arms more slender.

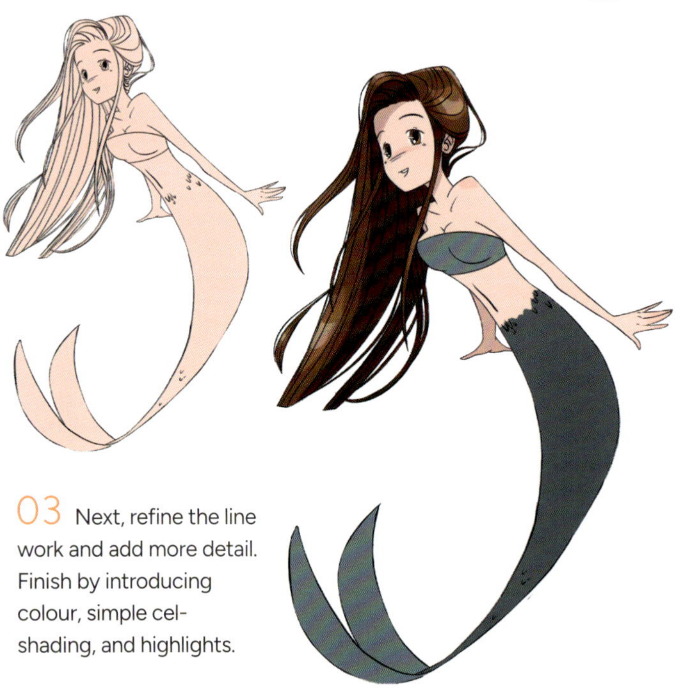

03 Next, refine the line work and add more detail. Finish by introducing colour, simple cel-shading, and highlights.

04 To reinterpret the character in a cubist style, experiment with bold, geometric shapes. Don't be scared to be a bit abstract.

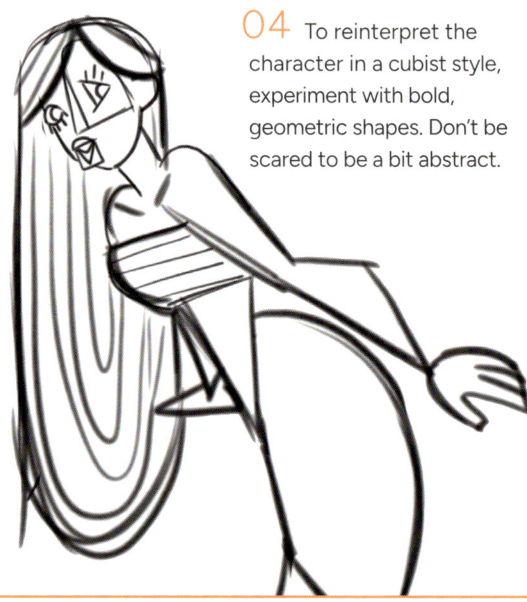

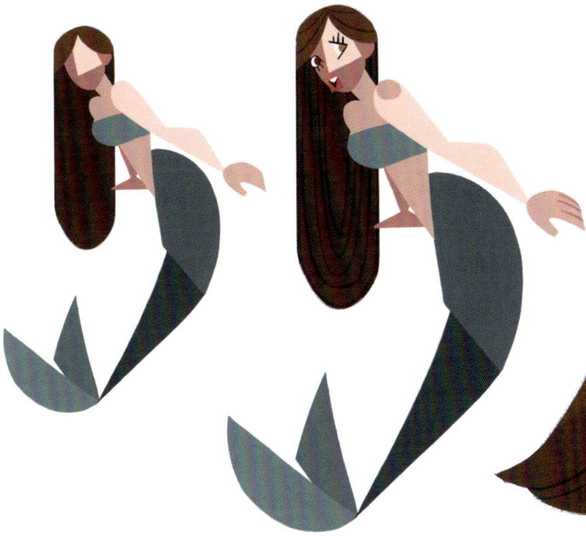

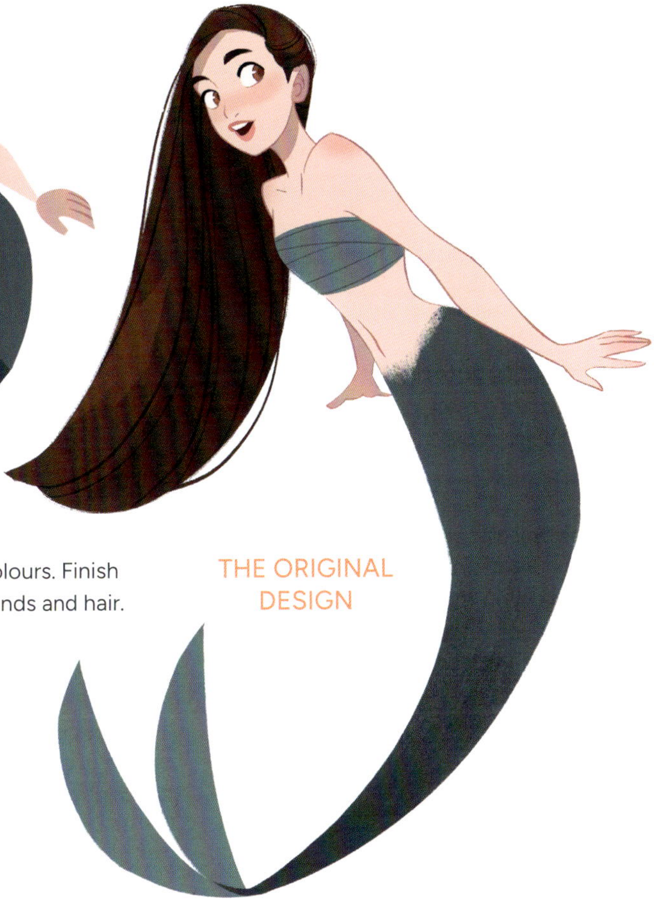

05 Next, refine the fragmented shapes and add flat colours. Finish by painting in the facial features, plus line work on the hands and hair.

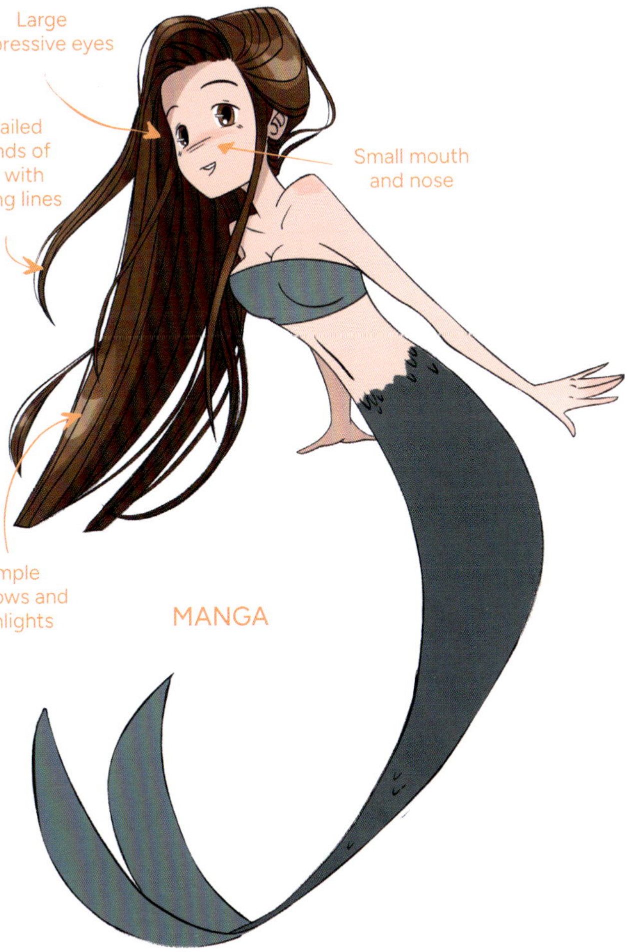

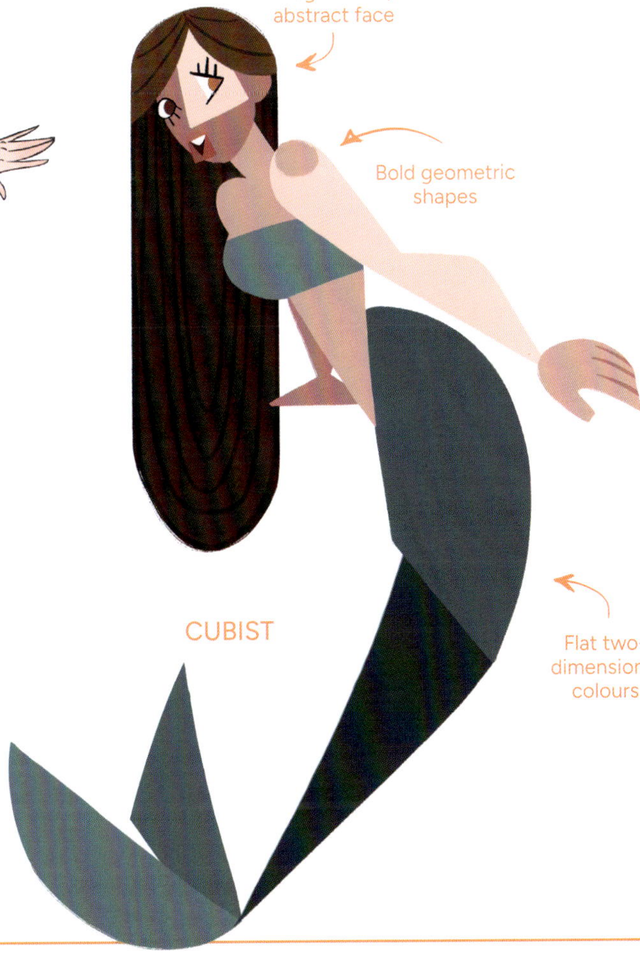

06 Compare all three designs. Consider what you do and don't like about each style, plus how you could incorporate certain stylistic choices into your character designs going forwards.

ART PERNILLE ØRUM

GENRE JUMBLE

ADVANCED ●●●

Create a character by combining your favourite and least favourite genres or themes.

This task will encourage you to come up with a unique and interesting design that you may not have previously considered. This example will merge a fairy world with a spaghetti western to create a never-before-seen gunslinger fairy.

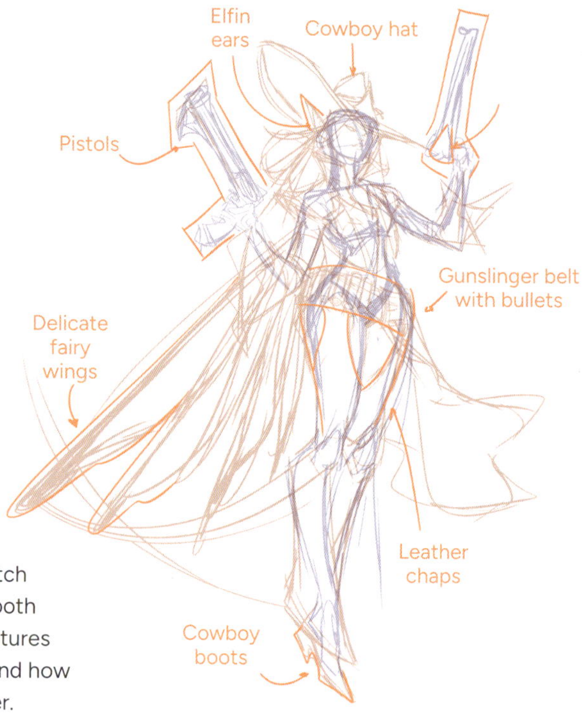

01 Create a rough sketch combining elements of both genres. Explore what features you can use from each and how they might work together.

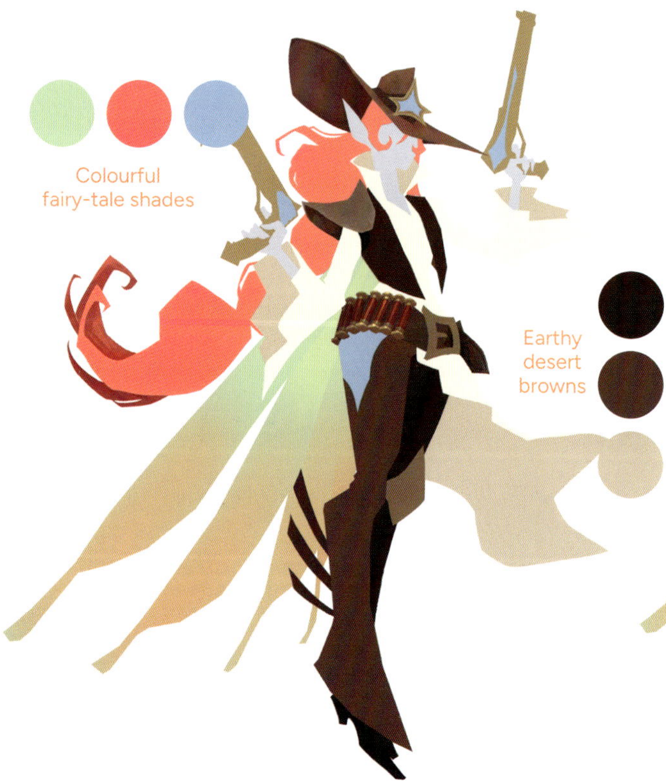

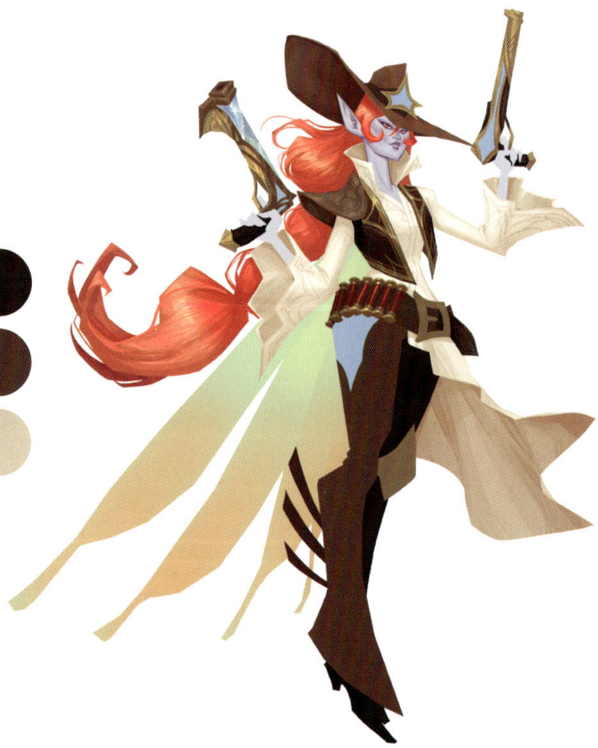

02 Think about the colours typically associated with each genre, then create a colour palette for the character that combines the two.

03 Begin to add light and shade to the various props and items of clothing, as well as additional detail. Note how the shiny fairy-tale plait and elfin ears sit alongside the cowboy vest and pistols.

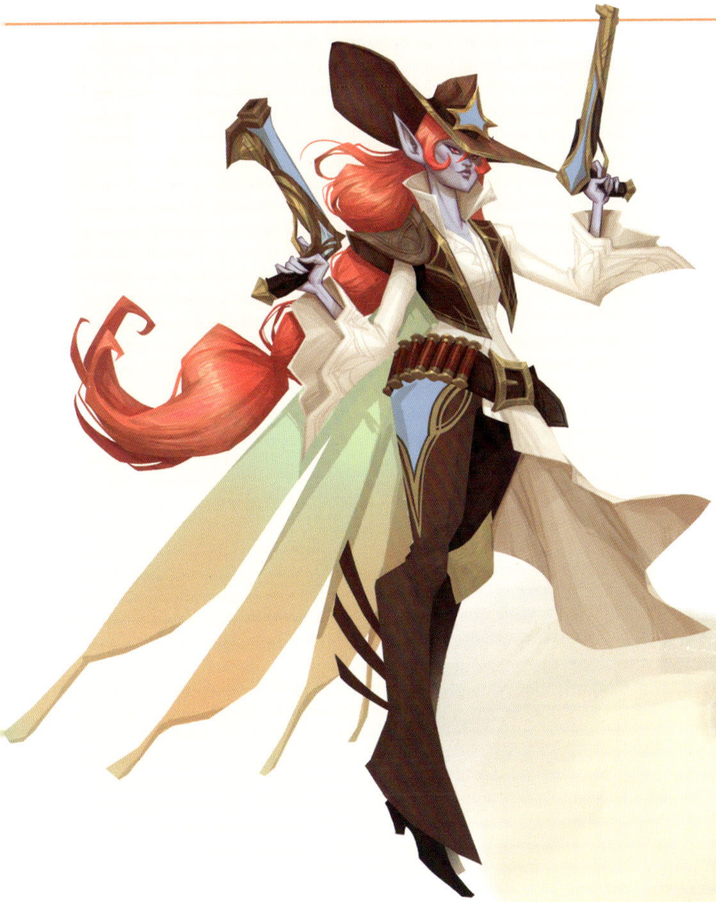

04 Continue painting light and shade on each element in turn, plus detailing that combines the two genres.

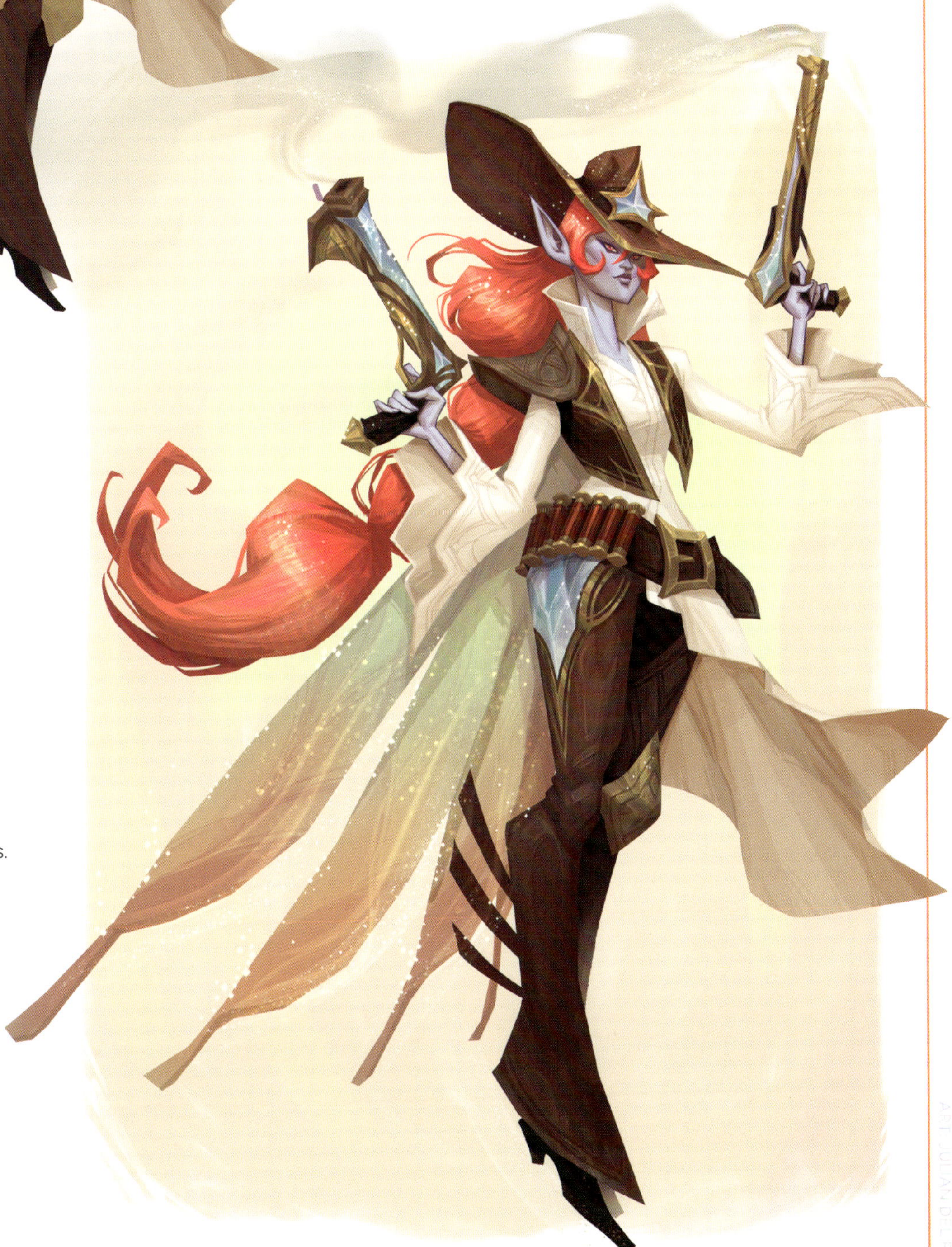

05 Add final touches, such as sparkly fairy dust on the wings and shimmering grey smoke emerging from the pistols.

ART: JULIAN DEL REY

AGEING A CHARACTER: PORTRAITS

ADVANCED ●●●

Design a character portrait at four different ages: infancy, young adult, middle-aged, and elderly.

When ageing a character, the challenge is ensuring they remain recognizable at each life stage. A certain hairstyle, facial feature, or accessory, such as glasses, can help to maintain continuity. By keeping these signature features consistent, the character is easily identifiable, even as they age.

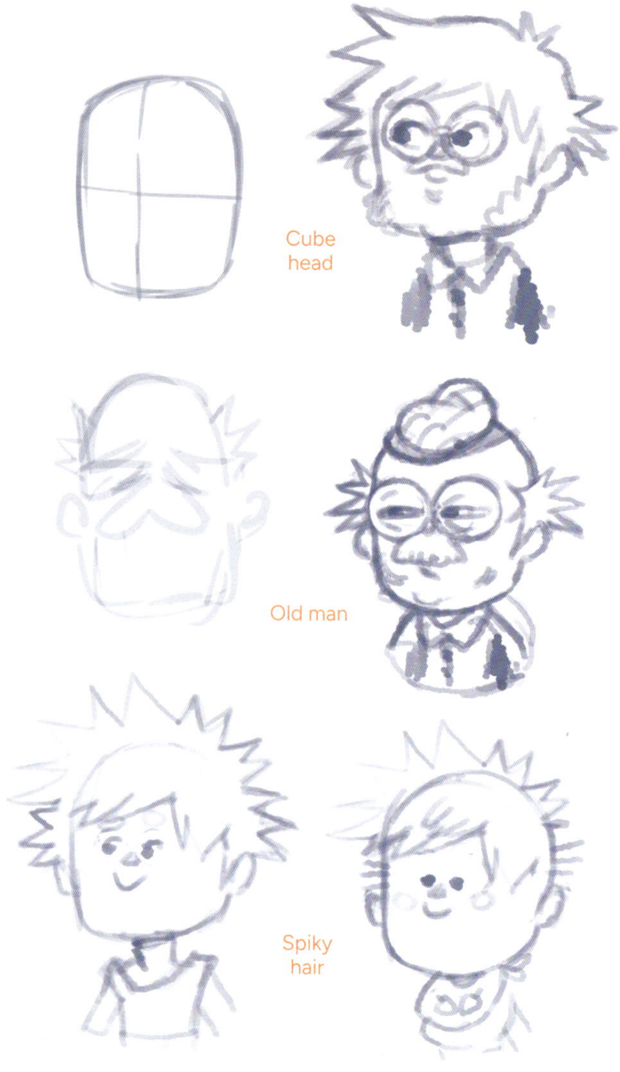

01 Start by sketching loose ideas for the character at each life stage. Don't worry if it's a little messy – this is just an initial concept.

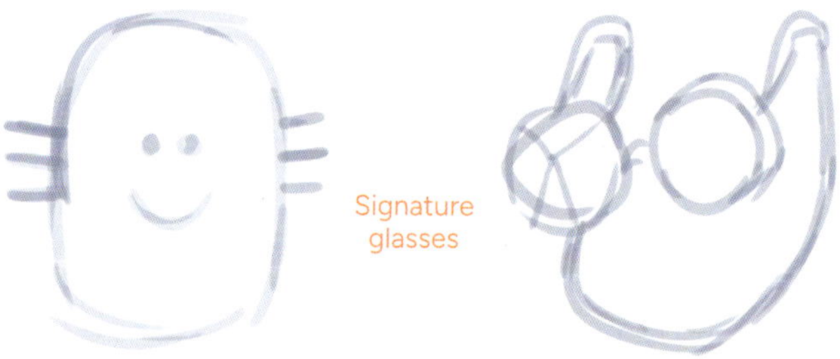

02 Redraw the character, refining the design to capture their personality. Notice how this character's face shape stays roughly the same as they age, though it is rounder in infancy and old age.

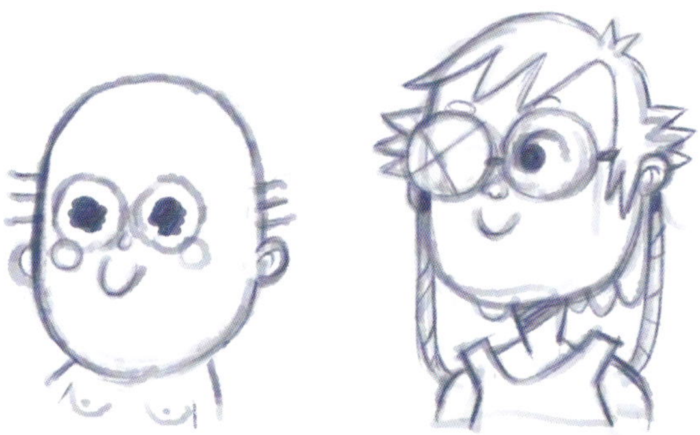

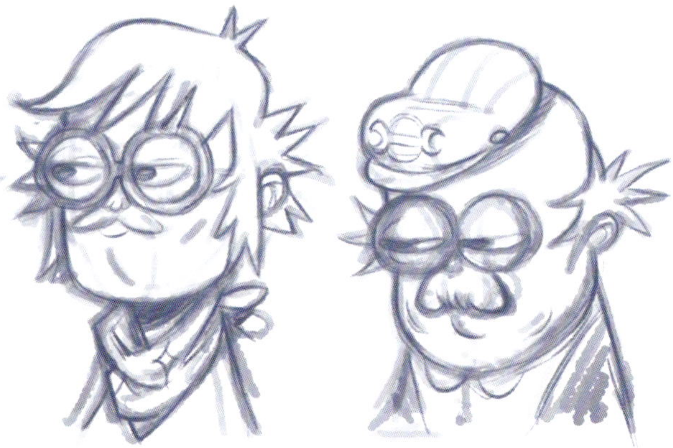

03 Draw neater line work, adding a base colour along with some tonal variations. The character's round glasses become a recognizable feature.

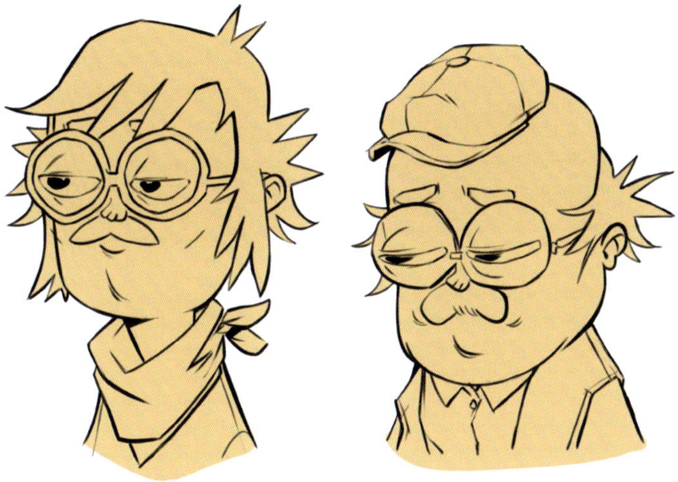

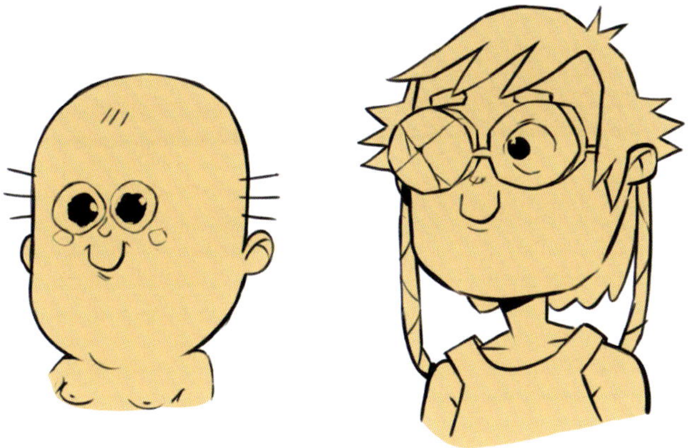

04 Apply flat base colours. Observe how the character's hair colour changes over the years, but keeps its spiky style.

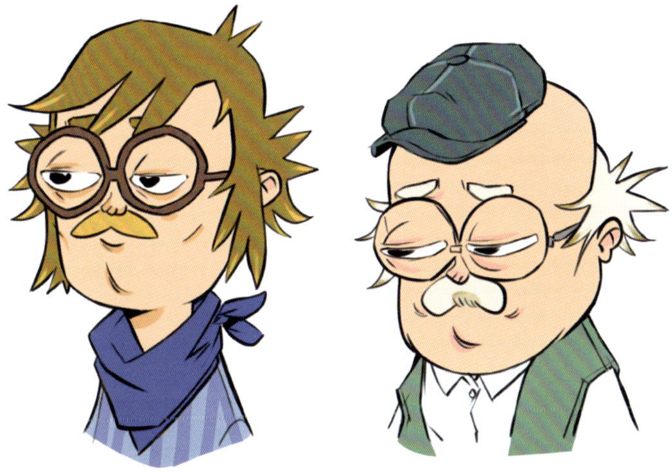

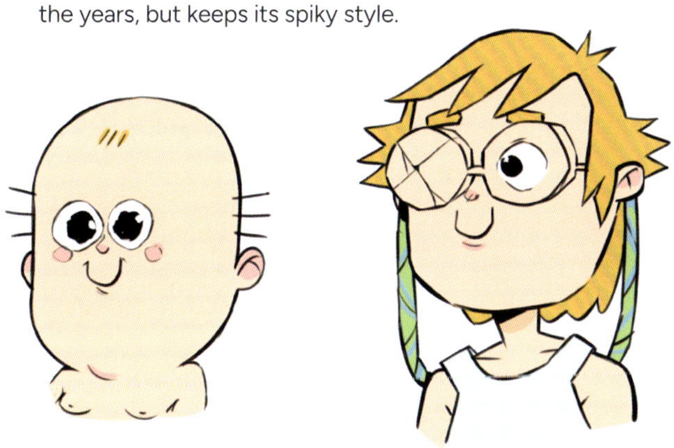

05 Add details that tell you more about the character at each age. As the years pass, this character increasingly likes a jazzy pattern or colourful stripe! Finish by adding highlights and shading to give the portraits some depth.

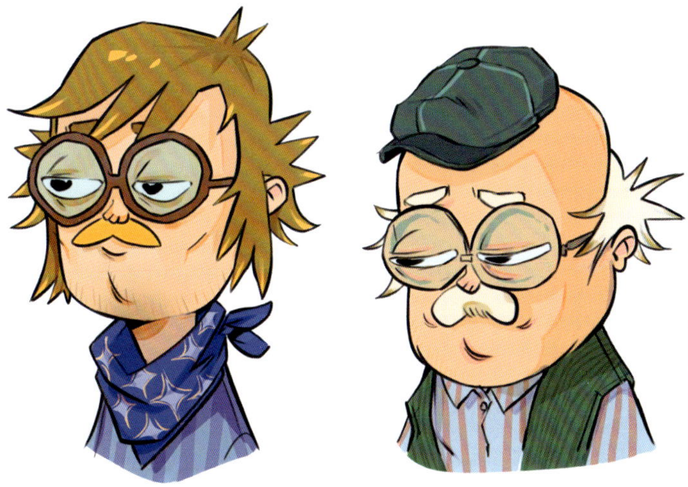

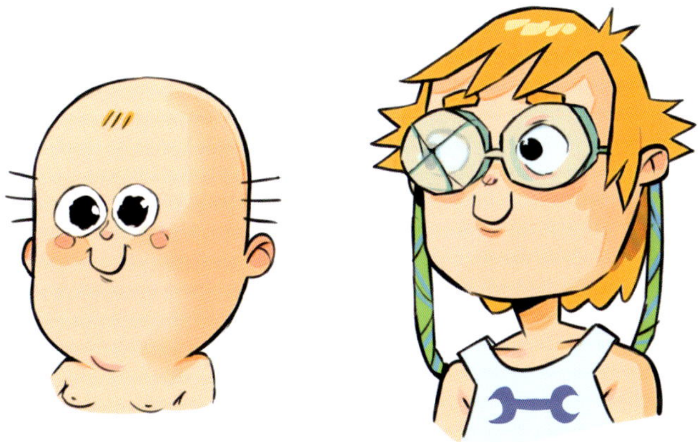

ART: LOBON LEAL

AGEING A CHARACTER: POSES

ADVANCED ●●●

Design the same character at four different life stages: childhood, teen, adult, and elderly.

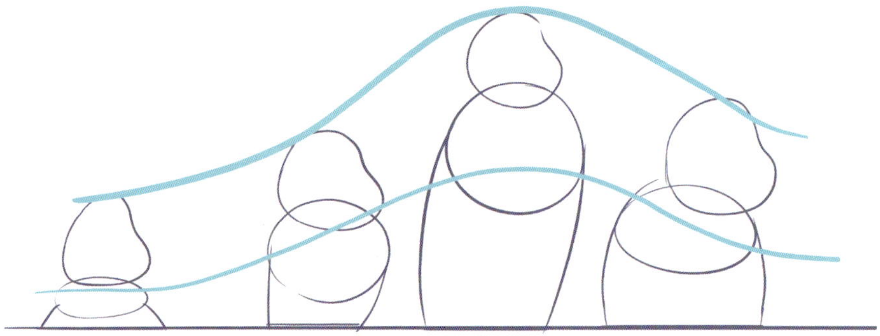

Consider how the body grows and matures over time and experiment with changes in shape, posture, weight, and wrinkles. Despite the changes, the character should still be recognizable at each life stage, perhaps through a specific hairstyle, colour palette, or certain facial features.

01 Start by sketching a rough age graph to visualize the character's shape and height at each of the four life stages. This will help you to analyse proportions and flow before committing to a final design.

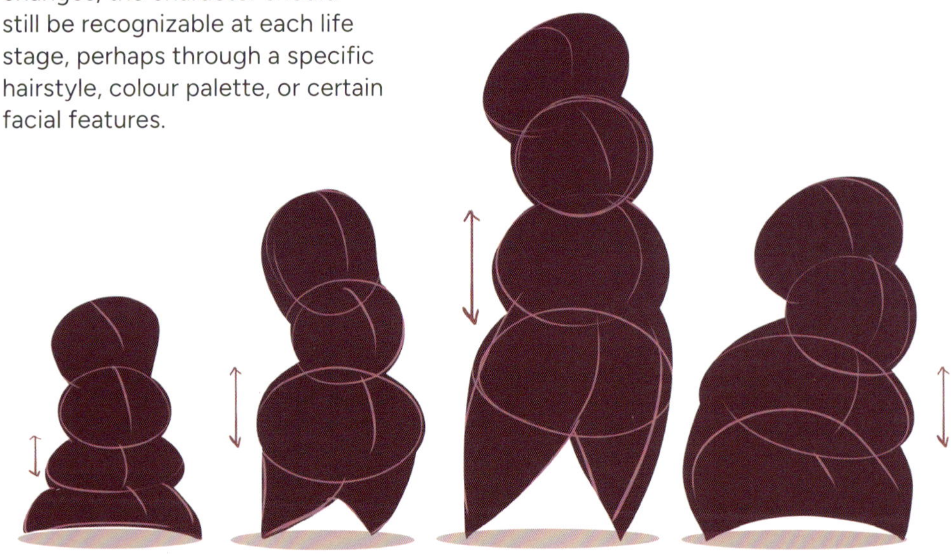

02 Whether a hunched or upright posture, weight gain or loss, proportions shift as you age. Identify overall shapes for the body and face at each life stage, experimenting with form and sizing.

03 Create a rough sketch for each stage, maintaining a visual connection by showing a consistent personality across the ages. Consistency in shape and form helps, but it's the attitude and essence that will truly make them feel like the same character throughout. You can also use this step to roughly paint in flat colours as a possible colour palette.

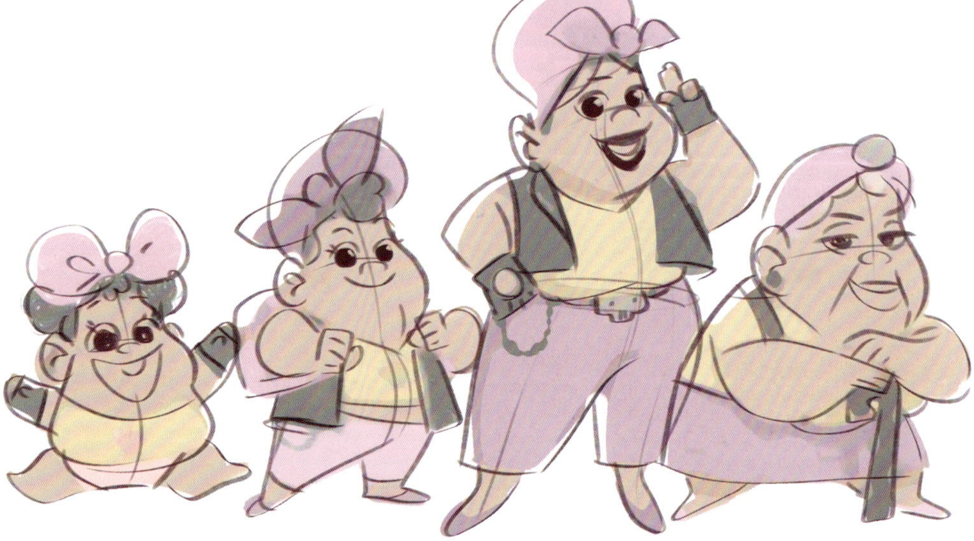

04 Draw more detailed line art, preserving the same vibe and energy across all ages. The characters must share a resemblance, no matter how young or old they appear.

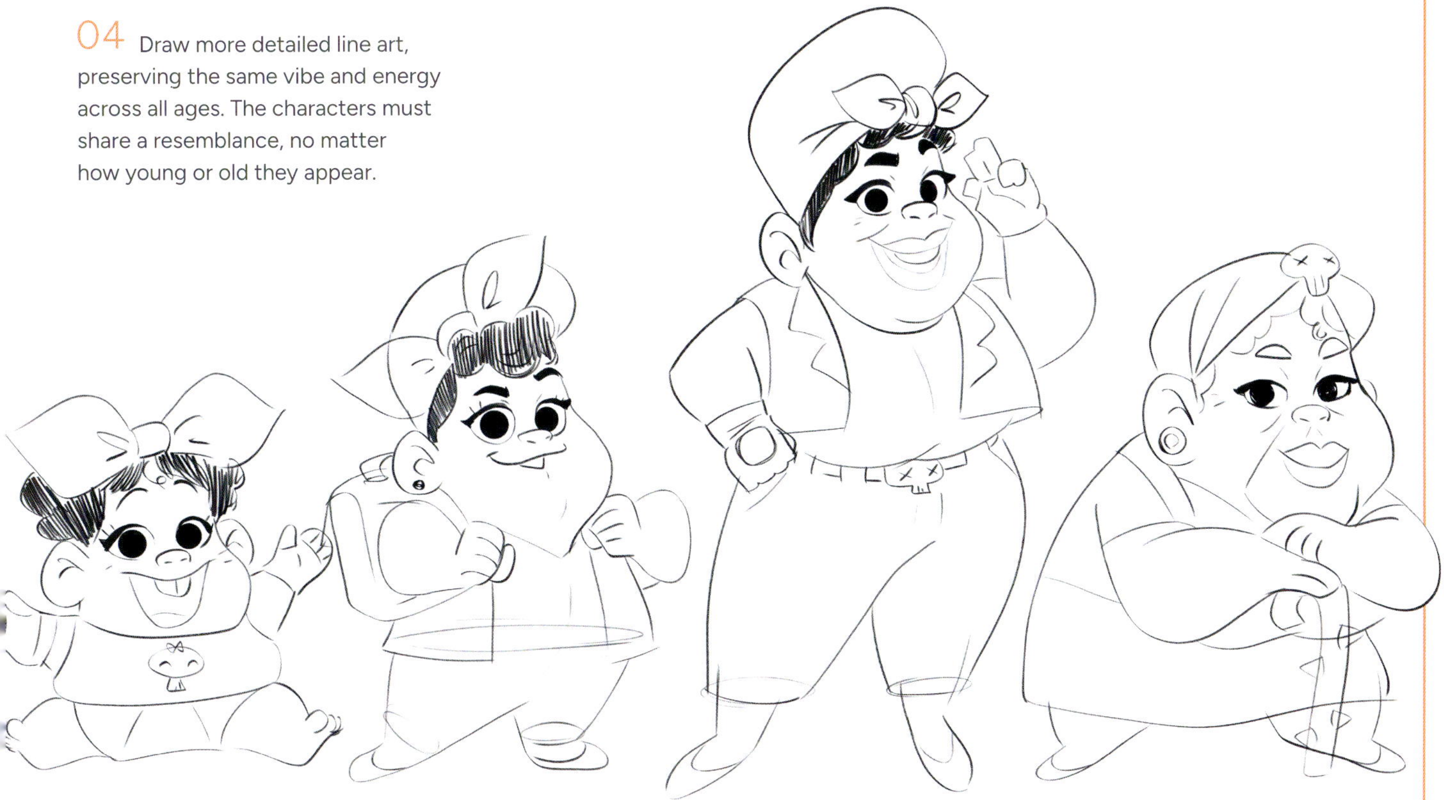

05 Refer back to your rough palette as you paint in the final colours, followed by light and shade. Finish with additional details and storytelling elements, such as her signature skull motif and upper-arm tattoo.

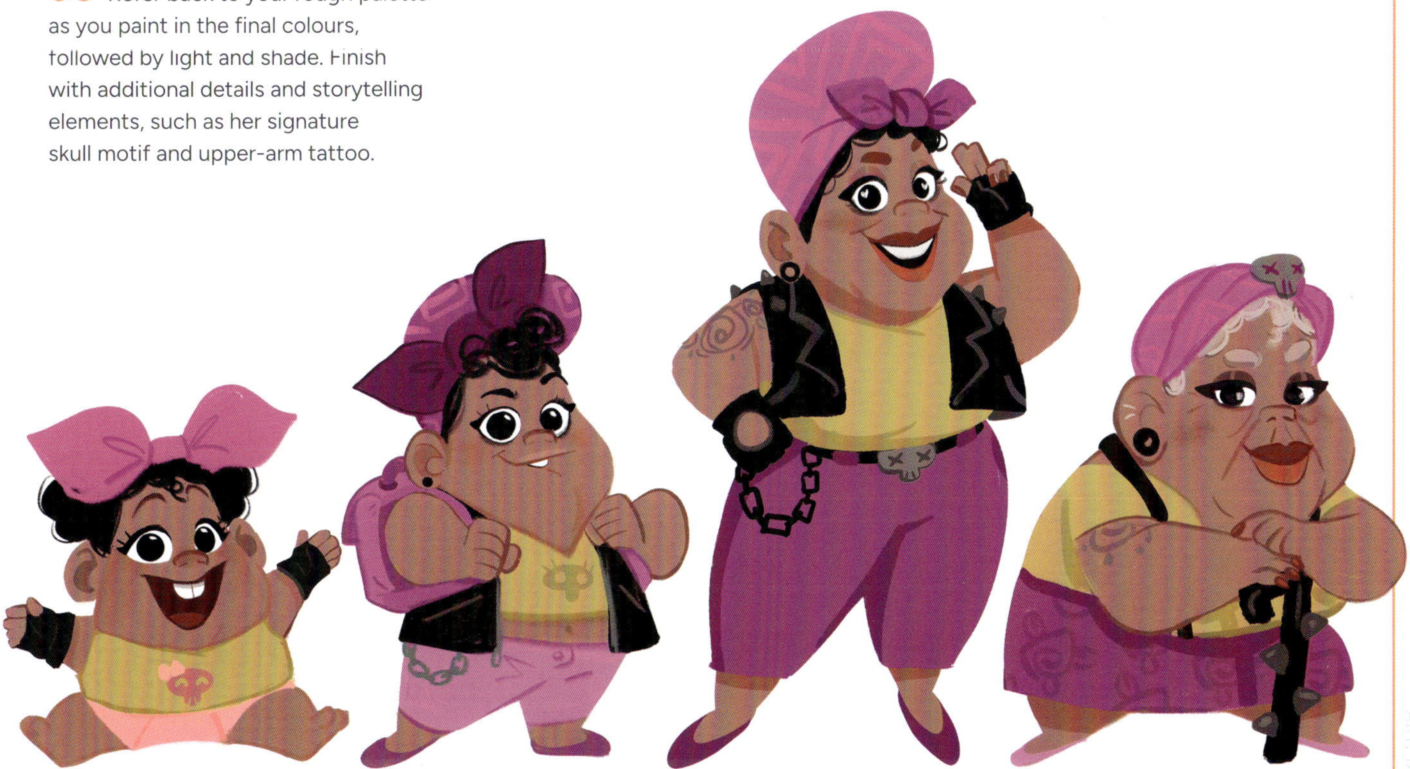

ART: TARANEH KARIMI

One-page challenges:

STARTING WITH SILHOUETTES

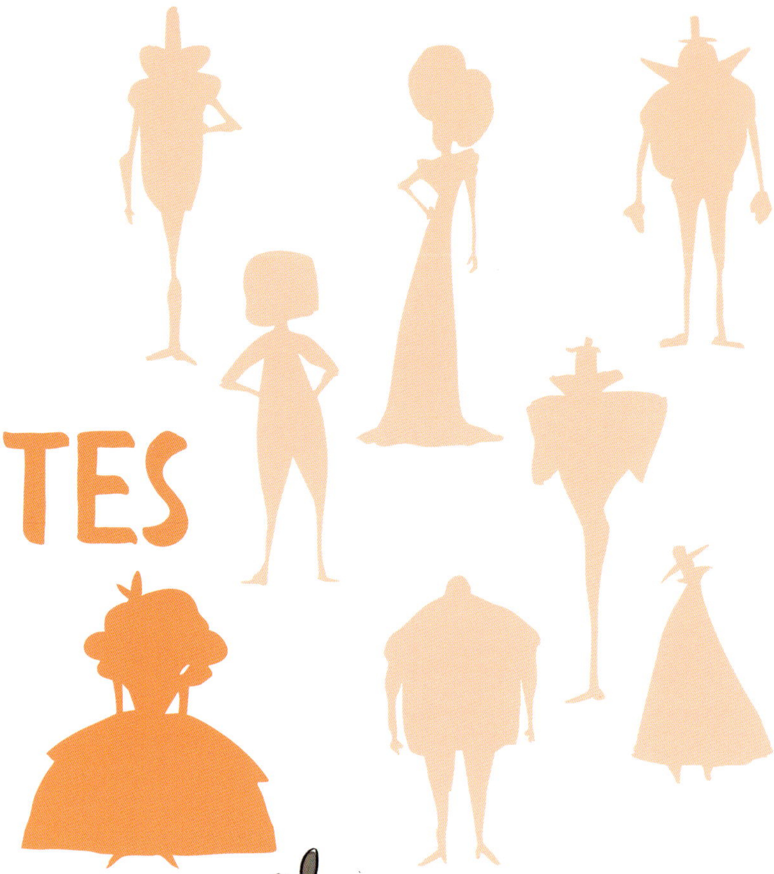

BEGINNER ●

Without sketching or outlining, use one solid colour to create silhouettes of thumbnail-sized characters.

Try to make the characters as abstract and interesting as possible – push proportions and shape language, include lots of negative space, and avoid uniformity. Finally, select one silhouette to turn into a character.

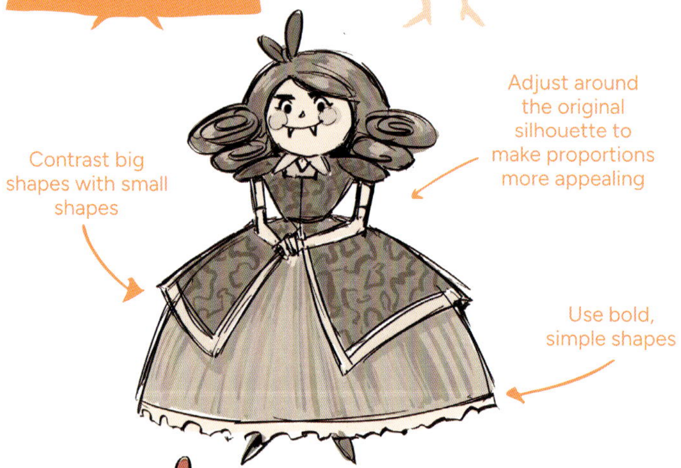

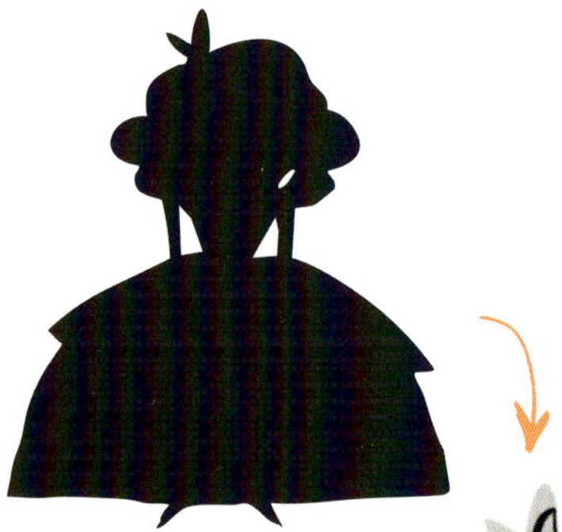

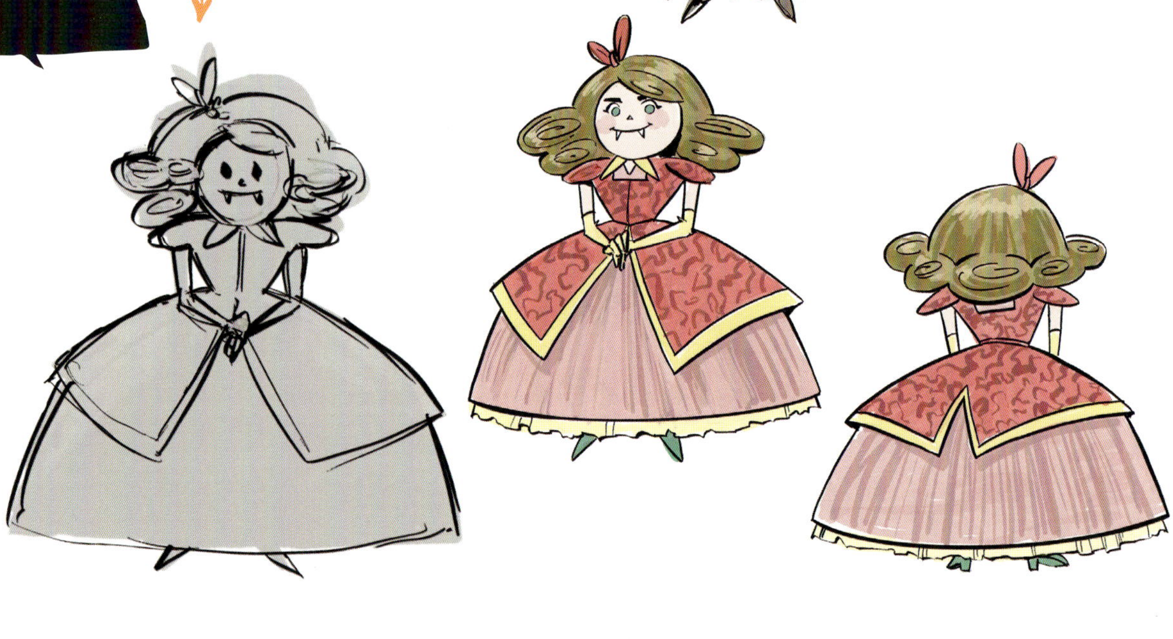

ANATOMICAL STUDIES

BEGINNER ●

Fill a page with studies of an anatomical subject that is outside your comfort zone.

This can be human or animal, hands, noses, feet, paws ... whatever you find difficult. This exercise is a great way to fast-track your practice in a certain area. For example, setting aside some time to get familiar with the anatomy of the foot, including all the different angles and ways it bends, will save you a lot of frustration in the long run. When you come to design a new character, you will already have that fundamental knowledge handy.

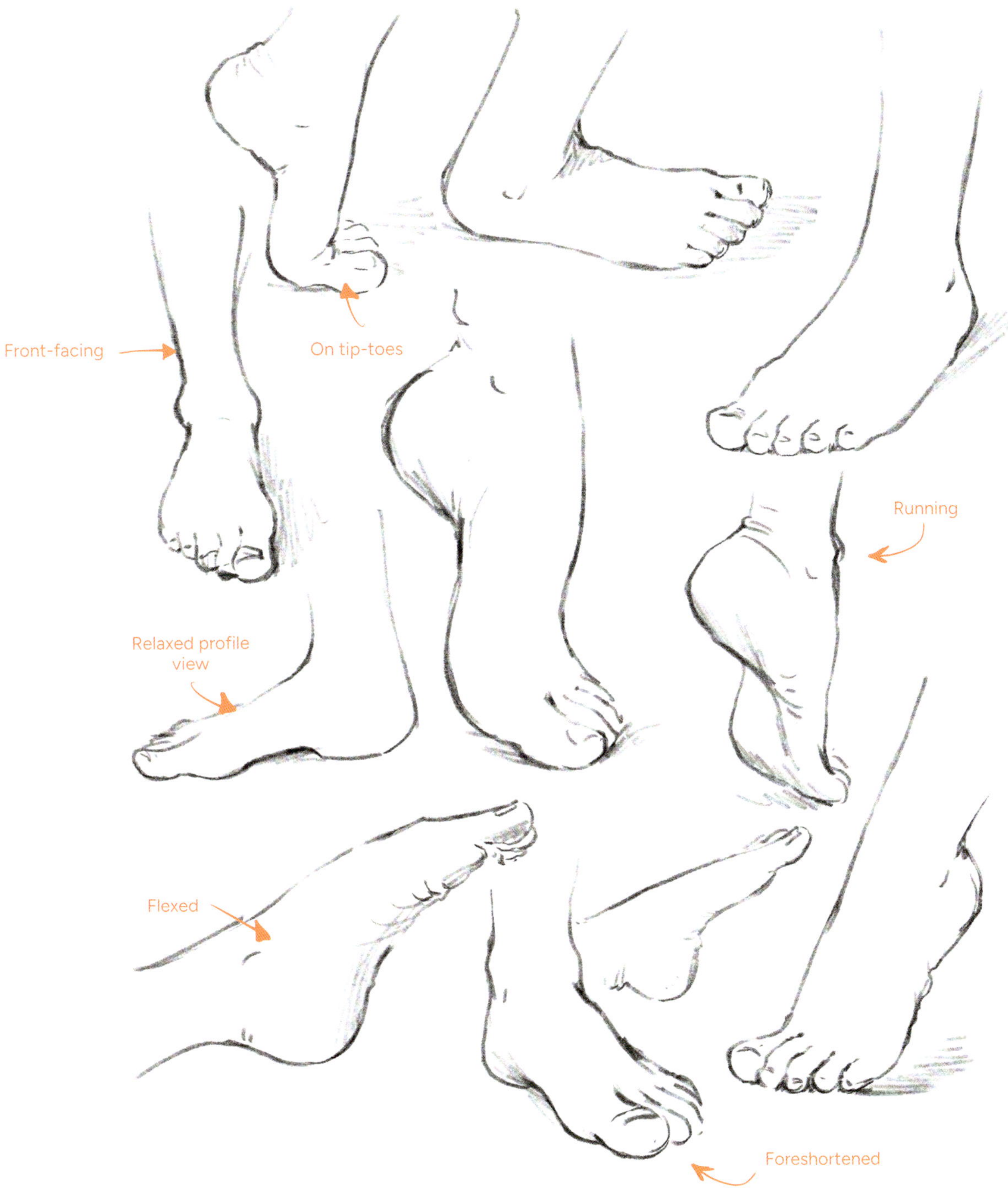

ART: MADI HARPER

CONTINUOUS LINE POSE

BEGINNER ●

Draw a pose without lifting your pencil from the paper/screen.

The technique of drawing with a continuous line allows you to capture the entire figure with energetic strokes. Use a light line weight to start, following the model's silhouette. Then with a second more controlled pass, define the volumes, focusing on the internal shapes and emphasizing curves and straight lines. Keep looking at your reference, making sure to spend more time observing the model than the drawing. By not lifting the pencil, you travel around the figure, enriching the drawing with multiple strokes rather than a single outline. This achieves a more visually appealing result.

Fill in details

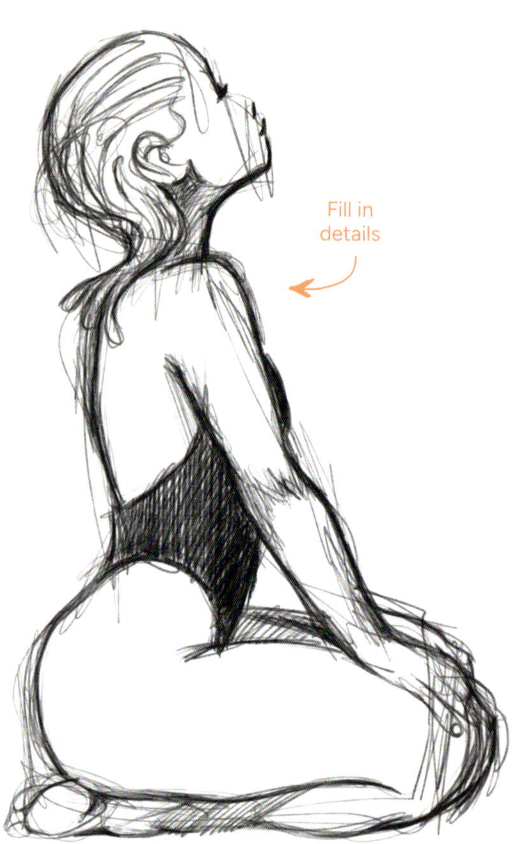

Use a light line weight to capture the silhouette

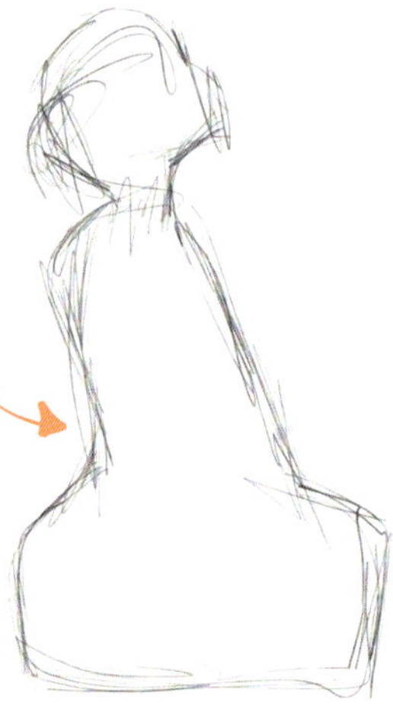

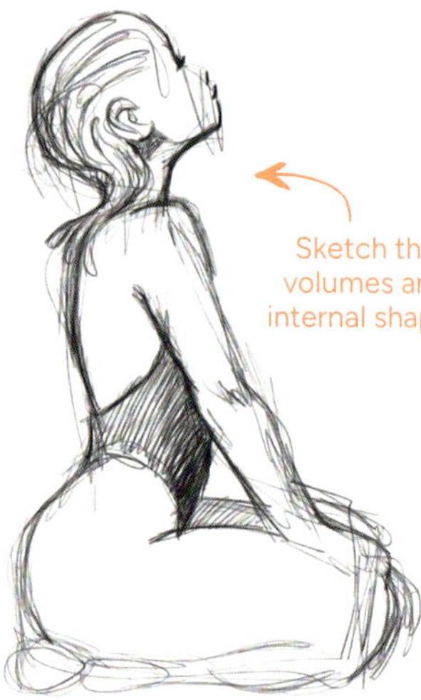

Sketch the volumes and internal shapes

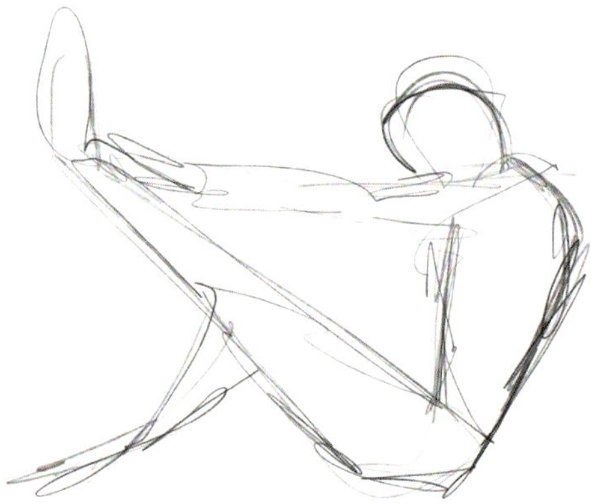

Multiple strokes enhance the drawing and provide visual interest

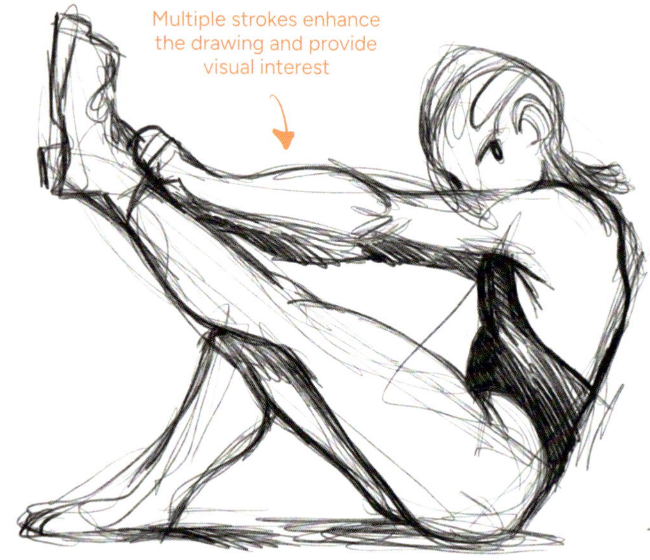

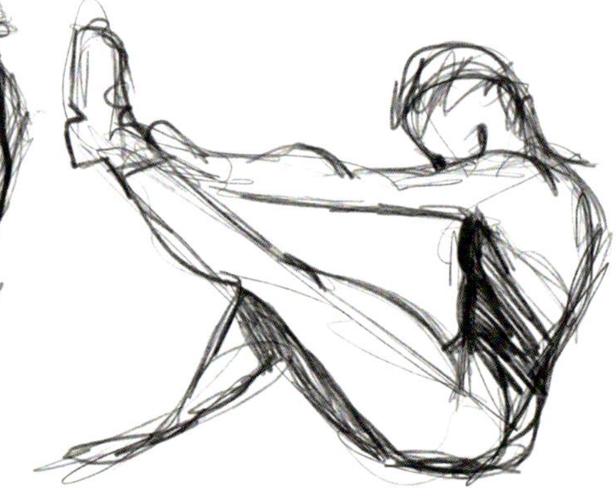

SHAPE LANGUAGE

BEGINNER ●

Design three variations of the same character: the first using only soft shapes, the second only angular shapes, and the third with a combination of the two.

Start by sketching a simple form from basic shapes, playing with sharp and curved lines to create different versions. How does this change the look and personality of the character? Shape language can be used to open up a realm of potential design possibilities.

ALL SOFT SHAPES

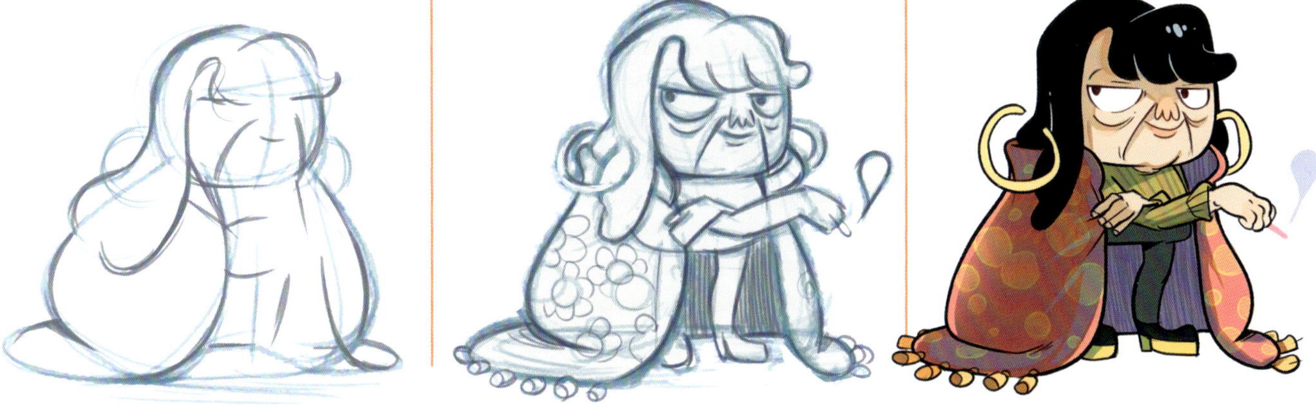

ALL ANGULAR SHAPES

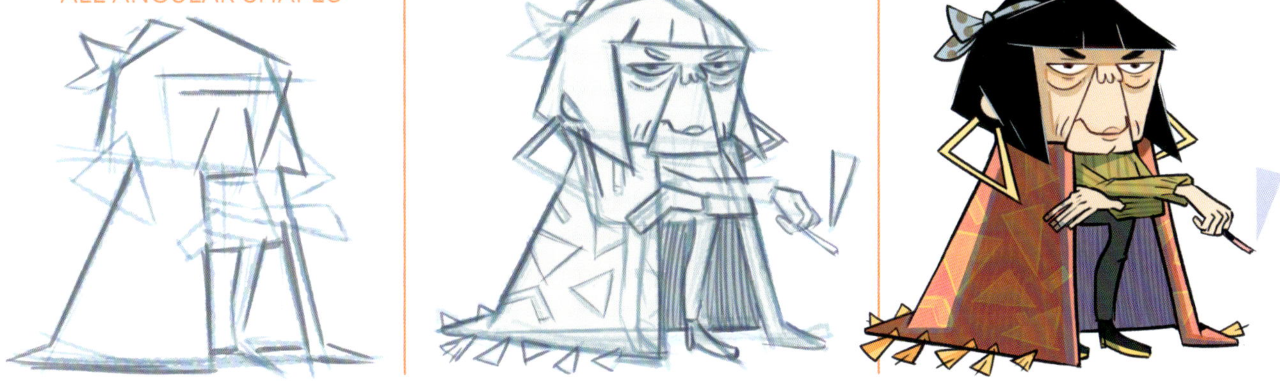

COMBINATION

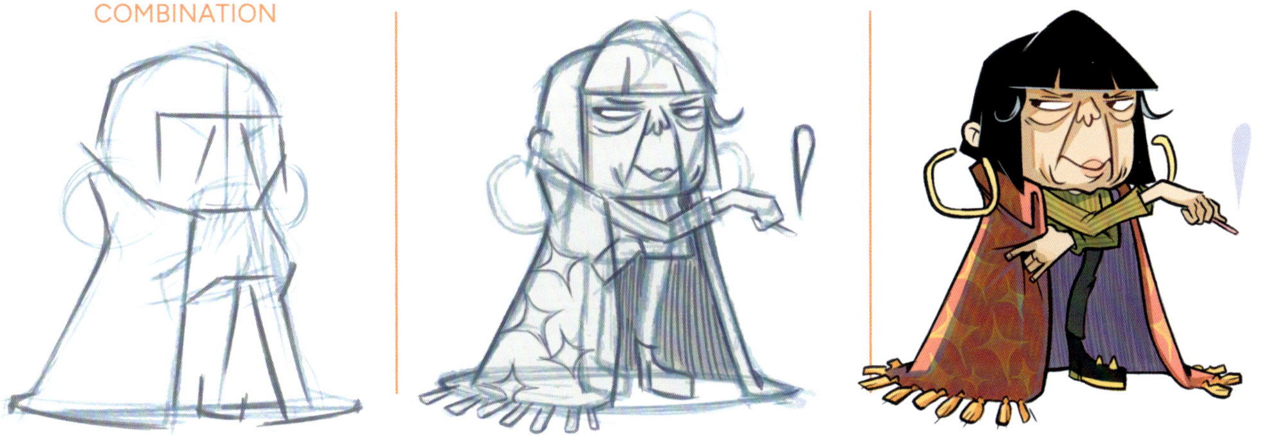

ART: LOBON LEAL

FROM ALL ANGLES

BEGINNER ●

Draw the same animal throughout the day from different angles, spending no more than five minutes per sketch.

Choose one of the animal's features to exaggerate in each drawing. For example, you could make the ears bigger or elongate the body. Use your imagination rather than relying on references. This exercise will encourage you to explore a subject from all possible viewpoints, rather than the most convenient angle.

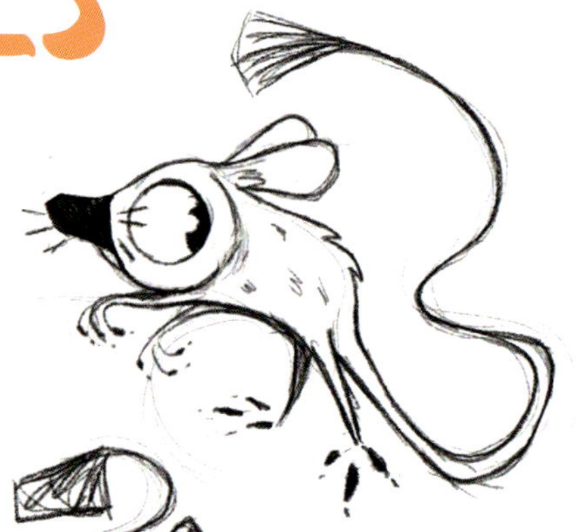

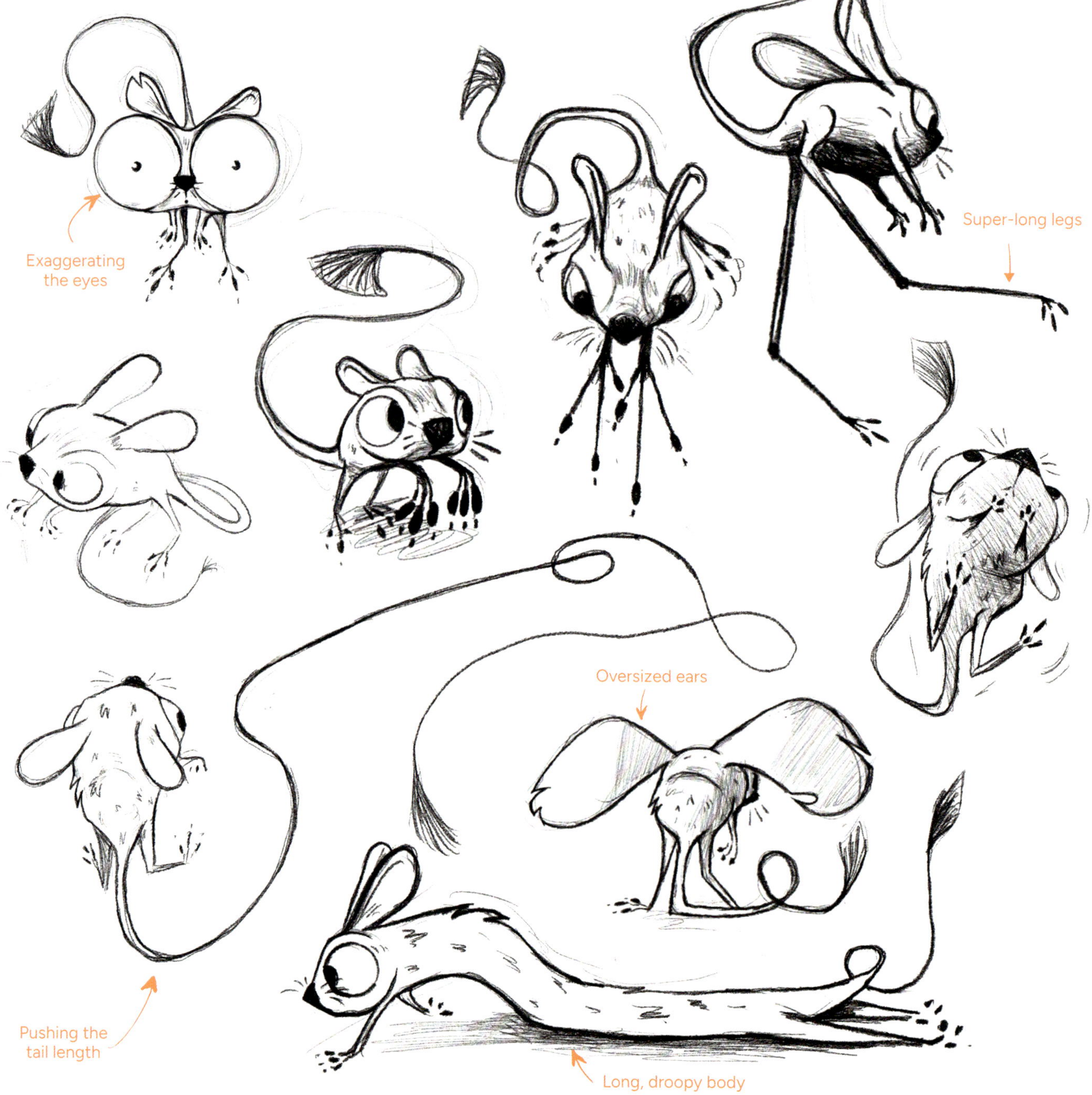

FACE PROFILES

INTERMEDIATE ●●

Draw five character profiles, experimenting with different proportions and facial features.

Play around with the size and shape of the nose, hairline, mouth, chin, jawline, and so on. Consider the position of the cheekbones and the angle of the forehead. Try not to repeat features among the five faces – each one should be drastically different. And don't be afraid to exaggerate the shapes. You can simply undo some of the exaggeration if you take it too far.

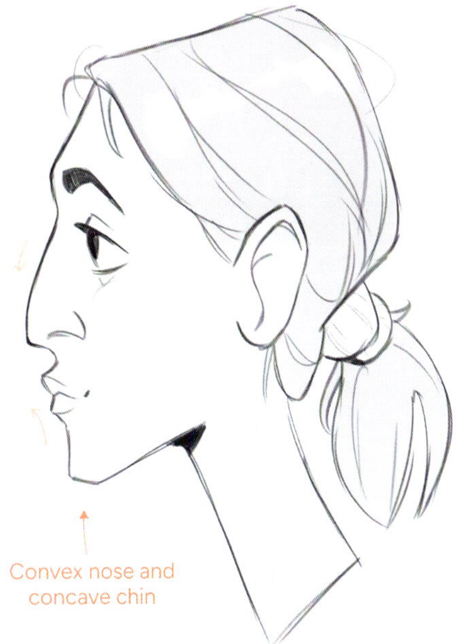

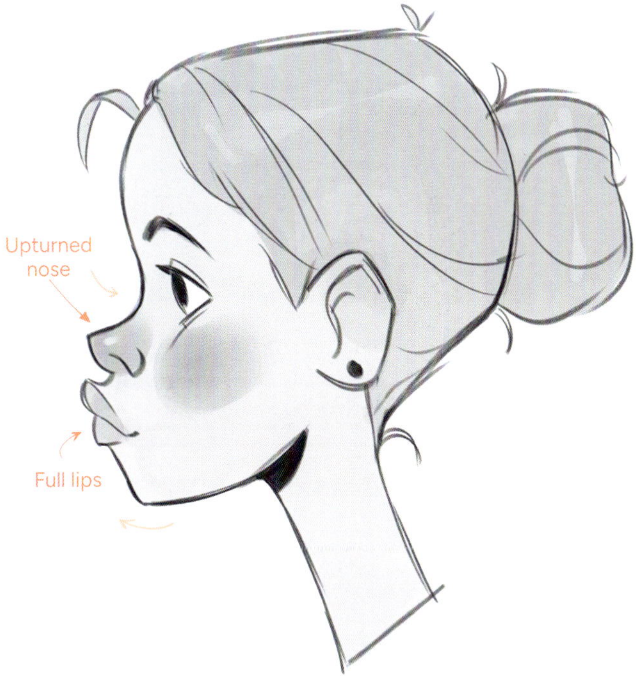

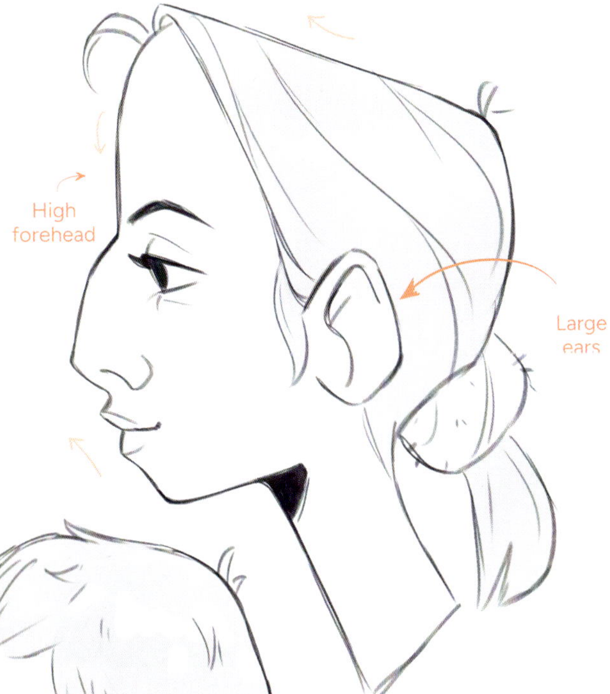

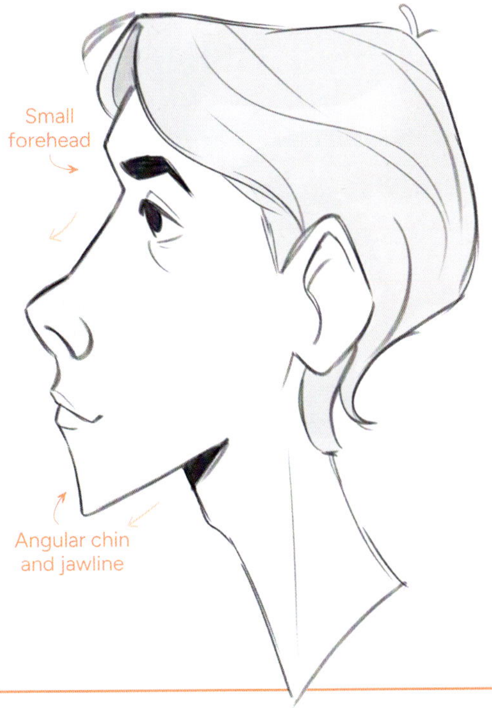

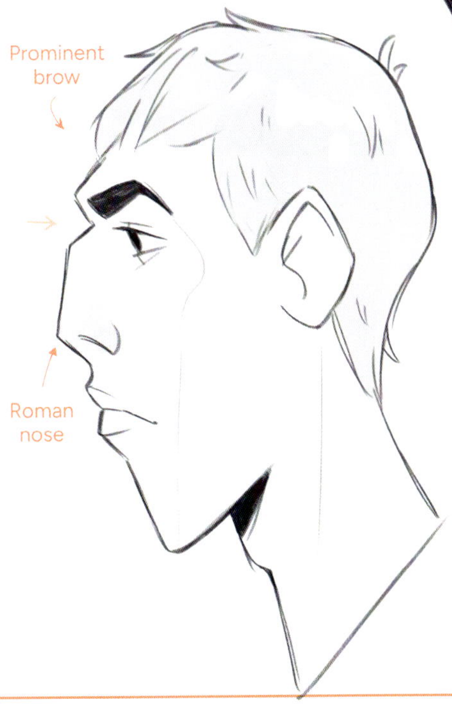

ART MAGDALINA LIANOVA

FACIAL EXPRESSIONS

INTERMEDIATE ●●

Fill a page with drawings of different facial expressions.

Start by practising different expressions in a mirror and notice which parts of your face change with each emotion. Next, draw a character with a neutral expression, sketching a simple guideline to ensure the overall size and shape of the character's face remains consistent with each iteration. Then it's time to experiment with emotion! Exaggerate certain facial features, but make sure to stay true to the original design.

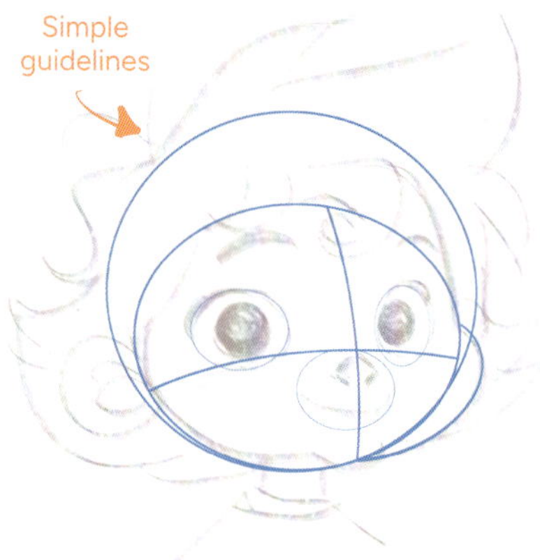

NEUTRAL EXPRESSION

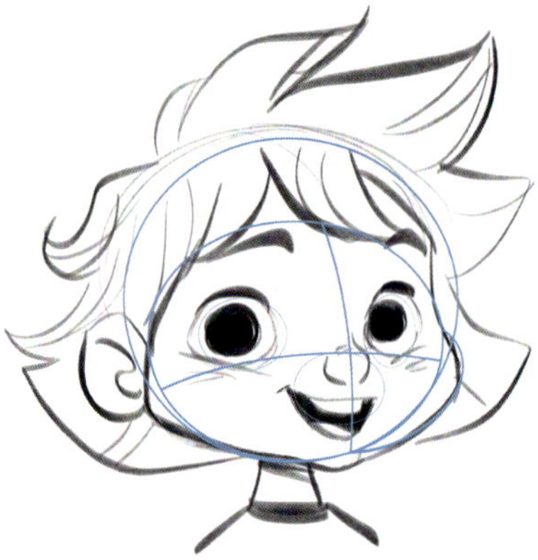

HAPPY

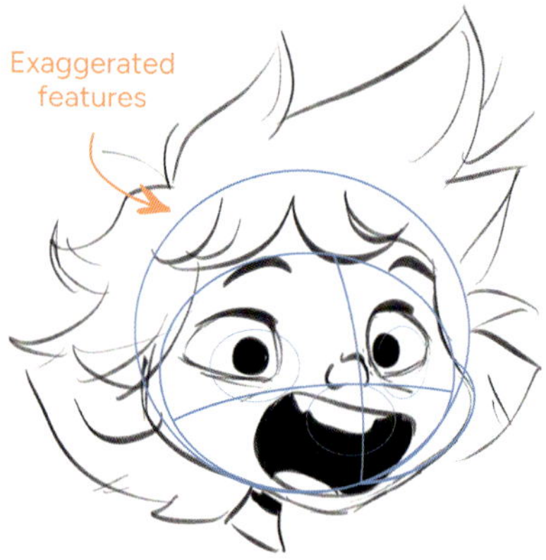

OVERJOYED!

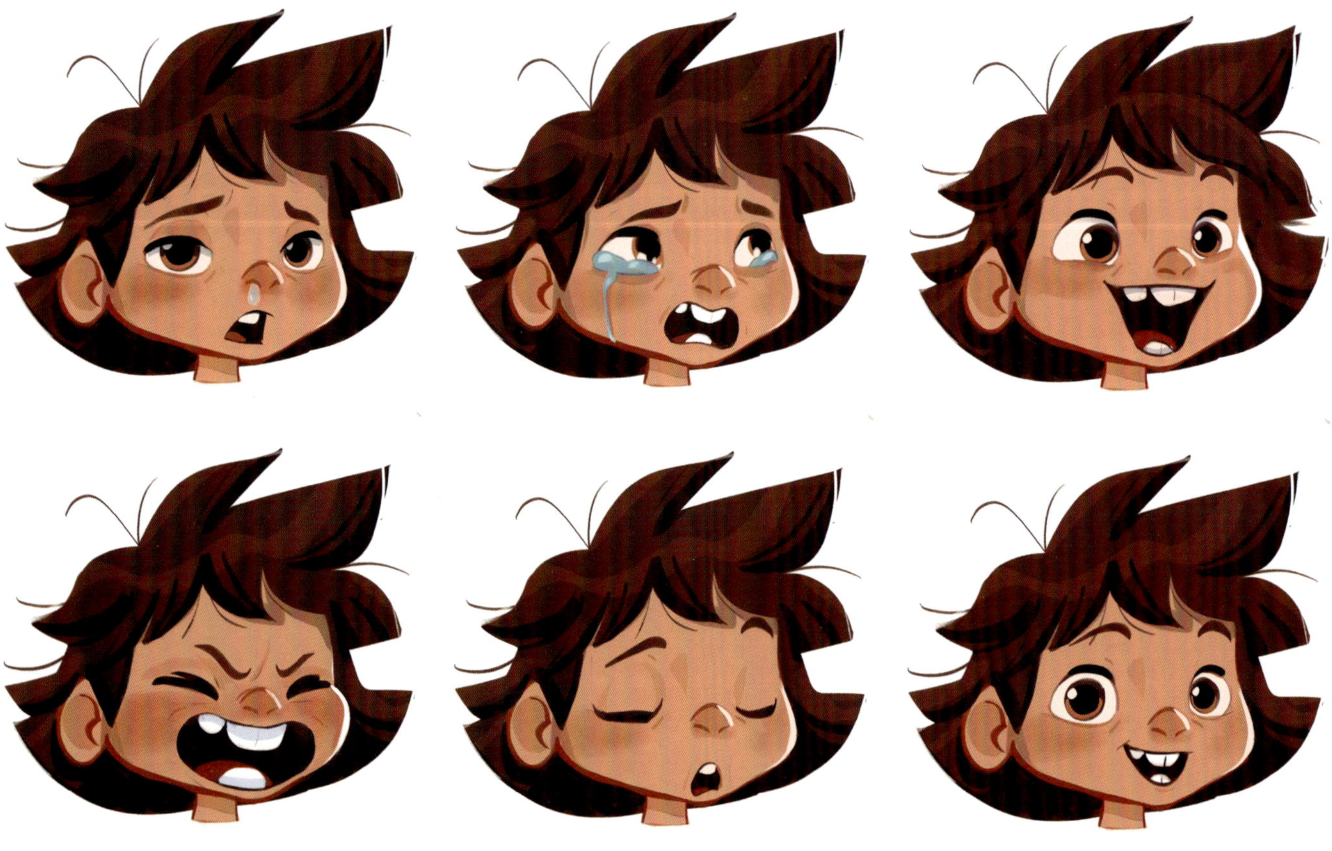

FAMOUS PORTRAITS

ADVANCED ●●●

Choose a famous portrait painting and redraw it in your own style.

This example shows *Girl with a Pearl Earring* by Johannes Vermeer. Focus on capturing the subject's expression, exploring how you can stylize their facial features. Draw the clothing and accessories using your preferred level of line work and detail. Consider what colours define your style. If you tend to use warmer palettes, see how you can incorporate this. Use your preferences and what you're good at to make the image your own.

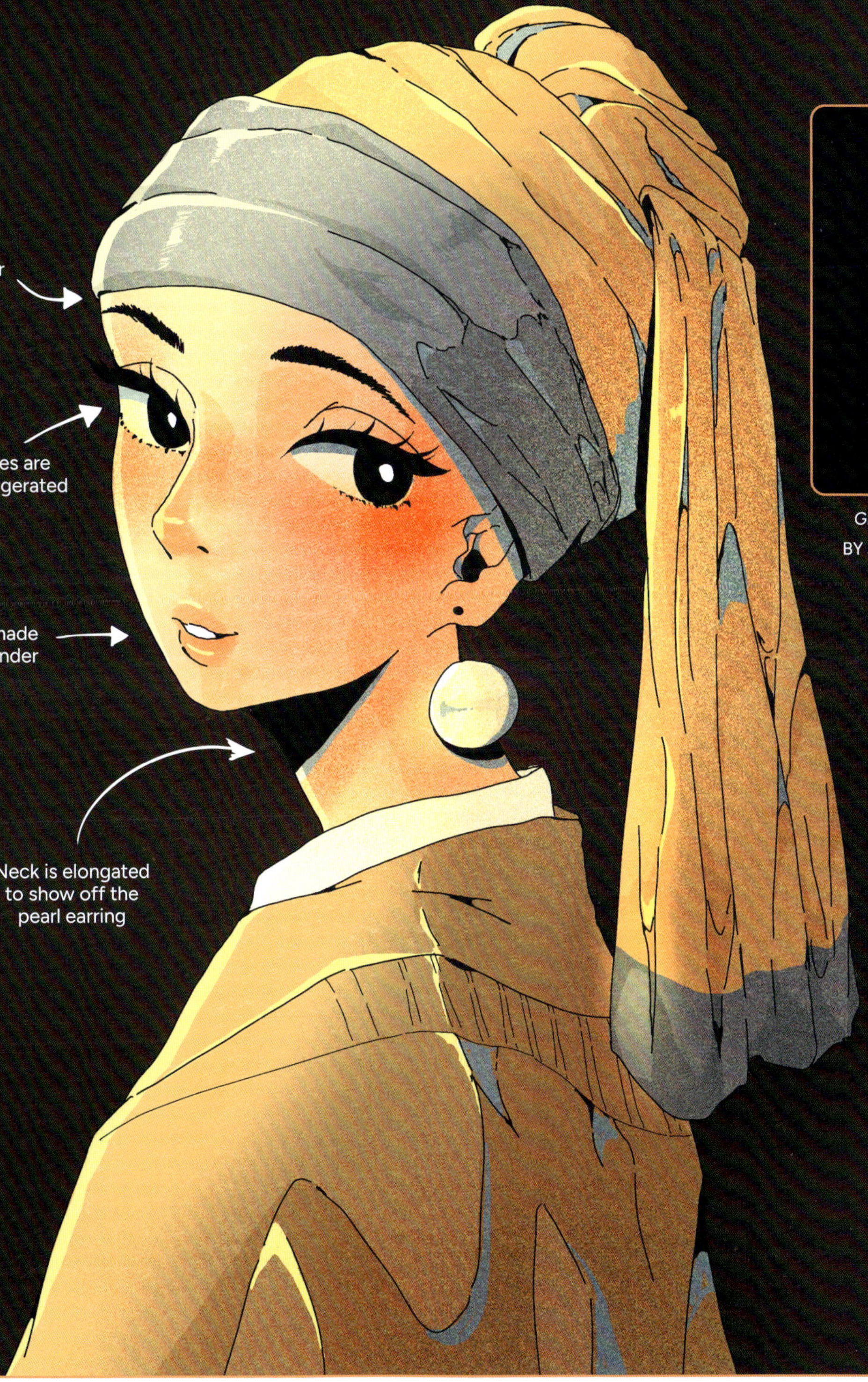

Colour scheme in keeping with the original ochre and blue

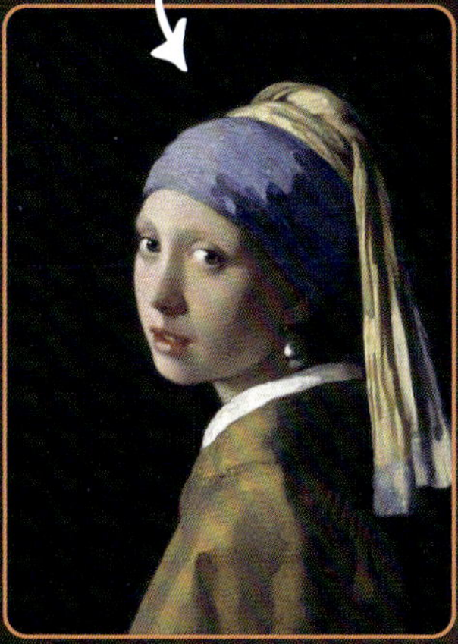

GIRL WITH A PEARL EARRING
BY JOHANNES VERMEER, 1665

ART: ELLA CHMIELLADAYS

STORYT

Step-by-step challenges:

ELLING

One-page challenges:

PACKED WITH STORY

BEGINNER ●

Design a backpack for a character, including storytelling details to communicate something about who they are.

A plain backpack won't tell the viewer much about its owner, so think of ways to add personality and interest. Every detail tells a story. This example will depict a backpack belonging to an animal-loving explorer.

01 Start by designing a simple backpack – this is your blank canvas.

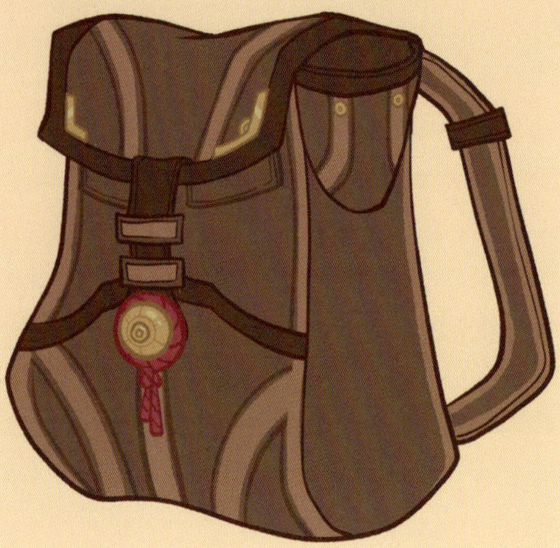

02 Start to introduce props and accessories. This sleeping mat suggests the character likes to camp under the stars, while the paw-print keyring hints at their love of animals.

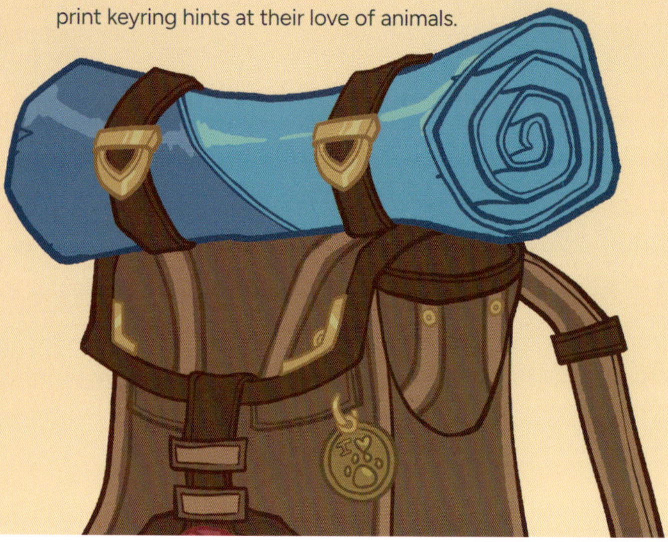

03 Continue to add objects, considering how they attach to the backpack. This water bottle and climbing pickaxe show the character's love of adventure and outdoor pursuits.

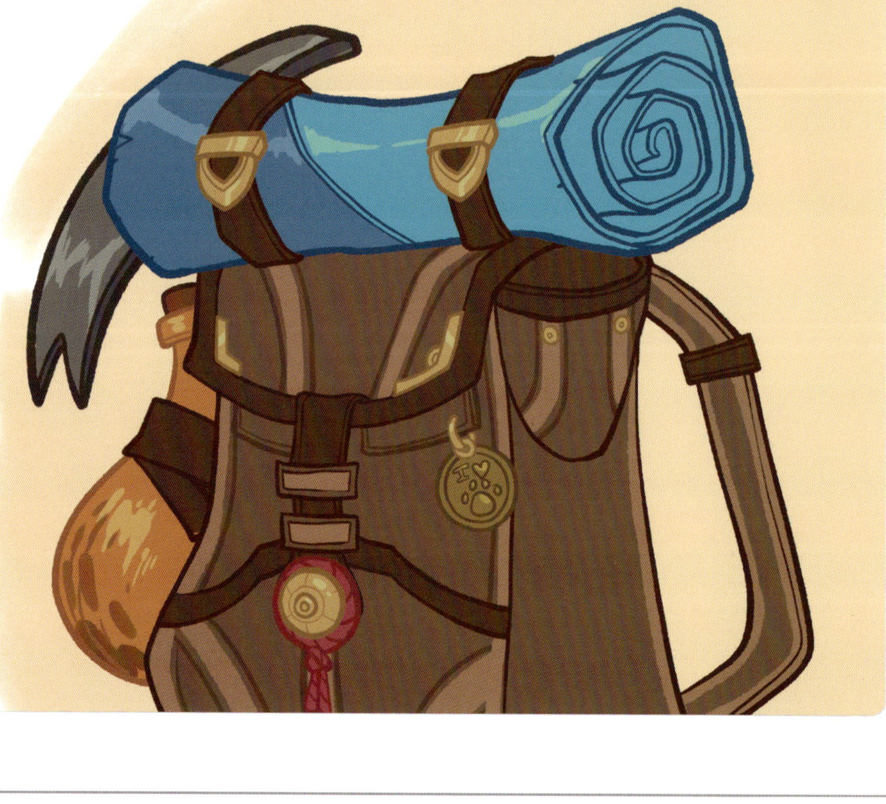

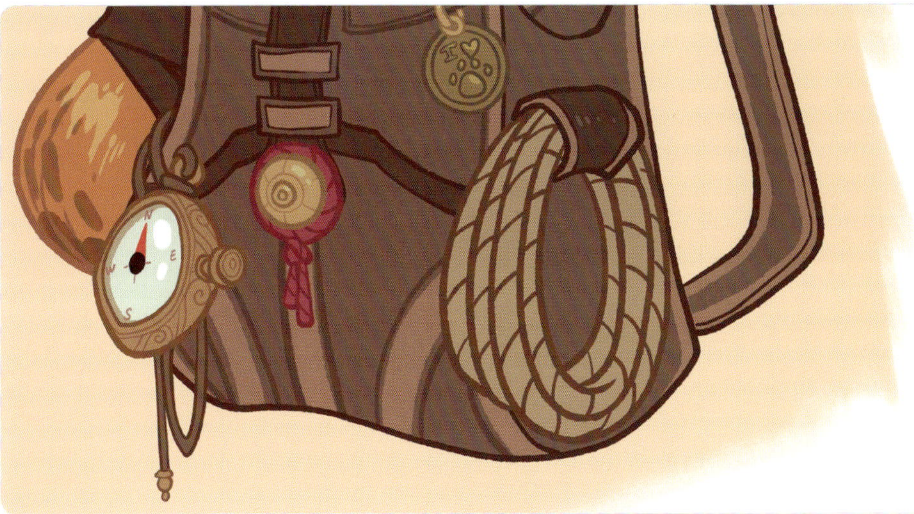

04 A compass and a rope complete this explorer's kit, working together with the other storytelling details to convey the character's intrepid nature and mountaineering skills.

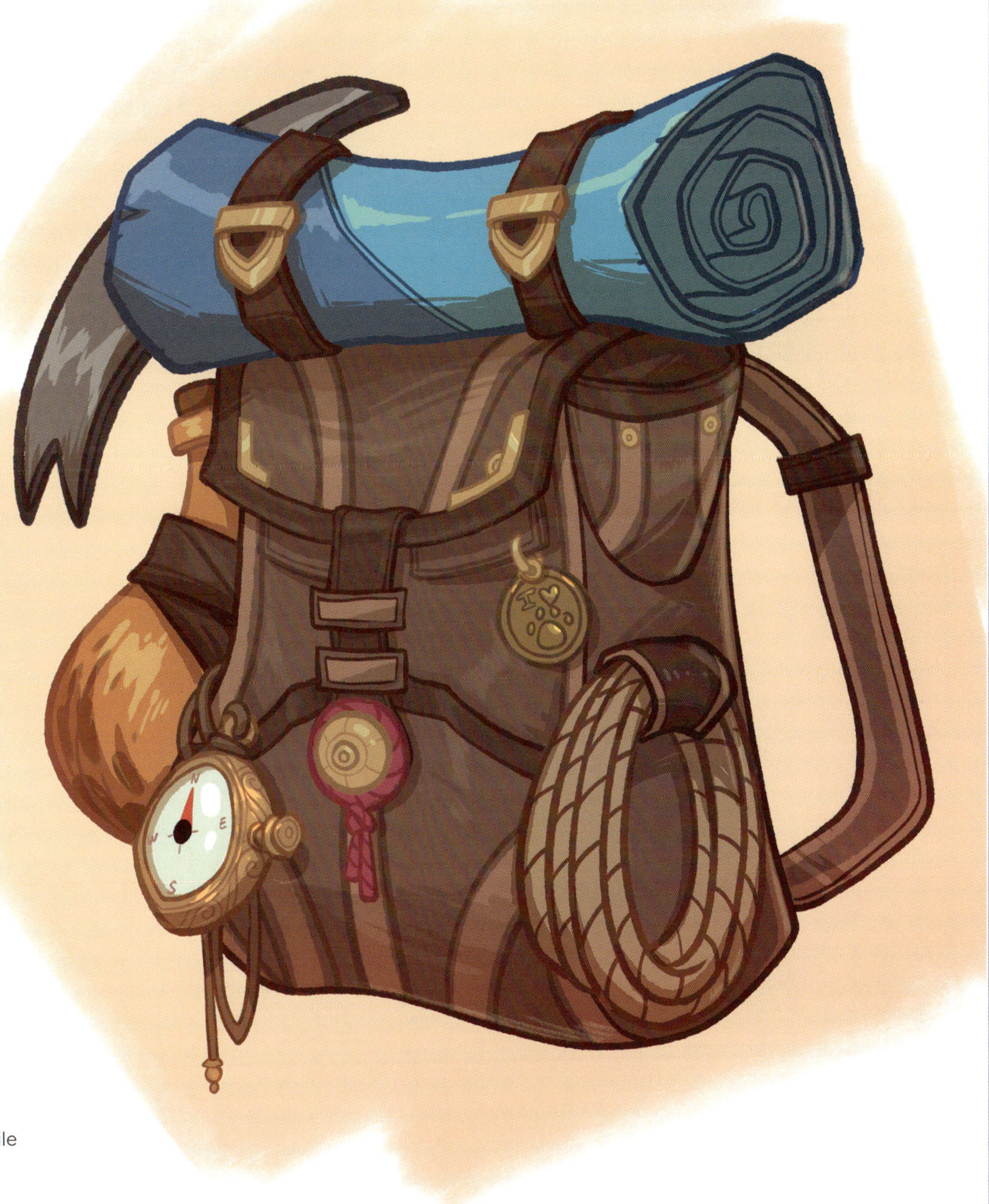

05 Finish by adding shadow and light, as well as texture and detail. The keyring and compass have a reflective sheen, while the rope is matt and worn.

ART: JULLIAN DEL RAY

THE LIFE OF THE PARTY

INTERMEDIATE ●●

Create a party scene (with no characters in it) and include five clear storytelling elements that let the viewer know what's happening.

These could be props or decor, clothing items or accessories, certain colours or lighting set-ups ... anything that communicates the story you're trying to tell. What visual clues can you include? What obvious or subtle details can you sneak in? Use your imagination to inhabit the party scenario and bring it to life.

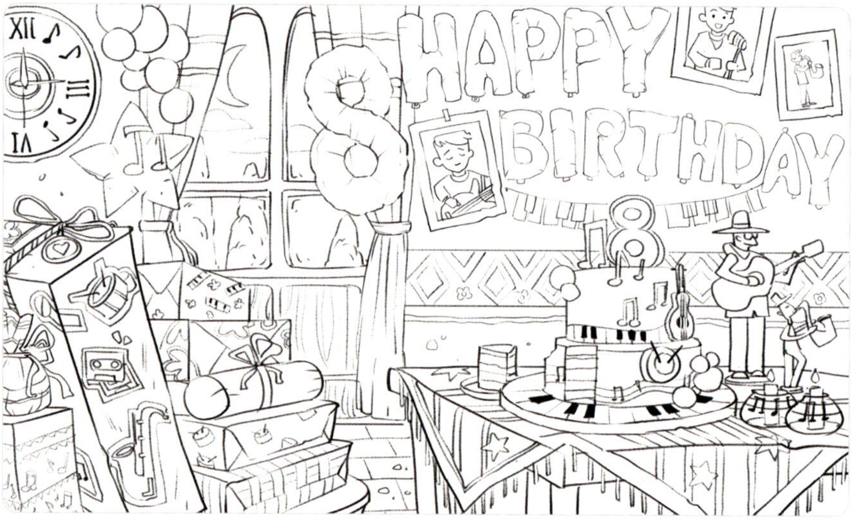

01 Start by drawing a rough sketch, carefully positioning each element in the composition. Try not to clump all the storytelling in one place – spread it throughout the scene.

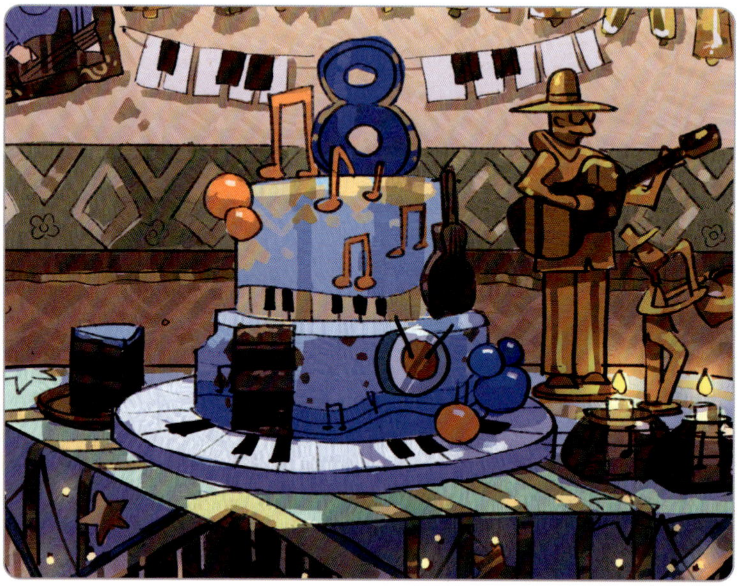

02 The first clear storytelling element in this example is a birthday cake. The number '8' reveals the child's age and the decoration hints at their love of music. Notice the chocolate guitar, fondant music notes, and piano-key cake board.

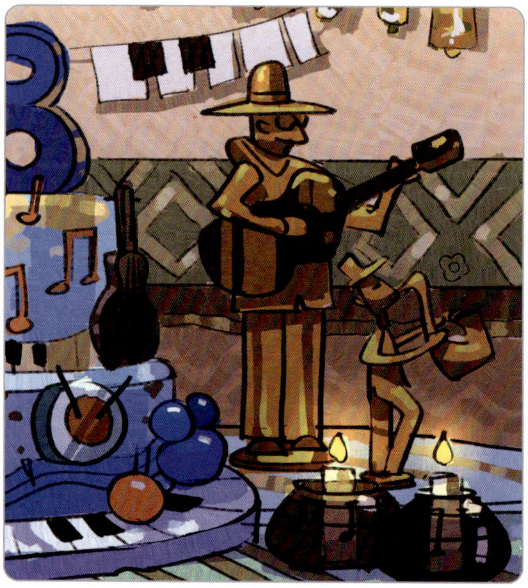

03 Two figurines playing musical instruments continue the theme of the party.

04 The large pile of presents conveys the celebratory occasion. Several of the gifts are wrapped in music-themed paper, showing how well the guests know the birthday child.

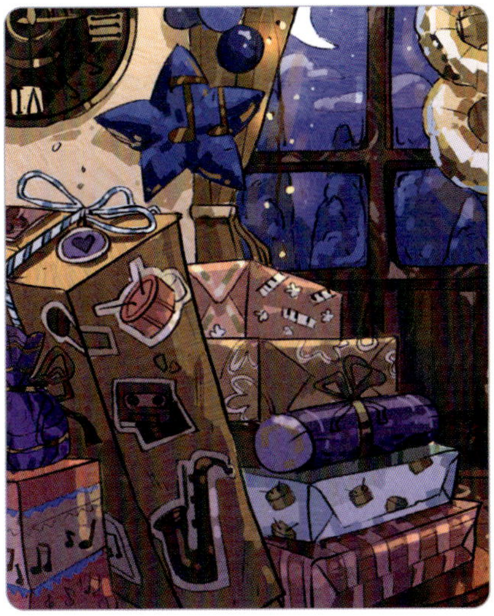

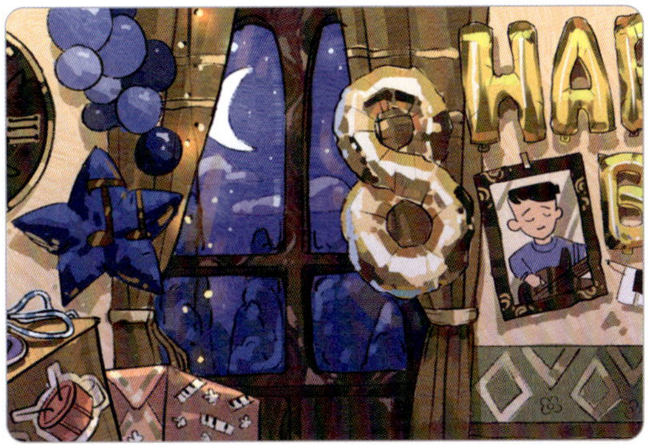

05 The window shows a dark night sky with moon and stars. It looks like the party has gone on late into the night! The balloon reinforces the child's age.

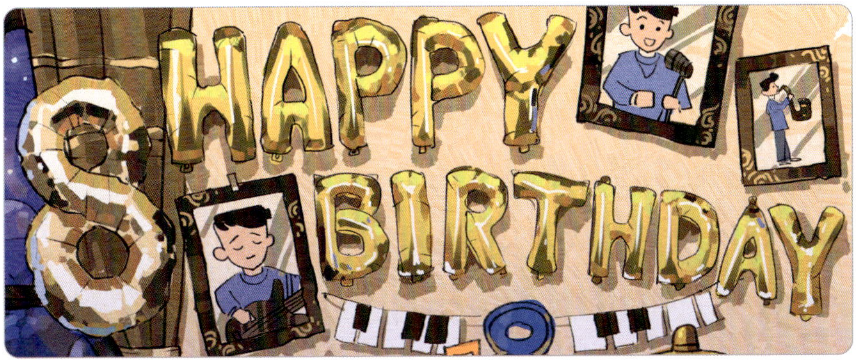

06 If the viewer hadn't guessed already, the 'happy birthday' balloons confirm the occasion. Framed photos show a young boy, which the blue balloons and cake icing had already hinted at.

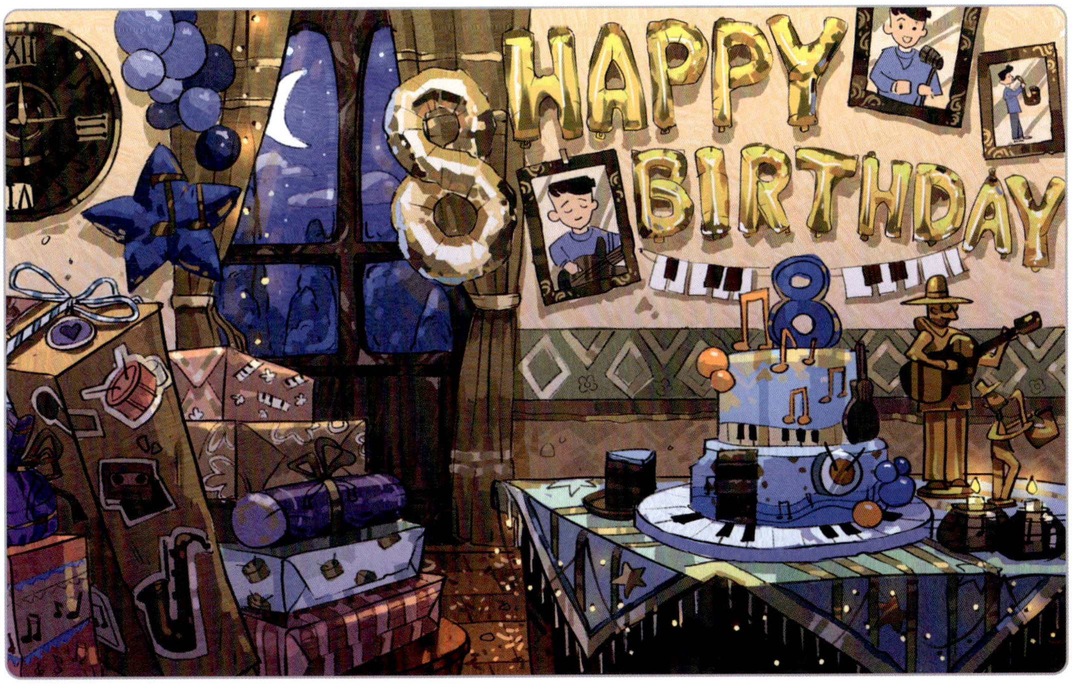

07 The final scene is a feast for the eyes, packed full of storytelling details. How might this approach inform the way you compose scenes in the future?

ART: ALFRED FERNANDES

ENDING/BEGINNING

INTERMEDIATE ●●

Create an image that clearly communicates a beginning and an ending in the same scene.

For example, a chick hatching as the sun sets, or a person laying flowers on a grave at sunrise. In this example, the crashed spaceship represents destruction and the end of a journey, while the mother and baby signify new beginnings. This contrast creates a powerful emotional narrative, reminding the viewer that even in the darkest moments, something beautiful can emerge.

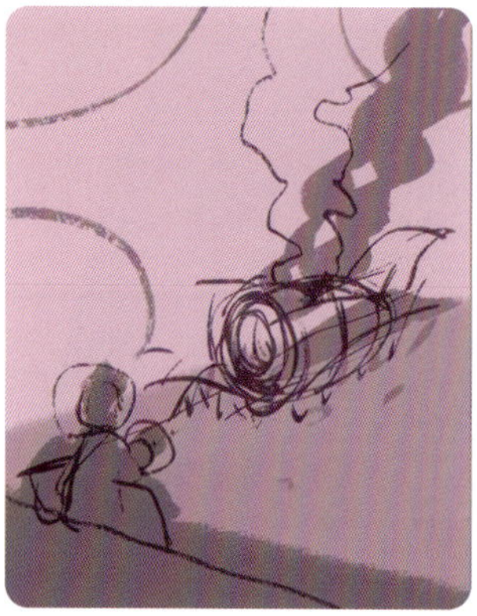

01 Decide on the story you wish to tell, then create a rough sketch of the scene. Position the most important element as a focal point in the foreground.

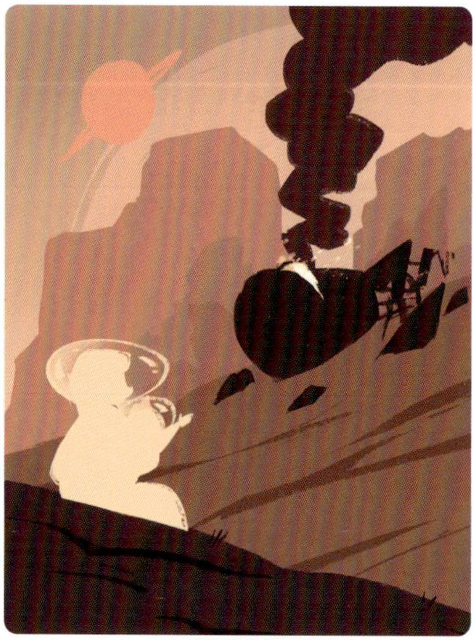

02 Use light and shadow to set the mood of the scene and create a sense of depth. Here, the background has a lower contrast to suggest an aftermath, while the mother and baby are highlighted to draw attention and create emotional variation.

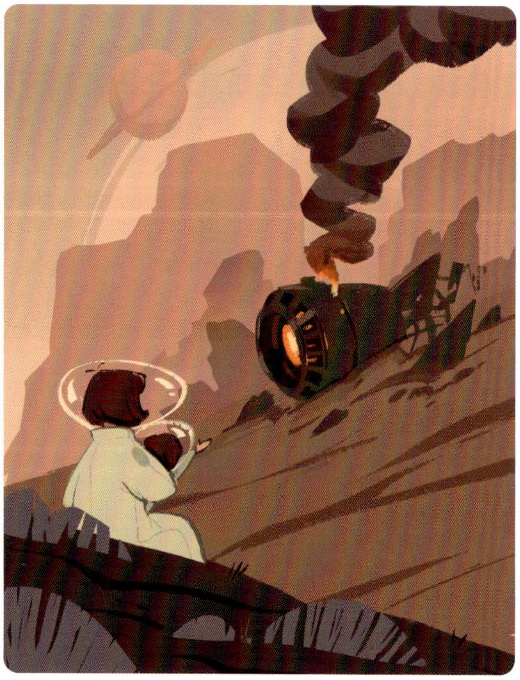

03 Introduce detail and texture to enhance the storytelling. This could include clothing and accessories, body language and gesture, or props and materials.

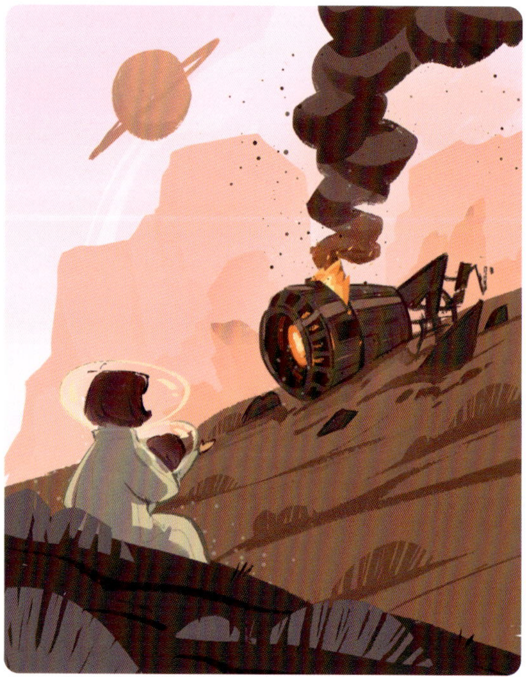

04 Add more environmental effects to communicate the intended message and mood, such as a fiery explosion and dramatic sky, in addition to highlights and shading.

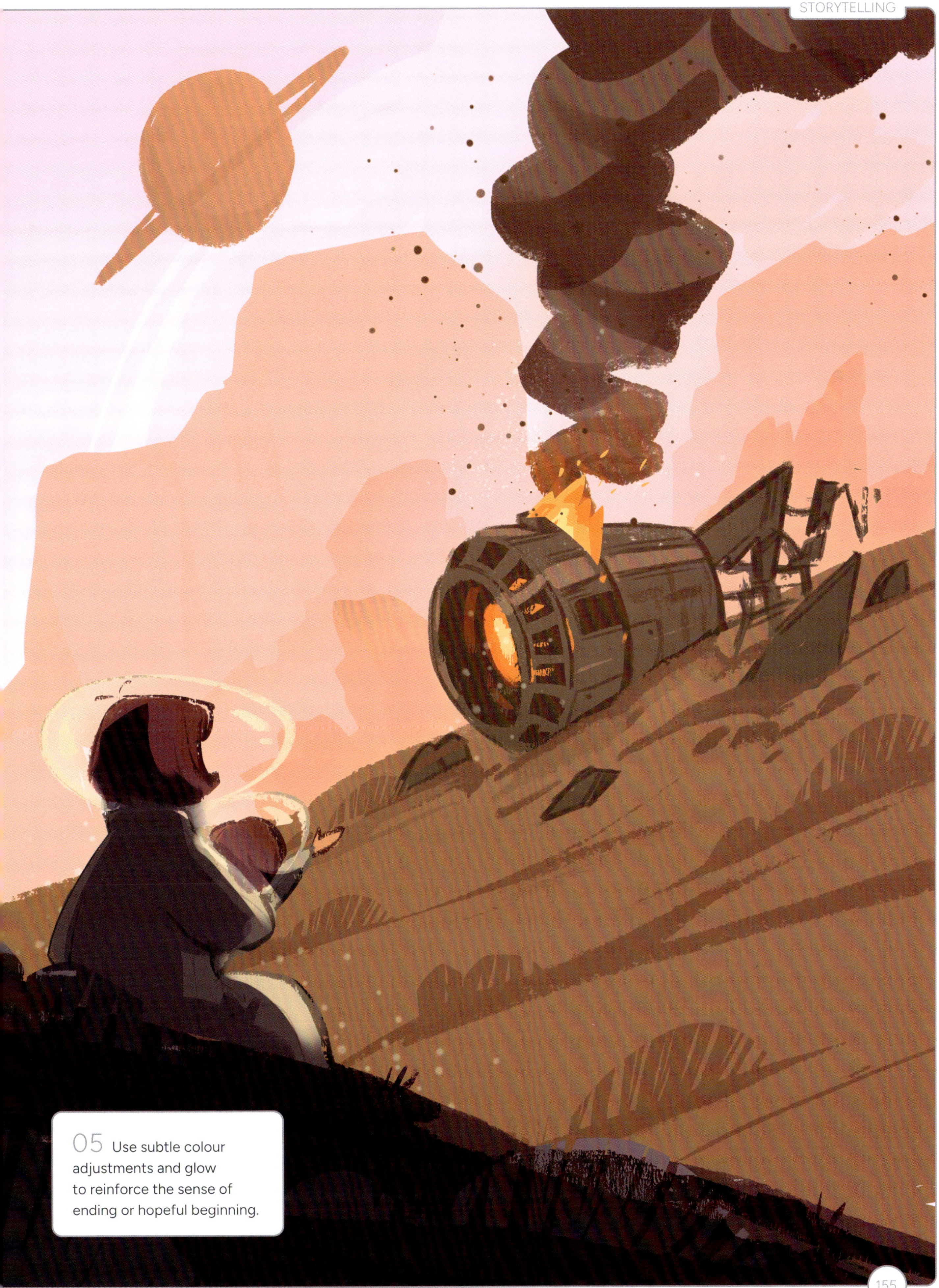

05 Use subtle colour adjustments and glow to reinforce the sense of ending or hopeful beginning.

ART: TARANEH KARIMI

HOME SWEET HOME

ADVANCED ●●●

Design a home for an imaginary character.

Take photos of an interesting or unusual environment, then think about what kind of person or creature could live there. Draw what this home might look like, choosing an element from the reference environment as a starting point. Why do they live there? What do they do? As well as sketching in obvious clues, such as props, see how you can convey their story through shape language and materials. A good piece of environment art will tell you all you need to know about the character that lives there.

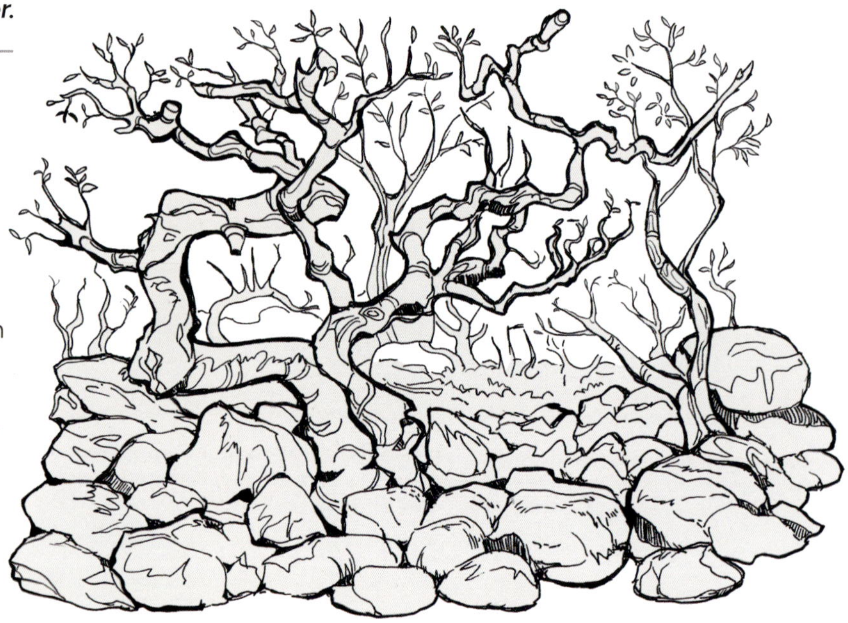

01 Create a sketch of your reference photo. With its twisted, gnarly branches, this woodland has a magical, slightly creepy feel to it. Perhaps a witch could live within...

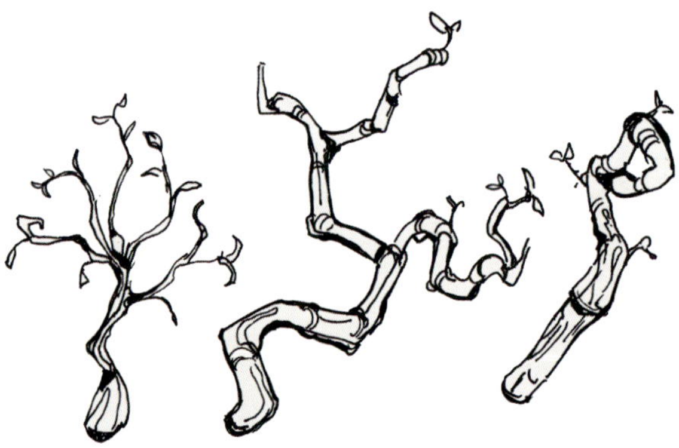

02 Study your initial sketch and consider what materials could be used to construct a home. In this example, the crooked branches and weathered rocks are perfect house-building materials.

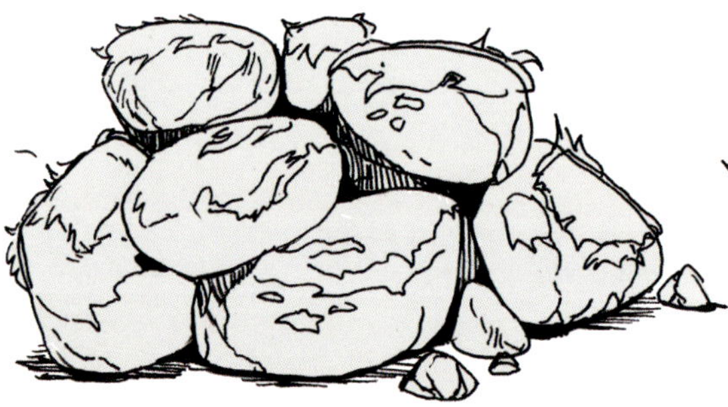

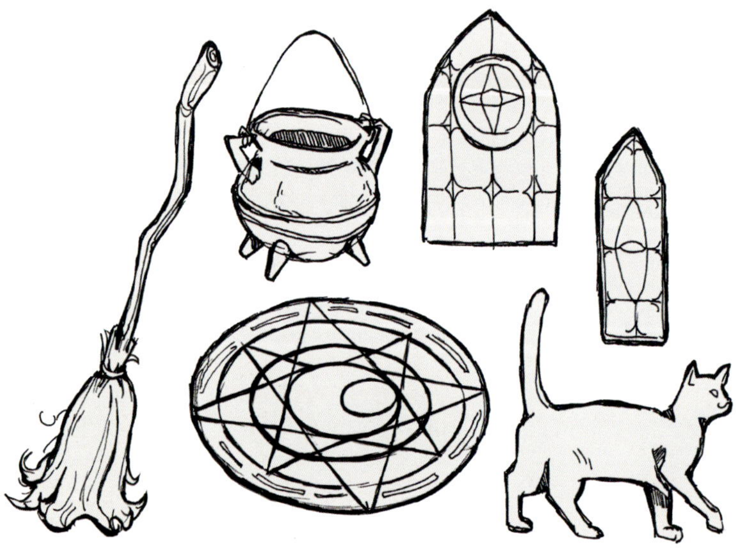

03 What props can you use to suggest who lives here? These should hint at the character's personality, interests, and how they exist in the space.

04 Now build your house with the elements you've chosen, making sure the silhouette is readable. Here, a tree forms the structure of the house, with stacked rocks for the walls. Adjust the scale of any doors and windows so a character could believably inhabit the space, then add extra elements that represent your character.

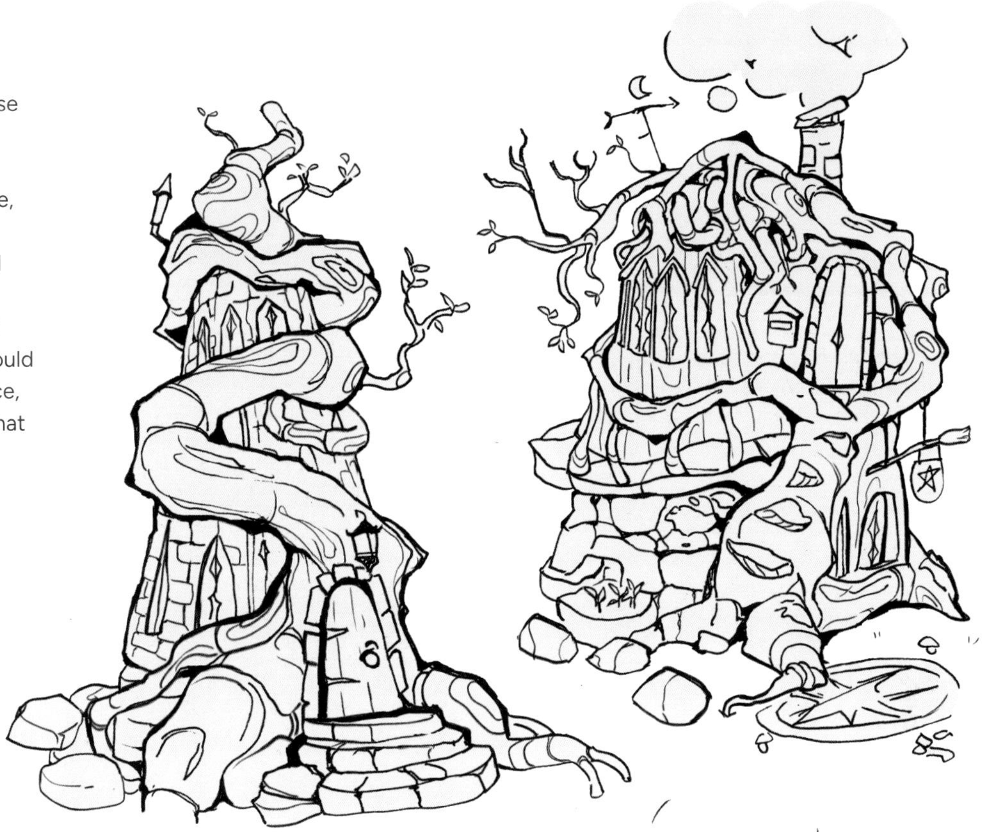

05 Behold the final design in all its witchiness! With your own piece, refer back to your reference photo or initial sketch to review how successfully you captured the environment.

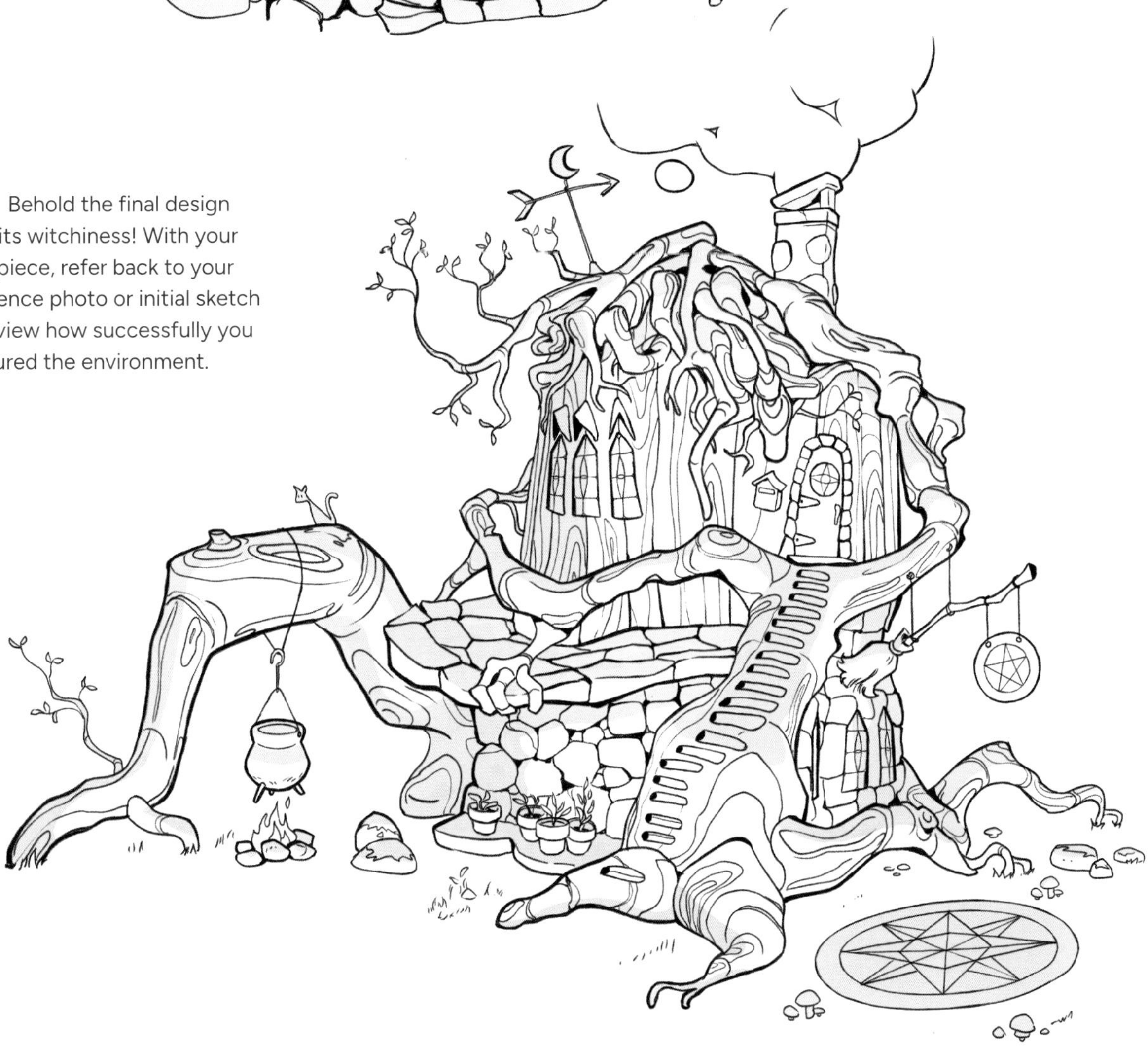

ART: MARIANA NORONHA

INTERIOR DESIGN

ADVANCED ●●●

Choose a character, or even a person in your life, and design the interior of a room for them. Add story elements that tell you about who they are and the life they lead.

For example, if they're into film-making, draw camera equipment, movie posters, studio lights, and other elements to communicate this. Ask yourself, when and where do they live? Is the room cramped or spacious? Think about their personality and general habits and reflect them in your design.

01 Begin by sketching a simple blueprint of the room to decide the layout without worrying about perspective.

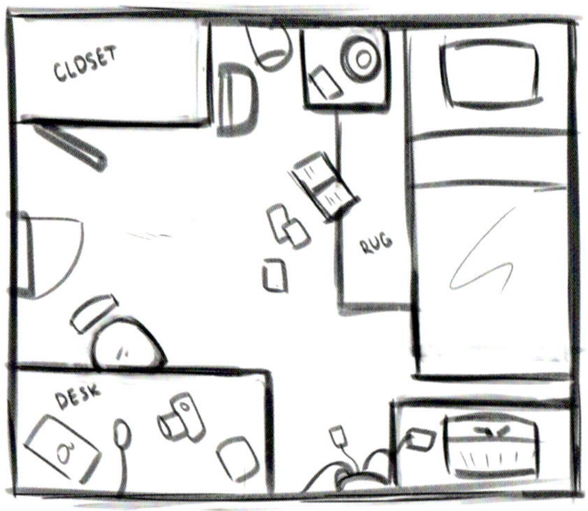

02 Make a perspective grid, then start sketching in the main elements as simple boxes.

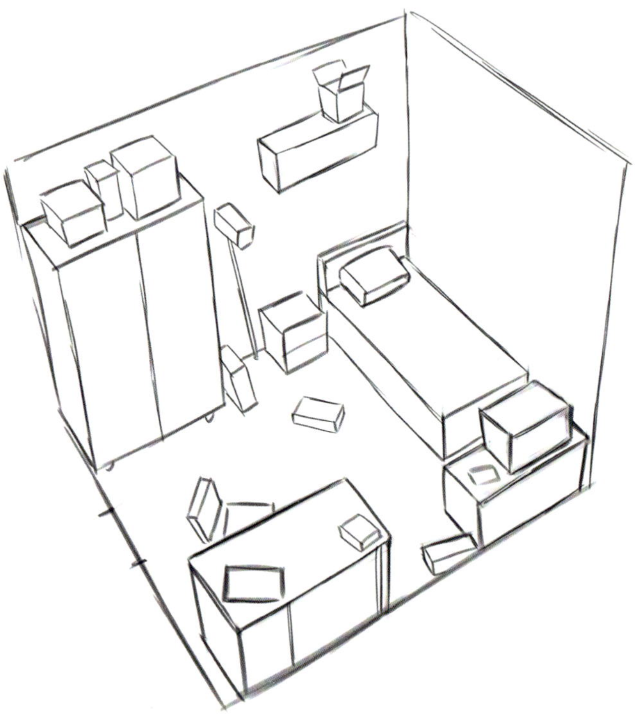

03 Once you have a solid base sketch, define the volumes and add more storytelling elements. Small details, such as an unmade bed or socks on the floor, tell you something about the room's inhabitant.

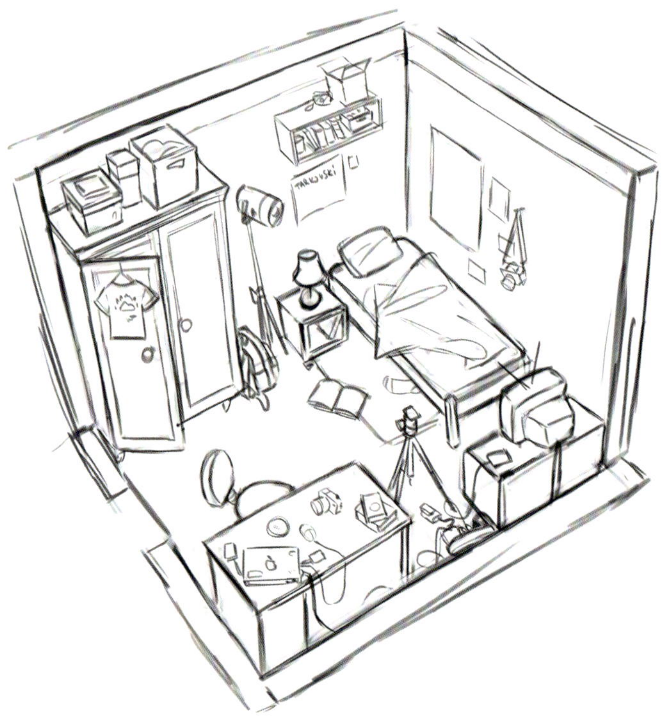

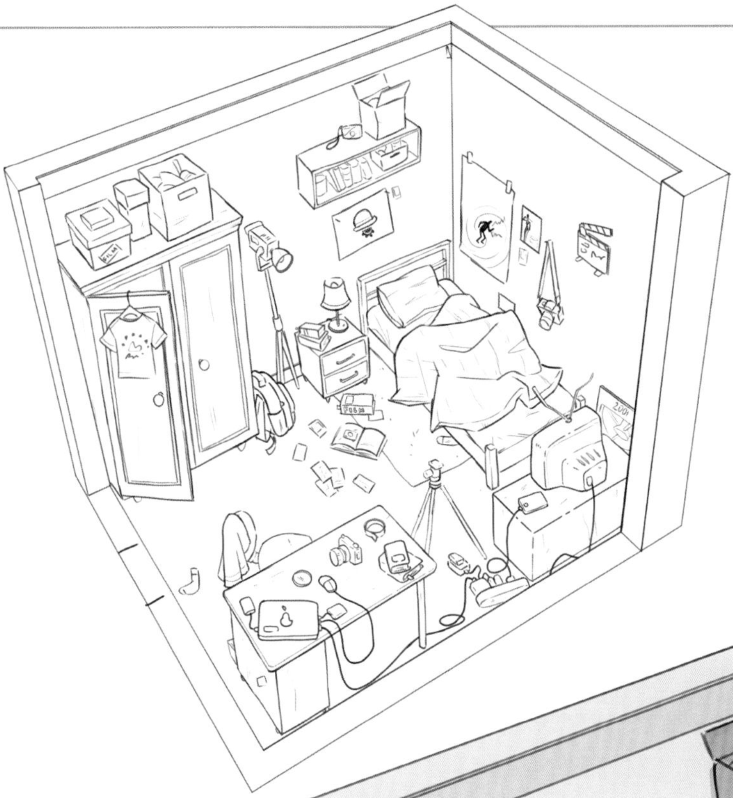

04 Refine the line work. Avoid adding too much detail to small objects, as this can be distracting. Make sure to include a few quieter areas for the eye to rest.

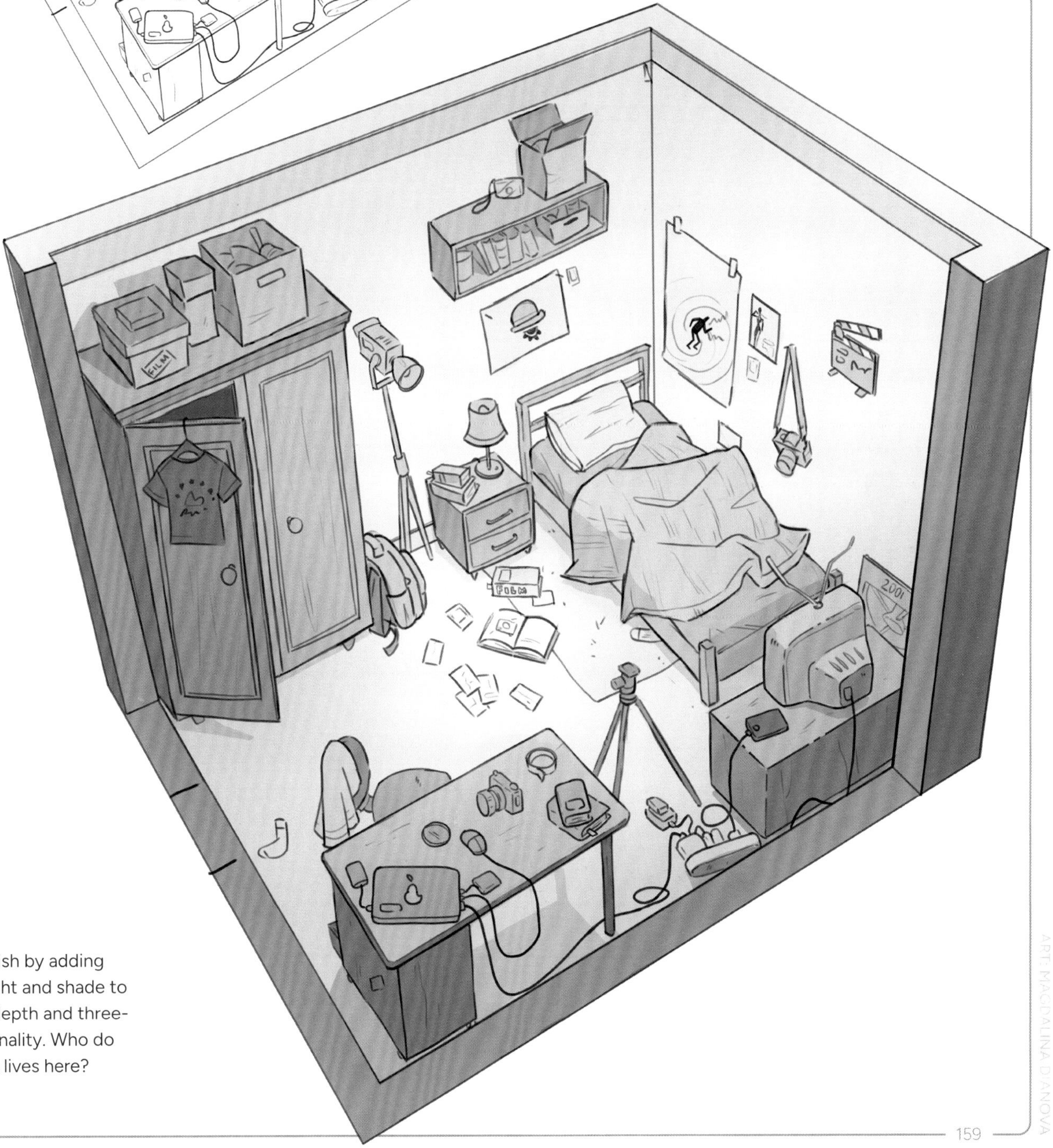

05 Finish by adding simple light and shade to provide depth and three-dimensionality. Who do you think lives here?

ART: MAGDALINA DIANOVA

THROUGH THE AGES

ADVANCED ●●●

Draw an outdoor scene in the present and then in three different time periods.

Use a photograph of your local area, or find a reference photo online, making sure it shows evidence of civilization. Do some research as you look back in time to illustrate historic eras, then let your imagination run wild as you step into the future! Include storytelling elements that clearly communicate each era.

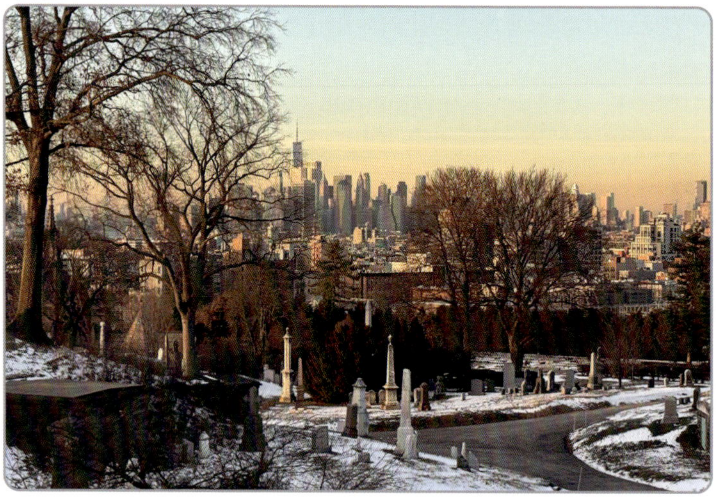

01 Choose a photo that successfully captures the current decade due to the infrastructure, buildings, or vehicles shown.

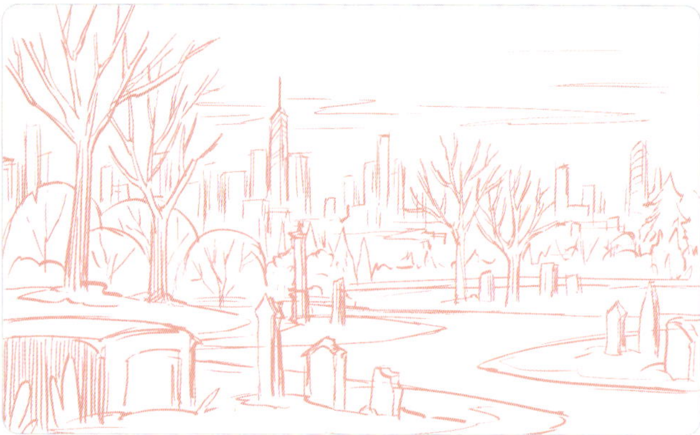

02 Draw a rough sketch based on your chosen photo. It doesn't have to be a perfect copy, but it should include details that suggest the time you're living in.

03 Sketch the same scene in three different time periods. In this example, the chosen eras are 200 BC, the late 1800s, and futuristic 2300. Research the two historic eras to include realistic details, such as the style of architecture. For the future, will you depict a brighter tomorrow or the end of civilization as we know it?

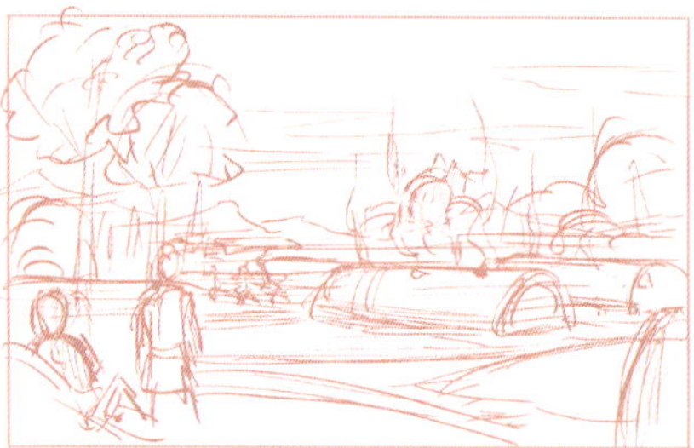

200BC

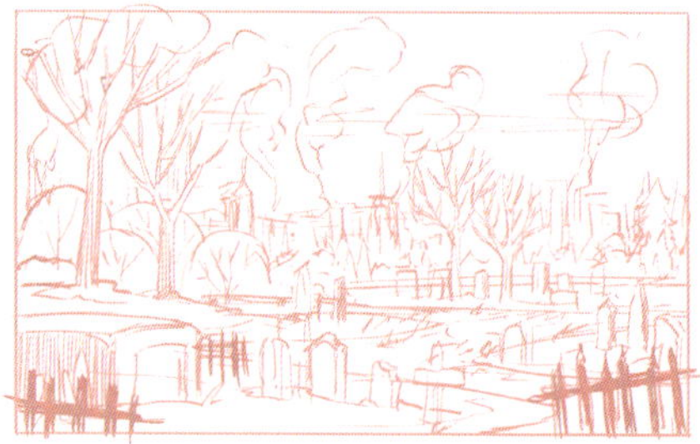

Late 1800

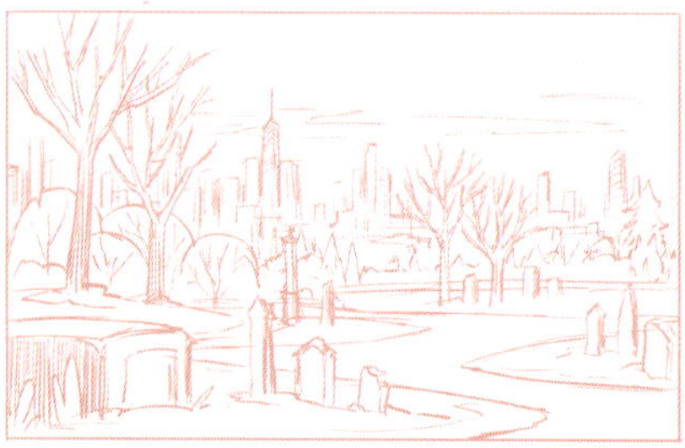

Present Day

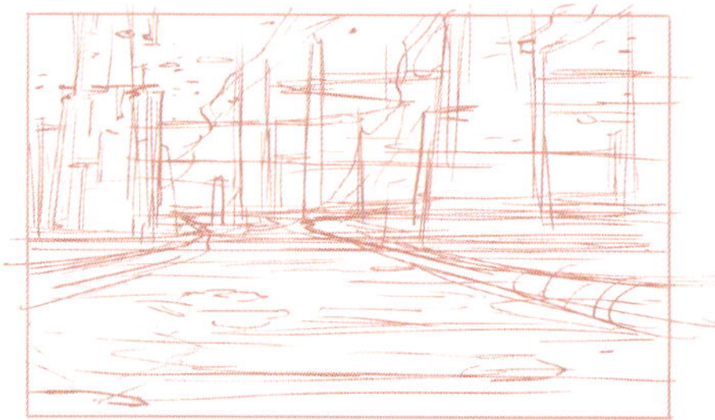

2300

04 Refine the line work in each of the drawings. Consider what storytelling details you can include.

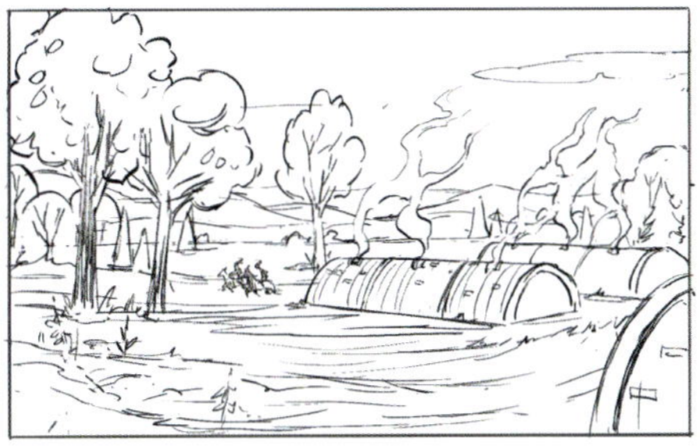

200 BC

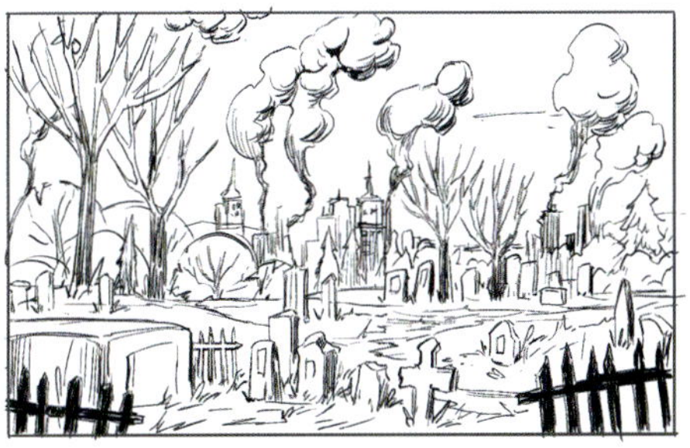

Late 1800

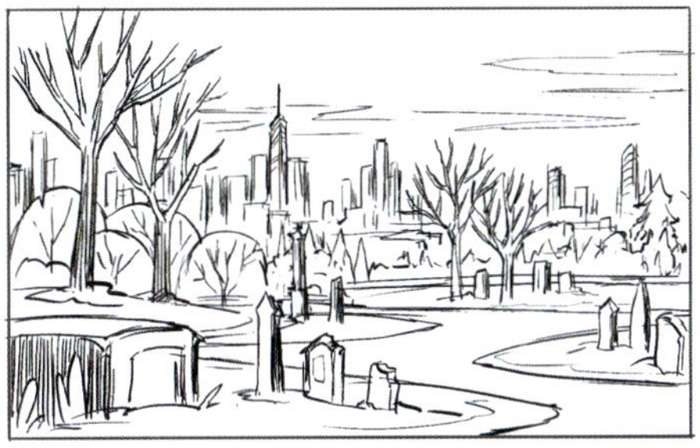

Present Day

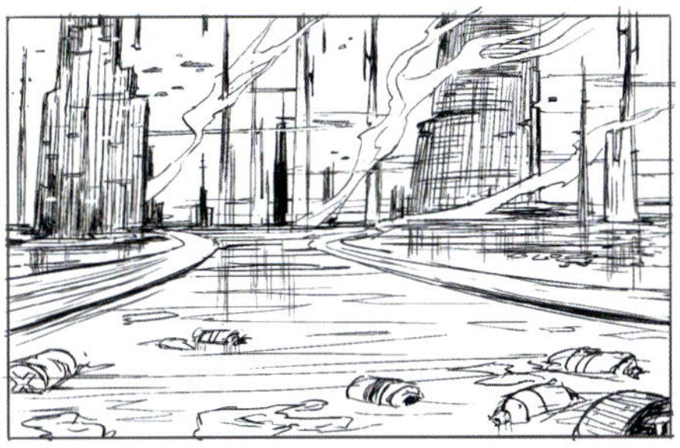

2300

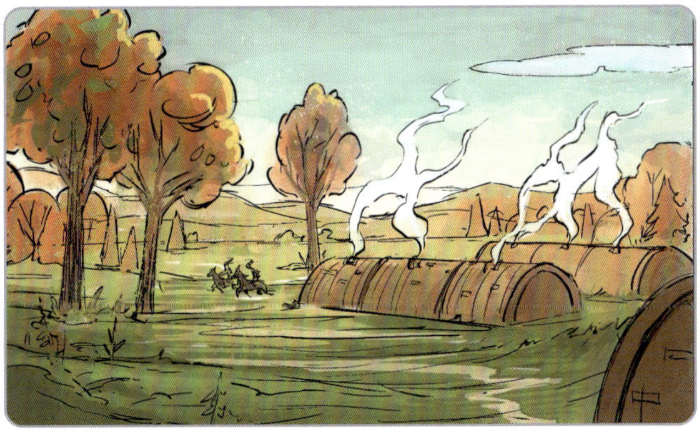

200 BC

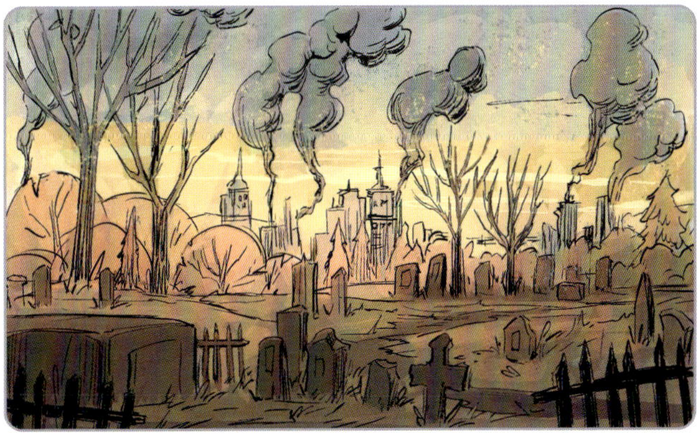

Late 1800

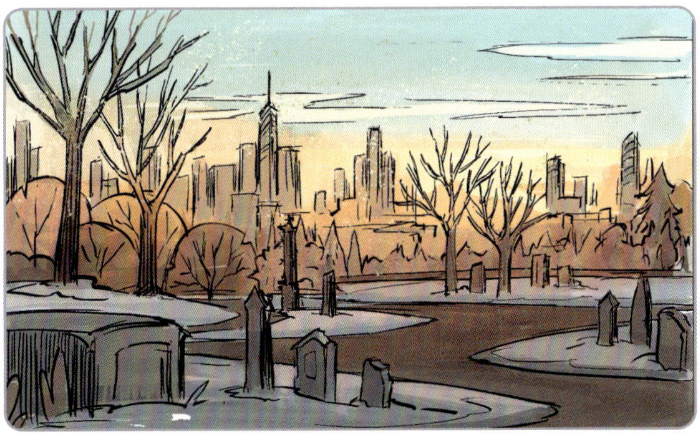

Present Day

05 Finish by adding colour, then step back and observe how the landscape changes over time. What story does each one tell? And which era's style did you prefer creating?

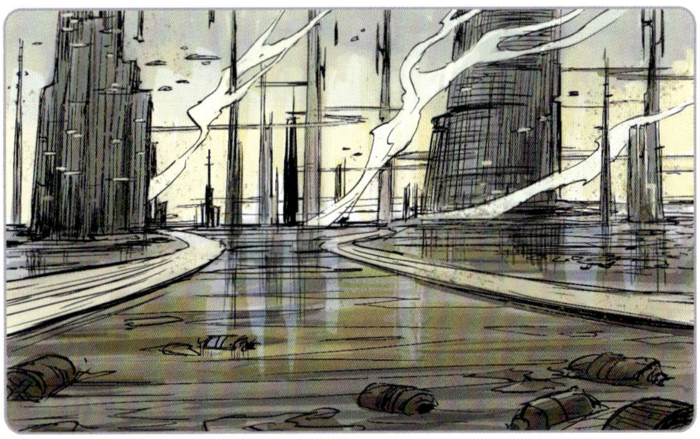

2300

ART: JOI TALUKDER

One-page challenges:

THE FOOD OF LIFE

BEGINNER ●

Think of a character then draw their favourite food in a stylized way.

Maybe it's what they eat for breakfast each morning? Or a familiar snack they're always seen with? What does the food and the style of the drawing tell the viewer about the character? Drawing everyday objects and food items related to a story or character can take you in new style directions!

What does this breakfast tell you about the character?

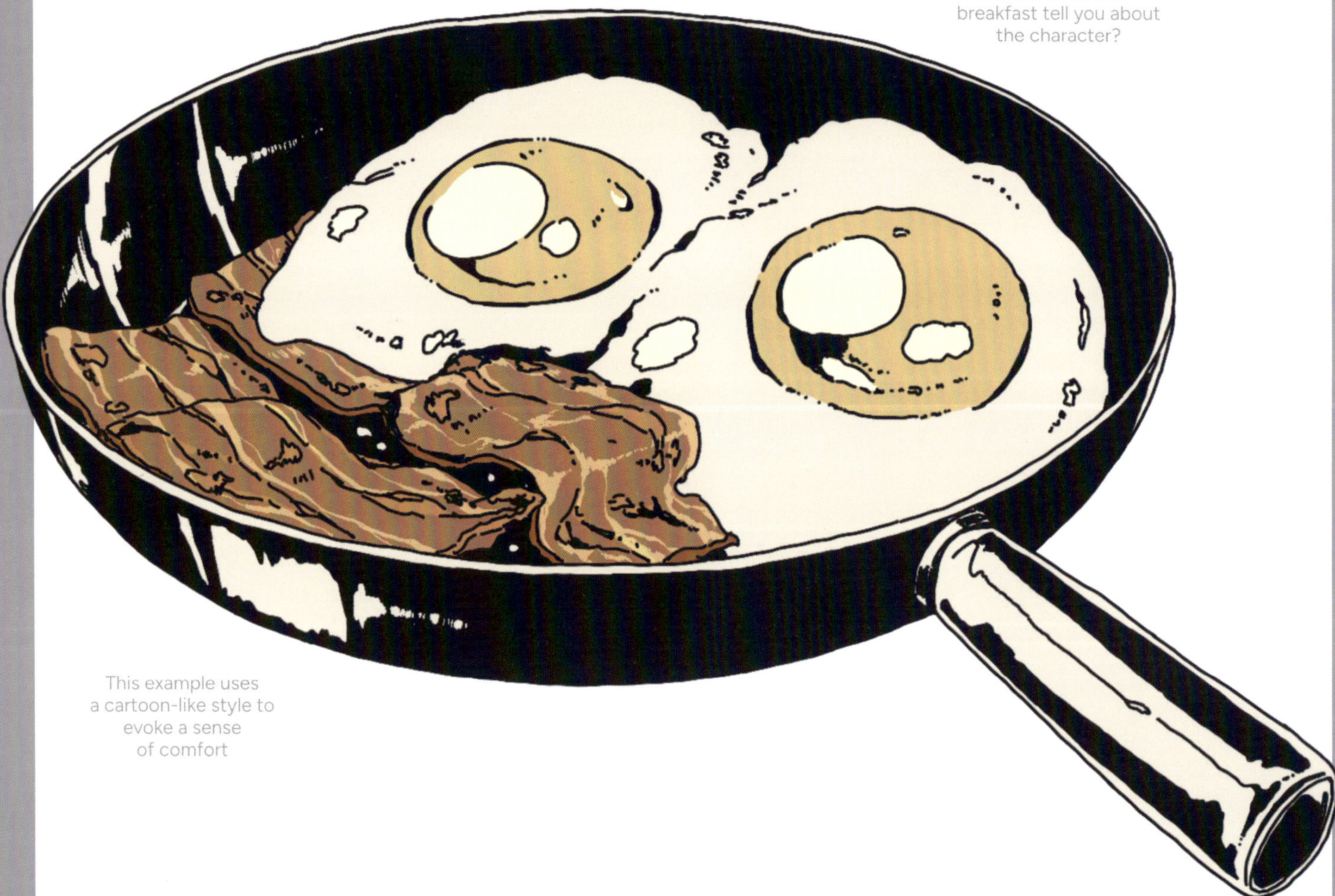

This example uses a cartoon-like style to evoke a sense of comfort

POIGNANT POSSESSIONS

BEGINNER ●

Draw three props that best describe who a character is.

These could be fashion accessories, food items, objects they carry around in their bag, or things that are otherwise important to them. Adopt the mindset of a detective and consider what can be deduced about a character based on the condition and style of their belongings. Scuffed, worn-down shoes might hint that they spend a lot of time walking or being outdoors. Shape language can also communicate a character's story. For example, objects with rounded edges might convey a character's warm, friendly nature, while sharp, angular-shaped items may hint at a spiky, fractious personality.

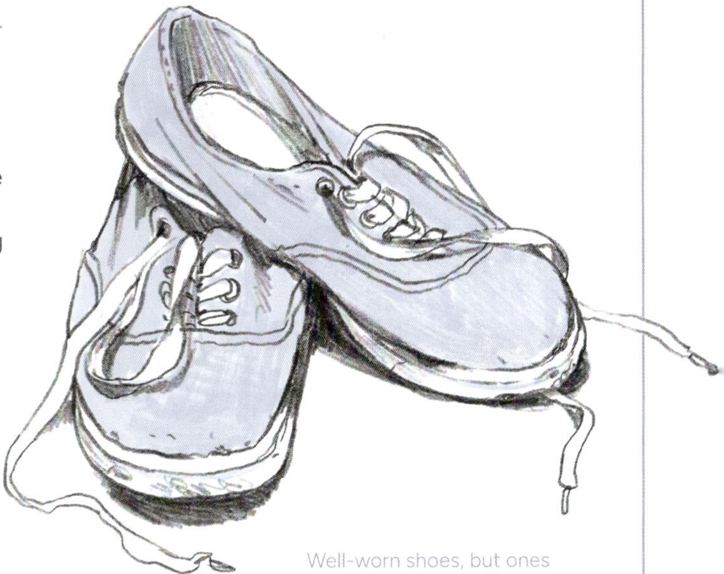

Well-worn shoes, but ones that aren't made for hiking. Maybe their owner walks around town a lot, and on unexpected adventures?

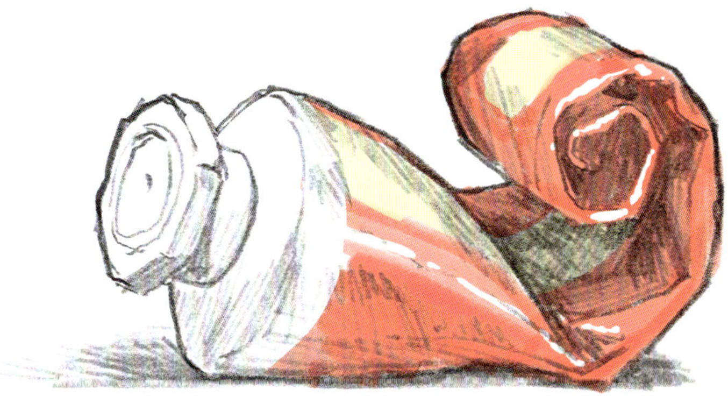

A well-used tube of hand lotion suggests the character is economical, getting every last drop out of it!

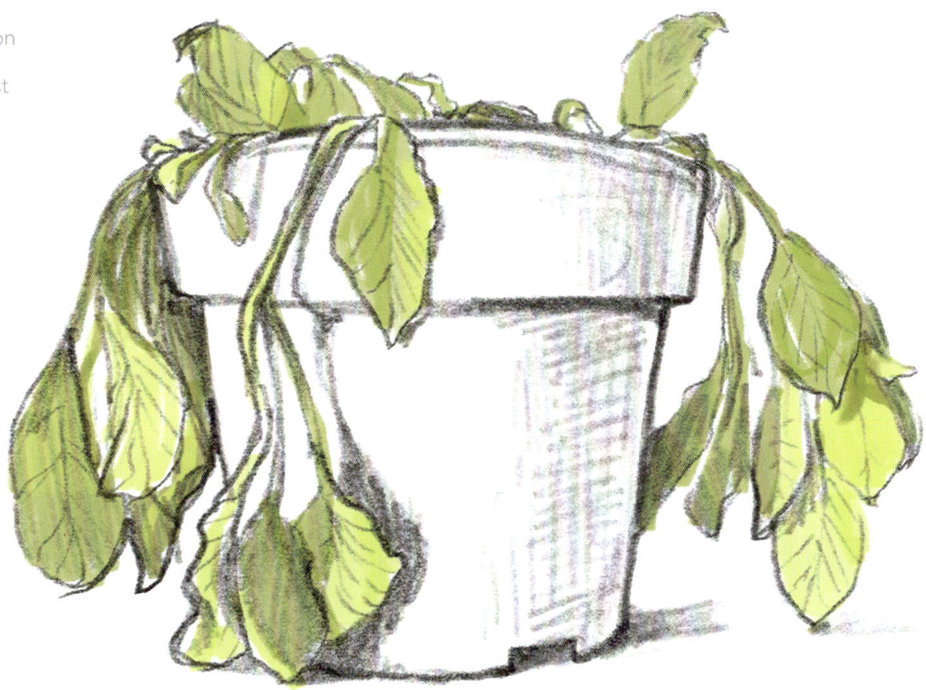

An unwatered plant shows the character has other things on their mind. Perhaps they're busy and never home? Or maybe just forgetful?

CHILDHOOD MEMORIES

BEGINNER ●

Draw three of your favourite things from when you were a child.

These could be toys, food, items of clothing, or any little trinkets that meant something to you. Choose objects that evoke a strong feeling of nostalgia and have a story to tell. Your style is not just how you draw, but what you draw too. The goal of this task is to remind you of the things that spark joy and inspiration.

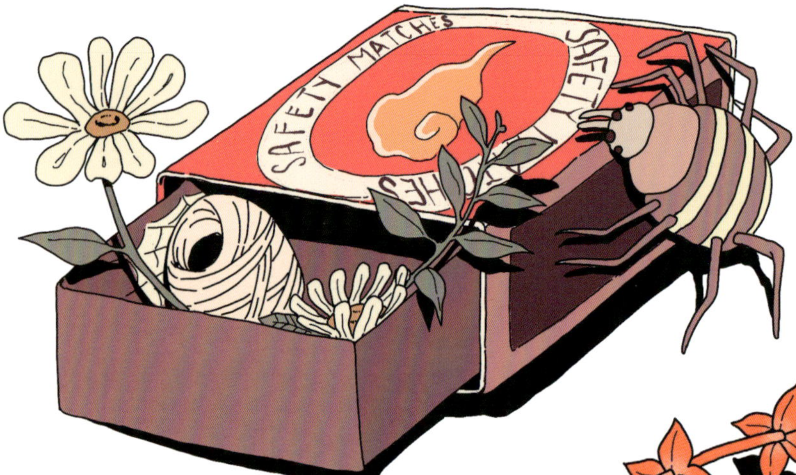

A matchbook full of odds and ends

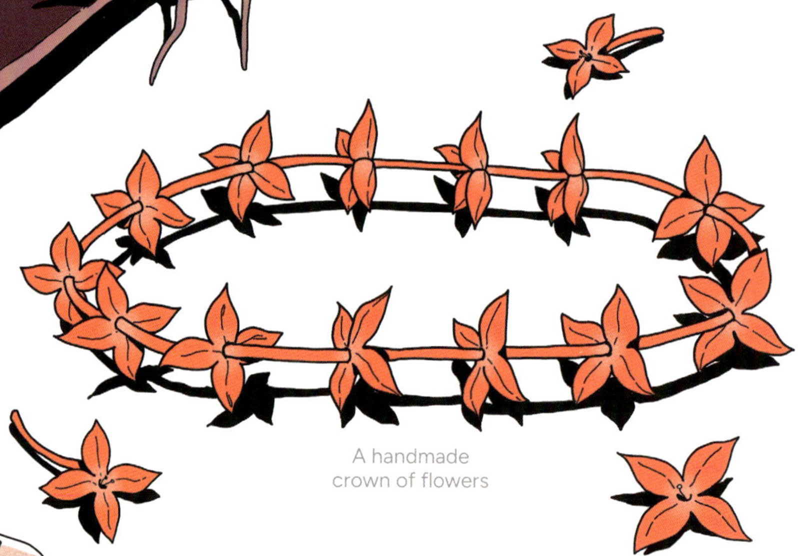

A handmade crown of flowers

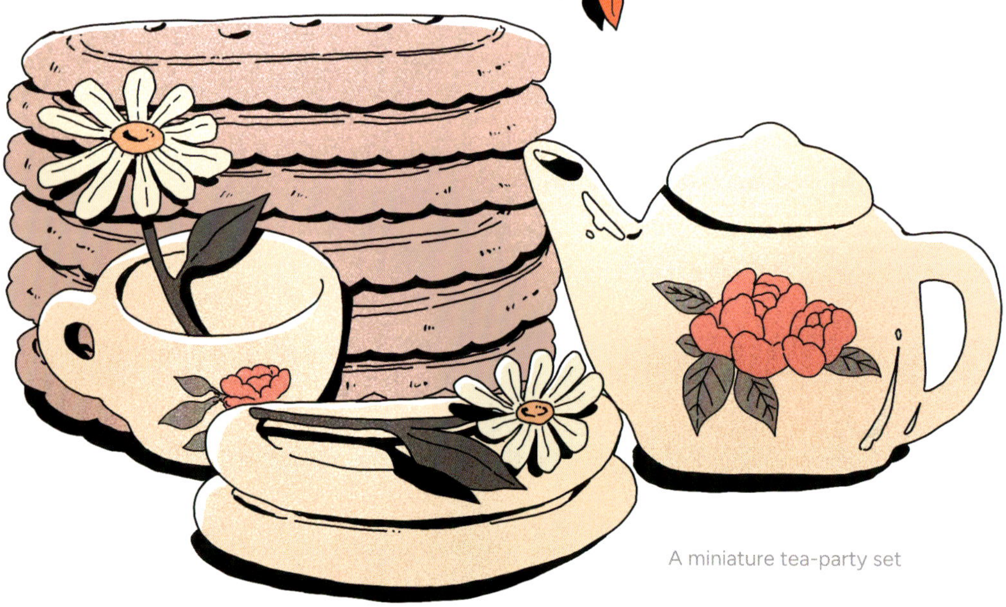

A miniature tea-party set

HAIRSTYLE STORIES

INTERMEDIATE ●●

Design three different hairstyles for the same character, each for a different scenario.

Start by drawing a neutral portrait of your character, then choose three different situations, moods, or events that might necessitate different hairstyles. Maybe they prefer it tied back and out of the way at the gym, but loose around their shoulders at home?

Do they spend time carefully styling their hair, or wear it wild and messy? Preserve the likeness of the original design by identifying the most characteristic shapes and translating them into each hairstyle.

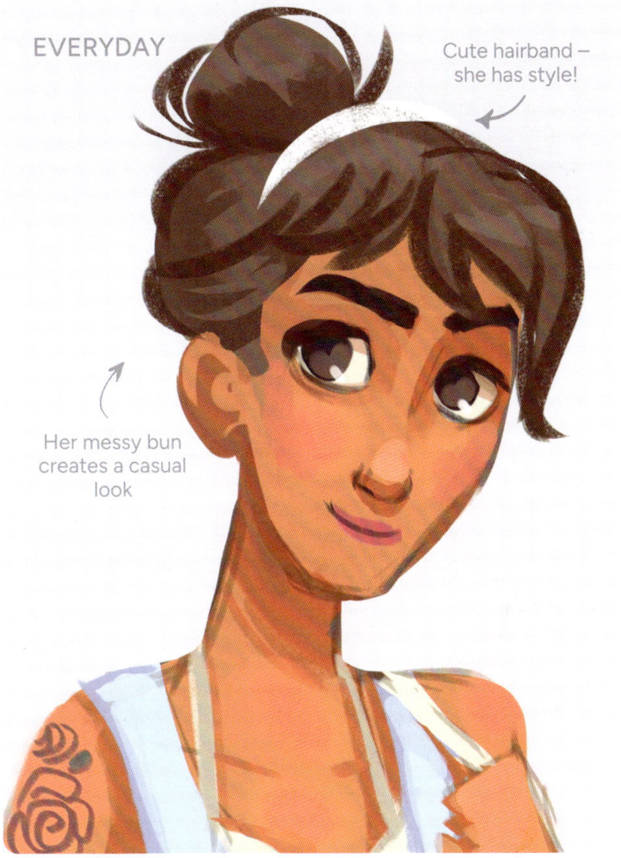

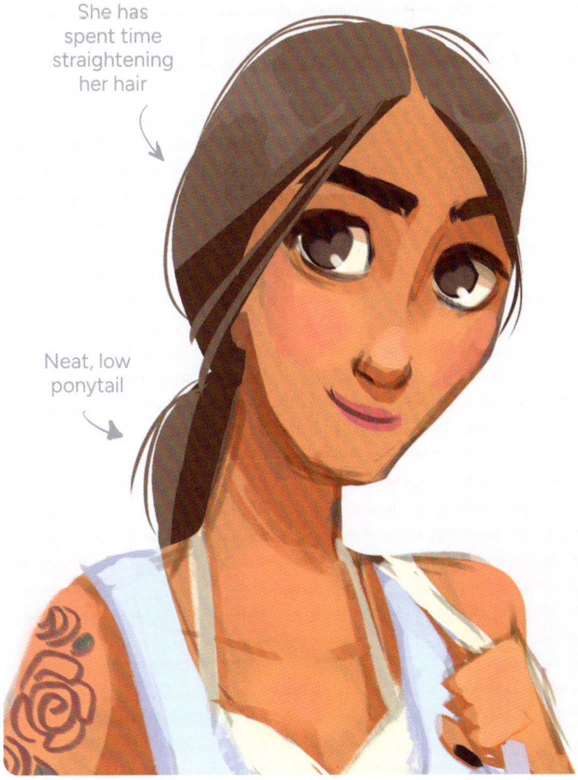

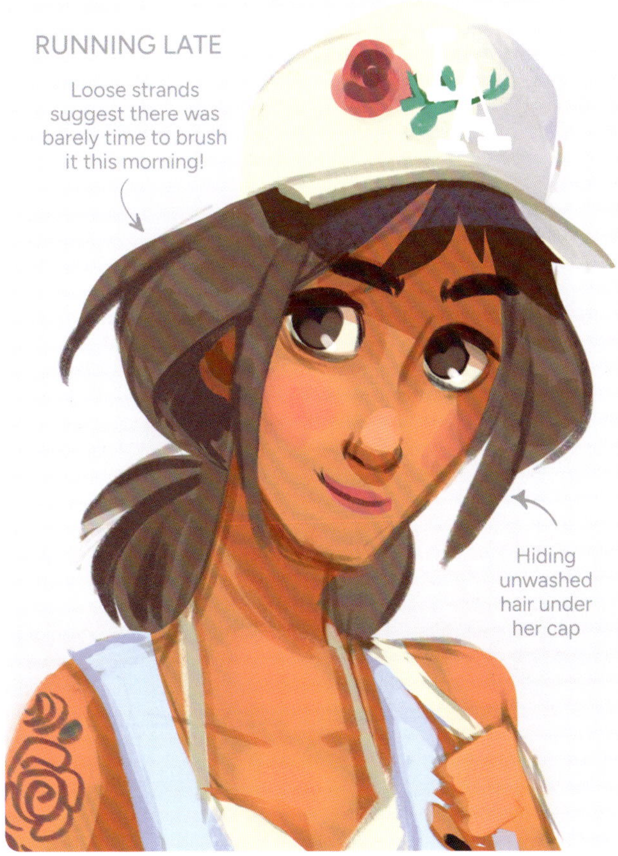

ART: TARANEH KARIMI

EMOTIONAL LIGHT

INTERMEDIATE ●●

Recreate the same illustration four times, each with an atmospheric lighting set-up that conveys a different emotion or mood.

Stronger emotions, such as joy and anger, can be expressed with bolder colours and stronger contrast. Softer emotions, such as peace and melancholy, can be communicated with more muted tones and softer contrast. A summer sunset will provide a more extreme, intense lighting set-up, perfect for conveying passion, romance, or rage, while an overcast dawn might better capture serenity, boredom, or depression.

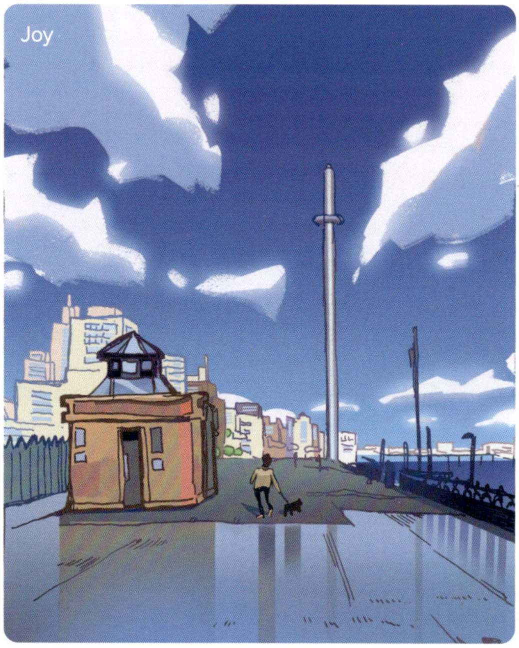
Joy

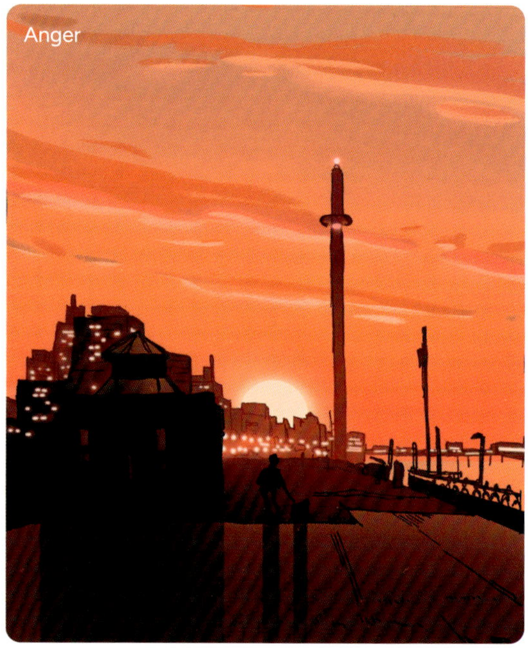
Anger

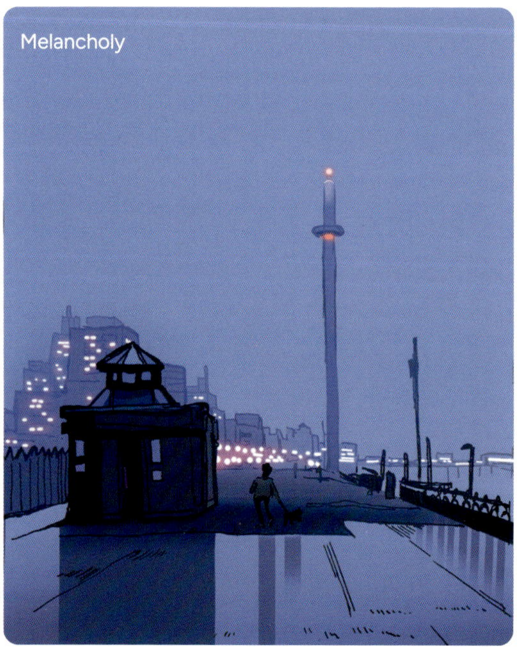
Melancholy

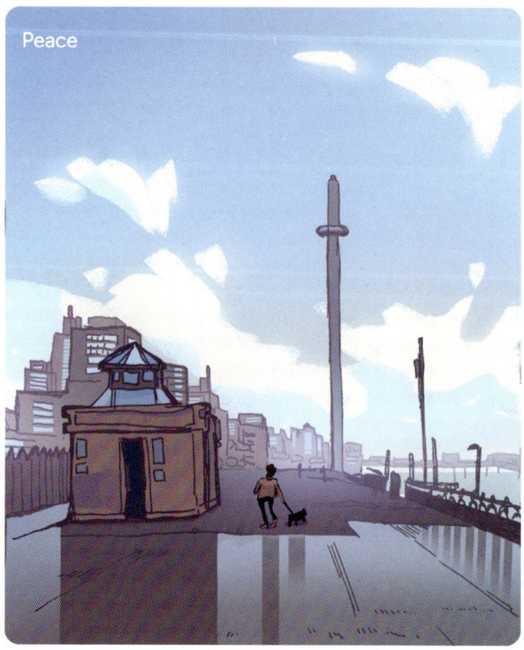
Peace

ONE CHARACTER, THREE OUTFITS

INTERMEDIATE ●●

Design three occasion-based outfits for the same character.

Start by thinking about your character's personality and lifestyle. What time period do they live in? What's their occupation, or where can they usually be found? Are they neat and organized, or messy and chaotic? What can they afford? Do they care about fashion? These answers should dictate not only your design choices, but your colour palette too.

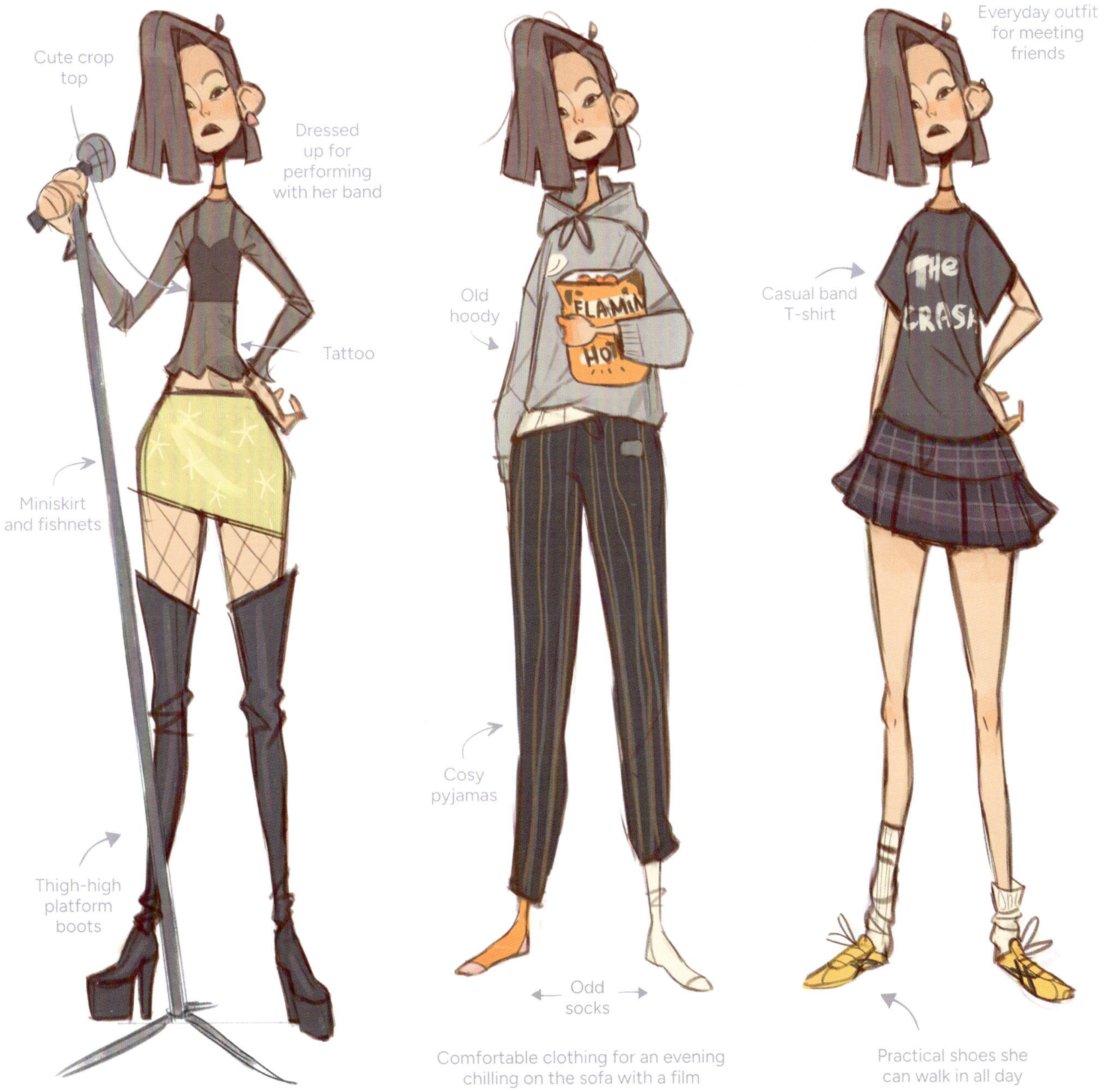

ART: MAGDALINA LIANOVA

WHAT IF...?

ADVANCED ●●●

Ask yourself a 'What if...?' scenario.

For example, what if gravity suddenly stopped existing? What if people kept dragons as pets? What if sea levels rose higher and higher? Draw a single image exploring this scenario. Consider what storytelling details you can include to pique the viewer's curiosity and let them know what's going on.

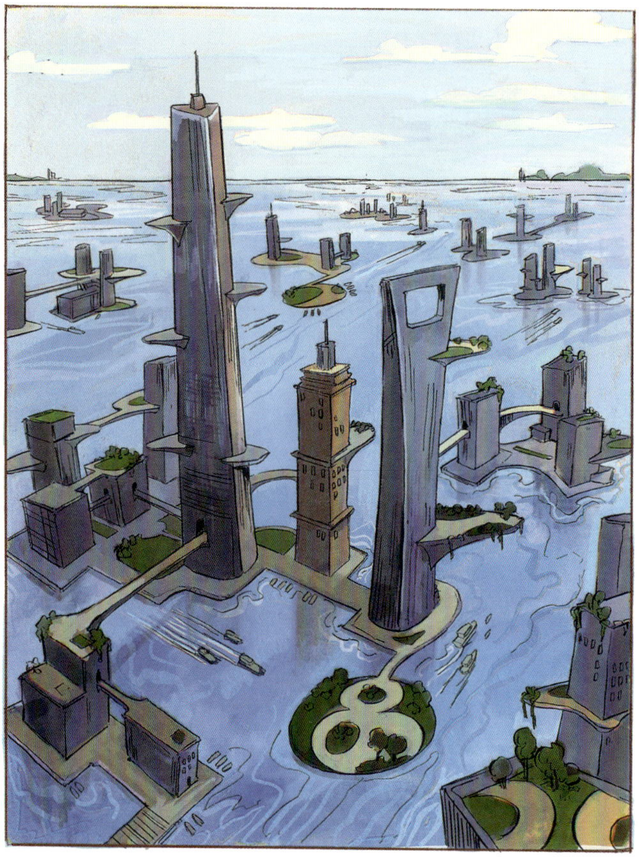

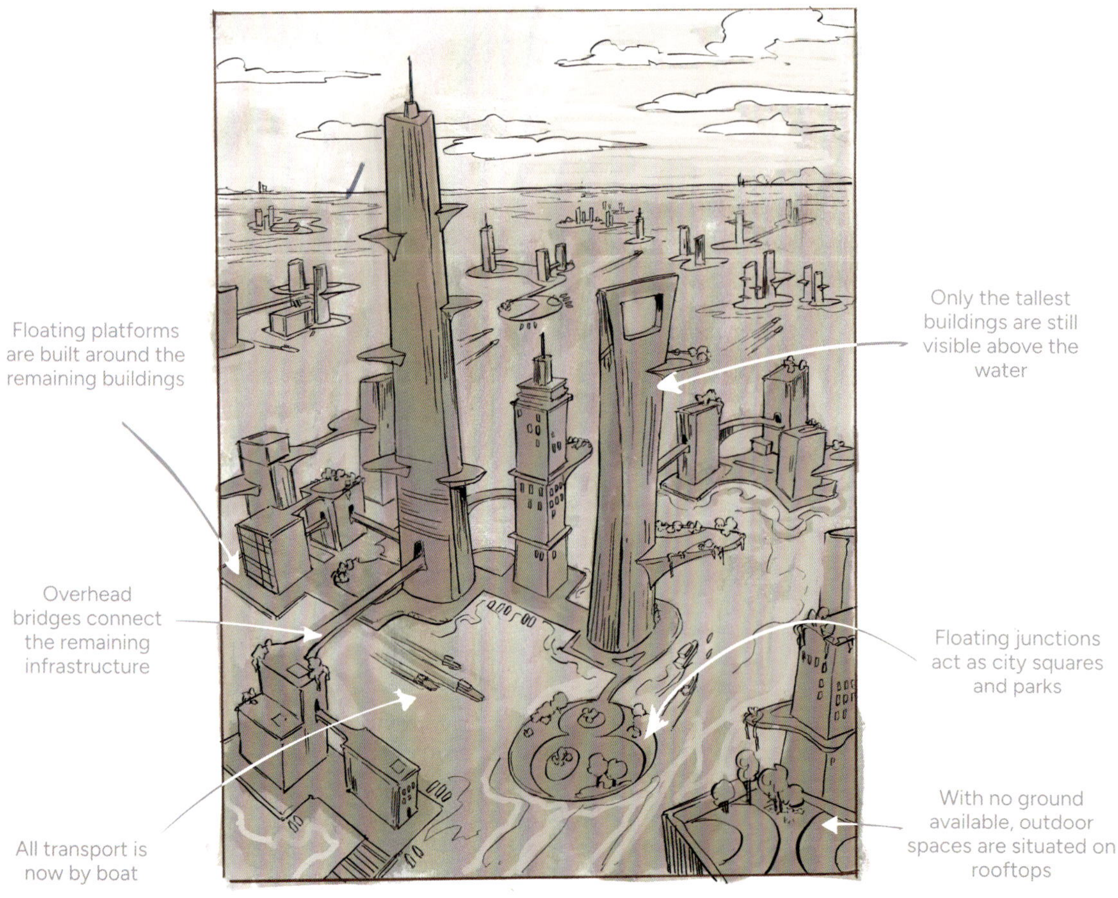

POV PANEL SEQUENCE

ADVANCED ●●●

Create a four-panel image sequence from a character's point of view.

The sequence should be chronological; for example, their morning routine, completing a task, or going on a quest. Try to show how the character sees and perceives the world. Think like a film director and use clear framing and flow. This task will build your storytelling skills and help you to think about how images can show time, suspense, and connection between moments.

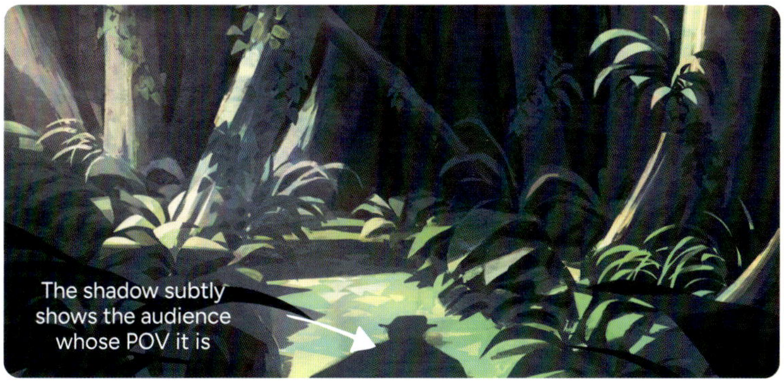

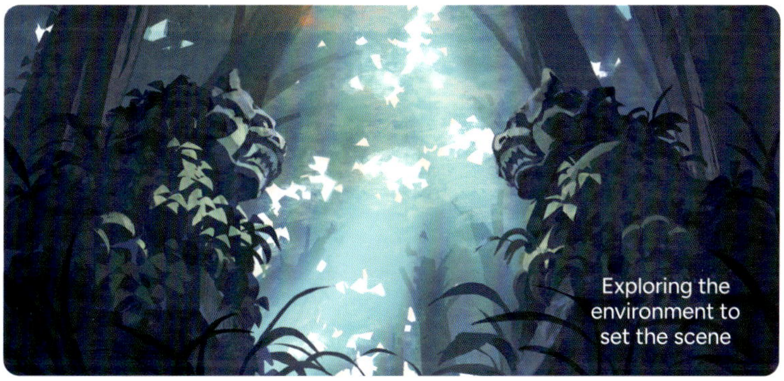

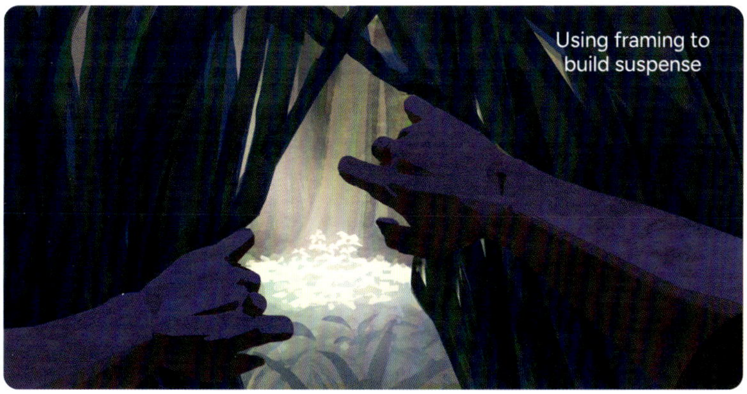

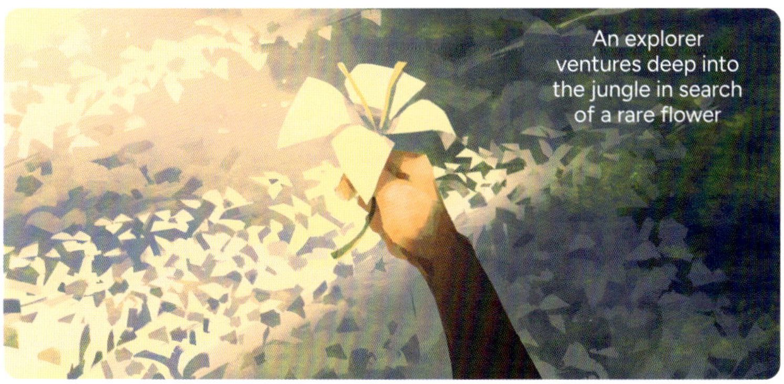

CONTRIBUTORS

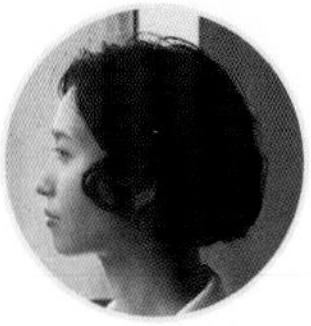

CHAVOOM (HITOMI TAMURA)

Visual development artist & background painter
chavoom.myportfolio.com

Chavoom is a visual development artist and background painter based in Japan. She focuses on storytelling through colour and light.

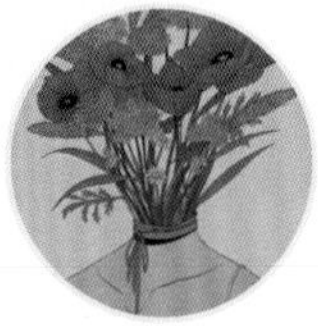

ELLA 'OHWELLADAYS'

Illustrator
instagram.com/ohwelladays

Ella enjoys making art inspired by everyday moments and the magic of the mundane from her home in the Philippines. She likes to evoke feelings of reminiscence, comfort, and sentimentality, one overgrown illustration at a time.

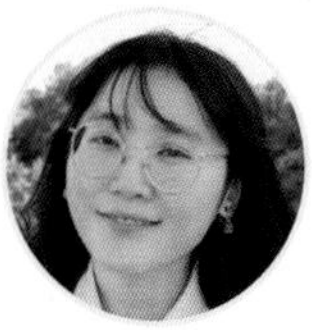

MICHELLE CHENG

Storyboard & visual development artist
lemoncholy.net

Michelle is a California-based artist currently working in the animation and games industry. She runs a YouTube channel called 'lemoncholy' where she enjoys creating videos about her art-making process.

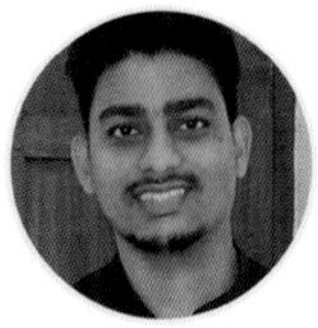

ALFRED FERNANDES

Concept artist & illustrator
artstation.com/alfredfernandes

Living in Goa, India, Alfred loves to create mystical, magical fantasy illustrations. He believes life without colour is boring and enjoys painting detailed environments, especially old architecture.

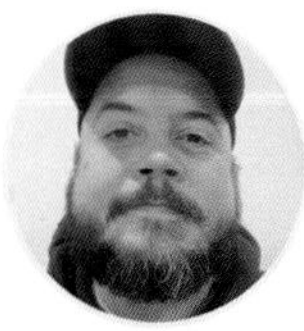

JULIAN DEL REY

Vis dev, concept artist & art director
juliandelreyart.carbonmade.com

Based in Spain, Julian has more than fourteen years' experience working in the entertainment industry for companies including Blizzard, Riot Games, and Disney.

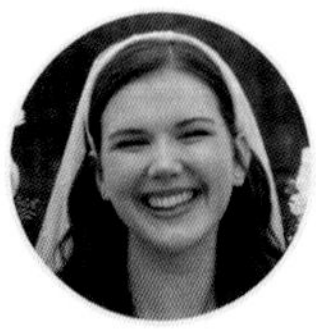

MADI HARPER

Illustrator
madiharpart.com

Madi is an illustrator based in the USA where she lives out her dream of bringing children's book stories to life.

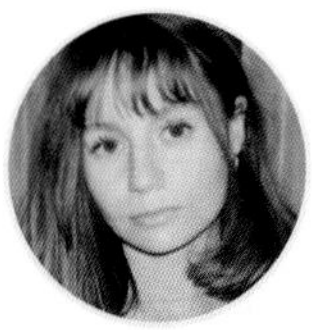

MAGDALINA DIANOVA

Character designer & illustrator
instagram.com/magdalina.dianova

Living in Bulgaria, Magdalina works on freelance projects for clients such as DreamWorks TV and Spin Master. She shares her creative process and personal projects on Patreon.

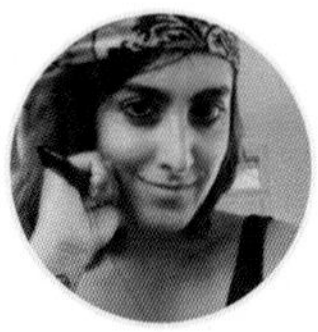

TARANEH KARIMI

Visual developer
taranehstudio.com

Taraneh has over a decade of experience working with numerous game and animation studios, including Disney Animation and Netflix. She loves the challenge of creating vibrant character designs.

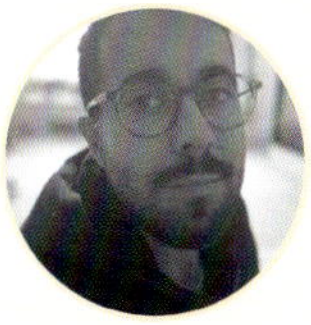

LOBÓN LEAL
Concept artist & visual development
instagram.com/lobonleal

Lobón works on animation and video-game projects from his studio in the coastal city of Cádiz, Spain. His days are filled with balancing professional work with his own comic-book endeavours.

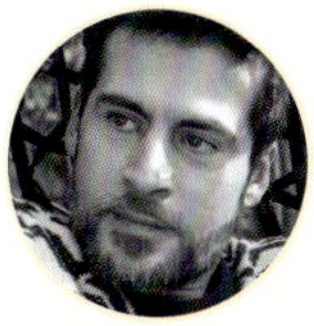

LANDER STRIJBOL
Visual development artist & illustrator
instagram.com/strijboll

Lander creates stylized illustrations for clients such as Wizards of the Coast and works on visual development for animation. Living in Bruges, Belgium, he likes to go plein-air painting with watercolour and gouache in his spare time.

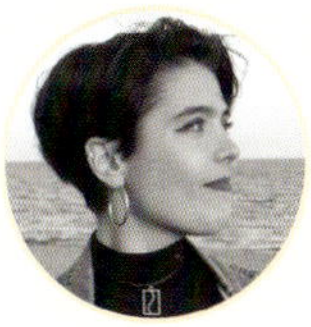

MARIANA NORONHA
Concept artist
mcnoronha.com

Mariana is a Portuguese concept artist based in the UK. She works across game, feature, and TV animation at various studios including Nickelodeon, Blue-Zoo Animation, and Wild Child Animation. She is also an avid plein-air painter.

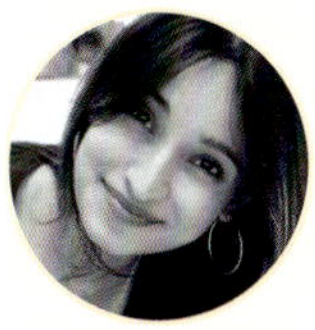

JUI TALUKDER
Illustrator & art educator
dewmanna.com

Jui is a Brooklyn-based illustrator who's worked with leading brands including PBS, Bonnier Books, the Hollywood Reporter, Faber & Faber, the Washington Post, Scholastic, and more. She is currently working on her first graphic novel.

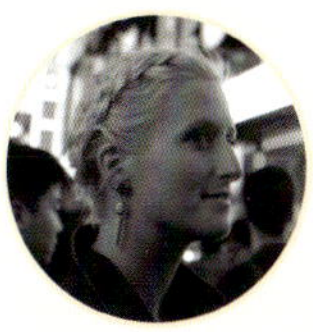

PERNILLE ØRUM
Character designer
pernilleoe.com

Based in Nairobi, Kenya, Pernille is a Danish illustrator celebrated for her dynamic, expressive style. A graduate of The Animation Workshop, she's designed for Disney, DreamWorks, Warner Bros' *DC Super Hero Girls*, and Image Comics.

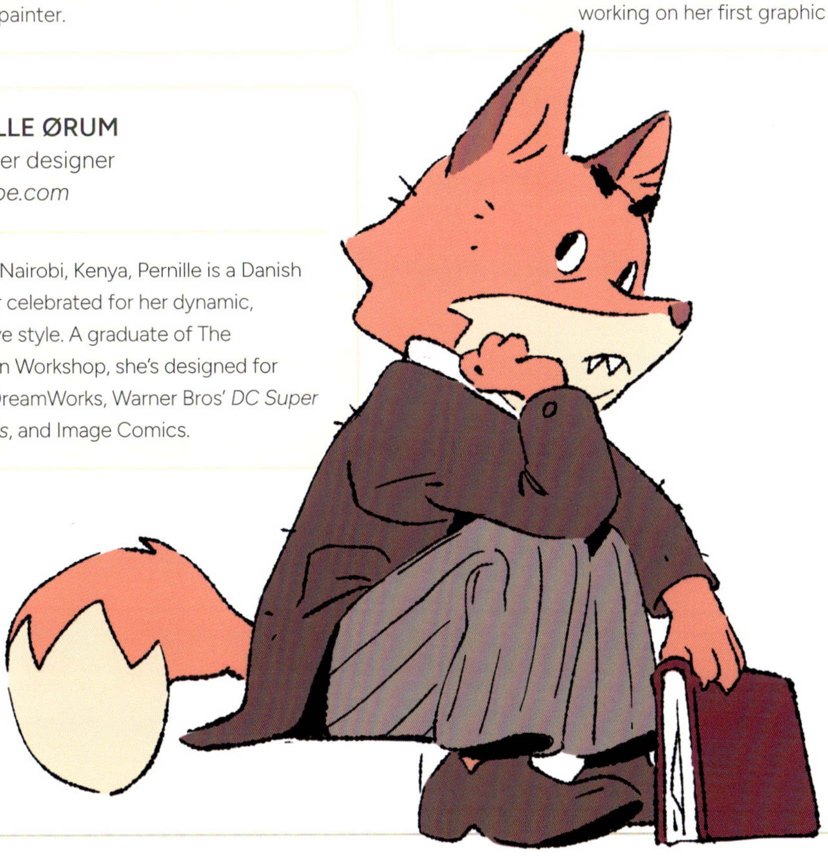

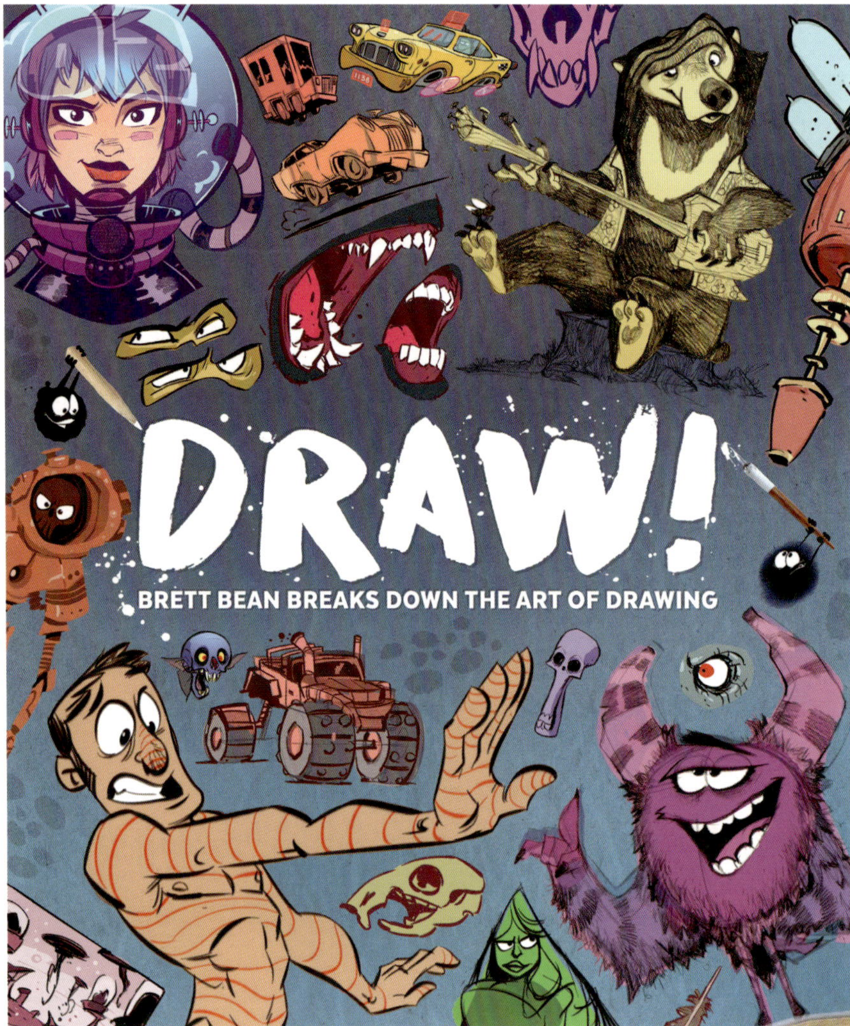
DRAW!
BRETT BEAN BREAKS DOWN THE ART OF DRAWING

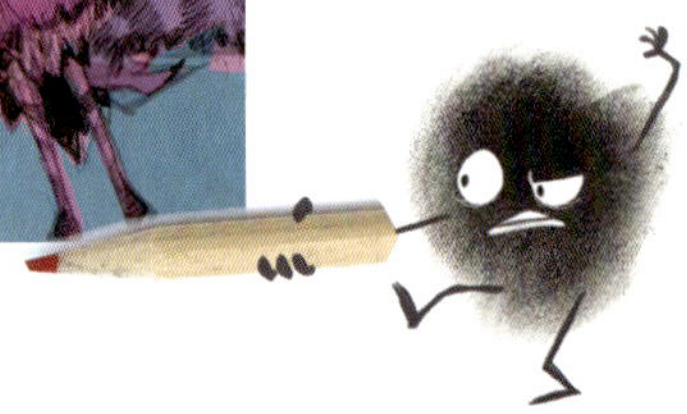

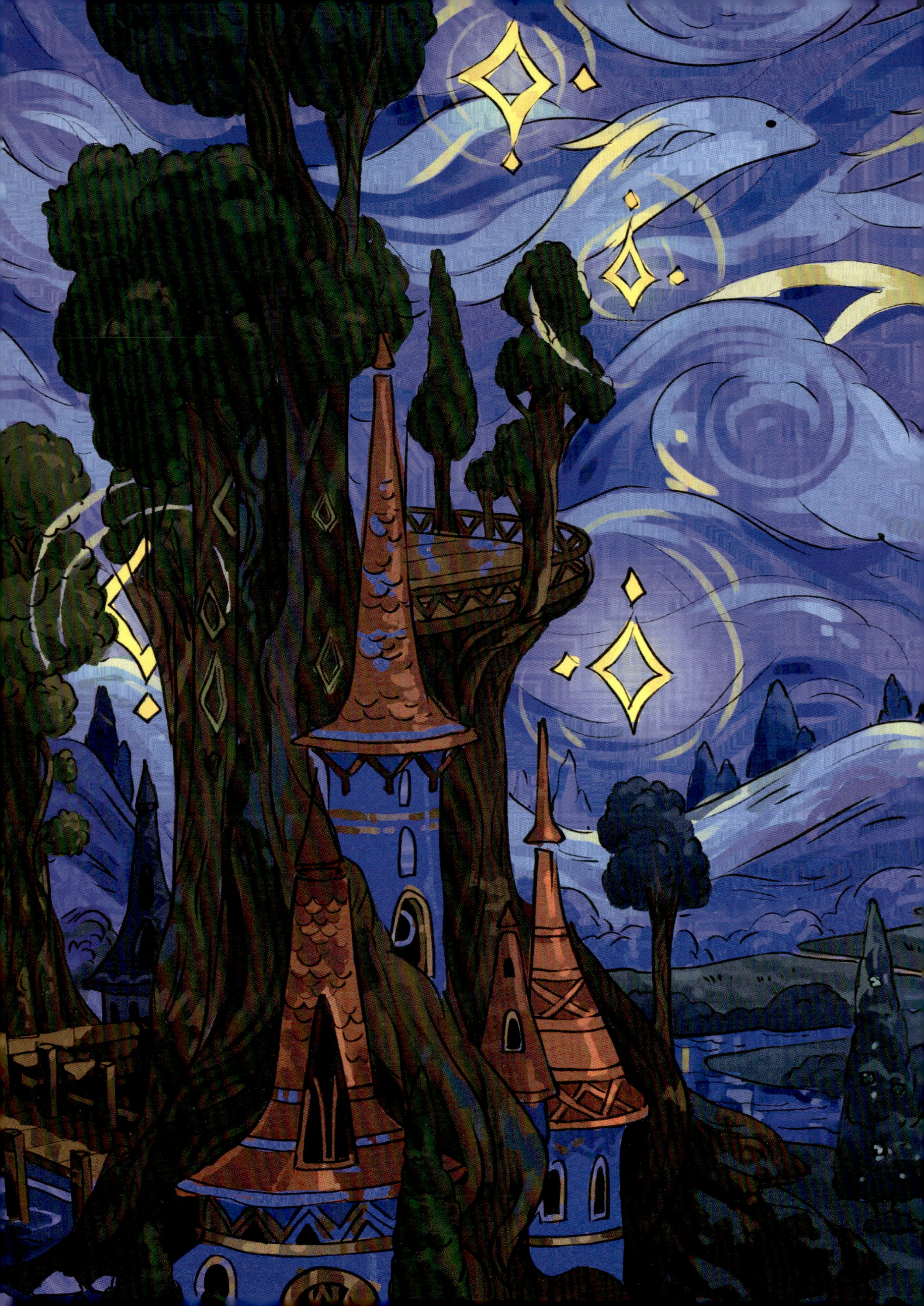

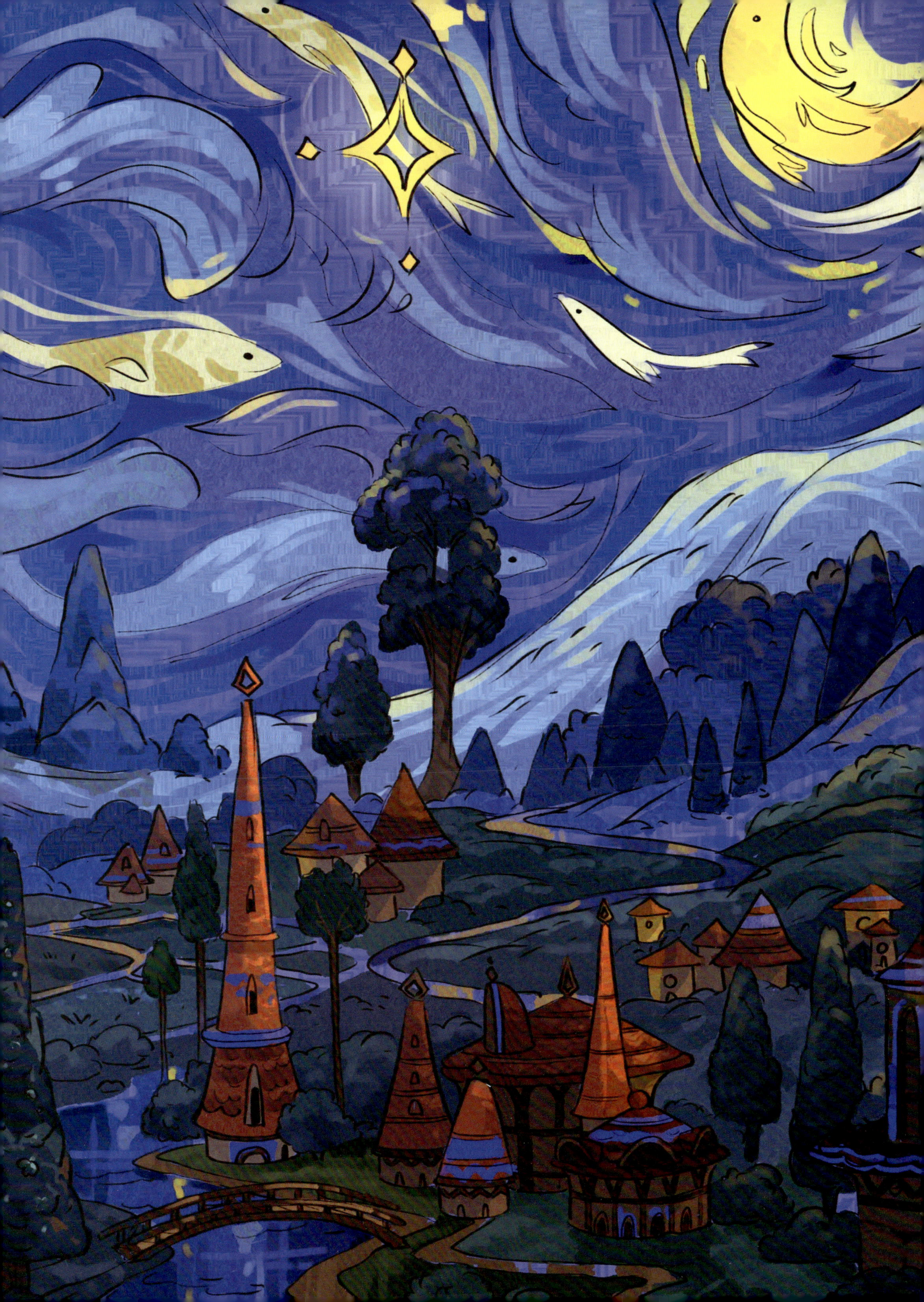

3dtotal Publishing

3dtotal Publishing is a trailblazing, creative publisher specializing in inspirational and educational resources for artists.

Our titles feature top industry professionals from around the globe who share their experience in skilfully written step-by-step tutorials and fascinating, detailed guides. Illustrated throughout with stunning artwork, these bestselling publications offer creative insight, expert advice, and essential motivation. Fans of digital art will enjoy our comprehensive volumes covering Adobe Photoshop, Procreate, and Blender, as well as our superb titles based around character design, including *Fundamentals of Character Design* and *Creating Characters for the Entertainment Industry*. The dedicated, high-quality blend of instruction and inspiration also extends to traditional art. Titles covering a range of techniques, genres, and abilities allow your creativity to flourish while building essential skills.

Well-established within the industry, we now offer over 100 titles and counting, many of which have been translated into multiple languages around the world. With something for every artist, we are proud to say that our books offer the 3dtotal package:

LEARN • CREATE • SHARE

Visit us at store.3dtotal.com

3dtotal Publishing is part of 3dtotal.com, a leading website for CG artists founded by Tom Greenway in 1999.

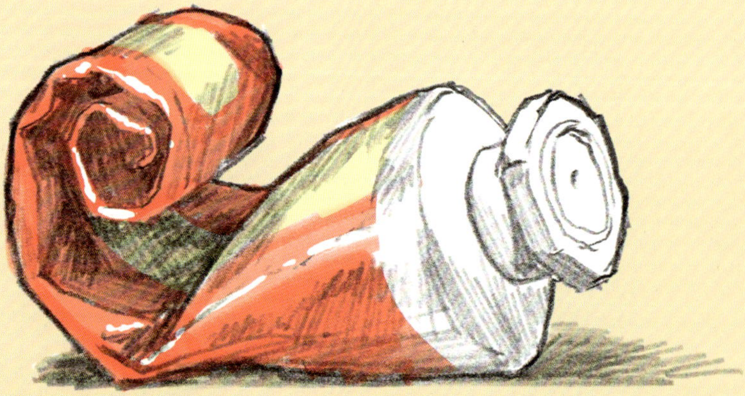